Backroad Mapbook

Welcome to the third edition of the Southwestern B.C. Backroad Mapbook!

The idea behind the Backroad Mapbook Series is simple. We like to participate in a wide variety of outdoor activities but we got frustrated with the number of maps and books we had to consult to plan each adventure. Equally, the government topographic maps are outdated and the maps found in the Freshwater Fishing Guide and the B.C. Recreation Atlas lack any detail to be useful. So we created one guide that tells you about all the outdoor activities in a particular area and shows you how to get there.

The third edition has been completely revised and updated including more detailed and up-to-date maps and an expanded reference section on all your outdoor activities. The maps in this book highlight the logging road networks, trail sytems and recreational opportunities found throughout Southwestern B.C. The reference section contains comprehensive information on activities such as freshwater and saltwater fishing, hiking and mountain biking trails, natural hot springs, paddling routes, provincial parks, wilderness camping and winter recreation (cross-country skiing and snowmobiling).

Southwestern B.C. is an area dominated by large wilderness parks all within a few hours drive of Vancouver. The natural beauty is waiting to be discovered. You can fish or explore the fjord-like coast, hike and climb the rugged coast mountains, sooth those road-weary bones in a remote natural hot spring, marvel at cascading waterfalls, or hike amongst large old growth trees to alpine meadows and volcanic formations.

The opportunities are endless! Whether you like to fish, hike, mountain bike, paddle, ski or just explore backroads, we are sure you will have as much fun using the Backroad Mapbook as we did in developing it.

Forward

The Backroad Mapbook is truly a unique product. No othe source covers Southwestern B.C. with as much detail or infor mation on all types of outdoor recreation activities as this book Further, no other guide book provides the detailed and accu rate maps this book contains.

The Backroad Mapbook is simple to use. There are two sec tions to the mapbook, a reference section and the maps. If yor know the activity you are planning, you simply turn to that ref erence section and find the area that you are interested in.] you are planning a trip to a specific area, you should consult th index to find the appropriate map(s) and look for the variou recreation opportunities highlighted in green and red.

Our maps have been developed and updated using a wide vari ety of sources including current forestry maps. To help you us our maps, we have provided a map legend. Continuous referra to this legend and the reference sections will help you get ac quainted with the area you are interested in.

Generally speaking, backroad travel on logging mainlines or for est service roads (FSR) is good. These roads are well main tained and can be easily traveled by a motor home or car. Thes roads are noted by the large black lines on our maps.

The most remote areas and spur roads should be left to the 4X truck, mountain biker or hikers to explore. These roads ar noted in thinner black lines on our maps. Some logging road have restricted access, and, if open at all to the public, allov access between 6 p.m. and 6 a.m. or on weekends and holiday: Always watch for logging trucks.

In order to limit public access, many of the logging roads ar gated or deactivated. It is recommended that you contact th Ministry of Forests or the local forestry company to determin which roads are gated or deactivated at the time you are plan ning your trip.

We emphasize that our mapbook should only be used as an ac cess and planning guide. We have gone to great lengths to en sure the accuracy of the book. However, over time, the roa and trail conditions change. Always be prepared!

Over 45,000 Southwestern B.C. Mapbooks In Print!

"...we can't think of a better book to have curled up in the glove compartment of the SUV."

Coast Magazine

"It's a book about access, a book that will aid any outdoor enthusiast in planning a backcountry adventure, whatever the reason for going off the beaten trail of Hwy accessible areas."

Squamish Chief

"There are a lot of recreation guidebooks on the market... but not anything to combine all the sources- until now."

Whistler Question

"... this book is invaluable."

The Revue

"Their amazing maps reveal a hidden world...a real do-it-yourself, no-budget guide to vactioning."

The Nirvana Report- Vancouver Magazine

Disclaimer

Mussio Ventures Ltd. does not warrant that the backroads and trails indicated in this mapbook are passable nor does it claim that the mapbook is completely accurate. Therefore, please be careful when using this or any source to plan and carry out your outdoor recreation activity.

Please note that travelling on logging roads and trails is inherently dangerous, and without limiting the generality of the foregoing, you may encounter poor road conditions, unexpected traffic, poor visibility, and low or no road/trail maintenance. Please use extreme caution when traveling logging roads and trails.

Please refer to the Fishing and Hunting Regulations for closures and restrictions. It is your responsibility to know when and where closures and restrictions apply.

Acknowledgement

This book could not have been produced without the dedication of our staff, Shawn Caswell, Kenneth Congdon, Trevor Daxon, and Brandon Tam. We would also like to thank the following individuals for helping with the project: Kelly Briggs, Leslie Bryant, Brian Do, Trent Ernst, Natalie Nicholson and Tim O'Hearn. Without their hard work and support, this mapbook would never have been completed as quickly and accurately as it was.

In addition, we would like to thank all those individuals, retailers, forestry companies and tourism personnel for their knowledge and assistance in the production of this mapbook.

Most of all, we would like to thank Nancy Jackson and Penny Mussio for their suggestions and support during the many hours when the authors, Russell and Wesley Mussio, were doing research.

ISBN 0-9697877-0-7

Cover and layout designs by Brandon Tam

Published by:
Mussio Ventures Ltd
232 Anthony Court
New Westminster, B.C. V3L 5T5
P. (604) 520-5670   F. (604) 520-5630
E-mail: info@ backroadmapbooks.com
or visit our web site:
www.backroadmapbooks.com

Canadian Cataloguing in Publication Data

Mussio, Russell, 1969-
	Backroad mapbook: an outdoor recreation guide

3rd ed.
Includes index.
Cover title.
Written by Russell and Wesley Mussio.
Originally published under the title: Backroad and outdoor
	recreation mapbook.
Contents: v. 1. Southwestern B.C. - v. 2. Vancouver Island
	(including the Gulf Island) - v. 3. Kamloops/Okanagan -
	v. 4. Kootenays - v. 5. The Cariboo.
ISBN 0-9697877-0-7 (v. 1) - ISBN 0-9697877-1-5 (v. 2) -
	ISBN 0-9697877-2-3 (v. 3) - ISBN 0-9697877-3-1 (v. 4)
	ISBN 0-9697877-4-x (v. 5)
	1. Recreation areas – British Columbia – Maps. 2. British
Columbia – Maps. I. Mussio, Wesley, 1964- II. Title.

G1170.B23 1997   912.711   C98-011809-3

Table of Contents

Natural Hot Springs

Southwestern B.C. is blessed with several natural hot springs that have not been commercialized. These hidden areas are often quite difficult to get to and/or difficult to find. Once you discover the pools, they offer a nice relaxing get-away. The pools are very rustic in nature and are usually found in a scenic wilderness setting.

Clear Creek Hot Springs (Map #14/D1)

Found next to an old growth forest near Clear Creek, these hot springs are accessed off the Clear Creek Main which, in turn, is found on the Harrison East FSR, 5.5km past the Silver Creek Camp. It is possible to drive approximately 7.4km up the Clear Creek Main using a 4wd vehicle or 2wd vehicle with great clearance (due to cross ditching). From there, it is about 5km (1.5hr) one way to the hot springs along the old road which now forms a rocky creek bed. You should expect a steady uphill walk along the road including forging the creek in several spots and skirting around the road and creek in one area. At the springs is an uninviting cabin together with three soaking pools and a camping area.

Plastic hoses and pipes were installed in 1991 to collect the hot water, carrying it to the 3 main soaking pools. The dingy log cabin has a wood stove together with a loft. It sleeps 10-12 people. People choosing to tent can use one of the tenting pads located along Clear Creek.

Keyhole (Pebble Creek) Hot Springs (Map #37/C1)

The parking lot leading to these undeveloped springs is found approximately 5.4km from the Meager Creek Junction along the Upper Lillooet River FSR (at the end of a flat stretch before the road climbs uphill away from the river). From that point, it is about a 1.5km scramble along the bank of the Lillooet River to the location where the hot water bubbles onto the small sandy beach next to the Lillooet River. At that location, it is possible to build a small swimming hole by scooping the sand away.

There are several vents where hot water flows out of the side of the river bank 15m from the river. For safety reasons, it is best to walk to these hot springs after spring runoff as you have to skirt the side of the river.

Meager Creek Hot Springs (Map #37/C2)

These hot springs use to be incredibly popular. However, the Ministry of Health took it upon themselves to close the hot springs several years ago and at this time, they are not opened to public bathing. When they were open, visitors used to camp next to the parking lot in the grove of old growth timber. From there, a series of well developed trails lead down to the creek and a series of hot spring pools. There are plans underway to install a new pool system and facilities, which would comply with Ministry of Health standards.

Pitt River Hot Springs (Map #21/C1)

Probably the most beautiful set of natural hot springs found in Southwestern B.C., the Pitt River Hot Springs are found in a spectacular canyon. To reach the hot springs, it is necessary to boat 25km to the north end of the Pitt Lake where you can moor at the dock to the right of the log dump. From there, it is about a 22km (2 hour) bike ride along the Pitt River FSR, a main haul logging road.

The first 16km are fairly flat and easy to ride but the rest of the ride involves some short hill climbing. Just past the 21km mark is a ditched side road (Pinecone Banch) that leads to the left and downhill to a concrete bridge spanning over the Pitt River canyon.

The trailhead to the hot springs leads up the west side of the river for 300m and is marked by a large white sign warning visitors of the potential dangers that lie ahead. The trail is not for the faint at heart. There are several steep spots and

a rope descent is required to get down to the three hot spring pools. The pools, set right next to the river within the canyon walls, are dammed by concrete retaining walls. During spring run-off (to early May), the pools are covered by water from the Pitt River.

Sloquet Hot Springs (Map #22/C4)

Recent road development in this area has really improved the access to this beautiful creekside hot springs. Unfortunately, this will probably lead to crowded conditions and vandalism. To reach the hot springs requires a long haul along gravel roads from either Pemberton or the Lougheed Hwy. The later requires travelling 74km along the Harrison West FSR to Tipella (including a 20km section of rough 4wd) before the 6.5km of smooth 2wd to Sloquet Creek. Allow 3.5 hours to reach the springs. North of Sloquet Creek turn left and left again and follow the 2wd road 8.6km to the parking spot. The new bridge and culverts take away the need to hike further than the 500m down the steep (blocked) road to the meadows above the hot springs. From the meadows (where rustic camping is possible), look for the hidden trail that leads across a fallen log. All trails leading to the pools require you to be fleet of foot.

Once you reach the site, you will find the main bathing pools right beside Sloquet Creek. The pools have been built-up by retaining walls made out some rocks from the creek bed. The hot water comes from a piping hot 10m high waterfall and flows along a creek bed to the pools. Since the water is extremely hot near the waterfalls (68 °C), you will find that the bathing pool cool as they get closer to the creek. Tenters are often found beside the sulphurous smelling pools. The lovely creek valley, the pretty waterfall and old growth timber around the pools make this a very scenic and relaxing site (especially after the long bumpy ride to access the pools).

St. Agnes Wells Hot Spring (Map #22/B1)

These hot springs are located approximately 3.2km south of the Rogers Creek Road off the Pemberton-Douglas FSR near B.C. Hydro tower #682. A muddy, rutted road leads several hundred metres down from the main road to the hot springs. Several undeveloped camping spots are located right at the hot springs which, in turn, are found in a draw beneath the main road.

The main tub, which is fed by pipes, is half of a septic tank and is found in an abused A-frame bath house. Several other tubs, including the other half of the septic tank, are found in an opening outside the A-frame. The whole area is generally unkept and usually littered with garbage. The area is certainly not as scenic as other hot springs but does offer an easily accessible place to camp and enjoy the rustic setting of a backcountry hot springs. The long drive to the hot springs discourages day-use from Vancouver.

Pitt River Hotsprings

Abbreviations Used Throughout the Book:

2wd: 2 wheel drive
4wd: 4 wheel drive
cm: centimetres
FSR: Forest Service Road
ft: feet
ha: hectares
hr: hours
Hwy: Highway
kg: kilograms
Km: kilometres
m: metres
min: minutes
Mnt: Mountain
Mt: Mount
Prov: Provincial
Rd: Road
Rec: Recreation
RV: Recreational Vehicle
X-C: Cross Country

Wilderness Camping

Created by the Ministry of Forests and various forest companies, a large number of wilderness camping sites have been built for use by the outdoor recreationists. The sites are rustic in nature and usually have camping pads, pit toilets, fire rings and picnic tables. Since the sites are usually located in more remote areas, other amenities such as power hook-ups or piped water are not available. Please remember to pack out whatever you pack in.

Below, we have described the recreations sites as found within southwestern British Columbia. If you plan to travel to one of those recreation sites, it is well advised to get there early as most of the sites are very popular and extremely crowded throughout the summer months, especially during long weekends. As road conditions and closures tend to fluctuate over time, you are well advised to phone the district office of the Ministry of Forests to determine up-to-date information on whether the area is accessible to the public.

Fraser Valley Rec Sites

Chehalis Lake Rec Sites (Map #14/A3)
Chehalis Lake is located north of Harrison Mills on the Chehalis FSR. At the lake are 3 popular rec sites.

Chehalis Lake South Rec Site is located at the 24km mark and at the south end of the lake. It is less busy than the rec site at the north end of the lake and has 25 camping spots together with a good concrete boat launch, a beach and picnic tables.

Skwellepil Creek Rec Site is along the western shores of Chehalis Lake at the 31km. It is a large, appealing site that offers wooded and open sites, creekside and lakeside sites. There is a rough boat launch and gravel beach at the rec site together with pit toilets and picnic tables. The site is often crowded during the weekends. Privacy is gained by camping in the overflow parking area away from the main camping spot.

Chehalis Lake North Rec Site is at the north end of the lake. Each of the 40 camping site is located in the forest in a rocky area next to the lake. There is a boat launch together with a nice beach during low water.

Chilliwack River Valley Rec Sites (Map #5)
Along the Chilliwack Lake Road are a series of rec sites, which allow visitors to camp next to the Chilliwack River. The valley is truly a great recreation area with excellent river fishing, good hikes and some challenging whitewater paddling. The Chilliwack River Road is paved for most of its length and provides good access for RVs, trailers and cars.

Allison Pool Rec Site is set in a nice 2nd growth forest next to the river. It is found at 15.5km along the Chilliwack Lake Road. The area is a popular Steelhead fishing spot with sand bars and rock walls surrounding the tepid green waters. The 5 vehicle access campsites are offered in addition to several trail access sites. The campsites have picnic tables and are far enough away from one another to allow for privacy. A parking area at the rec site allows for overflow camping.

Camp Foley Rec Site is found at the junction of the Chilliwack Lake Road and the Foley Creek FSR about 26km along the Chilliwack Lake Road. There are 3 camping areas with pit toilets and garbage cans but without picnic tables.

Chipmunk Peninsula Rec Site is set in a coniferous forest next to the Chilliwack River on the Chip-munk Creek FSR. It has 13 campsites with most having picnic tables. There are pit toilets and garbage cans at the rec site.

Depot Creek Rec Site is found 10km from the end of the pavement on the Chilliwack Lake FSR. The site offers 15 well spaced, treed sites and a sandy beach.

Eagle's Roost Rec Site is a tiny picnic spot next to the Chilliwack River. It marks the junction to the Mount Thurston Road. There is room for 1 or 2 camping parties.

Foley Lake Rec Site has two separate sites offering lakeside camping. The more popular western site offers good access via the Chilliwack-Foley FSR. A small boat launch is available.

Paleface Rec Site is on the eastern shores of Chilliwack Lake off the end of the pavement. It has 12 wooded camping spots, together with a paved boat launch and a gravel beach.

Pierce Creek Rec Site is really a parking lot with a couple of tables marking the trailhead for the Pierce Lake Trail. The rec site is found at 22km on the Chilliwack Lake Road.

Post Creek Rec Site is a medium sized rec site with about 12 nicely shaded campsites that receive heavy use throughout the summer so it is not a good choice if you want a quiet setting. This creekside rec site also marks the trailhead to Lindeman and Greendrop Lakes.

Rapids Rec Site is found on the Chilliwzack-Foley FSR and has 3 shaded campsites. The rec site is located right next to a nice stretch of whitewater on the Chilliwack River where you can watch kayakers paddle past.

Riverside Rec Site is a tenting-only site as it requires a short walk to reach the camping spots from the parking area. The 10 camping spots are in a thick Douglas-fir forest next to the Chilliwack River. The rec site is accessed at 29.5km on the Chilliwack Lake Road.

Sappers Park is a walk-in site found at the south end of Chilliwack Lake. It is known for its large white sandy beach. The small site provides access to the Upper Chilliwack River Trail and the surrounding ecological reserve.

Tamihi Creek Rec Site is 10.5km from the Chilliwack/Vedder River Bridge. It is a large, 30+ campsite, which is set in an open grassy area as well as a deciduous forest next to the creek. The open area is popular with larger camping units whereas the forested area is ideal for tenting. Most of the campsites have picnic tables. Steelhead and salmon fishermen use the rec site in late summer and into the fall.

Thurston Meadows Rec Site is another 3.5km along the Chilliwack Lake Road to the east of the Tamihi Creek Rec Site. There are about 20 campsites set in a large open meadow overlooking the river. Several picnic only sites line the river bank. The site is popular with RVs and campers.

Harrison Lake East Rec Sites (Map #14,15)

Harrison East FSR is reached by turning right at Harrison Hot Springs and travelling along Rockwell Drive. Once you pass Sasquatch Provincial Park, the road ascends sharply upward and then follows the lake in a northern direction.

Rainbow Falls Rec Site is the southernmost rec site. It can only be reached by walking down Slollicum Creek or by boating into Cascade Bay. There are several tenting pads at the rec site as well as a beach for swimming. The spectacular falls, the gravel beach and the peaceful surroundings are the main attractions to the site.

Cascade Peninsula Rec Site is accessed by hiking a blocked road from the FSR or by boat to Cooks Cove. It has several tenting pads set in a secluded cove as well as a small pebble beach for sunbathing.

Bear Creek Rec Site is located next to the FSR at the Bear Creek outflow. The site offers 12 quiet, shaded camping spots set in a second growth forest. Bear Creek Falls are nearby.

Cogburn Beach Rec Site is the northernmost rec site on the FSR. The treed camping sites stretch along the south end of beautiful Cogburn Beach. Hundreds of campers flock to the area during the summer weekends. Campers simply park on the side of the FSR and walk down the bank to the sandy beach, which is ideal for tenting and beach fires. Unfortunately, there is often a lot of garbage left behind by inconsiderate users.

Harrison Lake West Rec Sites (Map #4,14)

Access from Harrison Mills is along the Morris Valley Road and then the Harrison West FSR. There are several campsites within the area worth visiting especially since fishing is fairly good in some of the small lakes.

Chehalis River Rec Site encompasses 3 different areas with a total of around 50 campsites but no picnic tables. The largest of the camping area (found to the east of the road before crossing the river) has about 40 campsites. The area is nicely spaced in the forest next to the river allowing some privacy. The other 2 spots are less scenic and have around 5 camping spots each. From the camping areas, there is a short trail leading to a spectacular canyon. The river offers an opportunity to fish for Steelhead, sunbathe at one of the nice sandy beaches or enjoy a relaxing float down the river.

Francis Lake Rec Site is accessed by a 4wd road (Francis Lake FSR) and is a small site overlooking the lake. It offers a gravel boat launch and a better chance at seclusion (due to the access).

Grace Lake Rec Site is found on the Harrison Lake West FSR and has a total of 3 campsites, 2 of which have picnic tables. The rec site is located among the trees and rocky outcrops next to Grace Lake, which offers fairly good fishing. The rec site has been labelled incorrectly by the forest service.

Hale Creek Rec Site is a secluded, small site found in a dense forest between Hale Creek and a cove on Harrison Lake. Although it is known more as a boat access site, 4wd vehicles and hikers can access this beautiful site on the rough Hale Creek FSR. The site offers a sandy beach, a cartop boat launch and a unique barbecue hut.

Sunrise Lake Rec Site is an isolated site found on a rough 4wd road off of the Harrison West FSR. It is a medium sized open site located on the east side of the lake. A boat launch is available at the rec site.

Twenty Mile Bay Rec Site is found on the shores of Harrison Lake in a sheltered bay. It is a large, popular site that offers 2 pebble beaches and a boat launch. The large treed sites (25 in all) are well separated along the tip of land extending into Harrison Lake. Fishing, sunbathing and windsurfing are popular pastimes here.

Weaver Lake Rec Site is accessed by a rough 2wd road that climbs steeply to the lake over 3km. The rec site is set in a lush forest next to this picturesque lake. The site offers a separate day use area along with a gravel boat launch and excellent trail (see Denham Trail). Fishing is the primary attraction to the rec site.

Wolf Lake Rec Site has a total of 3 campsites and is accessed off the FSR. Each of the campsites has a picnic table with one of the sites located in a grassy area overlooking the small marshy lake whereas the other 2 sites are right next to the road. The forest service has labelled the site incorrectly.

Wood Lake Rec Site is a popular and pretty medium size rec site set in an opening next to this small fishing lake. Found 20km up the Harrison West FSR on a short but rough side road, there are 2 different sites with a total of 5 campsites. The north site is nicer and offers a boat launch.

Jones Lake Rec Site (Map #5/B2)

Jones Lake Rec Site is a BC Hydro campsite found at around 9km on the Jones Creek FSR. It is a large rec site with 15 camping spots ideal for RVs as well as for tenters. The rec site is popular throughout the summer months with fishing being the primary recreation pursuit. The popular sites are beside the creek whereas others are on a bank overlooking Jones Lake. The road into Jones Lake is steep and rough so an RV is not recommended.

Long Island Bay Rec Site (Map #14/D3)

Long Island Bay has a small tenting area, which is accessed by boaters on Harrison Lake. It provides a secluded camping experience. Moorage, a beach, a dock and a barbecue shack are all available at the site.

Ruskin Dam Rec Site (Map #3/B2)

At the south end of Hayward Lake at the Ruskin Dam, you will find a picnic site overlooking the lake. A popular hiking/biking route skirts the reservoir along the old railbed heading north to Stave Falls Dam. Hayward Lake is also popular with watersports.

Stave Lake East Rec Sites (Map #13/C4)

Lost Creek FSR leads past Davies Lake Provincial Park along the eastern side of Stave Lake. Within the area are 3 rec sites, which provide camping in an area that shows signs of poor logging practices of days gone by.

Salsbury Lake Rec Site is comprised of a small rec site on each side of the lake. The east side rec site is really only a pullout for one camping party overlooking Salsbury Lake. A 75 metre walk is necessary to reach the lakeshore. The west side offers a small lakeside parking space and gravel boat launch.

Cypress Point Rec Site marks the only public access on the eastern shores of Stave Lake. A 2wd truck is needed to reach the rec site, which has a small, open camping area as well as a tenting area set in the forest. Since the rec site is on a bench above Stave Lake, a short but steep trail leads to the shoreline where you will find a rough cartop boat launch. Launching a cartop boat is difficult because of the steep trail.

Kenyon Lake Rec Site is located on a 4wd road north of Salsbury Lake next to a beautiful sub-alpine lake. The rec site is set in a small flat opening found about 75m from the lake. It is possible to launch a small boat at the lake but you will have to pack the boat to the water. Bring your mosquito repellent!

Twin Bridges Rec Site (Map #14/A4)

This rec site is located on the Statlu Creek Road along the banks of Blacklock Creek. It is a small, functional 3 unit site at the convergence of three creeks. The rec site is used mainly by hunters during the fall or creek fishermen during the summer.

Widgeon Lake Rec Site (Map #12/C3)

Accessed by a 4.5km canoe trip from Grant Narrows Park, this peaceful site is found at the end of a grassy slough (actually 8km south of the lake). It is a flat grassy area that can hold up to 10 tenting parties. The rec site is popular with canoeists, hikers and those looking for waterfowl viewing opportunities.

Hope/Fraser Canyon Rec Sites

Nahatlatch River Rec Sites (Map #23,24)

This river valley is located west of the Fraser River and is reached by crossing the bridge north of Boston Bar and proceeding up the Westside Road to the Nahatlatch River FSR. The main haul logging road follows the north side of the river, which is a fast flowing popular whitewater kayaking river (see the paddling section). Along the road, you will pass by a total of 8 rec sites. These rec sites receive heavy use during the summer because of the scenic beauty of the valley and the great paddling.

Apocynum Rec Site is 3.5km from the Nahatlatch River Bridge. It has 3 campsites.

Fir Flat Rec Site is 2.5km to the west of Apocynum Rec Site. It has 2 picnic tables set in the forest next to the river.

Log Creek Rec Site is found next to the outflow of Log Creek into the Nahtlatch River. At that rec site, you will find 2 picnic tables set next to some rapids.

Francis Lake Rec Site is found at the outflow of Francis Lake. It is a small rec site with a couple of camping spots.

Hannah Lake Rec Site is set on the northern shores of Hannah Lake. There is one picnic table right next to the main road.

Old Ranger Station offers an old cabin on the shores of Hanna Lake. The cabin, which is very popular, is filled on a first-come first-served basis.

Nahatlatch Lake Rec Site is located on the northern shores of Nahatlatch Lake. There are 3 campsites with picnic tables as well as a boat launch at the site.

Salmon Beach Rec Site offers 2 campsites with tables next to the Nahatlatch Lake.

Squakum Creek Rec Site is found on a short spur road off the main haul logging road. At this rec site, you will find 10 campsites set in the forest next to Nahatlatch Lake.

Scuzzy Creek Rec Site (Map #24/C3)

This small rec site is located on the banks of Scuzzy Creek off the Scuzzy Creek FSR. A 2wd vehicle with good clearance is necessary to reach the site.

Skagit Valley Rec Sites (Map #6)

The Silver Skagit Road leads south of Hope past the Silver Lake Provincial Park and through the Skagit Valley, a spectacular valley with raging streams and meandering rivers set under snowcapped peaks. The valley offers a variety of recreational activities include camping, hiking, hunting, fishing, paddling and ski touring.

The Old Silver Hope Rec Site is a small site on an open gravel bank next to the creek. The Forest Service has recently closed the site but the area still remains popular with RV's and camper units.

Eaton Creek Rec Site is a tiny, 3 unit site found at 16.5km along the Silver Skagit Road (good access). Two of the camping spots are set in the forest next to the creek and all three have tables. The site marks the beginning of the trail to Eaton Lake.

Galene Lake Rec Site is a remote hike-in rec site accessed by the Galene Lake Trail from the north end of Ross Lake. The rec site is little more than an area to camp next to this beautiful alpine lake.

Lillooet/Goldbridge Area Rec Sites

Botanie Lake Rec Site (Map #33/B1)

This small rec site, used primarily by fishermen, is located right next to Botanie Lake off the Botanie Valley Road.

Carpenter Lake Rec Sites (Map #44,45)

Carpenter Lake is located to the east of Lillooet on the Carpenter Lake Road. The area is quite dry with ponderosa pine dotting the hillsides. Along the north side of the lake are a number of rec sites.

Mission Dam Rec Site is found near Terzaghi Dam at the east end of Carpenter Lake. It has 3 campsites and is the least scenic of the campsites on the lake.

Carpenter Lake Rec Site is on the south side of the lake past the dam and has several campspots next to the lake together with a boat launch.

B.C. Hydro Campground is located at around 19.3km west of the dam on the north side of Carpenter Lake. It is situated at the outflow of Bighorn Creek and has 10 campsites, a boat launch and a picnicking area.

Jones Creek Rec Site is 2km to the west of the hydo site. This rec site has 6 camping units next to Carpenter Lake at the outflow of Jones Creek.

Tyaughton Junction Rec Site is 22km further to the west. There you will find 2 camping units together with a rough cartop boat launch.

Gun Creek Rec Site is a large semi-open site east of Tyaughton Junction Rec Site. It is the last of the rec sites on the north side of Carpenter Lake.

Duffey Lake Road (North) Rec Sites (Map #40,41)

The Duffey Lake Road extends in a northeast direction leading from Duffey Lake to Lillooet. Along the road is a series of rec sites ideal for a rest stop or for overnight camping.

Cayoosh Creek Rec Site is the southmost rec site. It is a scenic site next to Cayoosh Creek and has 6 picnic tables.

Roger Creek Rec Site, which is located about 4km north of Cayoosh Creek, has 2 different camping areas. The southern campground has 4 picnic tables and one campsite set in a thick forest next to the creek. The northern site has 5 campsites, 4 of which have picnic tables. It is more open than the southern site and better suited for RVs.

Gott Creek Rec Site is 2km north of Roger Creek Rec Site. It has 2 picnic tables set next to the junction of Gott and Cayoosh Creeks.

Cottonwood Rec Site is located 7.5km further north, a short distance from Cayoosh Creek. It has a total of 7 campsites with picnic tables that are spaced away from one another allowing privacy.

Cinnamon Rec Site is 4.5km north of Cottonwood Rec Site. It has a total of 7 campsites with picnic tables. Several of the campsites are set next to Cayoosh Creek with the rest being are set back from the creek.

Seton Lake Rec Area is found next to Seton Lake after you descend down to the valley bottom and prior to reaching Lillooet. The rec site was created by B.C. Hydro. It has a total of 29 campsites with picnic tables, pit toilets, garbage disposal and free firewood. There is an area for both RVs and for tenters.

Gun Lake South Rec Site (Map #44/A3)

This rec site is a semi-open site on the western shore of Gun Lake. Access to the rec site is by 2wd vehicle. A boat launch is located at the south end of the lake where there is also a dam.

Goldbridge South Rec Sites (Map #44/B3)

South of Goldbridge and Carpenter Lake are several rec sites.

Lost Lake Rec Site is a medium size site located in an opening at the north end of the lake. A half kilometre hike is required to reach the rec site.

Kingdom Lake Rec Site is a small treed site which is accessed by a short trail south of Lost Lake. The rec site is used primarily by fishermen because the lake offers fairly good fishing.

Gwyneth Lake Rec Site is a forested campsite located at the north end of the lake. Visitors either visit the lake for fishing or use the rec site as a staging site to hike Green Mountain. Since the lake has a marshy shoreline, it is best to bring a boat if you plan to fish. A 2wd vehicle can reach the rec site.

Hurley River Rec Site is a small rec site located on the banks of the Hurley River to the southwest of Bralorne. The site is used mainly by hunters and is accessed by a 2wd vehicle.

Hogback Mountain Area Rec Sites (Map #45/D1, 46/A1)
Leon Creek Rec Site is a small rec site located on a 2wd road (Leon Creek FSR) leading to the Hogback Mountain area. It is located next to the creek and is used primarily by hunters during the fall. **Hogback Rec Site** is a small open rec site used as a staging ground for hikers to the Hogback Mountain. The rec site receives heavy use throughout hunting season as it is a popular area for deer hunting.

Kwotlenemo (Fountain) Lake Rec Sites (Map #41/D1)
Kwotlenemo Lake is situated to the southeast of Lillooet in a scenic valley above the Fraser River Canyon. It is accentuated by dry mountains that form the valley typical of the arid terrain of the area. **Kwotlenemo Lake South Campground** is the largest of the 4 sites. It is set in an open area next to the lake. **Kwotlenemo Lake North Campground** is set in a cottonwood stand next to the lake. There is also a medium size treed site on the west side of the lake and a small treed site on the east side of the lake.

All the sites have boat launches for fishermen wishing to try their luck on the lake. Please note that there is an electric motor only restriction on the lake.

Mud Creek Road Rec Sites (Map #44/D2,45/A3)
Mud Creek Road leads off the Carpenter Lake Road and provides access to several rec sites worth a visit.

Carol Lake Rec Site is this region's southernmost rec site and is found on a short spur road about 2km along the Mud Creek Road. The rec site is located next to the small fishing lake and provides a nice area to fish or picnic. A cartop boat launch is available at the site, which can be accessed by RVs. An extensive trail network leads to the northwest from the rec site providing access to the Hog Creek Trail and eventually Lac La Mare and Burkholder Lake.

Marshall Creek Rec Site is 13.5km along the Mud Creek Road, just before Marshall Lake. This is a very small treed site next to the creek, which can be accessed by small RVs and campers.

Marshall Lake Rec Site is found at the northwest end of the lake on a 2wd spur road leading from the Mud Lake Road. The campground, situated on the shores of the lake, is fairly open and has several picnic tables. An old road/trail leads from the rec site southward to Carpenter Lake.

Liza Creek Rec Site is a small site on the creek near Liza Lake. From the rec site, a trail leads to the west end of Liza Lake where you can fish.

Tyaughton Creek Rec Site is the northernmost rec site and is a semi-open medium size site next to the creek. It is used by hunters and creek fishermen.

Seton Lake Rec Site (Map #41/A1)
On the south side of Seton Lake is a medium size rec site. The rec site is accessed by a 4wd vehicle leading from Duffey Lake Road or by boat. The rec site has a small narrow beach providing a good area to land your boat. Swimming and fishing are the primary attractions to the rec site.

Spruce Lake Area Rec Sites (Map #43,44)
To the northwest of Carpenter Lake is a vast, pristine wilderness area called the Spruce Lake Wilderness Area. It has an extensive network (164km) of hiking/biking trails (see trail section) which lead through several valleys surrounded by rugged mountain terrain. There are numerous areas ideal for camping within the Spruce Lake Area but the hub of the region is Spruce Lake, a shallow lake providing good fishing. At Spruce Lake, there are rec sites on the north and east end of the lake. **Spruce Lake North Rec Site** is a medium size site whereas **Spruce Lake East Rec Site** is a smaller rec site. **Hummingbird Lake Rec Site** is accessed off the Gun Pass Trail from Spruce Lake. It has a small tenting area on a beautiful mountain lake. **Trigger Lake Rec Site** is also on the Gun Pass Trail and has a small tenting area.

Tyaughton Lake Road Rec Sites (Map #44/B2)
From the Tyaughton Junction Rec Site on the northern shores of Carpenter Lake, the Tyaughton Lake Road leads to the north past 3 rec sites worth visiting.

The Mowson Pond Rec Site is at about 1.8km along Tyaughton Lake Road, as you reach the top of the hill. This is medium sized rec site next to a fairly good fishing lake.

Pearson Pond Rec Site is accessed by taking the Tyaughton Lake Road. At 3.4km along this road, is a spur road (going west) that takes you to the rec site. This is a small site next to another decent fishing lake.

Friburg Rec Site is the final rec site along the Tyaughton Lake Road. This site is found on the western shore of Tyaughton Lake. It is a medium size open site offering a place to camp while you are fishing the lake. Access to Tyaughton Lake is fairly good, the road deteriorates beyond the lake.

Yalakom River Valley Rec Sites (Map #45/C2)
Along the Yalakom River FSR is a series of rec sites. The southernmost rec site is the **Yalakom Rec Site** located next to the river. It is a small, open site that can be easily accessed by RVs given that the road is a mainhaul logging road to that point and beyond. **Lac La Marie Rec Site** is situated on a deteriorating 4wd spur road which is best hiked as opposed to driven. The rec site provides a remote camping area ideal for fishermen wanting to explore a small mountain lake. From Lake La Marie, the Burkholder Lake Trail leads northwest to the **Buckholder Lake Rec Site**. This rec site is another small tenting area next to a good fishing lake. If you are not interested in the hike-in lakes then continue further along the Yalakom River FSR from the Yalakom River Rec Site and you will find the **Beaverdam Rec Site**. This rec site is in a large grassy opening next to the river. A 2wd vehicle with good clearance is necessary to reach the site.

Pemberton and Area Rec Sites

Blackwater Lake Rec Site (Map #39/D2)
This rec site is located along the Blackwater Creek Road next to a small lake. It provides an area to picnic or camp while exploring the Birkenhead Lake Park or while trying your luck fishing at Blackwater Lake. The road to the rec site is fairly rough so RVs are not recommended. Given the proximity to Birkenhead Lake Park, the rec site does not receive as much use as other rec sites in the area. There are a total of 6 camping sites located in a brushy/treed area next to the lake. A total of 3 picnic tables are available at the 6 sites.

Duffey Lake East Campsite (Map #40/C4)
This old rec site is now part of the new provincial park on the lake. The campsite is located right next to Hwy #99 and is not very quiet. The campsite, however, is scenic as there is a dramatic glacier covered peak overshadowing the lake. There are 5 picnic tables next to the lake together with a boat launch. Most users of the rec site are traveling to other destinations on Hwy #99 or trying the reasonable fishing the lake has to offer.

Lillooet Lake Rec Sites (Map #31)
Scattered along the eastern shores of the Lillooet Lake are a series of rec sites. All the rec sites are accessed by the In-Shuck-Ch FSR, a good main haul logging road. You should be forewarned that the In-Shuck-Ch FSR is very windy and has numerous potholes making it a bumpy ride. Lillooet Lake is not a great recreation lake for watersports or fishing because it is cold and murky. However, the rec sites still receive heavy use during the summer months.

Driftwood Bay Rec Site is the southernmost rec site at 17.2km on the In-Shuck-Ch FSR. The 200m road leading from the main road to the rec site cannot be driven by RVs due to overhanging trees. The site is somewhat open and has 3 picnic tables. The site is better suited for group camping.

Lizzie Bay Rec Site, at 15.5km on the In-Shuck-Ch FSR, is probably the best of the rec sites along Lillooet Lake. It has a total of 9 camping spots complete with picnic tables. Those campsites are spread out, allowing some privacy. The sites are also right next to the lake and surrounded by forest making the setting quite attractive.

Strawberry Point Rec Site is the northernmost rec site. It is located in a small wooded area next to the lake and requires about a 5 minute walk from the parking lot to reach the rec site. The rec site has a beach together with 2 picnic tables and several tenting pads.

Twin One Creek Rec Site at 9.8km on the In-Shuck-Ch FSR, has 2 picnic tables in an opening beside the lake and 3 other picnic tables set in a stand of timber next to the lake. The camping spots are close together so privacy is non-existant. When you combine that with the popularity of the site, this site is not recommended for a quiet weekend getaway.

Lizzie Lake Rec Site (Map #31/B3)
Lizzie Creek Main (4wd access) leads uphill from Lillooet Lake through a narrow gorge before reaching this beautiful mountain lake. At the lake is a nice rec site complete with picnic tables and camping pads. The lake marks the access point for hikers wanting to explore the Upper Stein River Valley, some alpine meadows and several mountain lakes. Fishing at Lizzie Lake can be productive throughout the summer months.

Mosquito Lake (Map #30/B1)
This day-use site next to Mosquito Lake, has a wharf, hiking/biking trails, picnic tables and a beach. Despite its proximity to Pemberton, the site receives little use except by fishermen and a few sunbathers. The road into Mosquito Lake is usually quite rutted and muddy discouraging cars and RVs.

Owl Creek Rec Sites (Map #30/C1)

The two Owl Creek Rec Sites are located next to Owl Creek and the Birkenhead River. The best spot is next to Owl Creek where you will find 13 camping spots set in a deciduous/conifer forest next to the creek. Each spot has a picnic table and offers some privacy from other campers. The site next to Birkenhead River is simply an overnight pullout and is not as attractive as the Owl Creek Site. Both camping areas are located 350m off Hwy#99 across the railroad tracks.

Owl Lake Rec Site (Map #39/B4)

This rec site is accessed by the Mount Ronayne Trail. It is located at the south end of the lake and is an undeveloped tenting area used by fishermen and hikers.

Speetch Creek Rec Site (Map #39/C4)

This rec site is located approximately 300m to the east of Hwy#99. It has 6 private campsites complete with picnic tables set in the forest next to Speetch Creek. The rec site is a good choice if you are looking for an easily accessible camping spot.

Tenquille Lake Rec Site (Map #39/A3)

A steep 2hr hike off the Upper Lillooet River FSR or a shorter trail off the Hurley River Road leads to this sub-alpine lake. Tenquille Lake is a popular retreat for backpackers due to its spectacular beauty, fishing and mountain climbing opportunities. The lake is located in the alpine and is surrounded by rugged mountain peaks. There is an open site with a few tenting pads next to the lake.

Squamish/Whistler Area Rec Sites

Alexander Falls Rec Site (Map #29/C3)

Alexander Falls is a picnic site with two tables overlooking a scenic falls. It is accessed off the Callaghan Lake FSR (2wd or bike) and provides a quiet picnicking area. In the winter, the area becomes an active snowmobiling and cross country skiing location.

Brohm Lake Rec Site (Map #20/B3)

Brohm Lake Rec Site is a day-use site located right off Hwy #99. A short trek leads to the rec site along the eastern shores of the lake from the parking lot. At the rec site, you will find a swimming area as well as picnic tables. The main users are fishermen casting a fly or lure into the lake or hikers/bikers exploring the extensive trail system around the lake.

Cal-Cheak Rec Sites (Map #29/C4)

These four rec sites are located just off Hwy #99 on the Daisy Lake Road. They receive heavy use, as they provide a camping ground together with access to a series of hiking trails over Callaghan Creek. Many visitors hike south to Brandywine Falls Park via the Cal-Cheak/Brandywine Trail, which is 4km one way. Thre trail crosses over a suspension bridge at Callaghan Creek.

The **Callaghan Creek Camp** has 5 tables and an A-frame cooking shelter situated in a bit of a cul-de-sac cut out of the forest. It is located approximately 150m from the Hwy#99. At 0.5km from the Hwyis the Cal-Cheak **Confluence North Site** which has a total of 9 picnic tables situated next to the river. At 0.8km on the road is the **Cal-Cheak Camping Area**. This site has a total of 8 picnic tables situated in a clearing in the forest nearby to the river. The final site is the **Cal-Cheak Junction Rec Site**, which has a total of 4 picnic tables and a number of tenting pads.

Callaghan Lake Rec Site (Map #29/B3)

This rec site is situated at the south end of Callaghan Lake, is really a glorified parking lot with 3 campsites and 2 picnic tables. However, the dramatic setting of Callaghan Lake makes up for the campground. The lake is surrounded by some rugged peaks together with a glacier and a beautiful waterfall. The rec site receives moderate use despite its attractiveness and 2wd access along the Callaghan Lake FSR. Fishing, beginning in the early summer, is the primary attraction to the area. Given the snow accumulation, the lake is not usually accessible until early July.

Cat Lake Rec Site (Map #20/C3)

Cat Lake Rec Site is found at the south end of this tiny lake. It is reached by walking down a bank from the parking area to the lakeshore site. At the site, you will find a swimming area and dock, picnic tables as well as an extensive trail network around the lake. The trail network can be enjoyed by hikers, bikers and motorcyclists. A gate on the Cheekeye River FSR may be closed meaning you will have a longer walk to the rec site. People staying overnight tend to camp near the parking lot.

Upper Squamish River Rec Site (Map #28/D4)

Found at 44km on the Squamish Main, this campground offers camping right at the juction at the Elaho and Squamish Rivers. The rec site is used by kayakers or individuals exploring the Elaho River Valley or the Upper Squamish River Valley.

Sunshine Coast/Powell River Rec Sites

Appleton Creek Rec Site (Map #16/D1)
Found on the Theodosia FSR next to Appleton Creek, this rec site has several camping units together with pit toilets and picnic tables. From the rec site, a network of hiking trails lead towards Sliammon Lake and the ocean. To reach the rec site requires a short walk from the Theodosia FSR and is ideal for wilderness tenting.

Dinner Rock Rec Site (Map #16/C1)
This rec site is located directly on the ocean off a 2wd access road from Hwy #101. The road to the rec site is fairly rough and steep as it nears the ocean so it is best left to high clearance trucks. The well maintained rec site has a total of 12 campsites together with pit toilets, firewood and garbage cans. Camping areas range from from walk-in sites to vehicle sites directly overlooking the ocean.

Duck Lake Road Rec Sites (Map #17/B3)
Along the Duck Lake Road, there are several rec sites restricted to day use. The **East Lake Rec Site** is accessed by a side road off of the Duck Lake Road and then a short walk. It is a picnic only site on the eastern shores of East Lake. **Lang Lake Rec Site** is also accessed by trail and is a picnic site across from the Lang Creek hatchery. **Mud Lake Rec Site** is also a picnic site at the south end of Mud Lake and is accessed by trail.

Emma Lake Rec Site (Map #26/D3,27/A3)
The trail leading south to Emma Lake begins on B Branch off the Goat Lake Main. There is a cabin at the lake providing overnight accommodation for fishermen to Emma Lake or for hikers accessing the South Powell Divide Trail.

Lyon Lake Rec Site (Map #9/C1)
On the Halfmoon-Carlson FSR, this small rec site is used primarily by fishermen. A 4wd vehicle is neccessary to reach the rec site.

Klein Lake Rec Site (Map #18/B4)
This rec site is accessed off the North Lake FSR (2wd access) and is found at the northern end of Klein Lake. It receives heavy use throughout the summer months. However, because the campsites are spread out and in a forested area, you can still have some privacy. There are a total of 10 campsites with picnic tables together with pit toilets, garbage cans and firewood at the rec site. Some of the spots are located in a cleared area whereas others are in a treed area next to the lake.

Mount Steel Cabins (Map #10/B2)
The Mount Steel Backcountry Trail System offers four cabins next to the sub-alpine lakes in the area. The trail system is accessed from the Sechelt FSR and is found in newly established Tetrahedron Provincial Park. The park is used extensively by hikers and backcountry skiers. The Mount Steel Cabin is the most popular and largest of the cabins in the area. It is located north of Chapman Lake and necessitates a steep climb into the alpine. It sleeps up to a dozen individuals.

Powell Lake Canoe Route Rec Sites (Map #17,18,26)
Along the Powell Lake Canoe Route (see Paddling Section) you will find numerous recreation sites available not only for the canoeists but also for visitors accessing the area via the main haul logging roads.

Please note that vehicle access to the area is restricted. Public access is allowed between 6pm & 6am or on weekends and holidays.

Beaver Lake Rec Site is found at the west side of Beaver Lake, a small lake where paddlers can take a side trip from the main route. The rec site has a few tenting pads together with picnic tables and pit toilets.

Dodd Lake Rec Site is found at about 16km on the Goat Lake Road. The campsite, which is comprised of 12 units, is set in an opening beside the mainhaul road. It has pit toilets, firewood and garbage cans. The site is used by both vehicle travelers as well as paddlers.

Goat Lake Rec Site is found at the end of the steep portage from Windsor Lake. It is a boat access only site with picnic tables and pit toilets as well as tenting pads.

Haywire Bay Campsite is located in the regional park next to this sheltered bay on the eastern shores of Powell Lake. The site has several camping spots next to the lake together with a boat launch. Trails lead to Lost Lake or along the Powell Lake shoreline southward (via Matthews Trail).

Horseshoe Lake Rec Site is found off of Branch H Road at the south end of Horseshoe Lake. The site has picnic tables together with pit toilets. It is used primarily by paddlers.

Horseshoe River Rec Site is found along the waterway leading from Horseshoe Lake to Lois Lake. It has several tenting pads together with picnic tables and pit toilets. The primary users are paddlers on the canoe route.

Inland Lake Rec Site is found at the south end of the lake off of the Inland FSR. It is a unique site because it has 13km of wheelchair accessible trails circling the lake. There are a total of 16 picnic tables at the campsite together with 5 campsites/cabins for disabled people. A few of the campsites can be accessed by campers or RVs, while the rest are best suited for tenting. There is a wharf, litter barrels and pit toilets available at the site.

Khartoun Lake Rec Site is set on the north side of the lake and is accessed by canoe or 2wd vehicle. When you reach the rec site, you can find camping either in an opening on the lake shore or in a forested area. There are a total of 6 picnic tables together with pit toilets, boat launch and trash cans. The lake is spectacular with the hillsides descending sharply to the shoreline creating a bowl-like setting.

Little Horseshoe Creek Rec Site is found on the shores of the Horseshoe Lake at the outflow from Little Horseshoe Lake. It is used exclusively by paddlers on the route. The site contains not only picnic tables but also litter barrels and toilet facilities.

Lois Lake Rec Site has a total of 8 sites with picnic tables, 5 of which are in an open area near the lake. The other 3 are tenting pads set in the forest.

Lower Powell Rec Site is accessed by trail off of the Island Lake Trail or by boat on Powell Lake. It provides several tenting spots on the eastern shore of Powell Lake.

Middle Point Rec Site is found on the waterway between Nanton and Ireland Lake. It has several tenting pads together with picnic tables and pit toilets. It is used almost exclusively by paddlers on the route.

Nanton Lake Rec Site is found on the western shores of the lake. It has a total of 15 campsites with 2 lakeside spots and the rest being in the forest next to the lake. Of the sites, 13 have picnic tables. There is a boat launch together with firewood, pit toilets and trash cans available.

Nanton-Ireland North Rec Site is found at the south end of Ireland Lake at the inflow creek. It has several tenting pads together with tables and pit toilets.

Nanton-Ireland South Rec Site is found at the north end of Nanton Lake at the outflow to Ireland Lake. It contains both picnic tables, tenting pads and pit toilets.

North Dodd Lake Rec Site is found at the north end of Dodd Lake next to the channel between Windsor and Dodd Lake. It is accessed by a short hike off of the Goat Lake Main or by canoe. There are several tenting pads together with picnic tables and toilets available at the rec site.

Powell Lake Rec Site is found near the outflow from Giavanno Lake. It is a boat access only site used primarily by canoers on the route. It has picnic tables as well as pit toilet facilities.

Windsor Lake Rec Site is found at the north end of Windsor Lake prior to the steep portage down to Goat Lake. The rec site can be accessed by a short trail from a 36km mark on the Goat Lake Main or by canoeing from Dodd Lake. The rec site has a few tenting pads together with picnic tables and pit toilets.

Richardson Lake Rec Site (Map #9/D2)
This rec site is reached by 4wd road off the Mount Richardson Road. It is a medium size site used by hikers accessing Mount Richardson or by fishermen.

Texada Island Rec Sites (Map #8/C2)
On Texada Island, there are only 2 rec sites. **Bob's Lake Rec Site** is found on a 4wd road at the foot of Mt. Grant. It is a small tenting area used by hikers and mountain bikers. **Shingle Beach Rec Site** is located right on the ocean to the southeast of Davie Bay off the Davie Bay Road. The site can be reached by 2wd vehicle and provides a nice area to camp overlooking the ocean. The rec site marks a good scuba diving area and allows for boat mooring.

Trails

Southwestern B.C. offers a wide variety of trails that can be enjoyed by hikers, mountain bikers, X-C skiers, snowmobilers, horseback riders and all other trail users. The options range from short interpretative trails to rugged sub-alpine treks. Also, there are numerous "destination oriented" trails that lead to some great fishing lakes, mountain vistas, waterfalls and more.

Below, we have included information on over 250 trails and routes. To help you select the trail which best suites your abilities, we have included elevation gain, return distance and special features wherever possible. **Please note that all distances and times are for round trip hikes unless otherwise noted.**

A word of caution for hikers. Higher elevation trails (over 1000 m) may have a limited season due to late season snow so they are best hiked beginning in July until October. Also, if you are travelling on unmarked trails, we recommend that you have mountaineering knowledge and are equipped with a topographic map and a compass.

Finding the trailhead is sometimes half the fun (and half the work). For this reason, you should refer to the appropriate map in this book to determine where the trail begins. In urban and rural areas, trails often start off small side roads too small to mark on our maps. In these areas we recommend you get a city map to help locate the trailhead. Also remember, our maps are designed only as a general access guide not intended to navigate you through a hidden mountain pass or across an expansive ridge network.

On the maps contained in this book, you will find symbols identifying what mode of travel is possible on the trails (ie. by foot, horse, motorbike, mountain bike, snowmobile or X-C skiing,). Mountaineering & climbing opportunities are also noted. We refer to the level of difficulty of the trails in this section as the following:

Easy is a gentle grade excellent for family excursions;

Moderate is a fairly strenuous trail with climbing involved. These trails will challenge most trail users and should not be underestimated;

Difficult is for experienced users as the trails are often rough and or unmarked.

Fraser Valley Trails (Lower)

Centennial Trail (Map #3-6)
The Centennial Trail extends 420km from The Plaza of Nations in Vancouver to Joe Lake near Keremeos. Trail conditions vary in each area with the sections in the Fraser Valley interrupted by private land ownership and the sections near Manning Park being overgrown and hard to follow in places. The distances and elevation gain of the various sections of the trail are noted below:

From Fort Langley to Manning Park: This stretch is best done in 12 trips. Some of this section is overgrown and very hard to follow so it may be advisable to follow a logging road to avoid difficult stretches.

Fort Langley-Mt Lehman:	20km; no elevation gain
Mt Lehman-Sumas Mnt Trailhead:	19km; elevation gain of 140m (to 150m)
Sumas Mnt-Quadling Road:	14km; 130m descent
Quadling Road-Sweltzer Bridge:	19km; 30m elevation gain
Sweltzer Bridge-O'Byrne Road:	16km;10m elevation gain
O'Byne Road-Chilliwack Bridge:	23km; elevation gain of 260m
Chilliwack Bridge-Post Cr Road:	16km; elevation gain of 280m (to 600m)
Post Cr Road-Hicks Creek:	16km; 50m descent
Hicks Creek-Skagit R. Bridge:	19km; no elevation gain
Skagit Bridge-Skyline Divide:	14km; 50m descent

Centennial Trail (Chilliwack River Section) (Map #4/D4,5) is an easy trail following the north side of the Chilliwack River. Due to a mudslide on the western end, it is easiest to walk downstream from the signed trailhead on the Chilliwack Bench Road to the Obyrne Road trailhead. Allow 4 hours to walk 10km as you descend 130m.

Centennial Trail (26 Mile Bridge to Skyline Trail) (Map #6/B3) is a rugged 18km section has recently been cleared (1996) but remains quite challenging especially for mountain bikers. The trail climbs over 1000m over

the shoulder of the mountain before descending to the valley bottom. Currently, there is a closed sign at the Skyline Trail end for reasons unknown. The route is still marked and easily followed.

Cheam Peak / Mountain Trail (Map #5/A3)
Found at the end of the rough 4wd Chilliwack-Chipmunk FSR, the Mount Cheam trail is a beautiful alpine hike. You climb 632m over 9.5km (4 hours) return to the sheer peak and amazing view of the Fraser Valley. Along the way you pass Spoon Lake, rolling subalpine meadows dotted with wildflowers in July-August and the steep trail own to Bridal Falls. The trail is best from July to September since the area is prone to avalanches in the winter. The alternative route is a difficult 30km (day+) hike from the gated Bridal Veil Falls FSR gaining 2080m from the valley.

Elk Thurston Trail (Map #4/D3)
A grueling 14.6km (7 hour) return hike found on the Chilliwack Bench FSR at a small gravel pit. You climb over 1000m (mostly at the beginning) to the 1630m summit and the breathtaking panoramic views of the Chilliwack Valley and the border peaks. The trail begins in a forested setting before entering flowery subalpine meadows near the base of Elk Mountain. The trail then continues through the subalpine to Mount Thurston. The exposed alpine ridge can be windy. The trail is best hiked in July-October.

Flora Lake Trail (Map #5/C3)
A grueling overnight hike that climbs 1130m in elevation to the ridge before dropping 430m to the beautiful lake. Allow 11 hours return as you journey 14km return. This difficult hike with 2 steep sections offers breathtaking views of the Chilliwack Valley, old mining trails around the lake and fairly good fishing. It is possible to follow a rough, undeveloped trail past the Flora Creek Falls over to Greendrop Lake.

Ford Mountain Trail (Map #5/B3)
From the sign at the end of the Ford Mnt FSR (4wd access), a short 1.7km (1.5 hour) one-way hike follows the treed ridge to an old forestry lookout with panoramic views. The moderate trail leads sharply uphill for the first 30 minutes before levelling out somewhat. The trail gains 400m in total. Experienced hikers can continue along the bare ridge to the base of Williams Peak, which is an additional 12km (4.5 hours) return, climbing 460m along the way. If you do not have a 4wd vehicle, it is possible to hike the road but this requires an additional climb of 620m over 4.5km (2.5 hours) one-way.

International Ridge Trail (Map #4/B4)
Accessed off Vance Road within the International Ridge Provincial Park, this 18km (8 hour) ridge route leads to the summit of Mount Amadis at 1525m gaining 1325m in elevation. From the summit, you get a good view of the Fraser Valley and the U.S. border.

Ling Lake Trail (Map #5/C3)
The trailhead is found at the end of Foley Creek Road, but there is a gate located near the Foley Creek Rec Site so you will have to hike or bike up the logging road before actually starting the trail. From the gate, the trail is about 18km (day+) to the alpine lake. The principle users of the trail are fishermen.

Liumchen Lake Trail (Map #4/C4)
A beautiful alpine hike that starts at the end of the rough Liumchen East FSR (about 9.5km along this 4wd road). From the trailhead you climb sharply uphill (130m) through some forested areas and meadows to the ridge and a view of the Chilliwack Valley before dropping 280m into the Liumchen Lake bowl. Allow 5 hours to hike 9.4km return or prepare to camp and explore the trails to the surrounding peaks of Church and Liumchen Mountains. The hike is best done in late summer (for the flowers) or in early autumn. Church Mnt is an additional 1.5km along the ridge to 1714m. Liumchen Mnt leads south from the alpine meadows climbing 457m over 2.5km one-way to the great vantage overlooking the U.S.A.

Mount Laughington Trail (Map #5/A3)
The spur road leading to the base of Mount Laughington is usually gated so it is necessary to hike 19km (8 hours) from the Chilliwack-Foley FSR to the summit gaining 1340meters in elevation along the way. If the road is not gated then the hike is reduced to 5km (3 hours) return gaining 200m to the summit.

Pierce Lake / Mount McFarlene Trail (Map #5/A4)

A rough, steep trail that climbs steadily from the Pierce Creek Rec Site to the south end of Mt McFarlane. It begins by rising sharply through a second growth forest before breaking out into a rockslide. Soon the trail crosses Pierce Creek and begins to deteriorate before reaching the lake. On the way, you will pass two lakes, alpine meadows and spectacular viewpoints. It is recommended to allow for an overnight trip since you climb 1780m over 7km one-way. Day-trippers may wish to stop at Pierce Lake, a good fishing lake, which is 4.3km (3 hours) one-way climbing 1080m. The trail is best hiked in July through September.

Post Creek X-C Ski Trails (Map #5/D3)

A 7.3km trail system that offers varying terrain to suit all abilities of skiers. It is recommended to ski these trails in a counter clockwise direction. The trails are found adjacent to the Post Creek Rec Site across from the Chilliwack Lake Road.

Post-Greendrop Trail (Map #5/D3)

Part of the Centennial trail system, the Post-Greendrop Trail starts from the Post Creek Rec Site. From here you climb 370m over 10.4km (6 hours) return past Post and Lindeman Lakes to the south end of Greendrop Lake, where rustic camping is offered. This moderate trail leads along the steep valley and has some rough rocky sections. The lakes are popular fishing destinations or you can continue on the Centennial trail system to the mouth of Hicks Creek. The later trail leads 6km over Custer Pass. It is also possible to access Flora Lake on an undeveloped trail.

Radium Lake Trail (Map #5/C4)

From the end of Paulsen Road, a suspension bridge crosses the Chilliwack River to the start of this moderate trail which climbs 880m over 12km (6 hours) return. Along the journey you will pass the Centennial Trail, a unique suspension bridge and an old cabin. Tiny Radium Lake is nestled below 2 towering peaks. A forestry cabin at the lake can be used as a base to explore nearby MacDonald Peak (at 2244m) or Mount Webb (at 2163m). These routes are best left to the experienced hiker willing to climb at least 780m from the lake.

Sumas Mnt Trail (Map #3/D3, 4/A3)

To reach the trailhead from the west, take Exit 95 off Hwy #1. The trail begins at the sign marked "Centennial Trail" and then crosses Wades Creek before proceeding uphill past some waterfalls and Chadsey Lake to the summit. From the east side, start at the Sumas Dam beneath a rock bluff off Quadling Road. From there, the trail leads uphill through an old cutblock before reaching Chadsey Lake and eventually the summit. Regardless of which route you take, the hike is about 12km (5 hours) return gaining about 700m in elevation. A great view of Sumas Prairie and Vedder Mountain is offered from the top. Some hikers prefer to save the extra effort of the 280 meter climb to the summit and circle peaceful Chadsey Lake. The trail can be hiked or biked by expert riders from May to November.

Upper Chilliwack River /
Hanging Lake Trails (Map #5/D4)

From the Depot Creek Rec Site at the south end of Chilliwack Lake, the main trail leads along the shores of the lake to the estuary of the Chilliwack River. From that point, there are two options.

Upper Chilliwack River Trail is a rewarding trail that meanders among an ecological reserve with old growth cedar, majestic Douglas-fir and amabilis fir next to the upper Chilliwack River. This flat, easy trail leads 5.4km (3 hours return) to the US border where you have a chance to continue south into the north Cascade Mountains. From here, a difficult route can bring you to Mount Baker after two fabulous days of hiking.

Hanging Lake Trail is a moderate 8km (4 hour) round trip hike to Hanging Lake, which is at the base of Mount Linderman. Hanging Lake provides good fishing and some rock climbing options.

Vedder Mountain Trail (Map#4/B4)

An excellent trail found off an old spur road on the Vedder Mountain FSR. It is a well developed, moderate 11.5km (6 hour) trail gaining 375m (mostly at the start) to the summit at 925m. Once you break out of the dense hemlock forest you will be rewarded with views of the Sumas Prairie, Vedder Canal and area. Spring flowers brighten the way. Once on the summit, other options are offered including: following

an old trail down to the old road and return along the road; or use the old trail from the Yarrow side to access the top.

For mountain bikers, this is the place to ride in the Chilliwack area. The main route follows the FSR from Parmenter Road 21.5km around the ridge and offers great views of the surrounding valley. This moderate ride climbs 490m along the way. Several side trails in the area have been developed by motorcyclists, and provide experienced mountain bikers with fast and twisty thrills. A popular option follows the Vedder Mountain Classic Route. This route heads south (left) from the FSR and follows several trails and old roads back to the main road and the start (some 17km 340m later).

Vedder River Trail (Map #4/A3)

A recently developed dyke trail leads along the north side of the Vedder River. It is found at the bridge marking the beginning of Chilliwack Lake Rd. The trail is a wide cart track that is available to hikers and bikers.

Williams Ridge Trail (Map #5/B3)

A grueling 11km (6 hour) trail found 32km along the Chilliwack Lake Road. The steep, undeveloped trail is marked by orange markers as it rises through a second growth forest past a clearing with a good view of the valley. From there, the trail continues along a forested ridge to connect with the Ford Mountain Trail. Overall, hike 1440m including 900m in the first 1.5km to the base of Williams Peak. It is possible to scramble up to the prominent Williams Peak (an additional 200m). The ridge route from Ford Mountain is the easier option.

Williamson Lake Trail (Map #5/B3)

Beginning at the Foley Lake Rec Site, the trail is a difficult 13km (7hr) hike gaining 1200m to the lake at 1660m. Not only will you feel like a mountain goat, you might actually see one. The trail begins by crossing Foley Creek and then it rises sharply along the ridge above Williams Creek to the lake. The hike is best left to late summer to the fall given the avalanche hazard in the spring and the creek crossing problems during spring run-off.

Fraser Valley Trails (Upper)

Belcarra Regional Park (Map #2/A1)

Accessed by the Bedwell Bay Road off Ioco Road, this regional park encompasses Bedwell Bay and Burns Point, which jets out into Indian Arm. A 5.5km (2 hour) round trip takes you along the shoreline past Burns Point to Jug Island. There is a pleasant secluded bay at the end of the trail. Views of Mount Seymour and Second Narrows Bridge are provided along the trail. Another pleasant walk circles around Sasamat Lake. This easy, one hour hike offers a cool, refreshing stroll through the heavy forest around the lake.

Mountain bikers will enjoy the **Burrard Thermal Trails**. This trail network starts near White Pine Beach at Sasamat Lake. A short 3km hydro road dips 165m

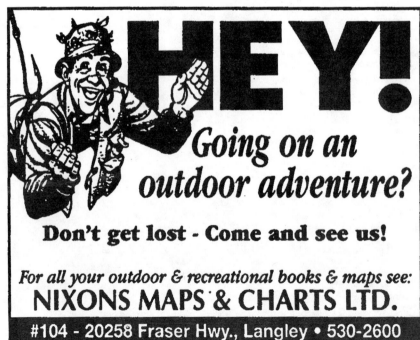

(after the initial climb) towards Bedwell Bay offering a view over Burrard Inlet. Off the access road, more challenging trails offer experienced riders some technical, downhill riding along well maintained motorcycle trails..

Blue Mountain Trails (Map #3/A2)
Found north of Maple Ridge at the end of McNutt Road, you access this challenging mountain biking area from the gate at the bottom of Blue Mountain FSR. Continue up the road and follow the first road left after the powerlines. From this road, several challenging trails cut down to the hill. For motorbikers and experienced mountain bikers, there are also many other routes to explore but expect loose surface, undeveloped trails which are steep and rooty.

The Bowl (Downes Creek Park) (Map #4/C4)
A neat 4km network of trails found in the bowl between Clearbrook Road and Trethewey St in Abbotsford. This small area offers great mountain biking for all levels of riders on short, well developed trails. The trail network also makes an enjoyable area to walk.

Buntzen Lake Trails (Map #2/A1,12/A4)
"Lake Beautiful" (the original name of the lake) is a popular recreation area that is easily accessed by Sunnyside Road to the north of Port Moody. Within the forest next to Buntzen Lake are a series of multi-use trails that range from gentle family strolls to difficult hikes. An on site map will help you pick your route.

The main bicycle route follows the Pumphouse Road from the main entrance to the recreation area. The route then crosses the floating bridge before leading along the South Beach Trail to the South Beach Picnic Area. Ultimately, the trail continues along the Powerhouse Road on the east side of Buntzen Lake to the north end. The easy route is 10km return and is mainly along dirt roads through the rainforest surrounding Buntzen Lake. The main hiking trails are as follows:

Academy Trail is a horse and pedestrian trail which leads from the Alpine Riding Academy at the main entrance gate all the way to the north end of Buntzen Lake. The road eventually connects onto the Powerline Road half way along Buntzen Lake. Overall, the trail is 10km (2 hours) return with minimal elevation gain.

Buntzen Lake Trail is a 12km (3 hour) route that circles Buntzen Lake. The best place to start is at the South Beach Picnic Area and proceed in a counterclockwise direction around the lake. At the south end, there is a floating bridge to cross. Generally, the easy trail is well maintained and has minimal elevation gain.

Buntzen Powerline Trail is a difficult mountain bike ride that is very difficult to find and follow due to the several side trails and new development in the area. The trail is found south of Buntzen Lake Park (off Sunnyside Road) and heads to Parkway Road (which leads to Golf Academy Way).

Diez Vista Trail is a moderate 13km (5 hour) hike with a 455m elevation gain. The trail goes up and down trail, and is quite steep and challenging in places. Ultimately, you reach the summit at 600m and will be rewarded with an excellent view of Indian Arm and Buntzen Lake. The trail leads from the Pumphouse Road to the north end of the lake.

Dilly-Dally Trial is a steep 24km (10+ hour) trail leading from the South Beach parking lot gaining 1100m to the summit at 1250m. From the summit, you can continue on to Eagle Peak or Eagle Mountain by following the ridge. The trail is best tackled in July to October.

Eagle Peak Trail is a steep 15km (6 hour) hike, which leads past Eagle Mountain to Lindsay Lake. Along the way is an elevation gain (1020m to 1160m). It is a small payment for the amazing view. From Lindsay Lake, you can continue on to Eagle Peak, which is another 5km return. An alternative route is to traverse down the slope to the north end of Buntzen Lake. The difficult hike is accessed off the gated Powerline Road.

Despite the climb, mountain bikers actually frequent the area. The smarter riders usually stick to the trails on either side of Noons Creek. These rough trails follow old creek beds and spill you out onto the powerline trail. From here, you can then make your way back to the start on Parkway Road & Sunnyside Road southeast of Buntzen Lake.

Lakeview Trail extends along the eastern slopes of Buntzen Ridge on the west side of Buntzen Lake. The trail is accessed just north of the Pumphouse Road from the south or from the suspension bridge at the north end of the lake. The trail is 5.8km (2 hours) in length, taking the hiker through up and down terrain. It is also very steep and rough at the north end. The trail can be used by both equestrians and hikers.

Nature Trail is a 1km self guided nature trail which circles a wooded knoll beginning south of the boat launch. The trail follows the shores of Buntzen Lake before leading through a forested area to the South Beach Picnic Area. Along the way, interpretative signs describe plant and animal growth.

Burke Mountain Trails (Map #2/C1)
Located at the south end of the new Pinecone Burke Provincial Park, the trailhead is reached by parking near the entrance to the Gun Club off Harper Road. The Burke Ridge Trail is 20km (8 hours) return gaining 880m to the height of land at 1225m. The trail begins on a gated old road and then marked trail eventually climbing steadily uphill to the ridge. From the top, you will get a great view of Coquitlam Mountain and the surrounding area. The **Woodland Walk** is a less strenuous option as the trail dissects the second growth forest at the base of the ridge with little elevation gain (200m). This trail is 7km (3 hours) taking you past some spectacular waterfalls, over a moss covered bridge and through remnants of logging from the turn of the century. Other hiking trails in the area include:

The **Coquitlam Lake View Trail**, a 9.4km (5 hour) hike gaining 200m.
The **South Slope Trail**, a 18km (6-7 hour) trail climbing 880m.
The **Village Lake Trail**, a 15km (7 hour) hike gaining 680m.

Mountain bikers should expect difficult rocky trails which require a lot of climbing. **The Sawblade** is the most popular (but misused) trail which heads north (left) from the main road. This 11.5km difficult trail climbs 400m and eventually meets up with the **Coquitlam River Trail**. An easier option is to continue along the main road past the second gate and follow the trail heading south. This is the start of **The Triple Crown**; a great moderate ride, which climbs 550m over 15km. This trail actually combines three shorter trails and will take you down to Galloway Road (south of Harper Road).

Campbell Lake Trail (Map #4/D1)
A rugged trail that climbs from the sign on Hwy#9 across from Balsam Ave. south of Harrison Hot Springs to a remote mountain lake. This difficult 3 hour hike climbs 630m over 4.8km with good viewpoints of the Harrison Lake and the Cheam Range along the way. Since the average grade of the trail is a steep 16%, it is recommended to arrange for a pick up at the top via the rough 4wd Mount Woodside FSR. Fishing is possible at the lake.

Centennial Trail (Map #3-6)
The Centennial Trail extends 420km from The Plaza of Nations in Vancouver to Joe Lake near Keremeos. Trail conditions vary in each area with the sections in the Fraser Valley interrupted by private land ownership and the sections near Manning Park being overgrown and hard to follow in places. The distances and elevation gain of the various sections of the trail are noted below:

From Vancouver to Fort Langley:
This section is best done in day trips. The trail follows The Seawall and then The Baden Powell Trail before requiring a water taxi over Indian Arm. From the east side of the Arm, the trail continues along the Pitt River Dikes eventually making its wat to the Albion Ferry and Fort Langley. The distances are as follows:

Plaza of Nations-Cleveland Dam:	16km, 160m elevation gain
Cleveland Dam-Lynn Canyon:	12km, 30m elevation loss
Lynn Canyon-Deep Cove:	12km, 120m elevation loss
Deep Cove-Port Moody:	14km, 10m elevation loss
Port Moody-Pitt River Bridge:	16.5km, 0 gain
Pitt R. Bridge-Maple Ridge Park:	16km, 10m elevation gain
Maple Ridge Park-Fort Langley:	11km, 10m elevation loss.

Davis Lake Park (Map #3/C1)
Reached by the Lost Creek FSR off Sylvester Road, this small provincial park offers a 5km (1.5 hour) easy, flat walk which circles the lake.

Denham Trail (Map #14/C4)
From the Weaver Lake Rec Site, a 6.2km trail loops around this picturesque fishing lake. Relatively flat, it makes for an easy 3 hour hike with several chances to access or view the lake.

Dewdney Trunk Trails (Map #3/C2)
Dewdney Trunk Road is a scenic rural road that is used by recreationists to access backcountry adventures between Maple Ridge and Mission. Near the Rifle Range and Mill Pond outside of Mission, a series of trails exist. These route can be enjoyed by hikers or expert mountain bikers.

Caswell (Red Mnt) Trail is a 9.8km loop trail that climbs 310m. This trail heads west from the Mill Pond and combines old roads with single-track trails.

Pioneer (Bear Mnt)Trail is found to the east of the Dewdney Trunk Road but is best accessed from Saunders Road (off Richards St.) to the south. This trail hosts the Bear Mnt Challenge Downhill Mountain Bike Race. From the microwave road you head back to the Mill Pond some 3.2km later. It is also possible to cycle up to the microwave and cruise down a single-track.

Hoover Lake Trail is found 2km east of Stave Falls Dam. This trail follows an old road and trail as it climbs steadily to the lake. The trail is 7.4km return with an elevation gain of 250m. Allow 1 hour to reach the lake as you hike through a heavy forest.

Stave Dam Forest Interpretive Trail is found just east of Stave Falls Dam and is marked by a large sign. This is a short 1.7km trail that raises 150 metres as it cuts through a second growth forest.

Fool's Gold Route (Map #12/C3)
Heavy lobbying for conservation of the extensive untouched forest to the west of Pitt Lake resulted in the creation of the Pinecone Burke Provincial Park. Within the park is the rugged and difficult to follow Fool's Gold Route. The route runs some 50km (7 days) from the Widgeon Lake Trail all the way to the Mamquam River FSR.

The Widgeon Lake Trail is accessed by canoe to the Widgeon Lake Rec Site. From there, the route follows an old road and trail, which are well maintained by the Burke Mountain Naturalists. As the route departs the Widgeon Lake Trail, you will have to cross the creek and head in a northern direction towards Pitt Pass. After reaching the pass at 720m, the route descends into the DeBeck Creek drainage, which offers some of the best, untouched subalpine forests around.

Throughout the valley, the trail leads through some extremely rough sections where you will wonder if there is even a trail. Eventually, you will pass through Bull Pass at 1060m on your way to the Cedar Sprit Grove, a stand of 1000 year old cedar. Then, the route leads to the west and becomes easier to follow as it is marked by pink flagging. The trail culminates on a spur road off the Mamquam River FSR. This route is an excellent choice if you desire a challenging, remote wilderness experience. It is best left to experienced backpackers equipped with compasses, topographic maps and mountaineering knowledge.

Golden Ears Provincial Park Trails (Map #2/D1, 3/A1, 12, 13)
Named for the snow-capped peaks of Mt Blanshard which glisten like gold, this wilderness park offers several multi-purpose trails. The highlights include an abundance of wildlife and the scenic Alouette Lake.

Golden Ears Trail is a 24km (10 hour/overnight) trip gaining 1500m to 1700m. The hike begins at the West Canyon parking lot and follows Gold Creek and the West Canyon Trail. Then, the trail traverses up the ridge past a rustic mountain shelter to the summit of Panorama Ridge. Enjoy the views of Pitt Lake and the surrounding area as you climb to the top.

Alouette Mountain Trail is 22km (9 hours) return gaining 1100m to the summit at 1375m. The hike begins on the Incline Trail before heading along a fire access road. A marked trail leads from the access road uphill to the summit. Along the way, you will pass some scenic meadows and ponds. Mountain bikers and horses are allowed to follow the fire access road to the hitching post at Lake Beautiful. The steady climb of 440m over 11.5km is well rewarded with a downhill cruise back to the start. It is possible to bike the **Switchback Trail** down. But expect a fast, difficult trail that is noted for its berms (switchbacks).

Mike Lake Trail is an easy 8km (2-3 hour) hike gaining 100m from the trailhead on Fern Crescent. No bikes are allowed on this trail.

Menzies Trail is an easy 18km (5-6 hour) return hike leading from the Fern Crescent trailhead to the West Canyon parking lot. Horseback riders frequent this trail.

East Canyon Trail is a rocky, 11km trail that follows the banks of Gold Creek. This trail is open to mountain bikers but expect a difficult trail with rough sections and a 320 meter elevation gain.

West Canyon Trail begin at the West Canyon parking lot and heads north following the western banks of Gold Creek. A bridge over the creek at Lower Falls allows you to cross the creek and head down the East Canyon Trail back to the parking lot. This loop is 9km (5 hours) return with minimal elevation gain. To continue up the Gold Creek Valley, take the **Hector Ferguson Trail** on the east side of the creek. This trail leads to the headwaters and involves a 22km (day+) return hike from the West Canyon parking lot.

Green Mountain Trail (Map #4/D2)
A moderate series of mountain biking trails found off the Agassis By-Pass just north of the railway tracks (on the west side). A tough climb takes you 455m up the access road to the network of trails at the top of Green Mountain. The access road eventually turns into a single-track trail and will take you down to the farmers field on the other side. You can ride back up or return to the start along the hwy (about 1km).

Also in the area are the **Agassiz Dykes**, a series of gated access roads that run along the Fraser River to the south of Agassiz. These routes can be accessed off of Hwy #7 below Mt Woodside or south of Maria Slough or from several of the intersecting rural roads. These peaceful trails are bordered by farmland and offer views along the Fraser River.

Harrison Lookout Trail (Map #14/C3)
Located of the Harrison West FSR, this short, steep 4km (1 hour) trail leads to an old forest service lookout on a hill above Harrison Lake. You hike along an old road to a beautifully wooded trail past mossy knolls to the vantage point from the lookout some 350m later. The panoramic views of Harrison Lake and the Chehalis Mountains can be rewarding on clear days.

Hayward Lake Trails (Map #3/B2)
On the west side of Hayward Lake Reservoir are 2 different hiking trails, the **Railway Trail** and the **Pond Interpretative Trail**. The **Railway Trail** can be accessed either near Ruskin Dam from Wilson Road or off of the parking lot just south of the Dewdney Trunk Road. This easy trail leads 13.5km (3-4 hours) return along an old rail bed, which was used in the early part of the century while building Stave Falls Dam. The trail can be quite muddy at times and is set through a forest offering a view of the lake. The **Pond Interpretative Trail** is a short easy education stroll around a small beaver pond. The walk takes 30-40mins to complete and can be done all year round. There are educational numbered signs displaying different stages of the forest canopy's life cycle. The trails have little elevation gain and can be hiked or biked year-round.

Hemlock Valley Ski Area (Map #14/C4)
Although mountain biking is allowed in the area in the summer, you must grunt your way up to the alpine as the chair lifts are not in operation. From the top, access roads provide fast, fun descents. Old roads in the area can also be explored.

Heritage Park (Map #3/C3)
At this Mission park, found east of Stave Lake Road and 5th St., is a series of trails that can be explored by hikers and expert mountain bikers. The main trail leads up to a field below the Monastery. This 4km single-track trail offers bikers a rewarding downhill return. Other options include looping back along the side trail heading northwest and exploring the side trails off the loop.

Ledgeview (Buttafouco) Trails (Map #3/C4)
Starting at the Ledgeview Golf Course, continue west on McKee Road to the obvious trail heading north. This difficult mountain bike ride climbs 280m over 5.5km as you climb an old road to the top. The trail heads down from here and is known for its sudden drops and cliffs.

Minnekhada Park (Map #2/C1)
This regional park is located on Quarry Road northeast of Port Coquitlam. Within the park, there are numerous interconnecting trails dissecting the second growth forest of the park. All the trails are well maintained with little elevation gain. The main trail leads from the large parking lot on the west side of the park past a marshy lake to a picnic site. Eventually, you reach a viewpoint overlooking the Addington Marsh next to Pitt River. Another trail circles the perimeter of the park in a clockwise direction. This trail leads the hiker through some wet, boggy sections, and several brooks.

A further option is to cross the floating bridge in the middle of the marshy lake and head west to the viewpoint. If you are interested in a dyke walk, then take Oliver Drive off the Quarry Road and park at a convenient point after the gates. From there, you can explore the Addington Marsh for a return distance of up to 14km (5 hours). Along the dyke are several observation towers and plenty of waterfowl.

Mount Crickmer Trail (Map #3/B1)
From the Florence Lake FSR, the difficult 20km (8 hour) hike follows an old gated road to the trail gaining 1190m along the way. After crossing several gullies and creeks, you soon enter the open meadows below the rocky summit. From the top (at 1360m), there are fantastic views of Stave Lake, Mt Blanshard and Robbie Reid Mountain.

Mount St. Benedict Trail (Map #3/C1)
The trail leads from the Davis Lake Provincial Park and is 15km (7 hours) return gaining 1000m to the summit at 1280m. The hike involves traversing a mixture of old road and trails along Murdo Creek past McKay Lake to the summit. Good views of Mount Judge Howay and Robbie Reid are offered from the top. Snow limits the hiking season to July through October.

Munro-Dennett Lake Trail (Map #2/C1)

From the signed trailhead on Quarry Road, the hike begins along an old road for a few hundred m before the trail heads straight up the hillside covered with mature Douglas-fir. Eventually, the trail levels as you approach Munro Lake and then Dennett Lake. Overall, the hike is 10km (6 hours) return gaining 860m. The trail, which connects with the Burke Ridge Trail, is best climbed in May through October.

Pitt Polder Wildlife Area (Map #2/D1,12/D4)

The extensive dyke network begins at the end of Rannie Road in Grant Narrows Park. The dykes are flat, wide cart paths perfect for mountain biking, horseback riding and hiking. The distance of the walk really depends on how far you want to walk as there are 20km of dykes and side trails in the area. Waterfowl is abundant in the marshy wetland.

Pitt River Hot Springs Route (Map #12,21/C4)

From the head of Pitt Lake, a 43km return cycle will take you along the Pitt River FSR to the Hot Springs. The gentle valley ride only has a few rough spots and steeper sections. At 21km, look for the "Pinecone Br" sigh on the left and follow the road across the bridge to the trailhead. Allow 3 hours to ride and a few more to soak in the springs.

Sasquatch Park (Map #5/A1,15/A4)

The roads into and around Sasquatch Park offer enjoyable family style mountain biking or hiking in a wilderness setting. The more popular routes start from the various gated access roads.

  Deer Lake Trail leads along the north side of the lake and keeping straight you can access the hydro lines and some more challenging terrain.

  Hicks Lake Trail circles the lake and offers a relatively easy wilderness type trail. This route starts from the gated access road on the north side of the lake. The spur roads to the left access more challenging options and viewpoints in and around the gas and hydro lines.

  Moss Lake Trail is the most difficult route. It follows the steep and rocky access road past Moss Lake to several unnamed lakes and the gas and hydro lines.

Rolley Falls Trail (Map #3/B2)

Accessed from the Rolley Lake Provincial Park or the Florence Lake FSR, this short, 2km loop leads past two sets of falls providing a great view of Stave Lake along the way. The well developed trail climbs 130m as it meanders through a heavy 2nd growth forest. Allow 1 hour or you can continue around the **Lakeside Trail** (around Rolley Lake) which adds another 1.5km and 45 minutes.

Statlu Lake Trail (Map #14/A3)

From the 40km mark on the Chehalis FSR, a 8km (4 hour) hike leads along the creek draw past Statlu Lake and into the headwaters of Chehalis River. The main trail ends at a waterfall gaining 610m along the way. There are further routes along the north side of Statlu Lake up the **Brotherhood Trail** to the Upper Lake or on to the Mount Ratney climbing area.

U.B.C. Research Forest (Map #2/D1,12/D4)

Take 232nd Street north of Haney and park at the gate near the forestry headquarters. From that point, a series of low level roads/trails lead though a mixed second growth forest with elevation gains of up to 610m. The attraction to the area is some of the innovative forestry practices used in the research forest. Also, there are several viewpoints overlooking the Pitt River marshes. You must register at the office before heading out. Please note that no fishing is allowed in the forest.

Widgeon Falls Trail (Map #12/C4)

A popular boat access hike found across from Grant Narrows Park at the south end of Pitt Lake. From the end of the slough at the Widgeon Lake Rec Site, an easy 2.7km walk leads along the west bank of Widgeon Creek. Allow 1 hour to reach the falls gaining 40m along the way. The area also offers a couple of more demanding hikes.

  Widgeon Bowl Lookout Trail climbs 700m from the campsite to a spectacular view of Pitt Lake from the bowl below Widgeon Peak at 1430m. This is a difficult steep 4km (2 hour) trail.

  Widgeon Lake Trail is a 18.5km (7 hours) return hike along logging roads to this beautiful clear lake nestled by high ridges and the heavy forest. From the campsite, follow the main road 4km to the old road before the washed out bridge over Widgeon Creek. You climb 660m along this well maintained trail (thanks to the efforts of the Burke Mountain Naturalists).

Greater Vancouver Trails

Burnaby Mountain Area (Map #2/A1)

The maze of trails in and around Simon Fraser University is a must for any mountain biker in the area (despite the fact that these trails built by mountain bikers are closed to mountain biking). The multi-use trails are found to the north and east of the campus. Generally speaking, the trails offer short climbs, with sweet descents and a good combination of double track and single-track options. You can access these trails from the SFU Campus, Gaglardi Way or North Road.

Burns Bog Trail (Map #1,2/A3)

A 6km (3 hour) interpretive trail leads through the ancient Burns Bog. The trail starts along the gated service road west of the Sidetrack Pub (off River Road) and takes you to a path system through the unique fauna and eerily woods. Be prepared for wet trail conditions.

Coquitlam River Trail (Map #2/B1)

A scenic river trail that travels 13.5km along the Coquitlam River from the Mary Hill By-pass to the Orr Creek Falls. Several roads (Pitt River Road, Lougheed Highway, Shaughnessy Road) can reduce the hiking/biking distance. Outside of the few tricky sections, this gentle trail can be enjoyed by all levels of mountain bikers (even mud seekers and hikers). Beyond the falls, the trail narrows and gets more difficult as it climbs to meet up with the Burke Mountain Trails.

Delta Watershed (Map #2/A3)

The Delta Watershed is one of those great riding areas that has easy access and can be enjoyed by all levels of cyclists. The popular multi-use trail network is especially busy after work and on the weekends. There are several access points including 64th Ave to the north and Hwy 10 to the south. As a rule of thumb, the trails to the north of the service road are quite short and follow well developed trails. To the south, the less developed trails offer more of a challenge. Roots and logs are scattered throughout the trails.

Dyke Trails and Easy Rides

Found throughout Greater Vancouver and the Lower Mainland are several small urban parks and dyke roads. These parks and dykes provide easy family style trails which are ideal for hiking and biking in a peaceful setting.

  Aldergrove Lake Park (Map #3/A4) is found off of 272nd St and Huntingdon Ave south of Aldergrove. This peaceful regional park offers designated hiking and biking/horse trails that lead around the gravel pit, through the woods and along creek. Allow 1.5 hours to explore the Pepin Creek Trail.

  Boundary Bay Dyke Trail (Map #1/D4, 2/A4) starts from 17A Ave in Tsawwassen. This trail skirts Boundary Bay all the way to the southern railway tracks (Junction of Hwy 99 & 91) in Surrey. Along the 25km route, you pass Boundary Bay Airport, Delta Air Park and several access points which can shorten the route.

  Campbell Valley Reach Park (Map #2/C4) is a 14km loop around the Campbell River Valley offering hikers and horseback riders a view of Mount Baker. For those looking for a shorter trail, there are many other trails to explore. The park is accessed at the end of 208th St south of Langley. .

  Derby Reach Park (Map #2/C2) is found off Allard Cres west of Fort Langley. The wooded trails offer easy family riding along the Fraser River.

  Matsqui Trail (Map #3/C3) is another pleasant dyke trail leading 17km return along the Fraser River. The trail starts at the picnic area in this popular Regional Park (found at the end of Riverside Road below the Mission Bridge).

  Mundy Park (Map #3/D3) is found off Como Lake Road. This urban park offers well developed trails that can be enjoyed by the whole family. For the mountain biker, the short trails (about 10km in total) are smooth, flat and fast and can be ridden by all levels of cyclists.

  Nicomen Island (Map #3/D3,4) is a quiet little island that has a 5km scenic riverside dyke trail. From December to February, Bald Eagles are a common site.

  Pitt River Dyke Trail (Map #2/C1) is a fine year round dyke trail along the Pitt River. From the end of Kingsway in Port Coquitlam, the ride heads 11km north to the Debouville Slough Lookout Trail, which is a short walk to a tower for a fine view and a chance to view waterfowl. It is possible to continue north to Minnekhada Park.

Richmond Dyke Trails (Map #1/B3) has a section called the West Dyke path, which stretches 10km from north of Westminster Hwy to Garry Point. The wide gravel path takes you past radio receivers as you peer out on the Straight of Georgia. The South Dyke is found between Gilbert Road and No. 5 Road. The gravel trails can be windy.

Roberts Bank Dyke Trail (Map #1/B4) leads from River Road and 34th St to the Ferry Causeway (9.5km). The ocean views are wonderful.

Serpentine Fen and Dyke Road (Map #2/B4) is north of White Rock, this trail is found on 44th Ave off of King George Hwy. It is an enjoyable ride through a Wildlife Management Area that is home to several species of birds.

White Rock Area (Map #2/B4) contains parks that offer enjoyable hiking or riding for all levels of cyclists on well developed trails. **Centennial Park** is found at 148th St and 16th Ave. The trails here are a little more challenging and can lead to the beach. **Cresent Beach** offers a 4km (1hr) walk on a wide, packed trail that goes along the waterfront then along a small dyke. The trail is extremely popular. **Semiahmoo Heritage Trail** can be accessed at the Star of the Sea School on 24th Ave east of 148th St. The smooth rolling trails blend nicely with the Softball City network for a good evening ride. **Softball City** is found off 24th Ave west of 148th St. This area has recently been developed into a mountain biking area. Expect loose surface trails which can be wet and muddy.

Pacific Spirit Park (UBC Endowment Lands) (Map #1/A2)

This large urban park offers an enjoyable place to walk, jog, horseback ride or mountain bike. With easy access (4th Ave, 16th Ave or SW Marine Dr), these year-round trails dissect the lush vegetation and old growth forests of Pacific Spirit Park. There are designated trails throughout the area. Mountain bikers are asked to please obey the signs. If you are looking for more of a challenge, why not try the trails north of 4th Ave. These trails get more challenging as you head down the ravine to Jeriko Beach.

Hope/Fraser Canyon Trails

Botanie Mountain Trail (Map #33/A1)

The length of the hike really depends on how far you can drive along the old lookout road leading from the Botanie Valley Road. If you do not have a 4wd vehicle then it's a 17.5km (8 hour) hike gaining 1425m. Along the way to the lookout at 1995m, you will pass some open meadows with wildflowers in July along with some great views of the Stein Valley, Thompson River and Fraser River. The hiking season runs from June to October. Mountain biking or horseback riding is certainly possible.

Coquihalla Canyon Trail (Map #15/D4)

This is a very popular route through the spectacular Coquihalla Canyon Gorge on an abandoned rail grade (Kettle Valley Railway). The trail begins at some picnic tables by the parking lot and leads through some dramatic tunnels (Othello/Quintette Tunnels) cut out of solid granite. It is recommended that you bring a flashlight if you want to explore the tunnels. It is possible to continue 12km (3 hours) along the north side of the Coquihalla River all the way to the Hope Cemetery and back to the parking lot. You can also head east along the old railgrade as far as you want. Hikers, mountain bikers and horseback riders all use the railgrade.

Dewdney Trail (Map #6/C2)

Beginning at the Cascade Recreation parking lot, this historic pack trail extends 36km (2 days) to Hope Pass. The trail was constructed in 1860 by Edgar Dewdney and represents one of the first trade routes linking the coast with the interior. The elevation gain to the pass is 1131m. It is possible to hike over the divide into the Whipsaw Creek FSR along the Hope Pass Trail. The trail is a popular horseback destination with its panoramic views of the valleys and mountains. There are several side trails and overnight facilities along the well developed trail.

Eaton Lake Trail (Map #5/D2)

The trailhead begins at the Eaton Creek Rec Site on the Silver Skagit Road south of Silver Lake Provincial Park. The trail leads 4.1km (2.5-3 hours) one way to Eaton Lake where fairly good fishing is offered. Along the way, you gain 915m in elevation so the hike is fairly strenuous. The rewarding trail begins by approaching Eaton Creek before descending rapidly to a log bridge, where there are great views of the falls and rapids. From here, the hike extends upward towards the lake. Along the way, you can enjoy the second growth forest you pass through as well as some nice rapids and flowers. When you reach the lake, it is possible to camp at the south end or continue on to Eaton Peak.

First Brigade Trail (Map #24/D4)

Beginning 100m north of the Alexander Lodge, this steep 13km (5-6 hour) hike climbs 760m along an old pack trail from the Fraser Canyon to Gate Mountain. The trail begins along a stream and then ascends to a great view from some bluffs. The route then passes several small lakes before coming out on another bluff where the best view of the Fraser Canyon is offered. The trail is best hiked in June-October. Part of the trail is comprised of the historic Hudson Bay Pack Trail.

Galene Lakes Trail (Map #6/C4)

This trail begins off the Silver Skagit Road at the Chittenden Bridge parking area and takes you 32km (11 hours) return gaining 1250m along the way. The hike begins by crossing a foot bridge and then proceeding through some meadows along the Skagit River. Then, the trail leads across Galene Creek through some further meadows and then eventually up the creek draw to Galene Lake at 1750m. The lake has a rustic campsite and some decent fishing opportunities. The trail is best hiked from July to October.

Gate Mountain Trail (Map #24/D4)

Gate Mountain Trail represents a more strenuous option than the First Brigade Trail. It leads over 16km (7 hours) up a steep trail gaining 1200m along an old pack trail. The trailhead begins uphill from the Alexander Tunnel. You follow an old road before reaching a marked trail which leads sharply uphill. Eventually, the hike passes through a meadow with wild flowers before reaching the "notch" and then finally the summit of Gate Mountain. The "notch" and the summit both provide excellent views of the Fraser Canyon.

Ghost Pass Trail (Map #6/B2)

This trail begins at the western gate of Manning Park and leads along the old engineering road to a signed trailhead marking the route to Ghost Pass Lake. This hike leads 22km (day+) along 18 Mile Creek to Ghost Pass at 1400m in elevation. The trail continues on to Ghost Pass Lake and then eventually connects with the Hope Brigade Trail and the Rice Trail. Beyond Ghost Pass Lake, the trail is overgrown and difficult to follow.

Hope Mountain (Map #15/D4)

This trailhead is found at about 7km on a 4wd road opposite the Nicolum Campground. The 14km (8 hour) hike leads sharply upwards with some dangerous talus slopes and open rock faces to cross. Overall, the elevation gain is 800m to the summit at 1850m. Needless to say, there is an excellent view of the Fraser Valley and Hope from the top.

Hope Pass Trail (Map #6/D, 7/A1)

This trail leads from Cayuse Flats 26km (7-9 hours) one way to a branch road off the Whipsaw Creek FSR. The first 4km of the trail leads along an old fire access road before the trail heads in a northeastern direction along the banks of the Skagit River. Around 2 hours along the trail, the Grainger Creek Trail departs to the right. The trail reaches Hope Pass at 21km (6-8 hours) before descending to the Whipsaw Creek FSR. From Hwy#3 to Hope Pass, there is an elevation gain of 1050m. There is an interesting side route to Dick's Cabin on top of Skaist Mnt.

Stein Valley Heritage Trail (Map #31-33)

To reach the trailhead, cross the Fraser River north of Lytton and proceed along the West Side Road to the starting point. From there, the trail leads along the Stein River offering 7-8days worth of good backcountry hiking opportunities. The length of the trail is an easy grade gaining 765m. It is 27km (10 hours) one way to the cable car and 58km (2-3days) one way to the cabin at beautiful Tundra Lake. The route is unique because it brings you from the dry terrain typical of the Fraser Canyon area to some cool, lush old-growth forests along the river containing Indian Pictographs. Along the trail, you can expect some blowdowns (fallen trees), some brushy sections and a bear or two. The trail is best left to May through October.

Mount Lincoln Trail (Map #15/D2)

Off Hwy#1 to the east of Yale, this hike leads from the Fraser River to the summit at 655m gaining 580m along the way. The return distance is 5km (3 hours) The trailhead being quite intimidating as you are required to use ropes to ascend a steep hill and bare rockfaces. From the top, you get a great view of Yale and the Fraser Canyon. Be sure to bring some water as the hike brings you up a semi-arid landscape.

Mount Outram Trail (Map #6/B2)

This trail begins at the western gate of Manning Park and leads along the old engineering road to a signed trailhead marking the route to Mount Outram. The trail is 18km (9 hours) return and is best hiked in July-September. The total elevation gain is 1760m so it is best left to hikers who are in great shape. The trail begins in a forested setting before crossing the creek and then continuing through a series of meadows to a steep, rocky ridge and eventually up to the summit of the mountain. You get a spectacular view of the surrounding mountain peaks from the top at 2440m.

Silverdaisy Mountain Trail (Map #6/C2)
This 20km (9 hour) trail leads from the Sumallo Grove Picnic Area off Hwy#3. The trail begins by crossing the Skagit River before zigzagging up the steep hill to a saddle where you can enjoy a great view of the Skagit Valley. From there, the trail continues through a meadow to the summit Silverdaisy Mountain. Overall, there is a 1435m elevation gain with part of the trail following an old mining tram eventually leading to the top at 2040m. The trail is best left to July-September.

Skagit River Trail (Map #6/C2)
This trail begins at the Sumallo Grove Picnic Area and leads 13km (6 hours) one way along the east side of the Skagit River with minimal elevation gain (105m). Along the route, you pass through an ecological reserve on the east side of the river which has a nice grove of old growth cedar, fir and cottonwood. The trail is best hiked in mid-June when the wild Rhododendrons start blooming at Sumallo Grove. For the adventurous, you can hike 27km one way to the Silver Skagit Road over a deteriorating trail (at the southern end). Mountain bikers, hikers and horseback riders all use the lower section of the trail.

Skyline Trail (West) (Map #6/C4)
The trailhead is accessed off the Silver Skagit Road and is marked by a parking lot to the north of Ross Lake. The trail leads 26km (10 hours) from the valley bottom to an alpine ridge at Camp Mowich. Along the way, the trail rises sharply gaining 1310m. The hike initially begins in a forest and then crosses several creeks before proceeding into some sub-alpine meadows and then along a ridge leading to Camp Mowich. It is possible to continue onward to Lightening Lake in Manning Park via the Centennial Trail.

Spirit Caves Trail (Map #15/D2)
The trailhead is located next to a sign found on Hwy#1 across from the Pioneer Cemetery at the south end of Yale. The 5km (3 hour) hike gains 500m for a great view of the Fraser River and Yale.

Thacker Mountain Trail (Map #15/D1)
In the heart of Hope, this trail leads 5km (1.5 hours) along an old road to the summit of Thacker Mountain. You gain 160m in elevation up to the summit, which provides a good view of the Fraser Valley and Hope. Mountain bikers as well as hikers frequent the area.

Whatcom Trail (Map #6/D1)
From the Cascade Recreation Area parking lot off of Hwy#3, this trail follows the Dewdney Trail for 2.5km before heading off to the right. From there, the trail climbs steeply through second growth forest to the subalpine meadows of Whatcom Pass and the Punch Bowl. The trail then descends into the Paradise Valley and the Tulameen River. Overall, the elevation gain is 650m and the hiking distance is 17km (6-7 hours) one way. Unless you are on horseback, using a two car system is preferred. The hike is best left to July to September.

Island Trails (Bowen, Gambier, Texada...)

Cornell Trail (Map #16/D4)
On Texada Island, this is an easy walk along an old mining trail past Emily Lake. The trail leads from Vananda at Prospect Road and is ideal for both hikers and bikers. If you want to extend the route past Emily Lake then it is possible to continue along the gas pipeline for the length of the island.

Dorman Point Trail (Map #10/D4)
From the picnic grounds at the ferry dock in Snug Cove on Bowen Island, this trail leads 4km (one way) in an easterly direction to a small lookout near Dorman Point. The hike involves a steady uphill climb to the summit where you will be rewarded with excellent views of Whytecliff Park and the Vancouver shoreline.

Gambier Lake Trail (Map #10/C3)
On Gambier Island, this 17km (6 hour) trail leads from the ferry terminal past the general store and continues up the hill. After crossing Mannion Creek, the trail follows an old road leading eventually to Gambier Lake. The trail gains 475m in elevation and can be used by both bikers and hikers. It is possible to take a side trip to Mount Liddle which involves a 900m climb over 14km (7 hours). This trail follows an overgrown road past Muskeg Lake and along a ridge which some excellent views of the ocean.

Keats Island (Map #10/C4)
This small island east of Gibsons can be accessed by boat or ferry from the Langdale Terminal to the Keats Government Wharf. Once you reach the island, you will find a variety of roads and trails, which you can explore by mountain bike or by foot. These roads and trails all begin from the Keats Government Wharf and can lead to Plumbers Cove Marine Park or to a nice sandy beach at the southern tip of the island.

Killarney Creek Trail (Map #10/D4)
On Bowen Island, the Killarney Creek Trail follows the north side of the creek past the small set of falls at the head of the lagoon. You also pass a fish spawning channel and fish ladder. The best place to find the trailhead is at the Union Steamship Co. Store in Snug Cove or at St. Gerard's Catholic Church. The trail leads about 8km (2.5 hours) from the ferry landing around Killarney Lake, where picnicking is available. It involves little elevation gain and is an easy walk.

Killarney Lake Loop (Map #10/D4)
Located in Crippen Regional Park on Bowen Island, this 4km loop can be accessed either from Mount Gardner Road or Magee Road. The trail circles Killarney Lake through a red cedar/hemlock forest and a marshy area near the west end of the lake. The trail offers a fairly easy walk or mountain bike with a few uphill grades.

Mount Artaban Trail (Map #10/D3)
The trailhead to this Gambier Island hike is accessed by boat to the south end of Halkett Bay Provincial Park (near the scout camp). The hike involves a 600m elevation gain beginning on an old road before passing by a couple of streams and continuing uphill through the forest and some open meadows. As a rule of thumb, stay to your right along the rough trail until you reach the summit which involves a total distance of 17km (7 hours return). The area, like other trails on Gambier Island, can be hiked most of the year.

Mount Gardner Trail (Map #10/D4)
The trailhead to this popular network of trails is found on a 2wd access road between poles #490 and #491 off the Mount Gardner Road. From the end of the road, a series of trails used by hikers, bikers and equestrian riders begins. The main trail climbs 725m to the summit at 830m along paved, gravel and forested paths. From the top, you will be rewarded with a great view of Bowen Island and Howe Sound. Overall, the trail extends some 10km (3-4 hours) with many side trails to explore. The side trails follow old logging roads and fire roads carved in the hillside. From the ferry landing it is a long 17.5km (7 hour) hike.

For the experienced mountain biker, follow the access road to the receiver at the top. From here, the **Handlogger's Trail** heads abruptly down to the access road. Once on the access road, look for the **Skid Trail** on the right which continues down to Killarney Lake. This ride involves a tough climb with technical, downhill single-track trails.

Shelter Point Regional Park (Map #8/A1)
On Texada Island, the regional park is easily accessed by the Texada Island Highway. Within the park is a scenic 2km easy trail that leads along the ocean through some large windswept Douglas-fir.

Texada Island Loop (Map #8,16,17)
From the Blubber Bay Ferry Terminal, this is a long moderate 73km return bike ride that should take a day to complete. Cycling in a clockwise direction from Vananda, you follow Central (High) Road, to Bell Road and down to the hydro lines. Here a steep, technical downhill will bring you to the Davie Bay Road, where you head north to Gillies Bay and back to Vananda and the ferry. It is possible to take side trips to Bob's Lake Rec Site or Shingle Beach Rec Site to camp. For a little more variety, the **Gas Pipeline Trail** runs the length of the island. It is easiest accessed in Vananda along the **Cornell Trail** (to Emily Lake).

Lillooet/Goldbridge Trails

Brett-Hog Creek Trail (Map #45/A2)
On Mud Creek Road, you will find a series of 35km of trails taking you from Carol Lake along Hog Creek to the Brett Creek Trail. The trail continues on to Lake La Mare and Burkholder Lake.

Burkholder Lake Trail (Map #45/B2)
From the Lake La Mare Rec Site off the Yalakom FSR, this 10km (4 hour) trail takes you to Burkholder Lake, a good fishing lake. From Burkholder Lake, you can continue on to Shulaps Range, which is 20km+ one way.

Eagle Ridge Trail (Map #32/D3)
From the North Kwoiek Branch Road, this 13km (5 hour) hike takes you through some second growth timber to an alpine ridge above Kwoiek Lake. It is possible to continue on to the Stein Headwaters on a difficult unmarked route eventually leading to the base of Skihist and Antimony Peaks.

Hogback Trail (Map #45/D1, 46/A1)
Beginning near the end of the Leon Creek Road, this 6km (3 hour) hike leads you to the alpine meadows of Hog Mountain at 2155m.

Kwoiek Valley Trail (Map #32/C4)
From the end of the Kwoiek Valley Logging Road, an 11km (5 hour) hike leads past Kokwaski and Chechiwa Lakes before leading uphill to Tzequa and Haynon Lakes. Along the way, you pass by serveral waterfalls gaining 600m to the height of land at 2000m. The trail also accesses Chachiwa Glacier by an unmarked route.

Kwotlenemo (Fountain) Trail (Map #41/D1)
At the popular recreation lake is a series of 12km of multi-use trails. In the winter, X-C skiing is available whereas in the spring through fall, mountain bikers and hikers frequent the trails. The lake is accessed by the Fountain Valley Road.

Marshall Lake Trail (Map #44/D2)
A 10km (4 hour) scenic trail takes you up the hill from the east side of Marshall Lake down to Carpenter Lake. From here, you can arrange for a pick up or retrace your path.

McGillivray Pass Trail (Map #39/D2, 40/A2)
Beginning on the Kingdom Lake FSR, it's a 15km one way hike taking you along McGillivray Creek to an old road on the west side of Anderson Lake. The area is a good X-C skiing area in the winter.

Melvin Creek Trail (Map #40/C3)
From the Cayoose Creek Rec Site on Duffey Lake Road, this 6km (3 hour) one way hunting guide trail crosses Cayoosh Creek and accessing a large alpine basin containing several small lakes. Hikers and horseback riders enjoy this trail in the spring and summer.

Riverview School Trail (Map #41/B1)
Found in Lillooet, this difficult mountain bike ride offers everything from steep climbs to fast single-track, from snakes to cactuses. The trail starts from Riverside School in the heights of Lillooet.

Seaton Highline Road (Map #40/A3)
A nice scenic 4 hour mountain bike ride on the logging roads around Anderson Lake. The route stretches 30km from D'Arcy (and the end of the Sea to Sky Trail) to Seton Portage.

Seton Ridge Trail (Map #41/A1)
From a switchback on the Seton Ridge Logging Road, it's a 11km (5 hour) route taking you along the ridge between Cayoosh Creek and Seton Lake to some open alpine. Once you are in the alpine, you can access the surrounding mountains for even better views or explore the endless alpine meadows.

Spruce Lake Trails (Map #43,44)
The Spruce Lake area is an outdoor recreationists heaven. It offers world-class hiking and backpacking, horsepacking, mountaineering, fishing, X-C skiing and mountain biking. The 164km of wilderness trails traverse over gentle mountain pass, meander through lush alpine grasslands and flowers to destination trout lakes. Most of the area remains pristine wilderness except at the southern and eastern perimeters where extensive logging is being carried out. The main access points into the area are the Gun Creek Road, Mud Creek-Taylor Creek FSR and the Slim Creek FSR. The Forest Service offers an informative topographic map detailing the area.

> **Spruce Lake Trail** starts from the Jewel Bridge (off Gun Creek Road) and follows the north side of Gun Creek eventually breaking from the pine forest to the open grasslands and aspen trees. After a couple hours, the trail forks (at Cowboy Camp). The right trail climbs 200m on its way to Spruce Lake, which has a rec site and beach on its eastern side. The lake is an excellent fishing lake producing large rainbow trout.

Texas Creek Trail (Map #41/B4)
From the end of the Texas Creek Road, the trail leads in a southern direction 10km (4 hours) one way to the Stein Valley. The difficult hike leads through some expansive alpine area providing great views of the surrounding valleys.

Tommy Creek Trail (Map #44/D3)
This 10km hike leads along an old mining exploration tote road and then overgrown trail to the subalpine. The trailhead is accessed by boat to the south side of Carpenter Lake. This is Grizzly Bear country so come prepared with bells and bear spray.

Viera Creek Trail (Map #45/C4)
This is a 8km (3 hour) trail along a series of mining exploration tote roads and old hunting trails. The trailhead begins a few kilometres west of Mission Dam off the Carpenter Lake Road. It is possible to hike, horseback ride or even mountain bike this trail system.

Manning Park Trails
Manning Park is easily accessed on Hwy#3 east of Hope. The 65,884ha park has an extensive network of trails ranging from short, easy valley walks to week long expeditions. Below, we have listed some of the options available in the park. Please keep in mind that this is a high elevation park so the hiking season does not begin until June and lasts until October.

Cascade Lookout Trails (Map #7/B3)
From the end of the Cascade Lookout Road (Blackwell Peak parking lot), the **Heather Trail** is a popular 21km (7 hour) one way hike gaining 292m to the Nicomen Ridge overlooking Nicomen Lake. In mid-July to August, the subalpine meadows are full of wildflowers. Initially, the trail leads 5km (1.5-2 hours) along an old road to Buckhorn Camp before passing through an old burn to a subalpine ridge below the First Brother. Kicking Horse Camp is reached at 13.5km (6.5 hours) and is a good place to overnight. From the end of the trail, you can continue on to Nicolem Lake and hike the **Grainger Creek Trail** to **Hope Pass Trail**, eventually ending at Cayuse Flats near the west gate of the park. This route is 21.5km (1 day) one way and using a two vehicle system is a good idea.

A further alternative is to detour about 7km along the Heather Trail in an easterly direction along the **Bonnevier Trail**. This hike is 29km (10-12 hours) one way from the Blackwell Peak parking lot to McDiarmid Meadows. A two vehicle system is necessary.

Grainger Creek Trail from Cayuse Flats is a 952m elevation gain, taking 6-8 hours to reach Nicomen Lake. The trail follows an old fire access road for the first 4km before leading up the Skagit River. The Grainger Creek Trail departs the Hope Pass Trail at about 8km and climbs steadily to the lake up the Grainger Creek Valley.

Bonnevier Trail from McDiarmid Meadows is a 950m elevation gain taking about 10-12 hours to reach the Blackwell Peak parking lot.

Frosty Mountain Trail (Map #7/A4)
To reach the highest peak in the park, start at the Lightning Lake Day Use Area and climb 11.1km (5-6 hours) to the summit at 2410m. From the top, the trail loops over to the Windy Joe Trail before reaching the Similkameen River. Once at the river, follow the Little Muddy Trail in a western direction back to the start. Overall, the loop is 27.7km (9-11 hours). An alternative route is to start at the Beaver Pond but this is a much longer route.

Lightning Lake Trail (Map #7/A4)
This trail begins at the Spruce Bay or day use area and leads 12km (3.5-4 hours) one way past Lightning, Flash, Strike and Thunder Lakes. Overall, it is an easy walk with little elevation gain on well developed trails in a forested setting. Wilderness camping is offered at the Stake Lake Camp. For a shorter walk, try circling Lightning Lake on the Lightning Lake Loop. The loop involves a 9km (2.5 hour) walk.

Monument 78 (Castle Creek) Trail (Map #7/B4)
From the Monument 78/83 parking lot, it's a 12km (3.5 hours) one way hike leading in a southern direction along Castle Creek to the USA border and the monument. Along the trail, you will pass through several meadows gaining 200m along the way. From the monument, it is possible to connect with the Windy Joe Trail via the Pacific Crest Trail. Wilderness camping is available 500m south of the monument. The trail can be used by backcounrty skiers, horseback riders and hikers.

Monument 83 Trail (Map #7/B4)
From the Monument 78/83 parking lot, it's a 16km (5 hours) one way hike leading along an old fire access road to the US Forest Service tower. Along the trail, you will pass by an old cabin built in the 1920s by the US Forest Service as well as Pasayten Pete's grave gaining 850m along the way. It is possible to head east out of the park on the **Pasayten River Trail**, which begins 1km before the lookout. The Pasayten River Trail is part of the Centennial Trail. The trail can be used by backcounrty skiers, horseback riders, hikers and mountain bikers.

Pacific Crest / Castle Creek Trail (Map #7/B4)
Dreaming of Mexico? Well if you have 6 months of spare time, the first leg of the famous trail that cuts through the backcountry of USA to Mexico starts from Manning Park. This particular section is a 20km (8 hour) moderate hike which gains 200m along the way. Wilderness camping and a shelter as well as fishing are possible along the route.

Poland Lake Route (Map #6/D4, 7/A4)
This trail is an easy 8km (2.5-3 hour) hike from the gate at Strawberry Flats to Poland Lake at 1750m in elevation gaining 435m along the way. The area is a popular x-c ski area as well as backcountry camping retreat. From the lake, it is possible to hike 9km (3-4 hour) one way to Allison Pass rather than return to Strawberry Flats. If you choice this alternate route, the hike will lead you along an unmaintained trail (**Memaloose Trail**) through the Memaloose Creek drainage. A two car system would certainly be helpful.

Self Guided Nature Trails (Map #6,7)
Within Manning Park are five short nature trails idea for the elderly or for families with small children:

Beaver Pond Trail is a 500m (15min) long trail starting 500m from the visitor centre and leading around a small pond. In May and June, as the snow departs, the pond is full of waterfowl.

Canyon Nature Walk begins at the Coldspring Campground and leads 2km (45min) along both sides of the Similkameen River.

Rein Orchid Trail is a 500m (15min) long trail beginning at the parking lot on Gibson Pass Road. The trail leads through a bog, which is full of flowering orchids in June through July.

Paintbrush Nature Trail starts at the Naturalist Hut at Blackwell Peak, which is reached via the Cascade Lookout Road. The trail takes you through a subalpine meadow full of wildflowers in mid-July to early August.

Sumallo Grove Picnic Area has a 700m (25min) walk that takes you past some old growth cedar and Douglas-fir and through some blooming Rhododendrons (in June).

Skagit Bluffs (Map #6/C2)
This is a 5.6km (2-2.5 hour) (one way) easy trail leading along the bluffs above Hwy#3 within Manning Park. The trail connects Dewdney Trail at the Cascade Recreation Area parking lot with the Hope Pass Trail at Cayuse Flats. It is used by horseback riders, hikers and mountain bikers.

Skyline Trails (Map #6/D4, 7/A4)
Beginning at the Strawberry Flats parking lot, the Skyline Trail leads 12.5m (5 hours) one way to Mowich Camp. Initially, the trail climbs along the ridge with a good view of Manning Park and then leads through Despair Pass before reaching the camp. The elevation gain to the camp is 475m. From the camp, it is possible to hike 13km (5-6 hours) one way into the Skagit Valley via the Skyline II Trail. Another option is to return to Spruce Bay via the Skyline I Trail, which is 16.8km (6-7 hours) one way. The hikes are best left to July through October.

Three Falls / Strawberry Flats Trail (Map #6/D4,7/A4)
Beginning at the Strawberry Flats parking lot, the trail is 9km (2.5-3 hours) return gaining 125m in elevation. The trail is wide and well used at the beginning as it leads to the downhill ski area. From there, the trail is less used and continues on to Shadow Lake before reaching Nepopekum Falls. Eventually, the trail culminates at Derek Falls on Nepopekum Creek.

Windy Joe Mountain (Map #7/B4)
Beginning at the Beaver Pond parking lot, this trail leads 15km (4.5-5.5 hours) return along an old fire access road to the summit of Windy Joe Mountain where you will find an old fire lookout. An alternative route during the spring when it is difficult to cross the Similkameen River is to begin at the Canyon parking lot. This hike is 18km (5-6.5 hours) return. Either way, you will get a great view at the summit. The trail can be used by backcounrty skiers, horseback riders, hikers and mountain bikers.

North Shore/Howe Sound Trails

The North Shore offers a multitude of trails ranging from difficult mountain trails to easy forest walks. Generally speaking, the mountain trails are quite steep and demanding but offer spectacular views. Due to the possibility of snow, these trails have a limited season (from July to October).

The lower elevation trails, which are open year round, are more easily explored but can be quite confusing due to the interconnecting nature of the trails. It is recommended to use a Vancouver Street Map to help access some of these lower trails.

Mountain biking has certainly become a popular way to explore the lower North Shore Trails but unless you are an expert rider you should stick to the easier trails found in the Seymour Demonstration Forest. Overall, the plethora of North Shore Trails tend to be steep and muddy with obstacles, roots and drop-offs. Teeter-totters, berms and other man-made contraptions are found throughout the area. Although most areas allow riding year-round, muddy trails can be a problem.

Baden-Powell Trail (Map #1,11)
The main artery to the massive lower elevation trail network of the North Shore Mountains is the Baden-Powell Trail. Built in 1971 during B.C.'s Centennial Year, this popular 42km (18hr) one way trail leads through the lush second growth forests from Horseshoe Bay all the way to Deep Cove. The trail has numerous ups and downs, several footbridges and wooden stairwells and passes by several canyons. Along the way, some great views of Vancouver and the surrounding area are offered. The route is well maintained and marked and can be accessed from at least 12 different roads as well as numerous trails. The hiking season is best from March through November. Most of the route is open to mountain biking but riders should expect a very technical route with lots of ups and downs, tree roots and difficult creek crossings. Needless to say, this route is best left to experienced mountain bikers.

The route climbs steeply over Black Mountain then gradually descends to Deep Cove. Here is a brief breakdown if you are heading west to east:

Horseshoe Bay to Cypress Bowl is a 9km (3 hour) section gaining 1140m along the steep Black Mnt Route;

Hollyburn to the British Properties is 10km (4hours) with a descent of 470m;

Cleveland Dam to Lynn Creek is 12km (5-6 hours) with an overall elevation loss of 30m;

Lynn Creek to Deep Cove is a 12km (4-5 hour) descent of 120m.

Brothers Creek Trail (Map #11/B1)
From the end of Millstream Road, the trail leads 11km (6 hours) return along Brothers Creek. The moderate trail combines longer flat sections with short steep grades to gain 435m in total. This is a good year-round hike as the route follows a fire access road through some older second growth timber dotted by large old growth Douglas-fir and Cedar. The creek has three sets of waterfalls and a scenic canyon. Blue Gentian Lake, which is found on the trail, has picnic tables. Mountain bikers use the road to access some of the steep, difficult trails of the Lower Cypress Area.

Capilano Canyon Trails (Map #11/B4)
Serveral parking lots off the Capilano Park Road and the Capilano Road provide access to this network of trails leading along the Capilano Canyon, a deep, narrow gorge surrounded by sheer granite cliffs. The trails are all well maintained and wide so it makes for easy walking under the large Douglas-fir. Spawning Salmon can be seen in the fall.

The **Capilano Pacific Trail** is the main trail on the west side of the river and is accessed by either crossing Cleveland Dam or the suspension bridge, which charges a fee. This 7.5km trail heads south to Ambleside Park from Cleveland Dam.

The **Chinook Trail** meanders through the seccnd growth forest on the east side of the river.

The **Coho Loop Trail** is a 45min walk that takes you next to the walls of the canyon over two footbridges and through some old growth cedar, Douglas-fir and hemlock.

Cypress Park Area (Map #11/B4)
The Cypress Parkway provides easy access to the subalpine area of the provincial park but for the more adventurous, it is possible to hike up. Within the park are a number of trails as well as the Hollyburn X-C Ski Area and Cypress Bowl Ski Area to explore.

Black Mountain Loop is reached by taking the Baden Powell Trail from the downhill ski area. The trail heads up a series of switchbacks to the south summit for a great view of the ocean. Overall, it is a 7.5km (3 hour) return hike gaining 300m to the summit at 1218m. The best time to hike the trail is in June through October. An alternate, more challenging route is to hike up the mountain from Hwy#99 at the Whistler/Squamish Exit. From the highway, it's a steep 16km (6 hour) hike gaining 1140m.

Hollyburn Peak Trail leads from the trailhead sign at the x-c skiing parking lot some 20km (7 hours) return to the peak at 1325m. The trail heads east past the old Hollyburn Lodge next to First Lake before leading steadily uphill past the powerline and the Fourth and Fifth Lakes. Soon you will pass the junction with the Baden-Powell Trail before reaching the top. From the summit, you get a great view of the Gulf Islands and Vancouver Island. An alternate and less strenuous option is to follow the Baden-Powell Trail from the downhill skiing parking lot.

Howe Sound Crest Trail is the link between the northern and southern portions of the park. The trail is 29km (8hours) one way and is clearly marked with orange flagging and markers. It links a number of North Shore Mountain hikes and is best hiked between mid-July to the first snowfall. From Cypress Bowl, the trail raises 600m to Unnecessary Ridge, the highest point on the trail at 1525m. The trail follows an undulating ridge before dropping down to Porteau Cove. Excellent views of Bowen Island and the Howe Sound as well as The Lions are offered along the ridge.

Mount Strachan Trail begins at the downhill ski area and leads 10km (5hr) return to a double summit at 1450m. The trail gains 540m and is best hiked in July to November.

Yew Lake Trail is a 4km (1.5hr) wheelchair accessible trail around Yew Lake. It is a good choice for a family outing as it involves a generally flat walk (145m elevation gain) through a subalpine forest around a small lake dotted with lily pads. There is some old growth forest in the area as well as a good view of Snug Cove and Deep Bay. The trail becomes accessible in late June with the season ending in October.

Deeks Lake Area Trails (Map #11/B3)

To access the Deeks Lake area, there are two different trailheads right next to Hwy#99. The northern most trailhead, the more popular route, is marked by a pull-out and a signed trailhead. The southern most trailhead is just north of Deeks Creek at a small pull-out. Either way, you can expect a steep strenuous hike upward.

Deeks Peak Trail leads from the northern trailhead some 20km (10hr) gaining 1190m to the height of land at 1220m. On the trail, you pass a powerline and then meet an old logging road. Proceed right and follow the road for 40 minutes past a small pond. From there, the trail swings left and rises sharply to the base of the peak eventually leading to Deeks Lake. From the lake, it is possible to continue on to Brunswick Mountain. The trail is best taken in July through October.

Deeks Lake Trail begins at the same location as the Deeks Peak Trail but veers to the left on an overgrown washed out road. The trail soon crosses Kallahne Lake and then climbs steadily uphill to the lake. Overall, the trail is 17.5km (8 hours) return gaining 1626m to the height off land at 1674m. It is best in July through October.

Deeks Bluff Circuit begins at the southern trailhead and leads 10km (5 hours) return to the northern trailhead. The trail gains 400m and follows the bluffs overlooking Howe Sound. Unlike other trails in the area, it can be hiked year round.

Grouse Mountain / Mount Fromme Trails (Map #11/C4)

Grouse Mnt and neighbouring Mt Fromme offer a maze of trails which offer hikers and expert mountain bikers endless opportunities to explore. This area should be left to the expert riders as the trails are very steep, technically challenging and have numerous obstacles. To access the area, follow the Old Grouse Mountain Hwy from the yellow gate at the top of Mountain Hwy. This access road climbs steadily (820m) over 7.5km to a viewpoint at the top. From the seven switchbacks on the road, several difficult single-track trails take off in all directions. By making your way down to the **Baden-Powell Trail**, you can follow the orange markers east to the parking area.

From the Gondola Parking Lot, Vancouver's latest exercise trend **The Grouse Grind** begins. This steep, busy trail is easy to find. Just follow the flow of people. As far as hike, this 2km (1.5 hour) one-way climb of 930m is not very rewarding. Especially since the view from the top is home of annoying black flies. But it is an excellent workout. Most people take the Gondola Ride down (for a fee).

The original Grouse Grind trail also begins at the Gondola Parking Lot. The less busy hike follows the powerline above Grousewoods before the fun begins. The hike leads straight up the old lift line to the bottom of The Cut. From there, continue up the ski run to the top of the gondola and the ride down to the bottom or hike back down. Overall, it is 10km (5 hour) return hike gaining 825m. The views of Vancouver are breathtaking. The hikes can be done in April through November.

Mount Fromme Trail begins off Prospect Road near Mosquito Creek. This steep 15km (6hr) hike gains 870m to the summit at 1170m. The trail begins on the Baden Powell Trail and shortly turns onto a trail labelled To the Old Mountain Highway. From there, follow the steep Old Mountain Hwy past Meech Lake to the summit. Once you reach the top, it is best to descend

through Pipeline Pass to Old Mountain Hwy and walk down the road to St. George's Trail. Eventually, you meet up with the Baden Powell Trail and a return to the start.

Goat Mountain can be reached by taking the Grouse Mountain Gondola to the top of Grouse Peak (for a fee) and starting your hike from there. The hike is 8km (4.5 hours) return gaining 275m to the summit at 1400m. The hike starts on an old road before the trail heads up Goat Ridge. Continue past one of many viewpoint to Little Goat and from there, hike to the summit of Goat Mountain. The views of Vancouver along the trail are excellent. The hike is best in July to early November.

Hollyburn Heritage Trails (Map #11/B4)

From the west side of Lawson Creek Bridge on Pinecrest Drive, an extensive trail network leads through the second growth forest typical of the North Shore. The main trail leads 6.7km (3.5 hours) return to the Hollyburn Fir, an 1100 year old Douglas-fir which is 9.7ft in diameter. The trail crosses the Crossover and Baden Powell Trails. Within the area, the remains of logging from the 1920's are seen.

Another possible access point is at the junction of Eyremount, Crestwell & Millstream Roads. From here, a well-signed trail heads uphill.

Hollyburn X-C Trails (Map #11/B4)

Found in the Cypress Provincial Park just before the downhill ski area, this popular trail system offers a wide variety of trails. In the winter, the opportunites range from well groomed trails to less traveled backcountry routes. In the summer, the area opens up a fabulous hiking area.

Lighthouse Park (Map #1/A1)

From the parking lot at Lighthouse Park, an extensive year-round trail network leads through old growth forest to the wave washed rocky shoreline of Point Atkinson. If you hike around the perimeter of the park enjoying the ocean views then the hike is 5km (2 hours). The well developed trail system can be enjoyed by the whole family. Make sure you visit the famous lighthouse, which was erected in 1912.

Lions / Brunswick Mountain Trails (Map #11/B3)

The trailhead to these two popular hikes is found at Lions Bay by taking the Oceanside Road exit off Hwy#99 and driving to the gate on Mountain Drive. The difficult trails follows an old road upward until there is a fork in the road. The right fork leads to the Lions Trail, while the left fork accesses the Brunswick Mountain Trail.

Brunswick Mountain Trail begins by taking the trail leading to the left from the second fork along the main trail from Mountain Drive. The trail crosses Magnesia Creek and then leads upward by taking the right fork. The trail soon raises steeply to the summit at 1785m. Overall, it is a 15km (8hr) return hike gaining 1550m. The hike is best in July through October.

Lions Trail is a steep 15km (7hr) hike crossing Harvey Creek before reaching Lions Ridge. Eventually, the trail ends at a small summit to the south of the West Lion where it is possible to pitch a tent and enjoy the view of the Howe Sound. Overall, the elevation gain is 1280m to the height of land at 1525m in elevation. The hike is best in July through October.

Mount Harvey Trail leads off the Lions Trail and is marked by a sign saying Mt Harvey and by orange markers. The trail is a difficult 12.5km (8hr) hike gaining 1465m to the summit at 1705m. The trail involves a scramble through a second growth forest to the ridge where wildflowers are prominent in July. After admiring the great view of Howe Sound, continue through the timber and hike up to the summit. The hike is best in July through October.

Lower Cypress Area (Map #11/B4)

Found between Cypress Bowl Parkway and British Properties are several intermediate to advanced mountain bike trails, which also offer a fine area to walk. It is best to ride up the main trails or parkway and then ride down the technical, single-track trails found throughout the area. These difficult trails have many obstacles, roots and drop-offs. The main trails include:

Baden-Powell Trail is the well marked (orange markers) intermediate trail that stretches across the North Shore Mountains.

Brothers Creek Trail is an easier fire access road that climbs 250m over 1.2km from the top of Millstream Road.

Skyline Trail is actually an old service road for the power line that gains 375m over 7km. This difficult ride runs east to west between the two roads.

From these main trails several technically demanding and steep side trails are waiting to be explored.

Lower Seymour Trails (Map #11/D4)

Comparatively speaking, this is one of the easier areas to mountain bike on the North Shore. This large network of trails, which are also enjoyed by hikers and horseback riders, extends between Mt Seymour Parkway and Lynn Canyon Park. For the biker, it is easiest to cycle up the parkway and pick any one of the trails heading down or west. Generally speaking, the trails found below the **Baden-Powell Trail** should be left to the experts. These difficult trails should bring you out on McNair Road from where you can head east to Mountain Hwy. The trails above and to the west of the Baden-Powell Trail offer a good combination of moderate and difficult riding.

Lynn Headwaters Regional Park (Map #11/C4)

This popular park offers a wide variety of trails ranging from easy creekside walks to strenuous wilderness treks. The heavily wooded trails make for good wet weather walking. The park is accessed off the Lynn Valley Road past Dempsey Road.

Coliseum Mountain involves a steep 25km (11hr) route gaining 1245m to the alpine. The route is marked with orange markers as you pass through the steep forested area and enter the Norvan Meadows on your way to Norvan Pass. The difficult hike is best from July through October.

Grouse Mountain is reached via a steep 13+km (6hr) hike through Crown Pass gaining 900m. The rough trail leaves the Headwaters Trail at Norvan Creek.

Lynn Loop leads from the parking lot over a large suspension bridge high above the Lynn Canyon. On the opposite side of the canyon, the easy trail heads north through a second growth forest next to Lynn Creek. An intimidating staircase after a scenic falls and swimming hole discourages most of the crowds. After the staircase, the trail continues northward eventually crosses the creek and returning to the bridge on the opposite side of the creek. The loop is 8km (3 hours) with little elevation gain (168m) along a well maintained trail.

Narvan Falls is 18km (5hr) return gaining 340m elevation to the scenic falls.

Lynn Peak is a 9.5km (4hr) return hike on a well maintained trail/old road gaining 825m to the summit at 1000m. The views of Mount Seymour are spectacular. From the peak, it is possible to continue on to The Needles by way of a recently cleared and marked 8hr route.

Rice Lake is an easy 4km (2 hour) loop gaining 330m. The route, which can be mountain biked, involves a creek crossing.

Mosquito Creek Trails (Map #11/C4)

Mosquito Creek Trail is a great choice if you want to sample the North Shore Mountains without the usual elevation gain. From the bottom of the gondola, head east to find the trail. Hike along the powerline and avoid the temptation to climb the Grouse Grind, one of the most hiked but least rewarding trails on the North Shore. The Mosquito Creek Trail heads across the mountain on an uphill incline crossing MacKay Creek and then Mosquito Creek. The trail ends by following the east banks of Mosquito Creek to the Cascades. Overall, the hike is 8km (4 hours) return gaining 320m. Since the trail intersects with the Baden Powell and BC Mountaineering Club Trail, the direction of travel can become quite confusing.

Mount Capilano Trail (Map#11/B2)

Park at Porteau Provincial Park and walk 100m south to the end of the concrete wall. From there, the hike leads 26km (10hr+) return gaining 1600m to the summit at 1685m. The trail initially leads steadily uphill through a second growth forest to an old gated logging road. This road leads to Phillis and Marion Lake if you stay right or to the summit if you take the left branch. Eventually, the trail takes off to the right and leads pass Beth Lake to the summit. The hike is best left to July through October. An alternative route is to follow the logging road from just north of Furry Creek Golf Course. Please note that access south of Phyllis Lake is restricted. Beyond the gate is the Greater Vancouver Watershed. The lakes offer some descent fishing particularly in May- June. Mountain bikers can use the road to gain access to the lakes.

Mount Seymour Area (Map #11/D4, 12/A4)

The 3508ha provincial park is easily reached by way of the Mount Seymour Parkway. The park contains a variety of hiking trails from easy strolls to rough backcountry excursions. All the trails are very popular given their scenic surroundings, views of Vancouver and proximity to the population belt. The best time to hike in the park is in July through November due to snow accumulations at higher levels. Below, we have described the main trails in the park. Please note that the Old Buck Trail is the only trail where horseback riding and mountain biking are allowed:

Mount Seymour Trail is the main trail leading from the north end of the upper parking lot. The moderate hike is 9km (5hr) return with an elevation gain to 450m to 1450m at the summit of Mountain Seymour. The popular trail climbs steadily through a semi-open subalpine forest before breaking out into the alpine meadows and a climb to the Second Pump and then the summit of Mount Seymour. Since great views of the Lower Mainland are offered from any of the 3 pumps, most people do not bother climbing beyond the first pump.

Dog Mountain Trail involves a 6km (1.5-2hr) hike from the north end of the upper parking lot with little elevation gain. The less popular but easier hike begins along the **First Lake Trail** for 30 min before the Dog Mountain Trail leads to the west from First Lake. The trail passes through an old growth subalpine fir stand to the bluff overlooking Greater Vancouver. On the return trip, complete the First Lake Loop by taking the north branch of the trail at First Lake and connecting with the Mount Seymour Trail. A further option is to hike the short distance (750m) to Dinkey Peak for another great view of the Lower Mainland.

Elsay Lake Trail is a difficult 20km (12hr/overnight) hike through Canadian Pass and some rugged alpine country with an elevation gain of 885m to 1325m in elevation. The hike begins at the north end of the upper parking lot initially following the main Mount Seymour Trail. Take the left branch just before First Pump Peak. The trail is good until you are northwest of Gopher Lake at which time the trail narrows and is occasional marked with flagging and markers. A small backcountry shelter is found at the north end of the lake and the end of the trail. Please note that it is steeper on the return trip.

Goldie Lake / Flower Lake Loops are found to the east of the upper parking lot. The easy **Goldie Lake Loop** is 2km (1hr) leading past the Goldie Rope Tow area to Goldie Lake gaining 218m along the way. This trail meets with the Flower Lake Loop and the top end of the Perimeter Trail so you can take either of these trails to increase the length of the hike. The **Flower Lake Loop** is 1.5km (45min) return with an elevation gain of 150m. This trail passes through a subalpine bog and past a small pond filled with wildlife.

Mount Elsay Trail is no more than a bushwack from the Elsay Lake Trail and is not even marked on the government map. It is 16km (9hr) return from the upper parking lot and involves a 1050m elevation gain along a flagged route with some rock scrambling. From the summit at 1430m, you are rewarded by an excellent view. The hike is best left to experienced backpackers.

Mystery Lake Loop begins at the upper parking lot and follows the Mystery lift line before connecting with the Mount Seymour Trail and the return to the parking lot. The loop is 3km (1.5 hours) with an elevation gain of 180m. The beautiful subalpine lake is a good spot to swim during a hot summer day.

Old Buck Access Trail is a short, 1km (30min) one way trail leading from the Vancouver Lookout parking lot to the Old Buck Trail. There is little elevation gain.

Old Buck Trail climbs steadily uphill from the Park Headquarters connecting with the Baden-Powell Trail about 2.3km (45min) along the trail and to the Perimeter Trail near the Deep Cove Lookout at 5.5km (2 hours). Overall, the route involves a 670m gain along a washed out, rocky old road next to the Mount Seymour Parkway. Since this trail does not offer the beauty and views of the other trails in the area, the main users of the trail are mountain bikers.

Perimeter Trail is a 1.5km (45min) one way hike gaining 240m in elevation. The trail begins at the Deep Cove Lookout and climbs steadily uphill to connect with the Goldie Loop.

Seymour Demonstration Forest (Map #1/B1,11/B4)

The Demonstration Forest is a 5,200ha forest created in 1987 to educate the public about forest ecosystems and logging practices. Within the forest are several well maintained trails and a few hidden routes to explore. From the parking lot at the end of Lillooet Road, a series of easier routes exist including the popular, paved Seymour Dam Road. This road leads 11km one way to the Seymour Dam and can be walked, biked or even roller bladed. Off the road, several roads lead down to the Seymour River where it is possible to meet up with a series of trails leading through the second growth forest and along the Seymour River.

The **Fisherman Trail** is a moderate route that combines an old road with singletrack trail as you skirt along the scenic Seymour River. You follow the Twin Bridges Trail to the bottom of the hill and follow the trail that heads north (left) before the bridge. This 7km trail should take 2 hours but a side trip to the Seymour Dam can add more distance. Be forewarned that this trail is now closed to cyclists (although the main users of the trail are mountain bikers).

The **Integrated Resource Management Trail** is an easy walk through a mixed-age conifer forest illustrating different forestry practices. The **Rice Lake Connector** is an easy, short 1.2km gravel road with little elevation gain.

The **Twin Bridges Road** is a 2.6km trail that descends 100m (mostly one long hill) to the bridge. Once across the bridge, you can head south along the river to Riverside Dr. or explore the many Lower Seymour Trails in the area.

Sunset Trail (Map #11/A4)
The trail is found opposite the Sunset Marina on Hwy#99 and leads past a gate on the second road (ignore the no trespassing sign). You will soon find the trail leading off to the right raising steeply from the Hwyto Yew Lake and eventually into Cypress Bowl. Overall, the trail is 14km (6 hours) return to Yew Lake gaining 855m to the height of land at 915m. It accesses the north end of Cypress Provincial and is best hiked in May through October. An alternate route is to hike 22km (9 hours) to the summit of Mount Strachan at 1455m in elevation gaining 1400m along the way. Given snow accumulations, the hiking season to Mount Strachan is from July to October.

> **Three-Chop Trail** (Map #2/A1) begins at about 3.2km on the Indian River FSR. The trail is 13km (5 hours) return gaining 550m to a viewpoint overlooking Deep Cove. The hike begins along a hydro access road before the actual trail leads from the road into a second growth stand to the lookout. From the lookout return to the start via the Old Buck Trail. The hike can be taken anytime from May through November.

> **Upper Cypress Area** (Map #11/B4) starts from the upper parking lot and follows the fire access roads down 7.5km (735m elevation later) to the first switchback on the Cypress Road. Unless you brought a second vehicle you need to grunt your way back to the start along the parkway. It is also possible to ride/hike up the scenic access road or explore the numerous trails in the area. The side trails, which eventually bring you back to the parkway, should be left to expert mountain bikers.

> **Unnecessary Mountain Trail** (Map #11/B3) starts from the gate on Oceanview Road (right before the Harvey Creek bridge in Lions Bay), follow the paved and then gravel road to the trailhead marked by orange markers. From there, the steep trail takes you over many windfalls and through some brushy sections. Overall, it is a difficult 9.5km (7hr) return hike gaining 1310m to the summit at 1510m. The view from the top makes for a rewarding hike.

Powell River Trails

Appleton Canyon / Marathon Trails (Map #16/D1)
The trailhead is found approximately 20m north of the Sliammon Lake Trail on the Theodosia FSR. It is a well marked and well maintained trail that leads along Appleton Creek past some nice waterfalls and through an old growth forest. The trail culminates at the Appleton Creek Rec Site 2km along the way (30mins). The Marathon Trail continues on from the Appleton Canyon Trail and eventually leads to the Southview Road. The trail is 4km (1.5 hours) one way and leads past Rieveley's Pond. A side trip leads to a viewpoint marked "Gibraltar" which provides a fantastic view of the Strait of Georgia as well as a picnic area.

Beartooth Mountain Trail (Map #26/C3)
This trailhead is located by boat on Powell Lake. The difficult trail begins on the north side of Beartooth Creek and extends 8km (4 hours) from Powell Lake to the summit of Bear Tooth Mountain gaining 1720m along the way. The trail is generally well marked as it is blazed with flagging tape. The hike leads through an old growth forest until it breaks out into the sub-alpine where you will have to pick your own route to the summit.

Beta Lake Trail (Map #17/D1)
Leading from Branch E-100 off the Stillwater Main, this short, 1.5km trail (30min) leads from the end of the road to a small sub-alpine lake. The trail is not well marked and is best left for late summer and into the fall given snow accumulations. Black bears are common to the area so be very cautious. It is possible to continue on to the Knuckleheads, which is an excellent climbing area in the alpine with views of the surrounding lakes. The **Knuckleheads Trail** is steep and unmarked and will take 6-8 hours to complete.

Bunster Hills (Map #16/D1)
From Wilde Road off Hwy#101, this moderate bike ride initially climbs 750m over 12km. Enjoy the views of Okeover Inlet and the Georgia Straight before the descent. The 34km loop is well marked as you follow logging roads back to the Hwy. Allow 4 hours.

Confederation Lake Trail (Map #17/B1)
The trailhead is found on an old logging road that starts to the east side of Inland Lake. If you plan to hike this trail anytime between November and March, the gate near the Inland Lake Rec Site will be closed and so you will have to hike 1.5km (one way) to the actual trailhead. If you choose to hike the trail in the summer, you will be able to drive to the parking area before walking down the old road approximately 100m to the trailhead. From there, a well marked and maintained trail leads past Confederation Lake and eventually to Powell Lake. Along the way you hike through a stand of old growth cedar and Douglas-fir as well as catching glimpses of Inland and Powell Lakes.

A forest service log cabin is located on the east side of Confederation Lake and provides a wood stove and accommodation for 6 individuals. The distance to the log cabin is 8km (3.5 hours) one way. Beyond Confederation Lake, it is possible to continue on to Powell Lake on an overgrown road. The trail from Confederation Lake to Powell Lake is 7.5km (3 hours) one way and has been flagged but only partially brushed at the time of writing this book. The trail descend downward to Powell Lake ending at the Fiddlehead Farm where there is a bed and breakfast resort complete with showers. On the descent to the lake, you will be rewarded with spectacular views.

Diadem Mountain Trail (Map #18/A1)
This hike is located along a road leading up Lois River Valley. A gate located before the valley may impede travel by vehicle to the trailhead, which is marked by a cairn with flagging tape. The route proceeds through a deep gorge eventually leading up to a ridge. From there, you cross a creek at the end of a box canyon and proceeds up into the sub-alpine past a series of ponds. Eventually, the trail culminates at the summit for a total of 8km (6 hours) return.

Duck Lake Area (Map #17/B2)
The Duck Lake FSR provides access to several hiking/biking trail systems found just east of Powell River. The variety of activities and proximity of all the trails makes this a good area to explore.

> The **Blackwater Trail** begins approximately 100m south of the Y-fork on the Duck Lake Loop. The trail starts along an old rail grade for 750m leading to Blackwater Creek. As the trail leads along the banks of Blackwater Creek, it passes by a series of waterfalls. Eventually, the trail ascends over the divide on an old logging road to Washout Creek. At that location, you will enter a spectacular gorge and continue in a westward direction back to the start. Overall, the trail is 7km (2.5 hours) in length and is well marked.

> The **Blue Trail** is an easy 2km (45min) interpretive trail that follows an old railgrade south west of Duck Lake. The trail cuts through the woods about 6km along the Duck Lake FSR. It crosses **Fred's Trail**, which will bring you to Padgett Road outside Powell River, before descending back to the road. A self guiding brochure is available to help explore the trail network.

> The **Cable Trail** begins opposite to the Suicide Creek Trail. The trial starts by crossing a foot bridge and then meandering through a second growth forest before crossing Sweetwater Creek. From there, the trail follows an old rail grade up a steady incline eventually looping back to Sweetwater Creek and the trailhead. Overall, the trail is 8km (2.5-3 hours) and is highlighted by the MacGregor Falls.

> **Duck Lake Loop** is a 21km (2.5 hour) moderate bike ride along logging roads and the hydro lines east of Powell River. The route starts at 3.5km on the Duck Lake FSR. You follow the road north to the intersection at 7.5km. Keep right and follow the main roads to the hydro lines to return to the parking spot.

> **Hamill Hills Trail** starts from the Duck Lake Road near the Maple Springs Ranch. This network of trails leads 5km (1.5 hours) through ranch pastures and along an old road eventually culminating at the bluffs. When you reach the bluffs, you will be rewarded with a panoramic view of the coastline. The trail is used by equestrians as well as hikers. Some bushwhacking is necessary when walking along the overgrown road.

> **Lang Creek Loop** is an easy, well marked trail leads south from the 6km mark on the Duck Lake FSR past East Lake and along Lang Creek. The trail is 3km (1 hour) one way and is gently sloping so it is well suited for a family outing. Mountain bikers can expect a moderate route with some of the best single-track riding in the area. Both the Lang Creek and East Lake Rec Sites are found on the route. Spawning salmon can be seen in September and October.

> The **Mud Lake Trails** are generally flat and well marked so they are suited for a family outing. The total distance of the trail depends on the route you plan to take as there are several interconnecting trails to pick from. Each trail is well signed so you should not get lost. Be forewarned that the area

can be muddy during the spring. Wildlife viewing and the beautiful wild flowers around Duck Lake are some highlights as is swimming at Haslam Slough. Mountain bikers should be wary of the technical sections around Mud and Deer Lakes.

Suicide Creek Loop begins on the opposite side of the road from the Mud Lake Trail. The trail heads in a southeast direction approximately 8km (2 hours). Highlights of the trail include two sets of waterfalls (which can be reached on foot). The Fern Falls offer a picnic table and is below the first bridge, while the Mimulus Falls are found between the two foot bridges. Mountain bikers should expect a moderate trail with re-routes around the rougher sections.

Sweetwater Creek Loop begins on an old rail grade leading to Sweetwater Creek. The trail follows the creek draw eventually leading past MacGregor Falls. From there, the trail continues past Donelley Falls before heading south and back to Duck Lake Road. Overall, the loop is 7km (1.5 hours) along a well marked trail which is ideal for moderate mountain bikers as well as hikers. The trail provides access to the Blackwater Trail as well.

Elephant Lake Loop (Map #17/D3, 18/A3)
A long 48km (5-6 hour) moderate bike ride that follows the main logging roads north of Saltery Bay. The roads lead past several small lakes and offer views of Jervis Inlet, Lois Lake and the surrounding area. You return along Hwy#101. Do not be discouraged by the tough 8km initial climb, as the views are spectacular.

Emma Lake Trail (Map #26/D3,27/A3)
Emma Lake Trail begins off the B-Branch from the Goat Lake Main. The steep trail leads 7km (5 hours) to a forest service cabin set on Emma Lake. That cabin provides accommodation for 8 individuals but be forewarned that it is usually full. Emma Lake is a beautiful blue colour and is surrounded by sub-alpine meadows containing heather. If you stay overnight at the cabin, you can take day trips to Snowy, Thunder Dome and Crossroads Peaks. Also, the South Powell Divide Route leads southward and involves a ridge run from Triple Peaks to Center Lakes.

Freda Mountain Trails (Map #17/D1,18/A1)
To reach the summit of Freda Mountain, there are 3 possibilities. The southernmost route is a long trail leading from the Freda Mountain Main just north of the F-Branch. It involves a day+ hike. A more direct route is found on the J-Branch at the south end of Freda Lake. It is 8km (3-4 hours) return and leads through an old growth forest to the sub-alpine. The third trail begins on Jenna Branch Road at the east end of Freda Lake. This involves a 12 hour hike on a well marked (flagged) trail leading through the old growth timber to the sub-alpine.

Frogpond Lake Trail (Map #26/B4)
This steep, 5km (2.5 hour) trail leads from Powell Lake up to Frogpond Lake. The trailhead is accessed by boat to Cassiar Falls where the trail begins on the east side of the creek. Half way along the trail you reach a bench, which overlooks Powell Lake with a good view of Fiddlehead Farm and Tin Hat Mountain.

Gallagher Hills Trail (Map #17/A2)
The trail begins at approximately 100m along the Inland Lake Road. The trail leads along an old skid trail up to a rock bluff and then on to a radio tower overlooking Powell Lake. From the bluff, you get a great view of Powell Lake, Cranberry Lake and the ocean. The total distance of the hike is 5km (1.5 hours) return. It is possible to take a side trip off the bluff and walk down to Mowat Bay joining Tony's Trail.

Goat II Access Trail (Map #27/A4)
At the end of Goat II Road is the Goat II Access Trail, a difficult hike to a beautiful alpine area. If you proceed south you will see a trailhead marked by flagging tape. From here, you must do some bushwhacking past 2 small creeks to a rock slide which must be crossed before reaching the ridge and ultimately the traverse down to Skwim Lake. If you proceed in a northern direction from the Goat Lake II Road , you will have to walk along the deactivated road to an old trail heading up to the alpine at the base of Triple Peaks. There are alpine flowers in July and great views of the surrounding mountain peaks. From the alpine area, you can continue on the South Powell Divide Trail which is an extensive ridge route leading all the way to Emma Lake and beyond.

Haywire Regional Park Trails (Map #17/A2)
Leading from the regional park are two trails. The **Lost Lake Trail** is 6km (2 hours) in length and leads through old growth forest past Lost Lake to Inland Lake. There are several steep sections along the trail together with many gulleys to cross and

a muddy area to traverse. **Tony's Trail** leads along the eastern banks of Powell Lake in a southward direction. The trail is 8km (2.5 hours) one way any culminates at Mowat Bay.

Inland Lake Trail (Map #17/A1)
Inland Lake Trail is unique because it is a wheelchair accessible area complete with a cabin, picnic tables and a dock. The trail leads 13km (3 hours) around Inland Lake and begins at the Inland Lake Rec Site except between November and March when a 10min hike is necessary from the gate on the road leading to the rec site. From the west side of the lake, it is possible to connect with the Lost Lake Trail which culminates at the Haywire Bay Regional Park. At the north end of Inland Lake, you may wish to hike 700m (one way) along the portage route to Powell Lake. This is a well marked and popular family trail enjoyed by both hikers and bikers.

Mowat Bay Trail (Map #17/A2)
From the Powell Lake Bridge, a 2.3km (1 hour) trail leading to Mowat Bay where you can enjoy a nice swim on Powell Lake. The hike switch backs up the northern side of Valentine Mountain (100meters in elevation) before descending into Mowat Bay. From the bay, **Tony's Trail** leads up the eastern shores of Powell Lake.

Myrtle Springs Trail (Map #17/A2)
This 5km (1.5 hour) trail begins approximately 200-300m along the Haslam Lake Road from the Inland FSR. It follows an old road network eventually leading to Duck Lake Road near the Haslam Slough. You can either return along Haslam FSR or the way you came.

Okeover Trail (Map #16/C1)
This well marked trail is 8km (3.5 hours) long. The trail begins at the south end of Okeover Inlet off the Southview Road with the end point being on the Theodosia FSR. Rather than proceeding back the way you came, you can follow the forestry road along the eastern shores of the inlet. The trail is ideal for mountain bikers as well as hiking. Beautiful views of the inlet are provided along the route.

Saltery Bay Trails (Map #17/D3)
In Saltery Bay Provincial Park is a network of trails worth trying. The main trail leads 10km (4 hours) along an overgrown road and then a well defined trail. There is a steep climb at the beginning of the trail but you get a good view of Nelson and Hardy Islands from the summit. A less strenuous option is to walk 2km one way from the campsite at the provincial park to the beach.

Scout Mountain Trail (Map #17/A2)
This trail begins at the Kinsman Park near the Powell Lake Marina and is marked by orange trail markers. The hike leads uphill to the summit of Scout Mountain, which overlooks Powell Lake and Wildwood. The trail then drops steadily downward through a second growth forest and ends at Sutherland Street where the Sliammon Lake Trail begins.

Sliammon Lake Trail (Map #16/D1,17/A2)
The trail begins at the south end of Sutherland Street and proceeds northward eventually leading to the Theodosia FSR. The well marked trail leads through second growth timber and up some steep sections. The hike takes you past Little Sliammon Lake, where there is a nice beach for swimming, and Sliammon Lake. The trail connects with Appleton Canyon Trail, Marathon Trail and Rieveley's Point Trail so it is possible to walk up to 18km if you so choose. A side trail, which is 5km (1.5 hours) return, leads to Three Mile Bay and an old mine site.

South Powell Divide Trail (Map #26,27)
This high ridge route extends 20km (2days) from the Goat Access II Trail south to the B Branch Road. This route should only be considered by experienced hikers with the appropriate topographic maps. Along the way you can enjoy the splendid views of the surrounding lakes and mountain peaks. The Emma Lake Cabin makes for a good overnight destination.

Tin Hat Mountain Trail (Map #17/B1)
From approximately 300m north of Spring Lake on the Tin Hat Road, it is best to park your truck and walk the old road northward. Eventually, you will pick up a well maintained but difficult trail which leads to the summit some 13km (5 hours) return gaining 1600m along the way. Alpine flowers, bunch berries and great views of the Powell Lake area are offered. The hike is best left for July-October.

Toquenatch Trail (Map #16/D1)
This trail begins approximately 3.5km from Hwy#101 along the Southview Road. The hike extends in a northwest direction 5km (1.5 hours) one way. It leads past 2 large Douglas-fir trees following the creek to the south end of Okeover Inlet. The trail is well marked and offers a chance to see salmon spawning in the fall.

Walt Lake Ridge Route (Map #18/A2)

A 4wd spur road off Lloyd Road leads to the trailhead. From there, a difficult and unmarked route leads to some alpine country where you can proceed either to the north or south. Either way, you have miles of beautiful alpine meadows to explore. The north branch leads onto Beta Lake whereas the south branch leads to the northern shores of Khartoum Lake.

Wednesday Lake Trail (Map #25/B4)

This 8km (3 hour) hike leads along an old road from Malaspina FSR to tiny Wednesday Lake which drains into Okeover Inlet.

Wildwood Hill Trail (Map #17/A2)

The trail begins on the west side of the Powell Lake Bridge off Hwy#101. This trail switchbacks twice before it connects with the powerline and eventually leads back to the Petro Canada Service Station. The trail is easily followed and is wide enough for both mountain bikers and hikers.

Willingdon Beach Trail (Map #17/A3)

This trail begins at the Willingdon Beach Campsite and follows the shoreline for about 2km (30mins) one way. The trail is wide and well marked. Along the way, there is interpretive signs featuring historic logging machinery as well as coastal ecosystems.

Squamish Area Trails

Alice Lake Park (Map #20/C4)

This wilderness park offers good access to several trails in and around the area.

The most popular year-round trail is the **Four Lakes Walk**. This well developed 6.5km (2-3 hour) trail leads past 4 woodland lakes providing a leisurely stroll through a second growth forest and access to the lake. The trail joins with trails leading to Cat Lake, the hwy and Garibaldi Estates.

Mountain bikers looking for more of a challenge may wish to try the **Edith-Fawn Lake Loop**. This technically challenging single-track offers extreme downhill sections. The loop starts on the access road past the Alice Lake Campsite on Squamish Valley Road. In all, you cycle over 16km with an elevation gain of 255m.

Alice Ridge Trail (Map #20/D3)

Take the right fork when the road splits at the Alice Lake Provincial Park Headquarters and drive up the rough 4wd road as far as you can. From the end of the road, continue uphill to the Little Diamond Head and the base of Mount Garibaldi.

Overall, it is a 8km (5 hour) return hike gaining 700m along the way. The height of land is at 2075m and provides a great view of the Squamish Valley. The route, which is best hiked in July to October, provides an alternative route to the Diamond Head Area.

Brohm Lake Interpretive Trails (Map #20/C3)

From the parking lot off Hwy#99, an easy 5km (1.5 hour) trail circles the popular fishing lake with minimal elevation gain along the way. The trail provides access to the picnic area next to Brohm Lake and is used for shore fishing as well as wildlife viewing. Around Brohm Lake, you will also find a network of interconnecting trails used by mountain bikers and hikers. These trails lead away from the lake and through the second growth forest typical of the area.

Cat Lake Area (Map #20/C3)

Around Cat Lake, a series of motocross trails offer very challenging routes for the mountain biker. These trails can be accessed off of the Cheekeye River FSR at the old gondola base area or the Cat Lake Rec Site. It is possible to cross the Cheekeye River and follow the trails down to Alice Lake or Garibaldi Highlands.

Diamond Head Area (Map #20/D4)

The Diamond Head Parking Lot is found at the 16km mark off the Mamquam Road. The road to the parking lot is open year round as the road is generally plowed to allow backcountry skiers to access Garibaldi Park. From the parking lot, it's a 11.2km (3-5 hours) one way hike gaining 600m up an old road and trail. The route cuts through a forested setting to some attractive alpine meadows and then down to Elfin Lake.

Mountain bikers looking for a gruelling uphill bike can bike to the hut at Elfin Lake, which sleeps 40 and has a propane heater. The Red Heather Day Shelter is found near the end of the old road. The trail is open from July to October for hikers and then turns into a popular backcountry skiing area when the snow falls.

From Elfin Lake, it is 7km (5 hours) return to the Little Diamond Head through some open subalpine meadows (gaining 625m). From Elfin Lake to the Oval Cone, a spectacular volcanic outcrop, is 6.4km (4 hours) return gaining 250m. From Elfin Lake to Mamquam Lake is 6.5 (4 hours) return. This strenuous scramble gains 570m along the way.

Evans Lake Area (Map #20/B3)

North of Evans Lake Camp, a series of trails link up with Levette Lake. The wooded trails provide challenging single-track riding or enjoyable hiking in and around the park reserve and the wilderness lakes. You can access these trails off the Paradise Valley Road.

Garibaldi Highlands (Map #20/D4)

The most popular mountain biking area in Squamish. You can access the area from Alice Lake Park in the north or Perth Dr and Glacierview Road in the Garibaldi Highlands to the south. Overall, the moderate trails offer easier, smoother terrain. To really explore the area, try joining the trails to create a long loop ride.

Garibaldi Neve Traverse (Map #20/D3)

This is a classic ski touring route covering 42kms (allow 2-3 days) from the Red Heather Day Shelter to the Black Tusk Parking Lot. The best time to ski the route is in the early spring when Garibaldi Lake is still frozen. Along the route, there are several alpine huts, expansive icefields and interesting volcanic features. Overall, you climb from 1000m at the parking lot off the Mamquam Road to 2100m before descending to 700m at the Black Tusk Parking Lot. The roads to both parking lots are usually plowed.

High Falls Creek Trail (Map #20/A1)

From the 24mile mark on the Squamish Main , the steep trail leads 12km (6 hours) return to a view of the falls and the Squamish River Valley. The difficult trail, which gains 640m to the vista at 715m, has been recently cleared and marked so it is fairly easy to follow. The trail is best in May through November.

Hut Lake Trail (Map #20/B2)

With a 4wd vehicle, you can park at the north end of Levette Lake and walk the overgrown, washed out logging road to Hut Lake. It is a 5km (1.5 hour) easy walk gaining 105m. The lake offers very good fishing for small rainbow.

Lake Lovely Water (Map #20/A3)

The hike into this scenic subalpine area is difficult. It involves crossing an Indian Reserve to the Squamish River and then paddling a canoe across the river. Unfortunately, the cable car is no longer available for public use. From the west banks of the Squamish River, the poorly maintained trail follows the creek draw leading to the lake set in a large glacial bowl. The trail is 15km (12-16 hours) return gaining 1200m to the lake. The Alpine Club maintains a cabin at the lake, which can be used for a fee ($10-$12). The rec area also offers good fishing, wilderness camping areas and climbing opportunities.

Marion and Phyllis Lakes (Map #11/B2)

A long bike ride takes you along the gated access road north of the Furry Creek Golf Course past Marion Lake to Phyllis Lake. The 450 meter climb over 16km return is rewarded with good views across Howe Sound. The area beyond Phyllis Lake (the Greater Vancouver Watershed) is closed to the public.

Mount Mulligan (Map#11/C1, 20/C4)

From the Raffuse Creek Spur Road, this short climb (4km) leads to the summit of Mount Mulligan. Great views of the Stawamus River Valley are provided from the top.

Mount Roderick Trail (Map #11/A1,20/A4)

This long day trip requires you to take the ferry to the Woodfibre Pulp Mill before biking or hiking to the trailhead several kilometers up the main logging road. Here you cross a footbridge to join the trail that passes a helipad before narrowing. Continuing north, the trail climbs up the open ridge to the subalpine for a great view of Howe Sound. Overall, it's a 20km (10 hour) difficult hike gaining 1475m. The trail is best hiked in June through October.

Petgill Lake Trail (Map #11/B1)

The hike begins on the marked trail north of the parking lot of Murrin Provincial Park (on the opposite side of Hwy#99). This 11.5km (6 hour) trail begins by climbing steeply through the bluffs before entering a second growth forest. It soon meets an old logging road and heads south. Eventually, the road becomes completely overgrown at which time the trail departs the road and leads up a ridge to the lake. The trail is best hiked in March through November and gains 640m in elevation. From the lake, it is possible to access the Goat Ridge Route and several climbing opportunities.

Ring Creek Trail (Map #20/D4)
This difficult mountain bike trail is found just after the bridge over the Mamquam River on the Mamquam FSR. It begins on an old railbed and heads downhill for about half an hour to the Ring Creek crossing and onto the Diamond Head Road. Using our maps you can make a good loop ride along the various logging roads in the area.

Ross's Rip / Doris Burma Memorial Trail (Map #20/B2)
The Doris Burma Memorial Trail can be found on Hwy#99 at the salt sheds south of Daisy Lake. The trail is marked with orange markers as it follows the river to a unique pine tree bridge. A great 7km loop trail can be done when combined with Ross's Rip (part of the Sea to Sky Trail) which is found across the highway.

Shannon Falls Trail (Map #11/B1)
From the Shannon Falls Park parking lot, this 5km (2 hour) trail gains 445m along the creek to a great vantage point overlooking the spectacular 220m waterfall. The trail connects with the Stawamus Chief Trails to the north.

Sigurd Creek Trail (Map #19/D2, 20/A2)
The trailhead is found at the end of Branch A251 off the Ashlu Road (past the second bridge). The trail climbs 1322m over 14km (7 hours) return along the creek to Pelion and Ossa Mountains. Along the trail, you will pass by some waterfalls and some nice vistas. The trail is best hiked in mid-July to October.

The Smoke Bluffs (Valleycliffe) Trails (Map #20/D3)
These multi-use trails are located in Squamish around the Smoke Bluffs Climbing Area. From the parking area on Loggers Lane you wind your way through the Smoke Bluffs to the top of Plateau Dr. where a good variety of trails that will suit all levels of mountain bikers can be found. The single-track trails are generally quite technical and twisty.

Squamish Estuary Trails (Map #20/B4)
The sea-level dyke trails found in Squamish offer enjoyable year-round hiking or biking. Excellent views of the Stawamus Chief, Shannon Falls and Mount Garibaldi combined with the wide variety of birds (including Bald Eagles in the winter) make this area a nice retreat.

Stawamus Chief (Map #20/B1)
From the parking lot north of Shannon Falls Provincial Park, a trail system leads up the back of the Stawamus Chief, a dramatic 500m granite wall south of Squamish. The are is a very popular hiking/climbing retreat providing great views from the top. To hike to the top of the First Peak is 6km (3 hours), to the top of the Second Peak is 9km (3-4 hours) and to the top of the Third Peak is 11km (5-6 hours).

Regardless of which hike you choice, you should expect a steep uphill climb. The trails are best hiked in March to November. An alternative is to hike the Squaw (the peak behind the Stawamus Chief) by way of a 14.5km (5.5 hour) trail gaining 500m to the summit at 610m. For rock climbers, there is a choice of over 600 routes between The Chief & Little Smoke Bluffs (further North).

Stoltmann Wilderness Hiking Route (Map #28,37)
This new wilderness trail was built by the Western Canada Wilderness Committee and links Meager Creek with the Elaho River Valley. The trail is well marked with orange markers and offers pole and rope bridges. The chance to encounter Moose, Cougars and Grizzly Bears and the remote nature of the trail makes this an area for experienced, well-equiped mountaineers.

It is best to use a two vehicle system, parking one on the Meager Creek Branch and then driving back to the start at 99km on the E1000 Road (off the Elaho Main). The total distance of the trail is 29km (3-4days).

The route takes you from a gentle valley with rainforest draped canyons, past the Elaho Giant, a 10m round Douglas-fir near Sundown Creek and the Grizzly Fir, another large Douglas-fir next to Last Chance Creek. After a day and a half, you will reach the Hundred Lakes Plateau, which offers panoramic views of huge glacier-clad mountains, as you walk among the heather and flower meadows that connect the crystal clear lakes and ponds. By day 3, you will be overlooking the Meager Creek Valley and the 1/2 day journey to the closed hot springs.

Utopia Lake Route (Map #11/C1)
From Hwy#1 at Britannia Beach, it's a 17km (8 hour) difficult hike along a gated road then poorly maintained trail to the lake gaining 1390m along the way. Along the hike, you will pass by the abandoned mining townsite of Mt Sheer. Climbers can access Mountain Lake Hut and the surrounding peaks. Call Copper Beach Holdings before setting out.

Sunshine Coast Trails

Ambrose Lake Ecological Reserve (Map #18/B4)
To reach the trailhead, follow Timberline Road, which is about 500m from the Earl's Cove ferry terminal. The trail leads from the end of the road and follows the powerline to the lake. Overall, the trail is about 5km (2 hours) return and is fairly easy. The ecological reserve at the lake is home to an abundance of waterfowl.

Angus Creek Loop (Map #9/D3, 10/A3)
This mountain bike loop starts on the Sechelt-Crucil FSR, which is found south of the Porpoise Bay Park Campsite. The 22km moderate route follows the main roads in a counter-clockwise direction. The steep initial climb is rewarded with panoramic views and then a downhill ride back to the hilly Sechelt Inlet Road and the ride home.

Brodie Trails Loop (Map #10/B3)
Beginning from the Roberts Creek FSR, you follow the powerline west to the trail. Follow the markings back to the beginning or explore the many difficult side routes. This moderate 7.5km route is home to the Brodie Test of Metal Race.

Caren Range Trails (Map #9/C1)
The Trout Lake Road provides access to an excellent area for hikers and mountain bikers in the summer and X-C skiers during the winter. The best place to start is at the 12km junction or up to the 15km point after the road passes though a stand of old growth timber.

The extensive logging road network in the area provides easy backcountry skiing and hiking opportunities with some great views of the ocean and the Sunshine Coast as well as a chance to explore an ancient forest of yellow cedar, hemlock and balsam, believed to be the oldest forest on the coast. If you coming to the area in the winter or early spring, it is well advised to bring a 4wd vehicle with chains as the road may not be plowed.

Carlson Lake Loop (Map #9/C2)
Found 6km up the Halfmoon Bay FSR (4wd access) this moderate 21km mountain bike loop should take 2.5 hours to ride. The route is marked in a clockwise direction, which begins with a tough initial climb. Most of the route follows old logging roads that are overgrown. Along the way, you are rewarded with views of Carlson Lake and Sechelt Inlet. The loop eventually brings you back to the Halfmoon Bay FSR, after gaining 390m in elevation, where you cycle down to the start.

Chapman Creek Trails (Map #10/A3)
Along the banks of Chapman Creek are several multi-use trails:

Chapman Falls Trail is reached by parking at the top of Havies Road and walking along the chainlink fence. From there, the trail leads 6km (2 hours) return initially along a wide, muddy trail to the powerline before passing through some old growth Douglas-fir on the way to the spectacular falls. This part of the trails is best left to experienced mountain bikers.

The Hatchery Trail begins off Parkway Drive at the sign. The trail leads to a viewing platform to the left or to a series of spawning channels to the right. To reach the channels, it is about a 500m (30min) return trip along Chapman Creek.

Lower Chapman Creek Trail is considered one of the premier short hikes on the Sunshine Coast as it leads through an advanced second growth forest next to the creek. The trailhead is located at the parking lot of Brookman Park immediately east of Davis Bay beach on Hwy#101. Large red cedar stumps are seen along the 2.8km (45min) one way trail. Several swimming holes and sandy beaches are reached from the trail.

Clack Creek Loop (Map #10/B3)
From the junction of Lockyer and Gruman Roads, this 12.3km moderate ride is best done in a counter-clockwise direction. You follow Gruman Road then the Clack Creek FSR to its end. Here an old skid road heads down for 2km (hang on) to the East Wilson FSR and the ride home. Also found at the end of the Clack Creek FSR is the 3 Steps Trails which will take you down to Hwy#101 along a series of 3 trails.

Cliff Gilker Park (Map #10/A3)
This small regional park is easily accessed off Hwy#101 north of Roberts Creek and adjacent to the Sunshine Coast Golf and Country Club. It provides a series of easy hiking trails through a forested setting with little elevation gain. Wooden bridges cross several small streams and Roberts Creek in amongst some large

second growth timber. There are four well maintained and easily followed trails within the park (Washout Trail, River Run, Katimavik and Short Cut). The trails are very popular.

Dakota Creek Loop (Map #10/B3)
This mountain bike ride is found at the junction of Roberts Creek FSR and the Dakota Creek FSR. It is a moderate 11km (1 hour) ride. Following a counter-clockwise direction you will be rewarded with fine panoramic views.

Gray Creek Trail (Map #9/D2)
The Gray Creek Trail takes off just north of where Gray Creek crosses the East Porpoise Bay Road (Sechelt Inlet Road). The trail meanders along the creek leading past 2 sets of waterfalls and some nice pools and rapids. The trail is approximately 2km (1 hour) return and is fairly rough as you have to pass over some windfalls and boulders along the way. Experienced mountain bikers access this trail from the logging roads on the upper (eastern) side of the trail.

Halfmoon Creek Loop (Map #9/C2)
Found on an old road on the east side of Homesite Creek just off Hwy#101, this easier 8.5km mountain bike loop follows the logging road to the power line. From the power line you loop back along the Halfmoon Bay FSR and the highway.

Hillside Demonstration Forest (Map #10/C3)
This newly developed demonstration forest is located along McNair Creek. It illustrates different silviculture practices of the Sunshine Coast and provides a view of the Port Mellon Mill as well as Howe Sound. The demonstration forest is on the west side of McNair Creek and so it is best to park on the west side of the McNair Creek Bridge and hike up the hill. Overall, the trail is 4km (1.5 hours) return and has a number of interpretative sign along the way. Picnic facilities on the trail were in the works at the time of writing this book.

Homesite Creek (Gumdrop) Caves (Map#9/C2)
The trailhead is found on the Homesite FSR just north of the powerline and is usually signed as long as vandals have not removed the sign. The trail leads half an hour (one way) in a southeast direction from the road to a series of 12 limestone caverns, the largest one being 10m deep.

Homesite Creek Loop (Map #9/B2)
Starting on the Homesite Creek FSR, an 8km moderate bike ride follows the logging roads and power lines to the west of Homesite Creek. This 1 hour loop is best done in a counter-clockwise direction (start left from the FSR and follow the markers). This way you end with a fun 5km downhill, which takes you back to the highway.

Kinnickinnick Park (Map #9/D3)
This regional park is found off Trail Ave near the arena. Within the park are a series of easy walking trails, which are clearly marked. These trails are set in a second growth conifer stand with some larger trees to admire. The trailhead is found on the side road leading along the Sechelt Golf and Country Club off of Fairway Ave. It is a short distance (3.7km) from Sechelt. Mountain bikers often explore the more difficult trails over to and off of the Crowston Lake Road.

Lyon Lake Loop (Map #9/C2)
Found on a side road 16km up the Halfmoon Bay FSR (4wd access), this difficult 17km mountain bike loop trail should take 2.5 hours to ride. This well marked route is best cycled in a clockwise direction as you follow a series of logging roads that tend to be steep and rocky in places. The loop takes you through some old growth forests to beautiful, panoramic views.

Mt. Daniel Trail (Map #9/B1)
This trail is located off the Oyster Bay Road north of Pender Harbour. It involves a 2.5km (1 hour) one way hike to the top of Mt. Daniel with some scrambling over fallen trees. The highlights include a great coastal view as well as a chance to explore some Indian rock formations near the top. The trail is fairly steep on the way up.

Mt. Drew Trail (Map #18/D4)
To reach the summit of Mt. Drew at 1860m is quite a trek. It is necessary to cross the Sechelt Inlet from Egmont by boat to the mouth of Earle Creek. From there, hike or mountain bike up the network of logging roads and then scramble to the top of the summit. Given the distance, it is best to make the hike in 2 days.

Mount Elphinstone Loop (Map #10/A,B3)
A long 42km mountain bike route that follows the Hwyand a series of logging roads. Starting from the Langdale Ferry Terminal, you head north to the steep

climb up the Dakota Creek FSR. Turn left on the branch road 2011 and follow the signs back down to the Hwyand the ride back to the start. This difficult route has a few steep sections but the great views of Howe Sound and the islands are worth it. The Lower Elphinstone Area offers more variety as you cycle old roads and trails through old mining remains.

Mt. Hallowell Trail (Map #18/B4)
From the Halfmoon-Carlson FSR, a newly improved trail begins at the abandoned red cable spool about 19.5km from Hwy#101. The trail leads through a clearcut and some old growth timber to the summit and a newly restored forest service fire lookout tower. It is about 1km (1hr) to reach the summit. From the top, you will get an excellent view of the Sechelt Peninsula and the ocean.

Mt. Richardson Trail (Map #9/D2)
The best place to access Mt. Richardson is from the Richardson Lake Rec Site, which is 4wd vehicle access. From the lake, proceed in a southwestern direction by bushwhacking 2km (2 hours) one way to the summit along a deteriorating 4wd road. From the summit at 986m, you will get a great view of the Sechelt Peninsula and Inlet.

Mt. Varley Trail (Map #10/C1)
To reach the summit of Mt. Varley at 1639m, you must bushwhack off the end of Rainy FSR. In order to reach the best spot to begin your hike, it is necessary to use a 4wd vehicle. It is about 3km (2 hours) one way to the summit.

Mt. Wrottesey Trail (Map #10/D2,11/A2)
Mt. Wrottesey is a prominent land feature overshadowing Howe Sound. To reach the summit, boat to McNab Creek or to Camp Potlatch in Howe Sound. From Camp Potlatch, a well established trail leads along the creek to the Potlatch Road. Continue up the road to where a small creek drains off the southern side of the mountain. From there, bushwhack through the timber to the sub-alpine and then to the summit. From McNab Creek, your must hike/bike 3km up the main haul road and cross over to the Potlatch Road. It is a full day hike involving an elevation gain of 1625m.

Pender Hill Trail (Map #9/A1)
The trail begins about 60m east of Lee's Road towards Irvine's Landing Road. It takes about a half an hour to reach the summit of Pender Hill because the trail is quite steep. You get a great view from the top as you peer over the edge.

Princess Louisa Provincial Park (Map #27/D2, 28/A2)
The remote access to this hidden inlet discourages most hikers. However, the spectacular fjord-like setting is certainly worth the visit. In order to reach the inlet, it is necessary to take a long boat ride up Queen's Reach until you come to the Princess Louisa Inlet. Once you are at the provincial park, a short, well-used trail leads to the world famous Chatterbox Falls (a 10min excursion). From there, the trail continues beyond the falls and is called the Loquita Creek Trail. The trail passes by Old Henry's cabin at Snake Falls gaining 875m along the way. Eventually, the trail continues on to a gorgeous mountain lake. From there, it is possible to hike in the seemingly endless open alpine country with rugged snow-capped peaks nearby. Needless to say, there is a spectacular view of the inlet as you ascend the trail.

Redroofs Loop (Map #9/C3)
Beginning 100m before the Halfmoon Bay Store along Mintie Road, this 2km (30min) trail loops alongside the estuary of Halfmoon Creek before returning to Mintie Road via Rutherford Road and Redroffs Road. Along the way, you can enjoy the waterfowl that frequent the mud flats and the rocky shoreline of the estuary. A recently developed trail leads 4km (1.5hr) one way from Sargeant Bay Provincial Park to Triangle Lake leading through some old growth timber. Triangle Lake is a shallow boggy lake offering waterfowl viewing. Mountain bikers can enjoy an easy 15km loop starting from Sargeant Bay Park and following Redroofs Road to the logging workshed where you turn right. Follow the signs back to the park. Please stay off the nature trails that are designed for hikers only.

Roberts Creek Loop (Map 10/A,B3)
Starting on the Roberts Creek FSR, this difficult 2 hour mountain bike route actually climbs 800m over the 30km loop. You ride mostly along the B&K logging road. As expected with the elevation gain, the ride has terrific views. It also provides access to a few other trails in the area. For example, the difficult, steep Mexican Jumping Bean Trail heads down to the Brodie Loop Trails. This rough route actually follows an old creek bed.

Ruby Lake - Klein Lake Traverse (Map #18/B4)
This is a newly developed (December 1995) trail which traverses the saddle between Klein and Ruby lakes 4km (1hr) one way. To access the trail from the

south, park at Dan Bosch Park, walk 50m to the south on Hwy#101 and follow a deactivated logging road for a short distance before you pick up the trail. From the north, drive to Klein Lake and park. It is easier to, start at Klein Lake (if you start from the south end, you must climb a steep stretch of the trail to the saddle). The highlight of the trail is the excellent views from the rocky bluffs along the route.

Skookumchuck Narrows (Map #18/C4)
From Edmont Road, an 8km (2hr) easy walk leads along a well maintained trail to the narrows, which are one of the most popular areas on the coast. You can explore the tidal pools at low tide or watch the tide rip through a narrow, shallow channel during high tide. Consult the tide tables for the best viewing times.

Soames Hill (Map #10/C4)
This popular trail network is found to the northeast of Gibsons. The trails can be accessed off Bridgeman or Esperanza Roads, which are side streets off Chamberlin Road. From either trailhead, it takes about half an hour to hike several hundred stairs cut out of fallen logs to the top of the hill. The view from the top (at 240m) is worth the effort. It is also possible to walk the short wooded trails around the southern slope of the hill.

South Elphinstone Heritage and Rec Trails (Map #10/B3)
On the southern slopes of Mt. Elphinstone is a series of popular multi-use trails. These trails lead through a second growth forest and into some scenic backcountry bowls. Along the way, you can see the remains of the 1920s shinglebolt operations. The trails are used by equestrians, mountain bikers and hikers in the spring through fall. In the winter, the area now has groomed X-C ski trails as well as telemark routes on the north side of the bowl on Dakota Ridge (at 975m in elevation). Snow can last till June on the peak and ridge areas.

Cablevision Trail leads from behind the shed at the top of Gilmour Road. The trail is clearly marked with yellow aluminum diamonds for most of its length except towards the top. It takes about 1.5 hours (one way) to climb to the B&K Logging Road. From there, continue uphill to two abandoned receiver stations which both provide excellent vistas. From the second receiver, it is possible to continue on to the old ski hut and eventually the summit of Mount Elphinstone.

K2 Summit Trail is marked by pink markers and is accessed by either Stewart Road or Wharf Road. Either way, it is a steady climb to the K2 summit at 640m where you get a fantastic view of the ocean and the Sunshine Coast. The trail eventually culminates on a 4wd spur road at the base of the mountain. It takes about 1.5 hours (one way) to reach the end of the trail.

Langdale Creek Waterfall Trail begins 100m past the powerline off Stewart Road. The hike takes about 40 min one way to reach the falls. The trail leads through a second growth stand of Douglas-fir and along an old road next to the creeks. It is fairly steep towards the end but is easily followed because of the blue markers that show the way. An option is to walk down the Waterfall Trail to the Wharf Road trailhead.

Mountain Trail leads from the south end of the cemetery off Keith Road and is marked by red diamond markers and a sign. The trail leads about half an hour uphill to the remains of First Camp located next to Chaster Creek at 488m. The camp was used by shingle bolt workers in the 1920s. From the First Camp, it is possible to continue uphill to the Second Camp just north of Largo Road or to hike in a northwest direction to the Chinese Camp. In the area, there are remains of an old dam, tramway and wood flume along the trail.

Shaker Trail leads from the powerline off Stewart Road and is clearly marked by orange markers. It leads steadily uphill about 35 minutes (one way) to the B&K Logging Road. The highlight of this trail is the wooden flume used to carry shingle bolts to the First Camp.

Smugglers Cove Provincial Park (Map #9/B2)
This park is accessed by Brooks Road northwest of Sechelt. From the parking lot, an extensive trail network leads through the forest to the scenic cove and then continues along the shoreline for a total of 3km (40mins) one way. The trails are easy and generally flat although they do pass through a marshy area.

Sprockids Mountain Bike Park (Map #10/C3)
A unique community project has created a series of fun, short loops for the young riders of the Sunshine Coast to enjoy. These trails were actually developed by the original 'Sprockids' as a school project. The trails are accessed off Stewart Road which is found off of North Road in Langdale.

Suncoaster Trail (Map #9,10,18)
A new 33km long trail leading from Homesite Creek through the foothills to Klein Lake. The trail passes through abandoned railbeds, hydrolines, old growth forests, and rocky promontories. The views are incredible. At the time of writing this book, campsites are being constructed along the way.

Tetrahedron Provincial Park Trails (Map #10/B2)
This newly created provincial park is the home of an extensive network of alpine hiking, biking and backcountry ski trails. It also contains a series of small mountain lakes, which provide good fishing opportunities. The main area is reached off of several branch roads off the Sechelt FSR. The trail systems in the area are as follows:

Batchelor Lake Cabin is reached by a 1.4km (40 min) one way hike through old growth forest to the subalpine lake. Blueberries are abundant in July to August but so are bears.

Chapman Lake is approximately 1km to the northwest of McNair cabin through a sub-alpine meadow. It is also approximately 3.5km (one way) from Edwards Lake cabin through some old growth forest and an open meadow.

Five Lake Circuit involves a 10.4km (6 hour) hike that passes by 5 of the larger lakes in the provincial park. One of the highlights is Edwards Lake, which is a beautiful subalpine lake in a bowl surrounded by old growth timber. Edwards Lake has a nice cabin on its shores. Overall, the circuit takes you through old growth forest along an old logging road and a series of trails. This hike is not accessible until after June when the snow melts. The 4 other lakes are Tannis, Bachelor, Mayne and Gilbert Lakes. Most of the year, the trail network is quite swampy so it is best to bring some good hiking boots. In winter, this area makes a good cross country ski circuit.

McNair Lake Trail begins at the end of the McNair Creek Road (or as far as you can drive). The trail leads 3km (2 hours) uphill to the lake and one of the four cabins in the park. The trail parallels McNair Creek on its northeast side and passes through old growth timber. McNair Lake is surrounded by subalpine meadows with rugged mountain peaks looming in the background. Wildflowers are a highlight in July and August.

Mt. Steel Trails begins by traversing some old growth timber past Edwards and Gilbert Lakes. Eventually, you reach the open sub-alpine terrain and the Mt. Steel Cabin (after climbing 540m). To reach the cabin at 1500m in elevation, it is 18km (7 hours+) return. The trail is well marked and is best hiked in July-October because of snow accumulations in other parts of the year. The trail is very popular not only during the summer for hiking but also during ski season.

Panther Peak is at 169m and is south of Tetrahedron Peak. The best route to reach Panther Peak is to proceed up the McNair FSR (4wd required) to the end of the road. From there, it is a 2km walk through some old growth forest, past some rock slides to McNair Cabin, which is a sub-alpine cabin. From the cabin, proceed towards No Name Lake and then eventually climb steadily upward through a snow chute to the summit. Overall, it takes a minimum of 5 hours to reach the summit and another 3 hours to climb down. The difficult route is well rewarded with panoramic views and the beautiful sub-alpine terrain. Alternative routes involve climbing the peak from the Rainy River valley or accessing the peak from the McNair Lake cabin.

Tetrahedron Peak is accessed by several difficult routes. The easiest route is to travel up the Rainy FSR approximately 6.4km and then take the overgrown spur road that crosses Rainy River. Unfortunately, the bridge is no longer there so you have to either forge the creek or use a series of ropes, both of which are less than inviting given the roaring currents of the river. Once you have fordged the river, proceed for an additional 2km up the old road and then take a spur road to the valley between Panther and Tetrahedron Peaks. Eventually, an unmarked route leads northward to the open slopes beneath the peak where you can scramble to the summit.

Overall, there is an elevation gain of 1600m and it takes a good day just to reach the summit. Once you do reach the summit, which is at 1737m, you will be rewarded with a spectacular panoramic view from the highest mountain peak on the Sunshine Coast. An alternative route is to tackle the peak from the Thornhill Creek drainage which involves boating up the Salmon Inlet and then walking/biking up a series of old logging roads. A further route is to bushwhack from the McNair Lake cabin. Both of these latter two routes are less than inviting.

Trout Lake Loop (Map #9/C2)
From the Trout Lake parking lot on Hwy#101, a 15km moderate mountain bike loop will take you clockwise along a series of roads back to the hwy. Allow 1.5 hours. Between Trout Lake and Redroofs Road a sereis of moderate trails can be explored. The hydrolines above Trout Lake also offer moderate riding that turns quite difficult the further you head west.

Tuwanek Point Beach Trail (Map #9/D2)
The trailhead to this ocean front walk is found off Upland Road just before the gravel pit. The trail leads 2km (1 hour) one way from the road down to the ocean following the shore of Sechelt Inlet to the point.

Wilson Creek Trail (Map #10/A3)
The trail is found by parking on Jack Road and then crossing Hwy#101. The scenic trail leads through advanced second growth timber along Wilson Creek. At 1km along the trail, you will cross a bridge over the creek before continuing on to the powerlines for a 2km (1 hour) round trip. This route can be mountain biked by experienced riders.

Whistler/Pemberton Area Trails

With hundreds of trails scattered around your backdoor, the Whistler Area has quickly become one of the premier mountain biking destinations in the world. Similar to the North Shore, trying to find any trail by name may prove difficult unless you have a guide. For this reason, we recommend you obtain a copy of the Whistler Area Topographic Map and a local guidebook.

Alta Lake Road Trails (Map #29/D3)
Off of Alta Lake Road, numerous short trails for the mountain biker can be found. On the east side of the road, off of the gravel pit access road look for A River Runs Through It and Emerald Forest. A River Runs Through It is a short 2.5km technically challenging single-track that heads south back to the road. This heavily forested trail leads through the swamp between Alta Lake Road and the Valley Trail. It is often muddy, has lots of roots and a log bridge to cross which will deter most riders. Emerald Forest offers easier, dryer riding along several short trails around the gravel pit. This area is actually on private property so please respect your surroundings. Rebob Trail can be found 120m north of the Rainbow Lake Trailhead. This difficult trail climbs the bank to a series of old roads with lots of obstacles to hop. You can climb to Binty's High Trail or exit back out on the road. Whip Me, Snip Me is found about 100m south of the Rainbow Lake Trailhead. This is another challenging system that climbs north to the Rainbow Lake Trailhead and the cruise down.

Ancient Cedar - Showh Lakes Trail (Map #29/D3)
This trail network is located north of Whistler off the Soo River 03 Road (4wd). The trail is a 4km (1.5 hours) loop through some 1000 year old cedar trees found at the base of Cougar Mountain. The elevation gain is about 150m on the trail and so it is a fairly easy trail. If you do not have a 4wd vehicle then the walk/bike will be more than 4km. While you are in the area, try fishing Showh Lakes.

Binty's High Trail (Map #29/D3)
A Whistler Mountain Biking Classic. This difficult 7.5km trail climbs 510m from the top of Alpine Meadows (you start on Rick's Roost Trail). Once you reach the top enjoy the view and then hang on. The trail spills you out on Alta Lake Road but not before crossing several side trails which offer similar thrills.

Birkenhead Lake Loop (Maps #39/C3)
A popular, moderate ride along gravel roads through a Lodgepole Pine Forest to beautiful Birkenhead Lake. From Hwy #99, you start with a tough 3km climb up the Birkenhead Lake FSR. Look for the gated road on the east that eventually links up with the access road on the north side of the lake. Continue past the main campsite and back to the hwy. This loop should take up to 4 hours to ride.

Birkenhead River Trail (Maps #30/C1, 39/C4)
Starting from the Owl Creek Rec Site, the Birkenhead River Trail is a scenic 20km mountain bike ride that makes up part of the Sea to Sky Trail. The easy route follows a rolling road on the west side of the river (following the powerlines). From the river crossing at its end, it is further 15km to Birkenhead Lake.

Black Tusk / Garibaldi Lake Trail (Map #20/C1)
A paved road leads just south of Daisy Lake from Hwy #99 to the Rubble Creek parking lot. From here, it is a 18.5km (7hr) hike to Garibaldi Lake along a popular well maintained trail. The trail is best taken in July-October and provides fantastic views of surrounding glacier and mountain tops as you gain 940m to the lake. It is recommended that you either camp at Taylor Meadows or at the Battleship Lakes Camp if you want to explore the surrounding mountains includ-

ing hiking to the famous Black Tusk. From Taylor Campground, the 7km (5-6hr) hike to Black Tusk leads through a subalpine meadow and forest to a rocky slope and eventually onto the prominent volcanic pillar (gaining 820m along the way). In the winter, the area turns to a X-C skiing haven with an expansive trail network including the Garibaldi Neve Traverse, which extends from Garibaldi Lake all the way to the Diamond Head Trail near Squamish.

Blackcomb Mountain (Map #30/A4)

Like Whistler Mountain, the expansive subalpine terrain, which is frequented by skiers throughout the winter months, gives way to some great hiking trails in the summer. For a fee (about $21.00), take the Solar Coaster chair and walk up to the Rendezvous Restaurant and the start of the trails. Be sure to pick up the complimentary map that highlights the alpine walks available. For mountain bikers, there are guided descents from the top of Solar Coaster, which take about 2 hours to complete. Adjust your brakes and hang on. Unfortunately, Blackcomb only allows guided tours because it is felt that without guiding, there may be a detrimental effect to the ecosystem on Blackcomb Mountain. For hikers, the trails range from an easy 15min walk leading to the Fitzsimmons Lookout to more advanced trails leading into the Garibaldi Provincial Park:

Alpine Forest Trail is a 2km (1-1.5hr) trail which leads through a subalpine forest off the Fitzsimmons Meadow Walk to a road leading to Seventh Heaven Express. It is an excellent way to explore the treed setting and perhaps see some wildlife.

Fitzsimmons Meadow Walk is a 1.5km easy walk with a slight drop in elevation along the way. It leads through some subalpine meadows which have wildflowers in season. A good view of Whistler Valley as well as the Fitzsimmons Creek Valley is offered. If you are lucky, you may see some wildlife (bears or coastal blacktail deers).

Marmot Trail is a 2km (1-1.5 hour) trail that switchbacks through the subalpine meadows and forest into the alpine. It is called the Marmot Trail because you will frequently see marmots sunning themselves on the rocky faces in the alpine area.

Overlord Lookout Trail involves a steady climb along a switchbacking trail leading into the alpine from Seventh Heaven Express. The lookout is located in Garibaldi Provincial Park and provides incredible views of the Overlord Glacier and the Thistle. The elevation gain is 215m over a 1.5km (1.5 hour) hike.

Upper and Lower Lakeside Trails are found south of the Seventh Heaven Express Chair. They lead throughout the subalpine meadows which have stunning wildflowers in season (late July-early August). The trail network is 2.5km (1 hour) long and extends out of the subalpine into the barren terrain of Alpine Lake. Overall, the elevation gain is 105m.

Blowdown Lake Trail (Map #31/D1)

To the north of Duffey Lake on the Duffey Lake Road, the Blowdown Creek Main extends in a southeasterly direction. This is an old mining road, which leads to the alpine and the Stein Valley Provincial Park. The road, which can be biked, passes by the old Silver Queen Mine to provide easy access to the Cottonwood Creek Trail and several ridge walks, which connect to the Stein River Trail. The area offers beautiful alpine meadows with great camping and some classic ridge walks. It is a popular backcountry hiking and skiing area.

Brandywine Meadows Trail (Map #29/B4)

This 6km (3 hour) trail is steep and short with an elevation gain of 1000m. The trail leads sharply upward from the 6.3km mark on Branch 10 through the dense old growth forest to the alpine meadow with spectacular views and a rustic camping spot. From the meadows, it is possible to gain access to Brandywine Mountain and the Metal Dome by an unmarked route.

Brew Lake Trail (Map #20/B1, 29/B4)

The signed trailhead begins on the B.C. Railway tracks just south of the Brandywine Falls Provincial Park. It involves a 10km (7 hour) return hike gaining 1200m along the way. At the end of the steep trail, which is best hiked in July-October, is Brew Lake where you will find a maintained cabin available on a first come, first serve basis. From the lake, it is possible to explore Mt. Brew at 1740m in elevation or access the Brew Hut 1620m. These areas are popular backcountry ski retreats. Brew Lake is at 1430m in elevation and is a beautiful mountain lake offering reasonable good fishing.

Cal-Cheak Trail (Map #29/C4)

The popular Cal-Cheak Trail or **Brandywine Falls Trails** lead 4km (one way) between Brandywine Falls Provincial Park and the Cal-Cheak Rec Site. South of the suspension bridge, the trails split with the western trail (under the powerlines) being the preferred mountain biking route of the Sea to Sky Route. At the park,

be sure to take the side route to look at the spectacular Brandywine Falls. The trails cut through the 2nd growth forest and require little elevation along the way.

Cerise Creek Trails (Map #31/A1)

About 41km east of Mt. Currie, turn onto the Cerise Creek Road off Hwy#99 and drive approximately 10 minutes to the signed trailhead and the gateway to a popular backcountry hiking and skiing area. From the trailhead, you hike through the forest along Cerise Creek to some alpine meadows where you will find Keith's Hut. It takes about 2-3 hours to reach the hut although it is a fairly easy hike. From the hut, experienced mountaineers can cross over to the Matier Glacier or Joffre Peaks.

Cheakamus Trail (Map #20/D1, 21/A1, 29/D4)

This popular multi-use trail begins at the end of the Cheakamus Lake Road, some 8km from Hwy#99. The trail meanders through a boulder field and some slide alders before entering into a forested area following Cheakamus River to the lake, a turquoise coloured lake surrounded by rugged snow-capped peaks. From the 3.2km mark, the trail leads along the north shores of Cheakamus Lake, past some large timber, to the Singing Creek Camp.

Overall, the trail is 14km (5 hours) return to the Singing Creek Camp with little elevation gain. It is an easy trail and provides a good flavour of the Garibaldi Provincial Park as well as access to a descent fishing lake. Experienced mountaineers can hike up Singing Creek to connect with the Singing Pass Trail and the Musical Bumps Trail for access to Singing Pass and Whistler Mountain. Another route enjoyed by the more experienced is the **Helm Creek Trail**.

The hiking route requires crossing the Cheakamus River (before the lake), and continuing 20km (8.5 hours) along Helm Creek to Helm Lake. The elevation gain is 900m. The trail network, after Helm Lake, connects with the Black Tusk Trail system as it passes through the extensive subalpine terrain of the Garibaldi Provincial Park providing great views of the valley as well as an opportunity for wilderness camping. The hike is best suited for July to October. Mountain bikers follow the trail along the river to Westside Main.

Emerald Estates Trails (Map #29/D3)

The most popular mountain bike trail in this area is the infamous **Shit Happens**. This 7.5km trail links Emerald Estates to Alpine Meadows to the south.

Green Lake (Map #30/A3)

A moderate mountain bike ride that offers a few tough hills as you head south from the Wedgemont Creek FSR. The route is 11km and climbs 150m as you alternate from double track to single-track along the powerlines on the eastern shore of Green Lake. The trail brings you to the Lost Lake Trail system.

Jane Lake Trails (Map #29/C4)

The main access route to the Jane Lakes, a series of three mountain lakes, is now blocked by a fence built by the CP Rail. Therefore, mountain bikers, ATVs and hikers follow the rugged 18km return trip along the washed out road to the lakes at 930m in elevation. The lakes provide good fishing throughout the spring and fall as they are stocked regularly. See the fishing section for a more complete fishing summary.

Joffre Lake Trail (Map #31/A1)

The trailhead is located approximately 23km east of Mt. Currie on Hwy#99 next to a small parking lot. The very popular trail is well marked and leads from the parking lot past two smaller lakes on your way to the picturesque Upper Joffre Lake. The upper lake, which offers wilderness camping, is simply spectacular as it lies directly below the icefields of Matier Glacier. Overall, the trail is 11km (5-6 hours) gaining 400m. Some mountaineers hike to the glacier edge or climb Joffre or Matier Peaks.

A further option is to take the **Twin Goat Ridge Route** 22km (14 hours) one way from Upper Joffre Lake all the way to Lillooet Lake Road just north of the Twin One Rec Site. Initially, you ascend from Upper Joffre Lake at 1280m all the way to 2380m at the foot of the Matier Glacier. Then, it is a steady descent to Lillooet Lake at 200m in elevation. As this is a high elevation ridge route, it is only available to be hiked in July-September. From the ridge, you will get some great views of the alpine lakes as well as the Lillooet Lake Valley.

Lillooet River Dykes (Map #30/B1)
Starting from Hwy#99 on the east side of the Lillooet River Bridge, this gentle trail follows the river in a north west direction for about 5km. At the end of the dyke road, a moderate single-track loops around MacKenzie Lake. It is possible to return along the steep (1000 meter gain) MacKenzie Basin Road.

The Dyke Trail also extends for several kilometers in the opposite direction. This easy route cuts through the Indian Reserve, marshland and offers fine views of Mount Currie. These dykes offer a good walking, mountain biking, equestrian or X-C skiing network.

Little Spearhead (Map #30/A4)
From the Upper Village, follow the signs to the Singing Pass Parking Lot. Here you cross Fitzsimmons Creek (careful there is no bridge) and descend on Blackcomb Mountain. This 13km round trip climbs 325m and is rated as a moderate mountain bike ride.

Lizzie Creek Trail (Map #31/B3)
After ascending through a narrow gorge on the Lizzie Creek using your 4wd vehicle, you will reach beautiful Lizzie Lake. From there, it is a steep 5km (3hr) one way hike gaining 640m to the Lizzie Creek Cabin. Initially, you pass by Lizzie Lake and then proceed through the "Gates of Shangri-la" to the alpine meadows where the cabin is located. It is recommended to use the cabin as a base camp to explore the many alpine lakes and mountains in the area.

The trail continues upward past several small lakes, through Cherry Pip Pass, and then to Caltha Lake, which is about a 6-8hr one way hike from the cabin. Another 1.5-2.5 hours takes you over the Stein Divide to Tundra Lake. Further along the route are Stein Lake and Elton Lake.

Overall, the area provides exceptional hiking in the subalpine with endless backpacking and backcountry skiing options. The area is quite popular and is best left to experienced backpackers.

Lost Lake X-C Trails (Map #29,30/A3)
30km of well maintained cross country ski trails leads from the day skier parking lot adjacent to the municipal hall in Whistler or from the parking lot next to the Chateau Whistler. When the snow is gone, the trail network is heavily used by hikers, joggers and mountain bikers. Periodically, you will find maps to help mark the way.

The main trail leads around Lost Lake providing easy access to the north end where you will find a nice wharf and a doggie beach. At the south end of the lake, there is a large sandy beach with an expansive lawn and picnic facilities attracting hundreds of visitors daily. The trail network connects with the trails to Green Lake as well as the Valley Trail network.

MacKenzie Basin Loop (Map #30/B1)
This difficult mountain bike route starts with a climb up an old road above the lake. From here, a fun but bumpy single-track heads back down to the start. This route is usually accessed from the Dyke Trail.

Mosquito Lake Area (Map #30/B1)
A challenging network of short mountain bike trails that offer fast, undulating single-track trails with extreme descents. The trails are accessed by Ivey Road (at the crest near the sub-station), from the rec site or along the MacKenzie Basin Road. These trails, which should be left to the experienced rider, can also be hiked or ridden on horseback.

Madeley Lake Trail (Map #29/C3)
Maintained by the Rotary Club of Whistler, the Madeley Lake Trail offers a shorter alternative for hiking to Rainbow Lake. The trailhead is found south of Madeley Lake along the 4wd/bike access road. From here, the trail leads 6km (3 hours) one way to Rainbow Lake (at 1460m) gaining 500m. Along the way, the trail passes over two bridges, one at Madeley Creek and one at Beverley Creek before passing Hanging Lake, where there is a campsite together with outhouses. Some hikers bushwhack up the creek draw to Beverley Lake, a small mountain lake set below Rainbow Mountain.

Northwest Passage (Map #29/D3)
Found at the top of Nordic Estates off of Whistler Road, a dirt access road climbs under the Quicksilver Chairlift on the bottom of Whistler Mountain. At the crest of this steep climb, you head left for some downhill, roller coaster thrills. The difficult 7km mountain bike route, which climbs 420m, spills you out at Whistler Village.

One Mile Lake Trails (Maps 30/B2)
The popular One Mile Lake picnic area found south of Pemberton offers some enjoyable trails that can be used by mountain bikers or hikers. The One Mile Loop is an easy one km loop around the lake. The **Nairn Falls Trail** heads 2km south to the provincial campground. This moderate trail has a few sections which require dismounting (if you are on a bike) as you climb over roots and descend along a rocky trail. Side trails also lead to more challenging biking terrain.

Owl Lake Trail (Map #39/B4)
The trailhead to this hike is found off the Owl Lake FSR, which requires a 4wd vehicle. From the trailhead, it is a 7km (3 hour) return trip gaining 140m along the way. The trail leads through the Owl Creek Valley to the lake where you will find a rec site on the western shores.

Place Creek Trail (Map #39/D3)
From Hwy #99 just west of Gates Lake, this steep, rugged 21km (9hr) hike gains 1300m past several waterfalls to the beautiful Place Glacier. Near the foot of the glacier is an A-frame used for camping by both climbers and mountaineers. The hiking season extends from July to October.

Pemberton Icefields (Map #29/A1, 38/A4)
This is an extreme ski touring area, which can be accessed from several locations in the Pemberton Valley with the best access being the Ryan River Valley. The area is best left to expert mountaineers knowledgeable on avalanche hazards and extreme winter weather conditions.

Rainbow Lake Trail (Map #29/C3)
This alpine trail leads from the wooden map located on the west side of Alta Lake Road. The trail follows 21 Mile Creek through a hemlock forest before meeting with an old logging road. The trail then follows the road for a short distance before the trail takes off through a thick 2nd growth forest and eventually past the 21 Mile Creek Waterfalls and over a suspension bridge. Soon, you will enter the alpine meadows of Rainbow Lake at 1460m in elevation. Overall, the trail to Rainbow Lake is 18km (7 hours) return gaining 800m.

Rainbow Lake is extremely unproductive but has fast growing fish because of the low number of fish in the lake. The lake is not stocked and so it offers a chance to catch some wild rainbow. Given the fish numbers, fishing is quite difficult. A side trip on a less developed trail takes off to the left about 200m before the suspension bridge. The trail leads to Gin and Tonic Lakes, which are barren lakes without fish and which are at 1430m in elevation

Sea to Sky Trail (Maps #20,29,30,39,40)
Eventually, a 150km route will link the communities between Squamish, Whistler & D'Arcy. This route is being designed to suit families with spur trails being added to excite the more experienced riders. The route follows existing trails and forestry roads past waterfalls, canyons and glacier covered mountains. Here is a brief description of the majority of the route.

From Squamish, follow Government Road through Brackendale to the Squamish Valley Road. After the bridge over the Cheakamus River you follow the Paradise Valley Road to it's end. Here the Old Pemberton Trail takes you through the spectacular Cheakamus Canyon to Hwy#99.

Follow the Hwy to Ross's Rip, a nice trail through a deciduous forest. Again cross the Hwy at Chance Creek FSR to work your way north to Roe Creek. Follow the Hwy uphill to Brandywine Falls Park. Here you follow the Cal-Cheak Trail and Sugarcube Hill Road north. Back over the Hwy you connect with Alta Lake Road to pick up the Valley Trail.

Continue north to the Lost Lake Trails and Green Lake. Unfortunately, the section north to the Owl Creek still requires you to follow the highway. Here you follow the Birkenhead River Trail and continue past Birkenhead Lake to D'Arcy. The later 40km section was completed in 1997.

Shadow Lake Trails (Map #30/A2)
Shadow Lake Trails are located north of Whistler near the Soo River right off Hwy #99. There are a number of short trails providing examples of the various forest practices of the Whistler Valley. Highlights include a walk around Shadow

Lake (1.5km) or a stroll through a stand of old growth cedar next to Soo River. This trail network is a good choice if you want to get away from the crowds of Whistler and enjoy an easy stroll through a forested setting. The parking lot is clearly visible on the east side of Hwy #99 as you will see a large sign and toilet facilities. The trail system is a total of 6km long and dissects most of the 125ha demonstration forest.

Singing Pass Trail (Map #30,31)
Probably the most popular alpine trail in the Whistler Area. This beautiful hike starts from the end of the well signed Singing Pass Road. Here you follow Fitzsimmons the Melody Creek to the cabin at Russet Lake. The area offers alpine flowers in late summer along with spectacular glacier and mountain views. Allow 7 hours to travel the moderate 14km return hike which gains 600m. The cabin offers a good base for the surrounding climbing opportunites. You can also follow a difficult route over the pass to Cheakamus Lake. []

Spearhead Traverse (Map #21,29,30)
Another spectacular but rugged backcountry ski adventure that connects Blackcomb Mountain to the Whistler Mountain Ski Area. Basically, head to the top of Blackcomb using the over priced chairlifts and follow the high elevation ridges around Spearhead Glacier. After a few days of virgin powder you will emerge at the top of Whistler Mountain. Obviously, you must be well prepared and equipped with the proper equipment before attempting the route.

Tenquille Lake Trail (Map #38/D3,39/A3)
Tenquille Lake is a beautiful alpine lake set in some sub-alpine meadows surrounded by rugged mountain peaks. At the lake is a cabin together with a rec site for camping. The area is extremely popular with backpackers, mountaineers, snowmobilers and even extreme mountain bikers. The lake can be accessed four ways.

The easiest route leads from Branch 12 off the Hurley River Road gaining 450m over a 12km (4 hour) return route. The trail begins in an old cut block and then crossed a creek before joining with the other trail leading from the Lillooet Valley. In order to reach this trailhead, you need a 4wd vehicle. An alternative and more challenging route is to climb from the Lillooet Valley some 19km (7 hours) gaining 1460m along the way. The trailhead begins east of Wolverine Creek and winds uphill through open forests. Although the hike is extremely strenuous, you will be rewarded with excellent vistas of the valley below as well as the opportunity to walk through beautiful meadows filled with wildflowers.

The third route is a recent extension of the Mount Ronayne Trail. It leads from Ogre Lake to Tenquille Lake over 16km (5 hours) return gaining 330m along the way. As this is a rugged mountain route following a series of ridges, it should be left to the experienced backpacker. The final trail is an 11km (4 hour) hike from the Tenquille Creek Road gaining 427m along the way.

Tour de Soo (Map #29/D3, 30/A2)
30km of logging roads and 10km of single-track make up this 3 hour difficult mountain bike ride with a few hike-a-bike sections. From the Soo River 03 Road (Cougar Mnt Rd), you climb over to the Soo River Valley and onto Echo Lakes, Rutherford Creek and eventually out to the Hwy. From here, make your way north to Pemberton along trails found around and above the railway.

Tower Roads (Map #20,29)
There are two microwave towers that make for excellent but difficult mountain biking. The Black Tusk Tower requires a 1270m climb over 16km while the Whistler Tower is an 8km return route. The steep roads offer great views and fun descents.

Valley Trail System (Map #29/D3)
Within the Whistler valley is an extensive 20km network of well maintained gravel and paved trails. The trail network extends from Alta Lake along the River of Dreams to Green Lake. At most intersections, there are signs marking the various routes. The trail system is heavily used throughout the summer months by mountain bikers, joggers, hikers and in-line skaters and in the winter, by X-C skiers. The trails will take you through the heart of the Whistler Valley past creeks and lakes, forested areas and golf courses.

Wedgemont Trail (Map #30/A3)
A short but steep trail climbs to a beautiful lake set at the foot of a glacier below cascading peaks. From the end of the Wedgemont Creek FSR, you climb 1220m from the heavy forest, past a rockslide with a view of the falls on Wedgemont Creek, to the rocky subalpine meadows around the lake. At the lake, it is possible to camp or use the cabin as a base for further exploration. The 12km (5 hr) return trail is best tackled in July-September, after the trail drys.

Whistler Interpretative Forest (Map 29/C4)
The Whistler Interpretative Forest encompasses almost the entire upper Cheamanus River Valley and is easily accessed by the Cheamanus Lake Road. It is a total of 3500ha and ranges from the valley bottom all the way to the subalpine at 1600m. Through the interpretative forest are numerous short trails exploring the various silviculture practices and ecosystems of the Cheamanus Valley. The trails that can be used by hikers, X-C skiers and mountain bikers are the Ridge Trail, Lower Riverside Trail, Highline Trail and the Logger's Access Trail. Hiking trails restricting mountain bikers are the Crater Rim Trail, Riverside Interpretative Trail and Whistler West Ridge Trail.

Several signs within the interpretative forest allow you to decide on a route to travel. From the Westside Main, 4wd vehicles or mountain bike can access Logger's Lake, which is stocked annually. The trail around Logger's Lake as well as the trail through the old growth timber along the western banks of the Cheamanus River are very scenic. Snowmobilers, kayakers and fishermen also frequent the area.

Whistler Mountain Trails (Map #29/D4)
After the ski season and the snow departs, Whistler Mountain becomes a spectacular hiking destination. The glacier covered peaks and the rugged treeless terrain makes the area a gorgeous place to visit. During the off season, Intrawest runs the Whistler village gondola to the Roundhouse Lookout for a significant fee (around $21). Be sure to pick up the complimentary map that highlights the routes available. There are 4 different guided bike routes that lead from the Roundhouse Lookout to the Whistler Village. Regardless of which route you take, adjust your brakes before your descent and hang on. For hikers, there are the following options:

Glacier Trail is a 2.5km (1 hour) trail leading to the foot of Glacier Bowl at 1987m in elevation. You gain 150m as the trail switchbacks up the barren alpine under the T-bars.

Harmony Lake Trail is a 3.5km (1-1.5 hours) fairly challenging route. This popular route begins by descending 100m to Harmony Lake before looping into the meadows set below Harmony Bowl. A fantastic viewpoint at 1887m provides a great view of the Whistler Valley.

Little Whistler Trail ascends sharply up the ridge to the top of Little Whistler Peak at 2115m in elevation. As you ascend the ridge, you leave a subalpine forested area and enter the treeless alpine. The return hike is 3.8km (1.5-2 hours) and involves a 265m elevation gain. From the top of Little Whistler Peak, you get a fantastic view of Black Tusk and the Whistler Valley.

Musical Bumps Trail is a 19km (5-6 hour) hike leading to Singing Pass. The trail leads past Harmony Lake and Burnt Stool Lake over a challenging rock slide and into Garibaldi Provincial Park. Along the way, you get great views of Cheakamus Lake and the Cheakamus Glacier. An alternative route to Singing Pass begins at the end of the Fitzsimmons Creek Road (about 5.5km from Blackcomb Way). This popular trail, which is called the **Singing Pass Trail**, is well marked and leads through the creek draw passing by an old gold mine and eventually entering some alpine meadows. It is 14km (5-6 hours) return to Singing Pass gaining 600m along the way. Both trails eventually connect and continue on to Russet Lake where you will find a rustic cabin used by mountaineers. The last part of the trail leading to Russet Lake (at 1890m) is steep and switchbacks up the mountain. It is an additional 8km (3 hours) return from Singing Pass.

Ridge Lookout Trail is a 1.2km (30-50mins) leading to the Ridge Lookout at 1922m. Along the way, you gain 85m in elevation and have a nice view of the Glacier Bowl and the Whistler Village. It is a steep hike.

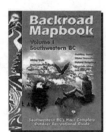

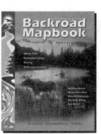

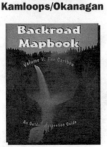

Southwestern B.C. Mapkey

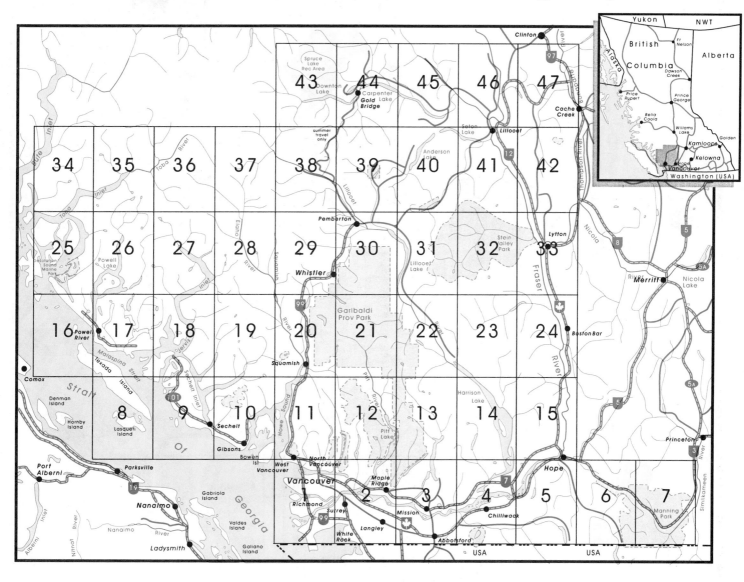

Legend for the Maps

Scale 1:150,000   1.5km   0km   3km
1 cm = 1.55 km   1 km = 0.6214 mi.

Roads:

Highways	
Paved Secondary roads	
Forest Service/Main road	
Active logging road (2wd)	
Logging road (2wd/4wd)	
Unclassified road (4wd)	
Trail/old road	
Route (undeveloped trail)	
Ferry Route	
Powerline	
Pipeline	
Railway	

Boundaries:

3-17

Wildlife Management Units	
Park Boundaries	
Indian Reserves	

Miscellaneous:

Airport/airstrip	
Cabin/lodge/resort	
Closed/restricted road	○
Deactivated road	☒
Gate	=
Forestry Lookout	
Lighthouse	
Microwave Tower	
Mine Site (abandoned)	✗
Parking	Ⓟ
Point of Interest	★
Town, Village, etc.	●
Waterfalls	
Wildlife Viewing	★

Recreational Activities:

Anchorage	
Boat Launch	
Campsite (Full Service)	
Campsite (Wilderness/Recreation Site)	△
Campsite (trail/boat access only)	▲
Cross Country Skiing	
Downhill Skiing	
Fishing Hotspot	
Float Plane	
Golf Course	
Handgliding	
Hiking Trail	
Horse Back Riding	
Mountain Biking	
Motorbiking	
Paddling (canoe-kayak)	
Picnic Site	
Rock Climbing/Mountaineering	
Scuba Diving	
Snowmobiling	

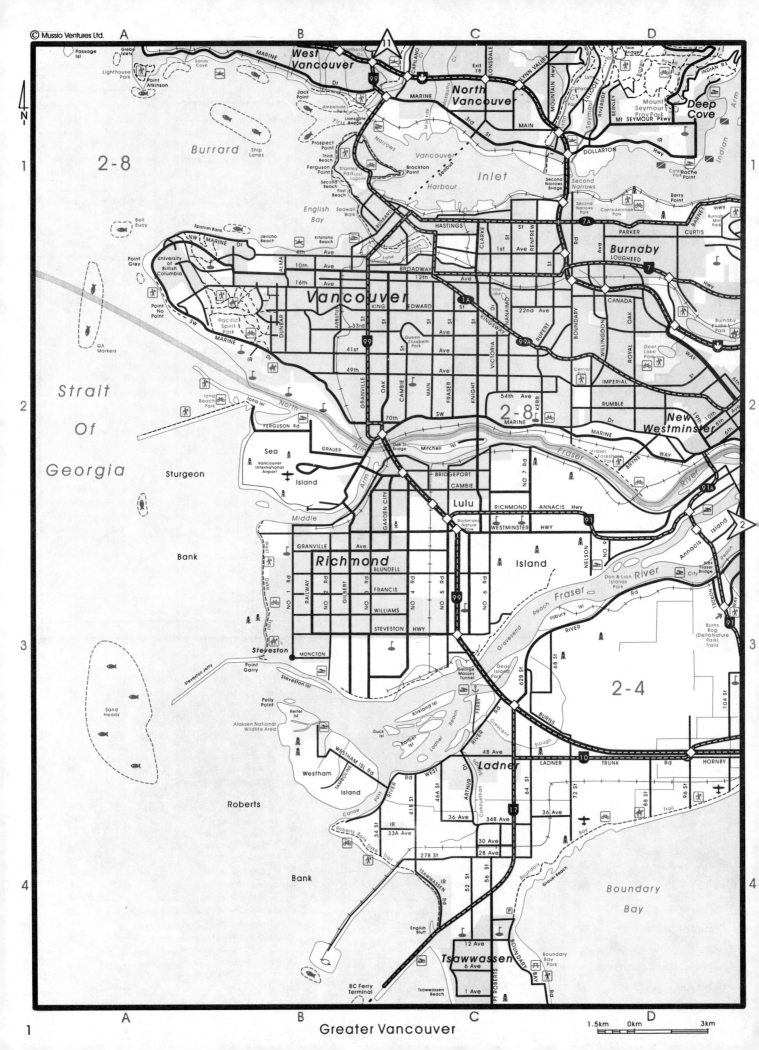

Greater Vancouver

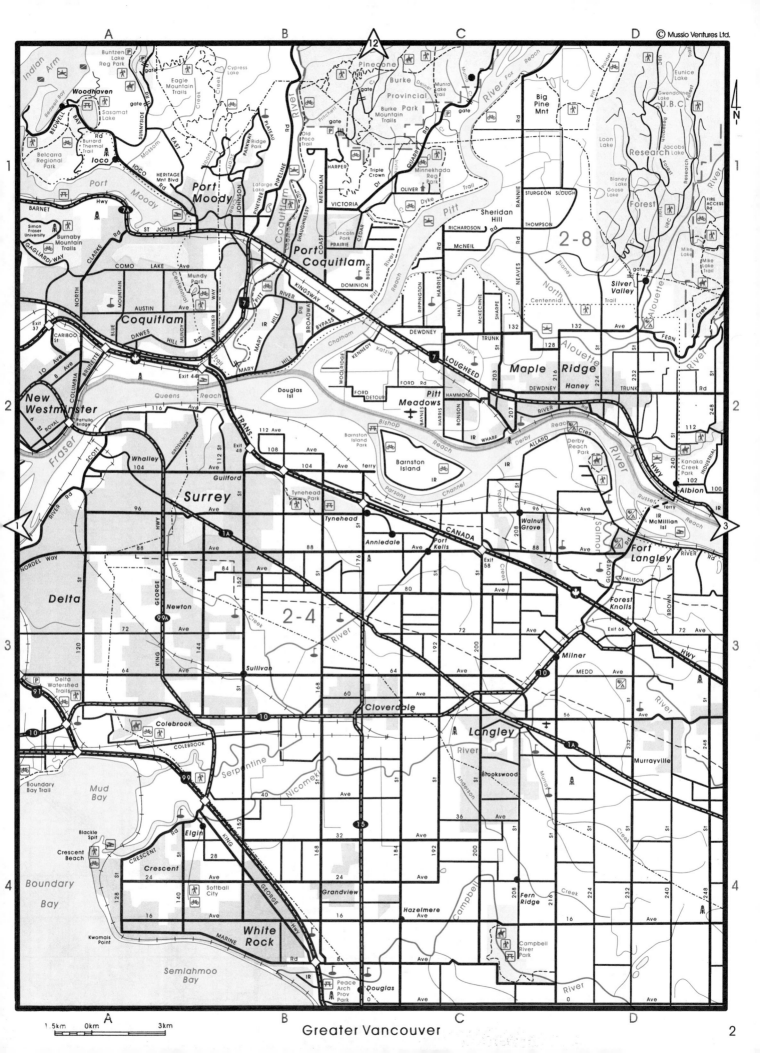

Greater Vancouver

1 1.5km 0km 3km

2

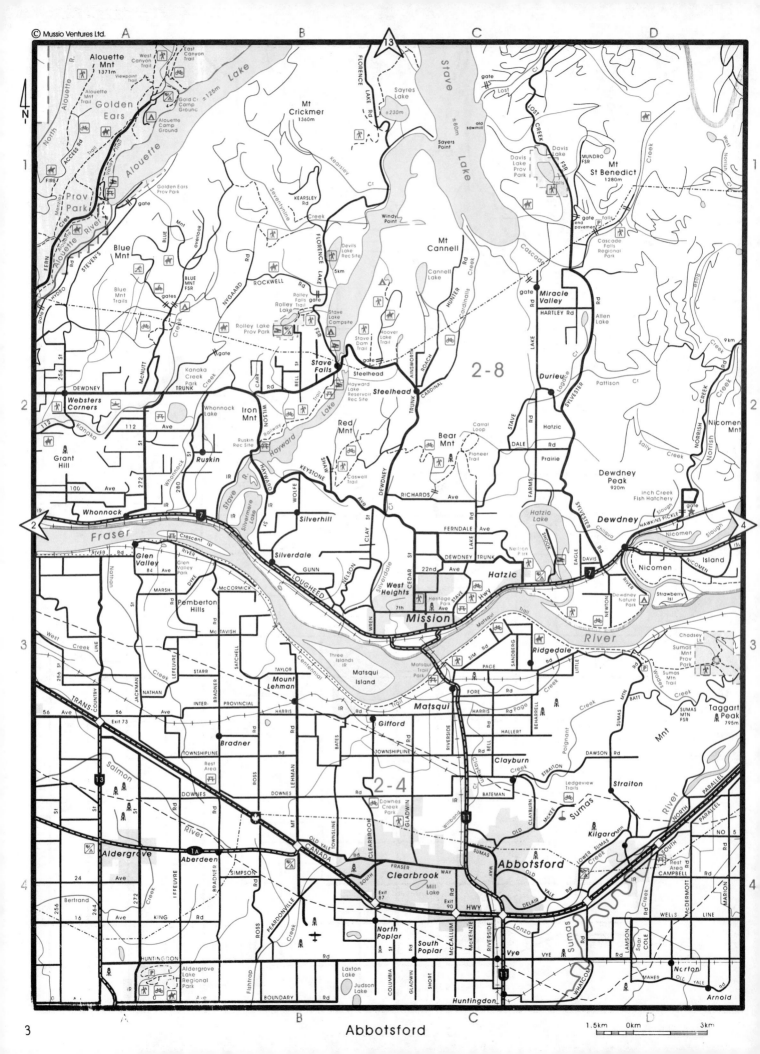

Abbotsford

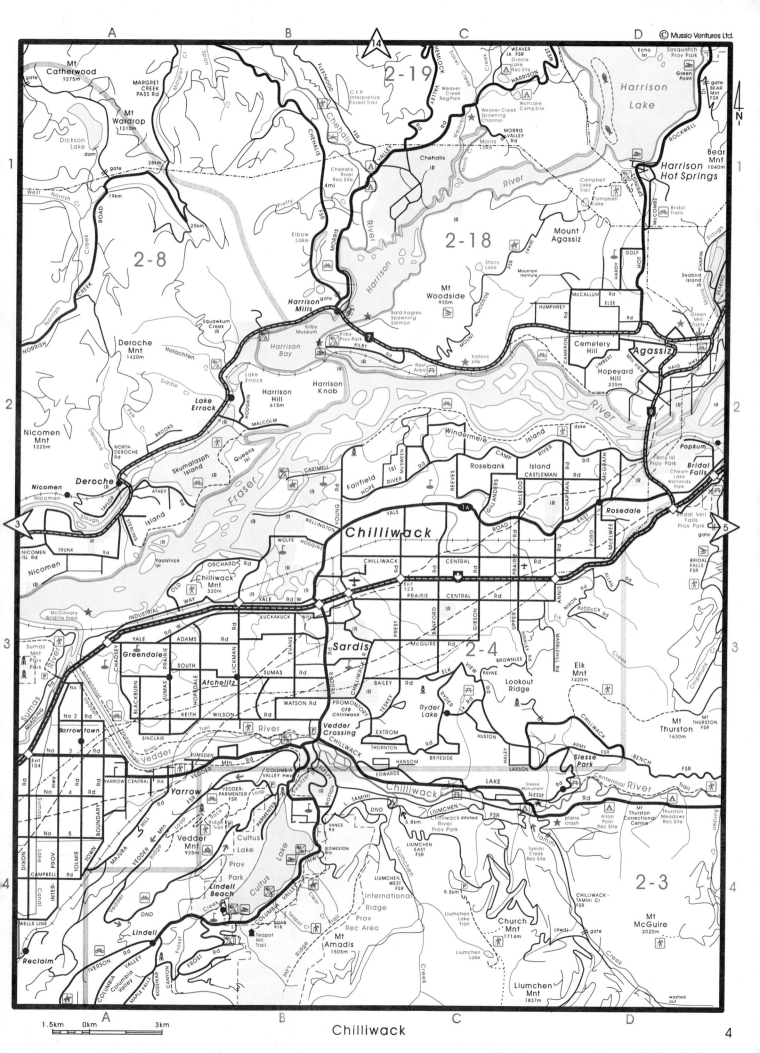

Chilliwack

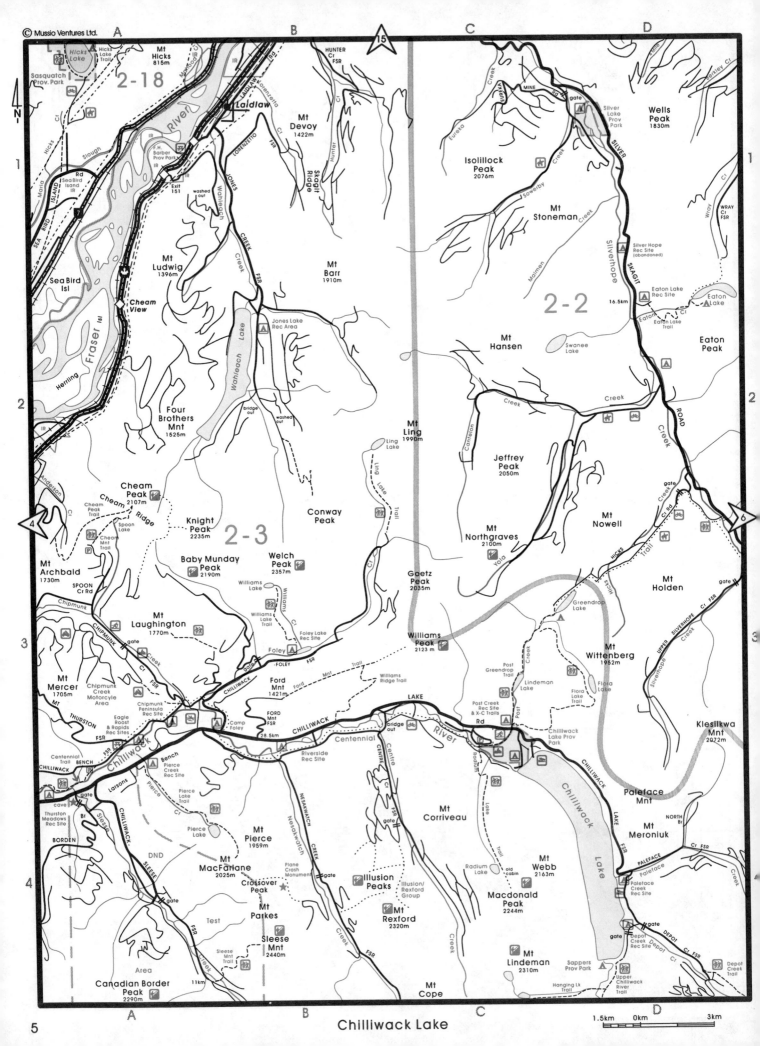

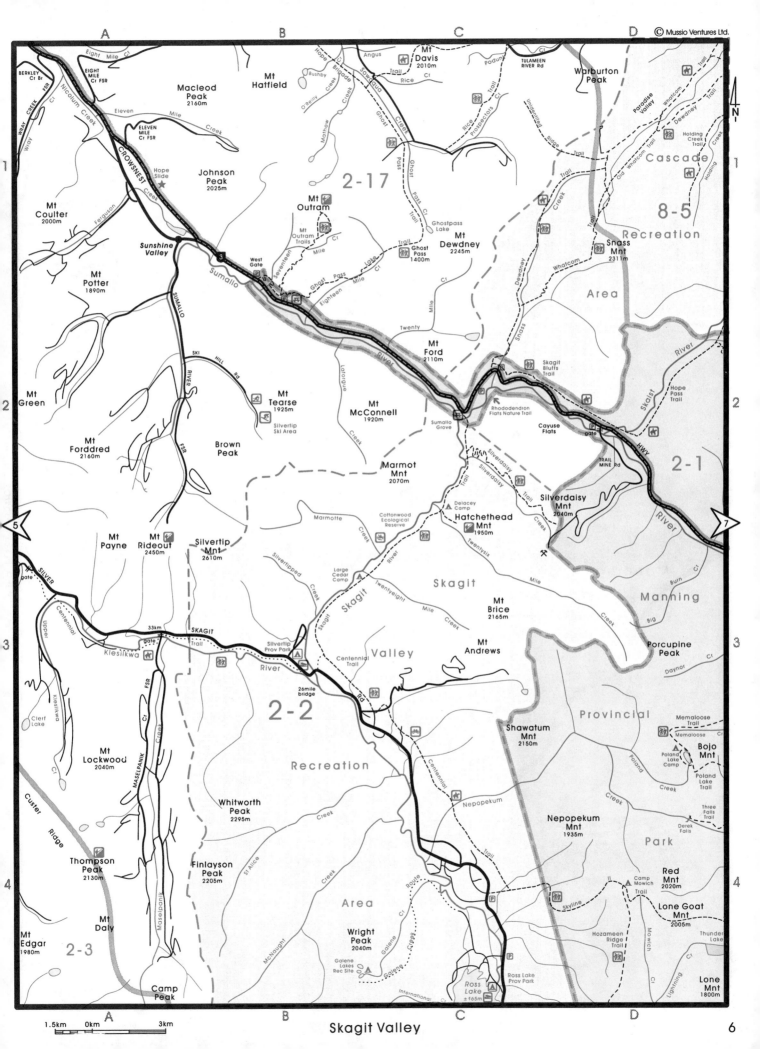

Skagit Valley

6

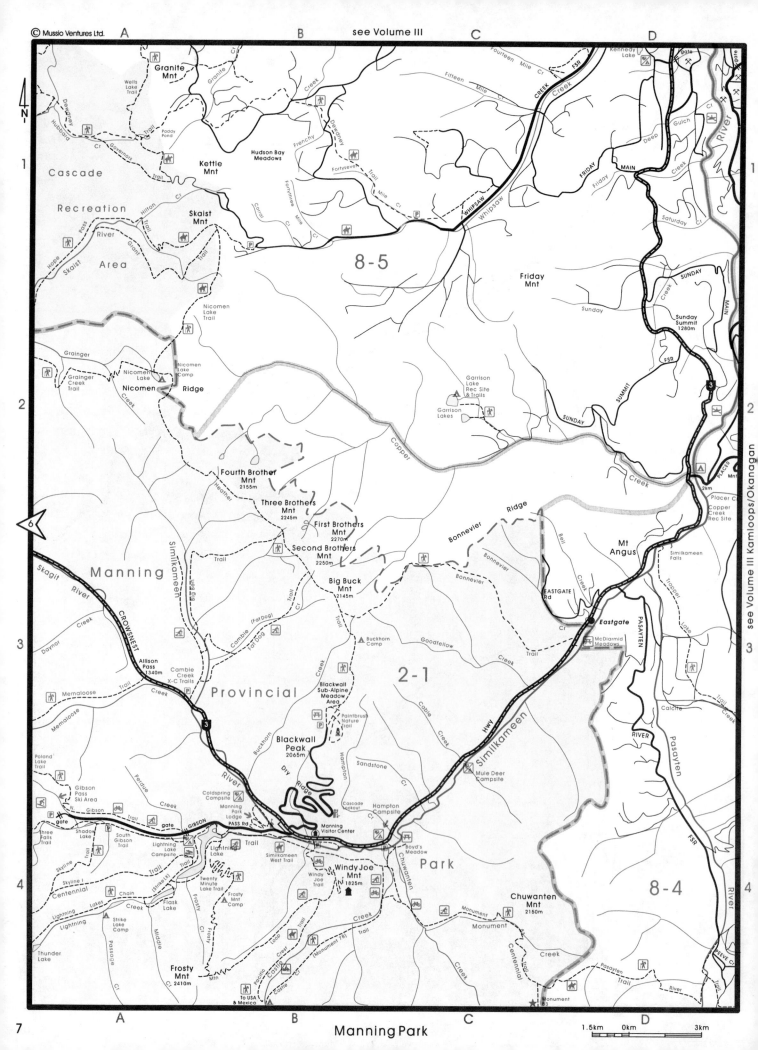

© Mussio Ventures Ltd.

A   B   C   D

N

Granite Mnt

Wells Lake Trail

Cascade

Recreation

Area

Kettle Mnt

Skaist Mnt

Hudson Bay Meadows

8-5

Friday Mnt

Nicomen Lake Trail

Grainger

Grainger Creek Trail

Grainger Lake

Nicomen Lake Camp

Nicomen Lake

Nicomen

Ridge

Garrison Lake Rec Site & Trails

Garrison Lakes

Sunday Summit 1280m

3

Copper

Fourth Brother Mnt 2155m

Three Brothers Mnt 2245m

First Brothers Mnt 2270m

Second Brothers Mnt 2250m

Bonnevier

Ridge

Mt Angus

Placer Creek Rec Site

Manning

Skagit River

Big Buck Mnt 2145m

Bonnevier

Bonnevier

EASTGATE Rd

Eastgate

PASAYTEN

Similkameen Falls

Buckhorn Camp

Goodfellow

McDiarmid Meadows

Allison Pass 1340m

Camble Creek X-C Trails

Provincial

2-1

Blackwall Sub-Alpine Meadow Area

Paintbrush Nature Trail

Cascade Lookout

Mule Deer Campsite

Poland Lake Trail

Gibson Pass Ski Area

gate

Three Falls Trail

Shadow Lake

South Gibson Trail

Blackwall Peak 2065m

Dry Ridge

Hampton

Sandstone

Coldspring Campsite

Manning Park Lodge

PASS Rd

Manning Visitor Center

Hampton Campsite

Boyd's Meadow

Park

Lightning Lake Campsite

Lightning Lake

Similkameen West Trail

Windy Joe Mnt 1825m

Chuwanten Mnt 2150m

8-4

Twenty Minute Lake Trail

Frosty Mnt Camp

Windy Joe Trail

Centennial

Skyline

Chain

Flask Lake

Lightning Lakes

Strike Lake Camp

Thunder Lake

Frosty Mnt 2410m

To USA & Mexico

Monument 78

Monument

Pasayten Trail

Monument 83

A   B   C   D

1.5km   0km   3km

see Volume III Kamloops/Okanagan

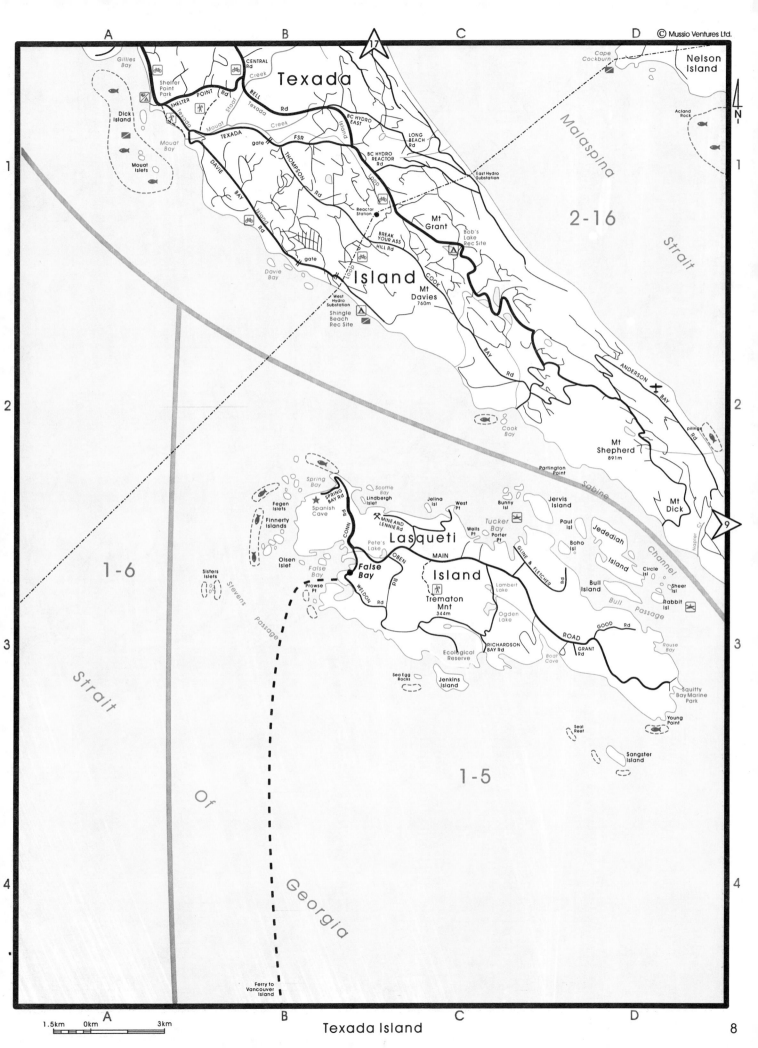

Texada Island

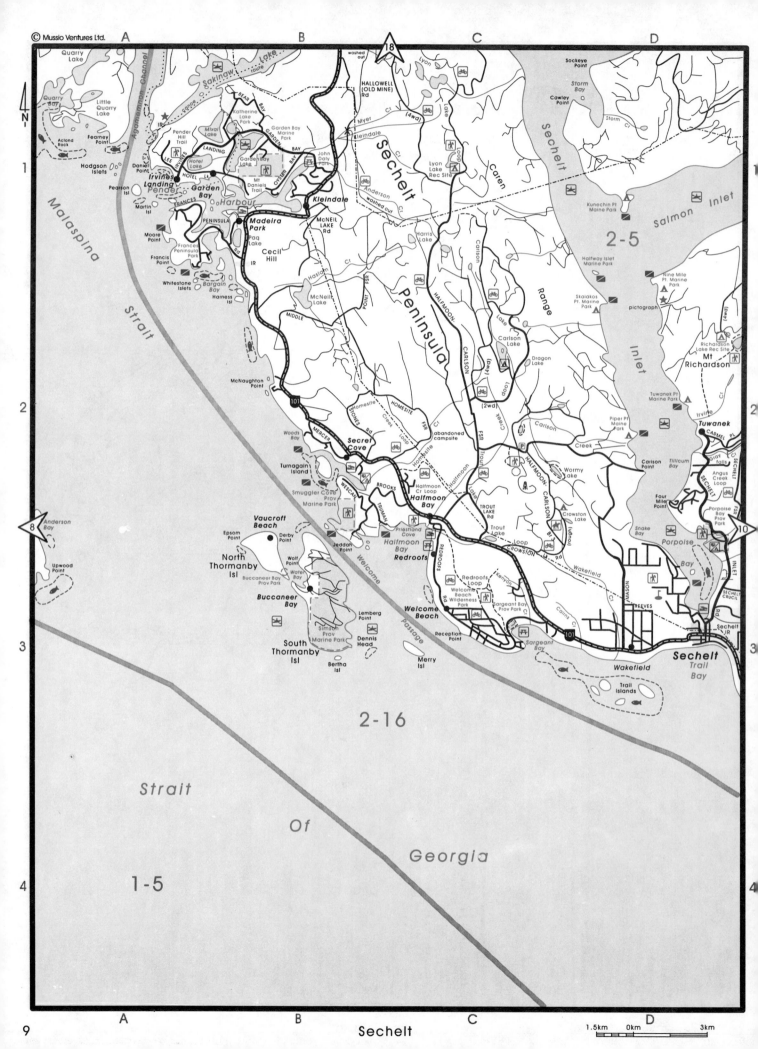

© Mussio Ventures Ltd.

N

Sechelt

9

1.5km 0km 3km

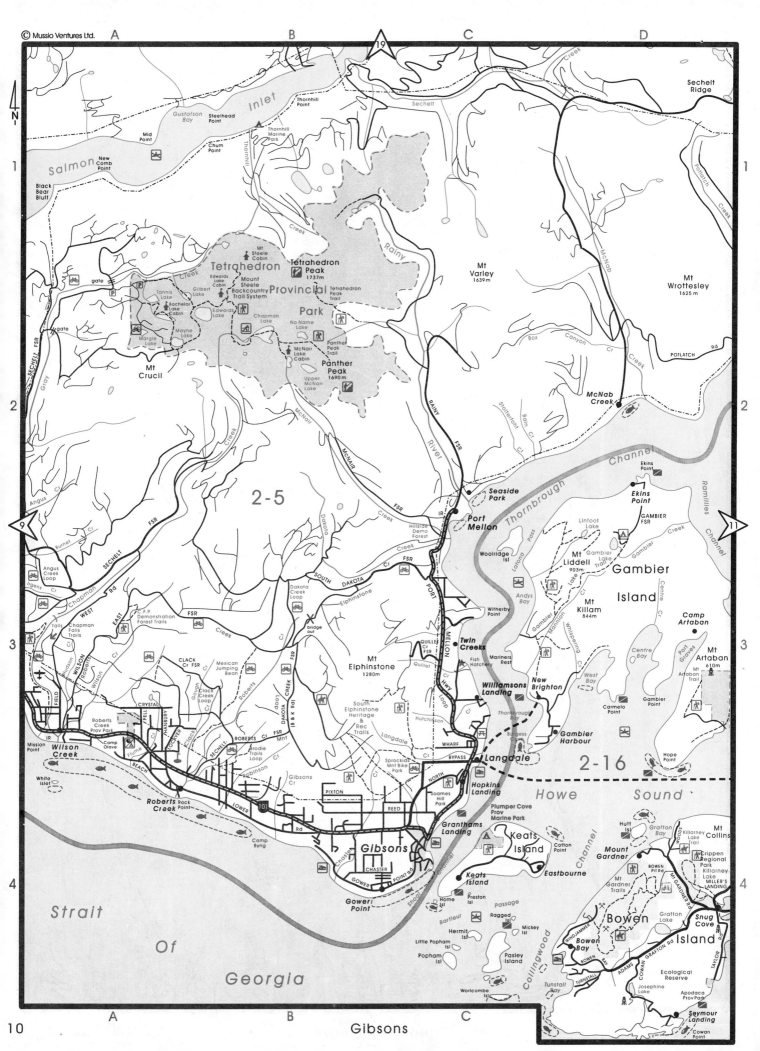

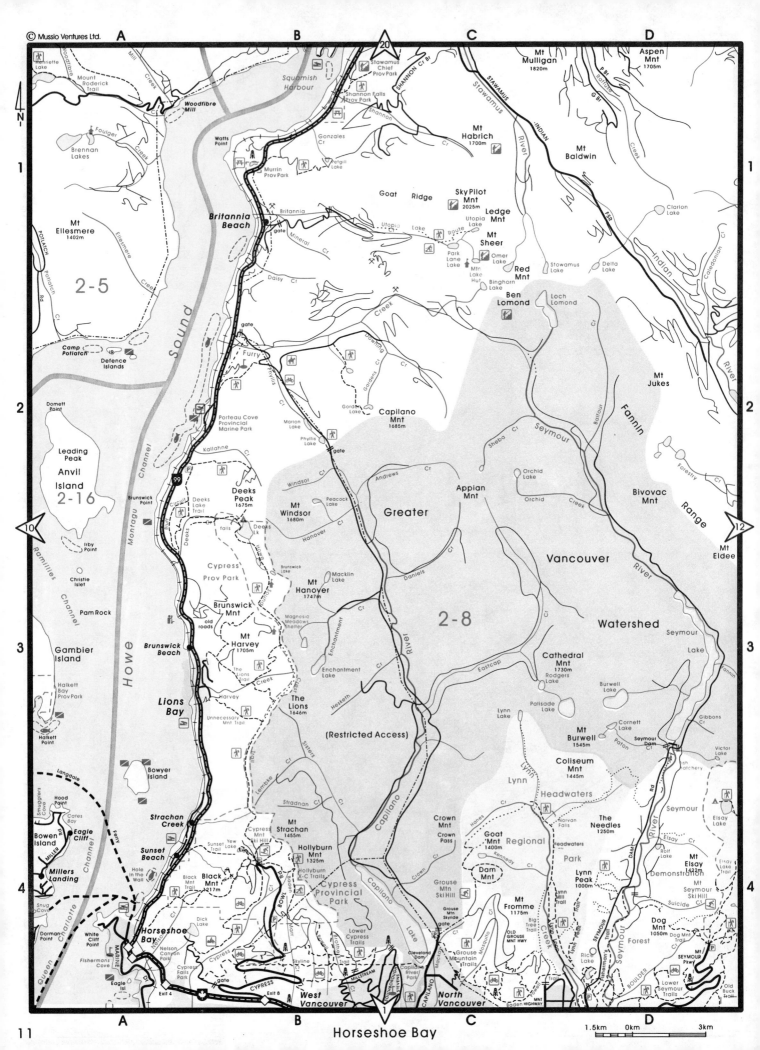

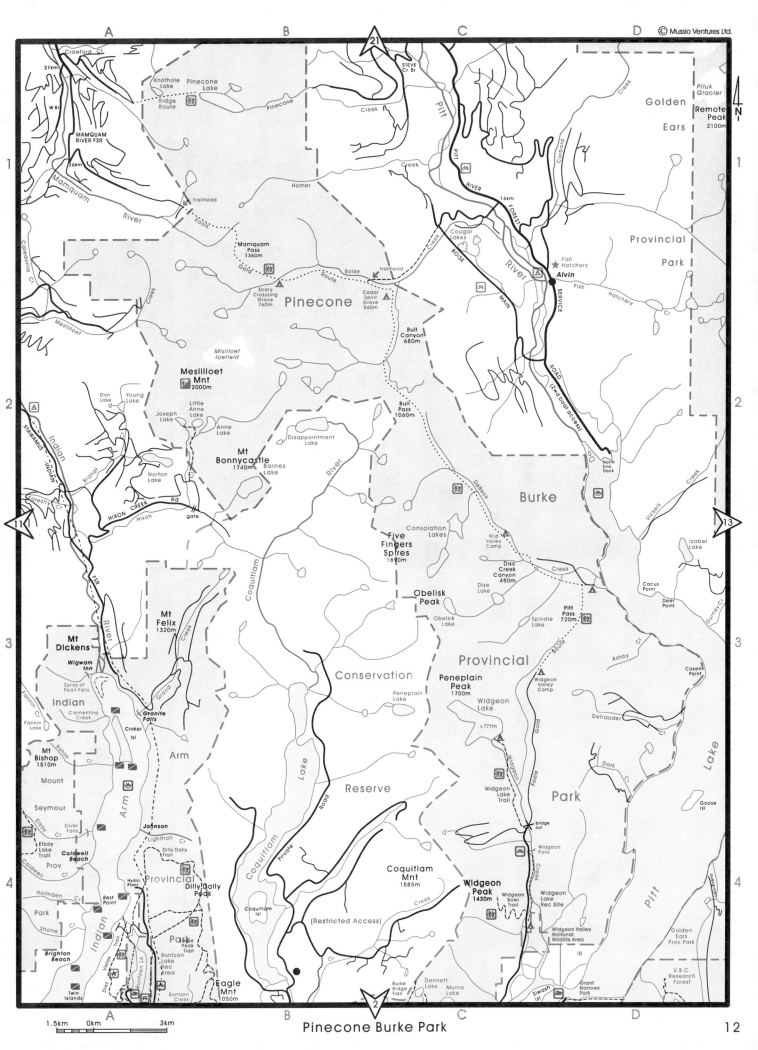

© Mussio Ventures Ltd.

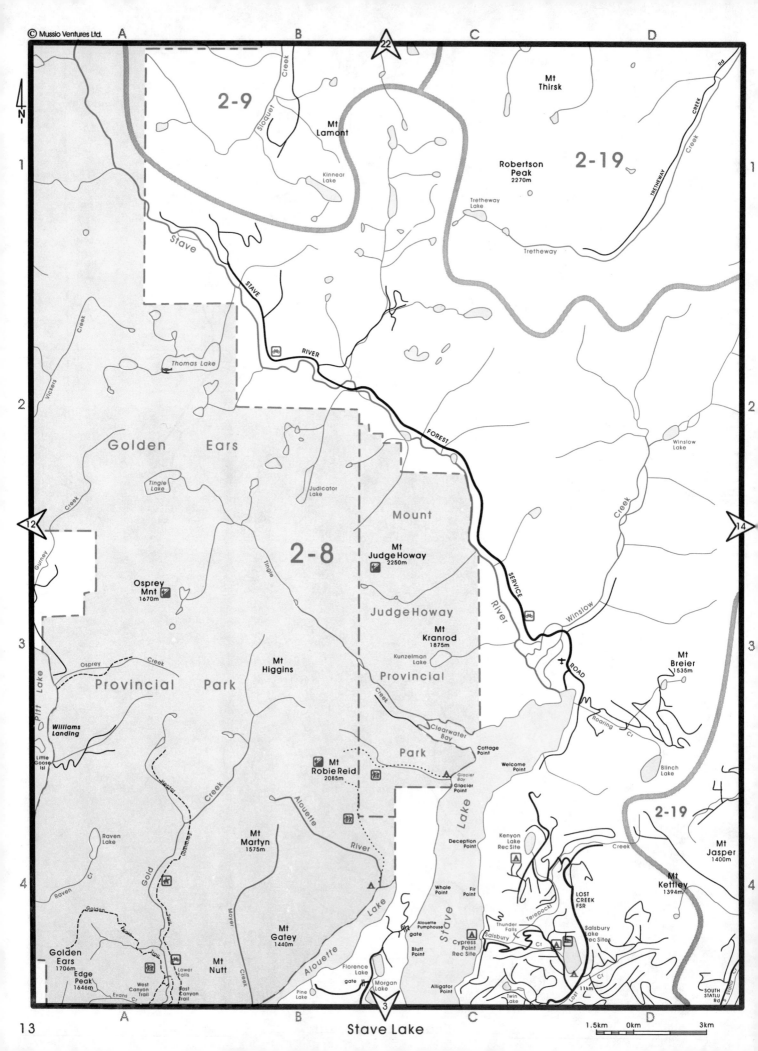

© Mussio Ventures Ltd.

A   B   C   D

N

2-9

Mt Lamont

Kinnear Lake

Sloquet Creek

Stave

STAVE

Thomas Lake

RIVER

Vickers Creek

Golden   **Ears**

Tingle Lake

Judicator Lake

FOREST

Mount

Mt Thirsk

Robertson Peak 2270m

2-19

Tretheway Lake

Tretheway

Tretheway

Winslow Lake

TRETHEWAY CREEK Rd

12

14

Gurney Creek

Osprey Mnt 1670m

Tingle

2-8

Mt Judge Howay 2250m

Judge Howay

SERVICE

River

Winslow Creek

ROAD

Pitt Lake

Osprey   Creek

Provincial   **Park**

Mt Higgins

Mt Kranrod 1875m

Kunzelman Lake

Provincial

Mt Breier 1535m

Roaring Cr

Williams Landing

Little Goose Isl

Jacob

Gold

Creek

Mt Robie Reid 2085m

Clearwater Bay

Park

Cottage Point

Welcome Point

Glacier Bay Glacier Point

Lake

Blinch Lake

2-19

Raven Lake

Raven Cr

Commerce

Golden

Mt Martyn 1575m

Alouette

River

Deception Point

Kenyon Lake Rec Site

Creek

Mt Jasper 1400m

Lake

Whale Point

Fir Point

LOST CREEK FSR

Mt Kettley 1394m

Mt Gatey 1440m

Alouette

Stave

gate

Alouette Pumphouse

Bluff Point

Terepocki

Thunder Falls

Salsbury

Cr

Salsbury Lake Rec Site

Golden Ears 1706m

Edge Peak 1646m

West Canyon Trail

Lower Falls

Mt Nutt

East Canyon Trail

Evans Cr

Moyer Creek

Pine Lake

Florence Lake

gate

Morgan Lake

Lake

Cypress Point Rec Site

Alligator Point

11km

Lost Cr

Twin Lake

SOUTH STATLU Rd

13

A   B

3

Stave Lake

C   D

1.5km   0km   3km

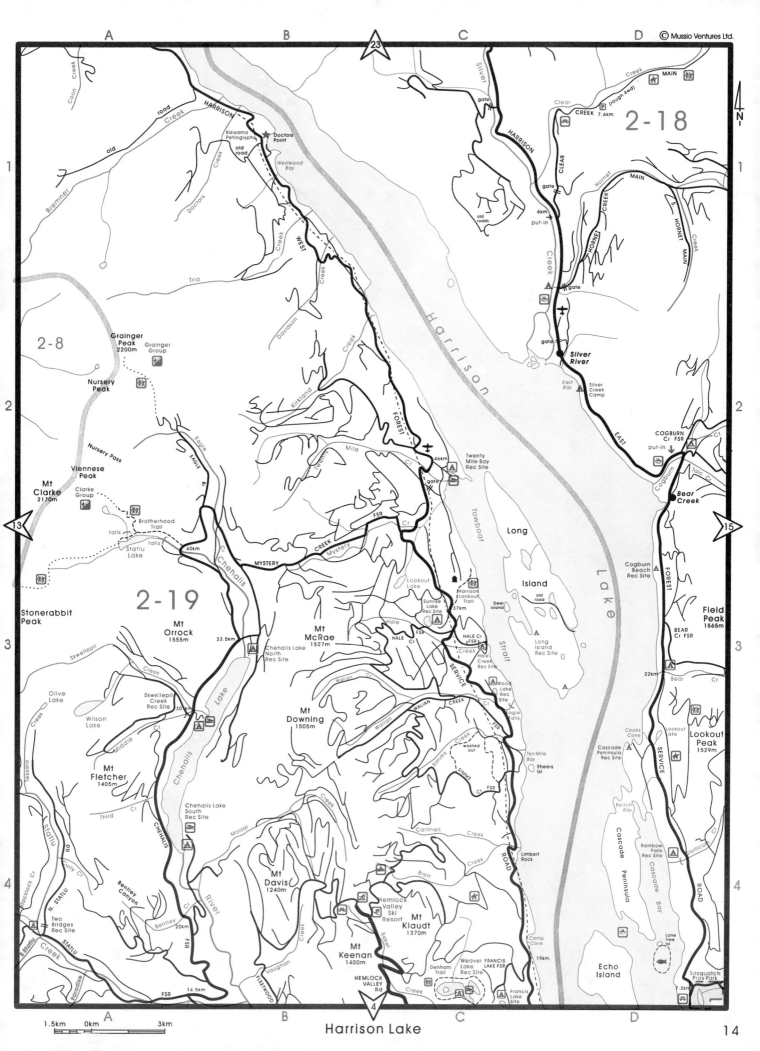

Harrison Lake

14

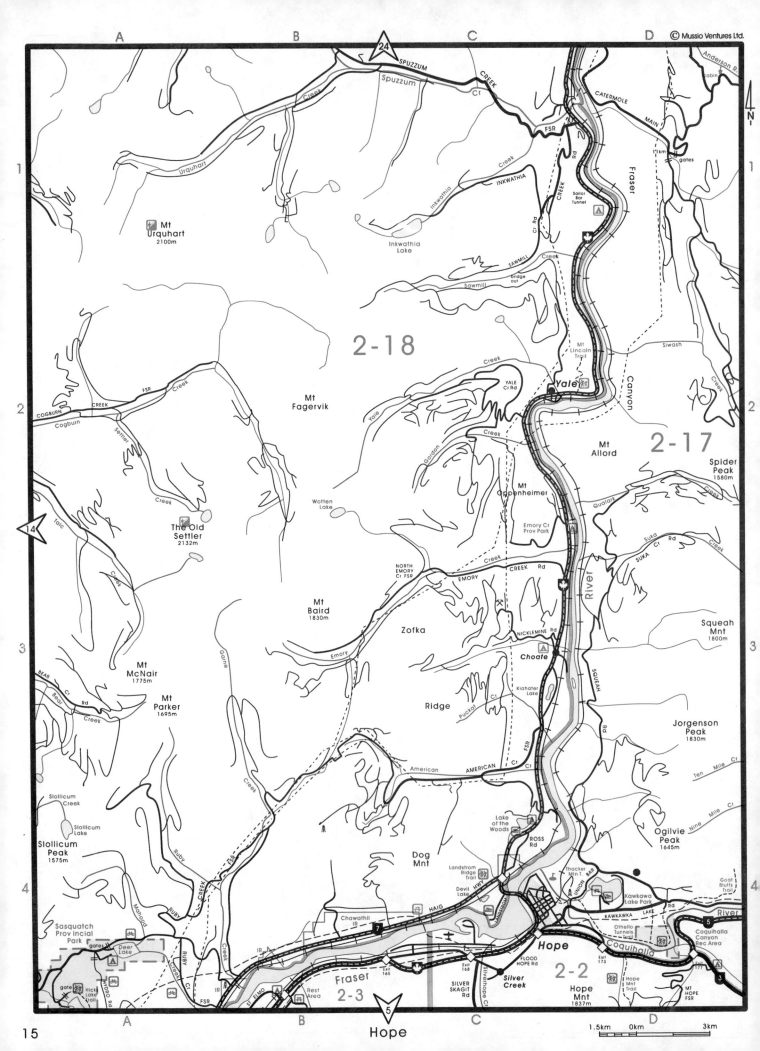

A   B   C   D

1   1

2-18

2

2-17

Mt Urquhart
2100m

Inkwathia Lake

INKWATHIA

SPUZZUM

Spuzzum
Creek
Creek

Cr

CREEK

FSR

CATERMOLE

Anderson R.

cabin

MAIN

gates

1km

Fraser

Sailor Bar tunnel

Mt Lincoln Trail

Yale

Siwash

Canyon

Mt Allord

Spider Peak
1580m

Urquhart

COGBURN   CREEK

Cogburn

FSR   Creek

Settler

Creek

Creek

Talc

The Old Settler
2132m

Mt Fagervik

Yale
Cr Rd

Creek

Gordon

Creek

Wotten Lake

Mt Oppenheimer

Emory Cr Prov Park

Qualark

Creek

2

3

4

Mt McNair
1775m

Mt Parker
1695m

BEAR   Cr Rd

Bear

Creek

Game

Creek

Mt Baird
1830m

Emory

NORTH EMORY Cr FSR

EMORY

Emory

CREEK   Rd

Creek

Zofka

Ridge

Kiahater Lake

Puckat   Ct

Choate

NICKLEMINE Rd

SUKA   Cr Rd

Suka   Cr

SQUEAH

River

Squeah Mnt
1800m

Jorgenson Peak
1830m

Slollicum
Creek

Slollicum
Lake

Slollicum Peak
1575m

Ruby

RUBY   CREEK   FSR

Creek

Mahood

Dog Mnt

American

AMERICAN   Ct   Ct

FSR

Lake of the Woods

ROSS   Rd

Ogilvie Peak
1645m

Ten   Mile   Cr

Nine   Mile   Cr

Goat Bluffs Trail

Sasquatch Provincial Park

gates

Deer Lake

HYDRO   Rd

gate

Hicks Lake Trail

Cogill   Ct

RUBY   CREEK   FSR

ST   ELMO

FSR

IR

IR

Rest Area

Chawathil IR

HAIG

Landstrom Ridge Trail

Devil Lake

Thacker Mtn T.

UNION   BAR

Hope

Silver
Creek

FLOOD HOPE Rd

Hope Mnt
1837m

KAWKAWA

LAKE

Kawkawa Lake Park

Rd

Othello Tunnels Rec Area

Coquihalla

Coquihalla Canyon Rec Area

River

Hope Mnt Trail

MT HOPE FSR

5

Exit 165

Exit 168

SILVER SKAGIT Rd

Silverhope Cr

Exit 173

Exit 177

2-2

Fraser

2-3

Hope

24

5

N-

1.5km   0km   3km

15

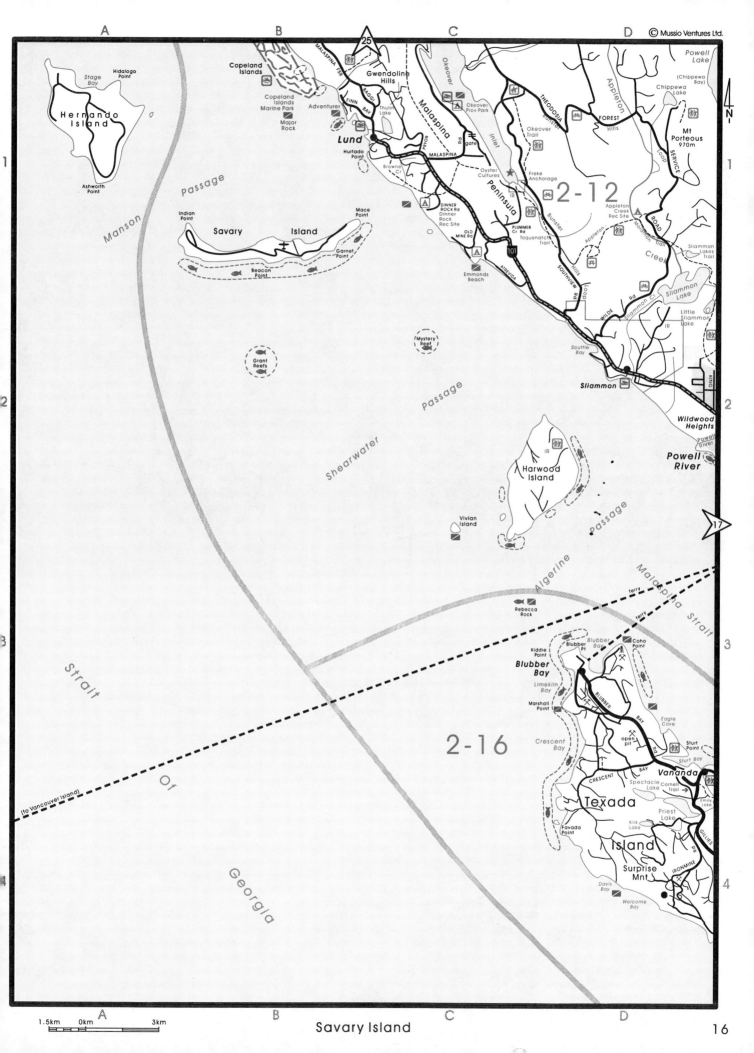

Savary Island

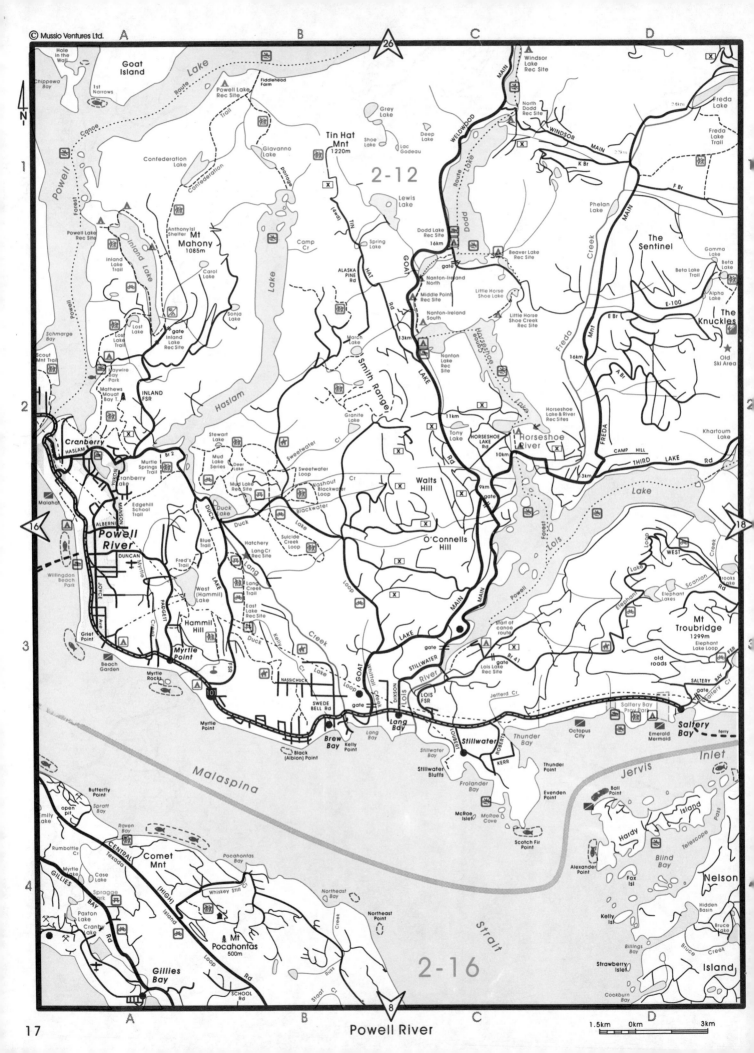

2-12

2-16

1.5km   0km   3km

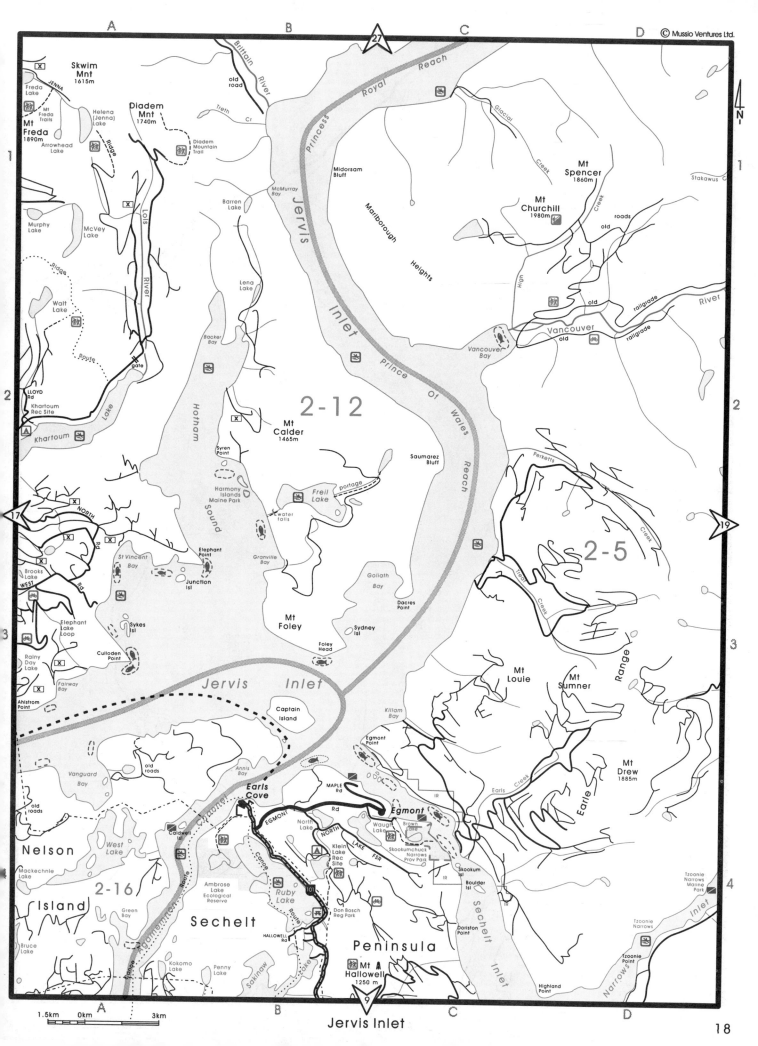

A B C D

Skwim Mnt
1615m

Freda Lake

Mt Freda Trails

Mt Freda
1890m

Arrowhead Lake

Helena (Jenna) Lake

JENNA

Ridge

Diadem Mnt
1740m

Diadem Mountain Trail

old road

Brittain River

Treth Cr

Murphy Lake

McVey Lake

Barren Lake

McMurray Bay

Midorsam Bluff

Marlborough Heights

Mt Spencer
1860m

Mt Churchill
1980m

Glacial Creek

Stakawus C

roads
old

High Creek

railgrade

Vancouver River

railgrade
old

Ridge

Walt Lake

Route

LLOYD Rd

Khartoum Rec Site

Khartoum

Lena Lake

Hotham Sound

Backer Bay

gate

Lois Lake

Lois River

Mt Calder
1465m

Syren Point

Harmony Islands Maine Park

waterfalls

Freil Lake

portage

2-12

Saumarez Bluff

Prince Of Wales Reach

Vancouver Bay

Princess Royal Reach

Jervis Inlet

27

NORTH Rd

Brooks Lake

WEST Rd

Elephant Lake Loop

Rainy Day Lake

Fairway Bay

Ahlstrom Point

St Vincent Bay

Elephant Point

Junction Isl

Sykes Isl

Culloden Point

Granville Bay

Mt Foley

Sydney Isl

Foley Head

Goliath Bay

Dacres Point

2-5

Teal Creek

Perketts

Creek

Mt Louie

Mt Sumner

Range

Earle

Mt Drew
1885m

17

19

Jervis Inlet

Captain Island

Annis Bay

Killam Bay

Egmont Point

Earls Cove

MAPLE Rd

Rd

North Lake

EGMONT

NORTH LAKE FSR

Klein Lake Rec Site

Egmont

Waugh Lake

Brown Lake

Skookumchuck Narrows Prov Park

IR

IR

Earls Creek

Vanguard Bay

old roads

old roads

Caldwell Isl

West Lake

Agamemnon Channel

Nelson

Mackechnie Lake

Green Bay

Bruce Lake

Island

2-16

Sechelt

Ambrose Lake Ecological Reserve

Ruby Lake

Kokomo Lake

Penny Lake

Sakinaw Lake

Canoe Route

Ruby Lake Route

101

HALLOWELL Rd

Don Bosch Reg Park

Peninsula

Mt Hallowell
1250 m

Skookum Isl

Boulder Isl

Doriston Point

Sechelt Inlet

Tzoonie Narrows Marine Park

Tzoonie Narrows

Tzoonie Point

Tzoonie Inlet

Highland Point

Narrows

1.5km   0km   3km

9

Jervis Inlet

N

2   3   4

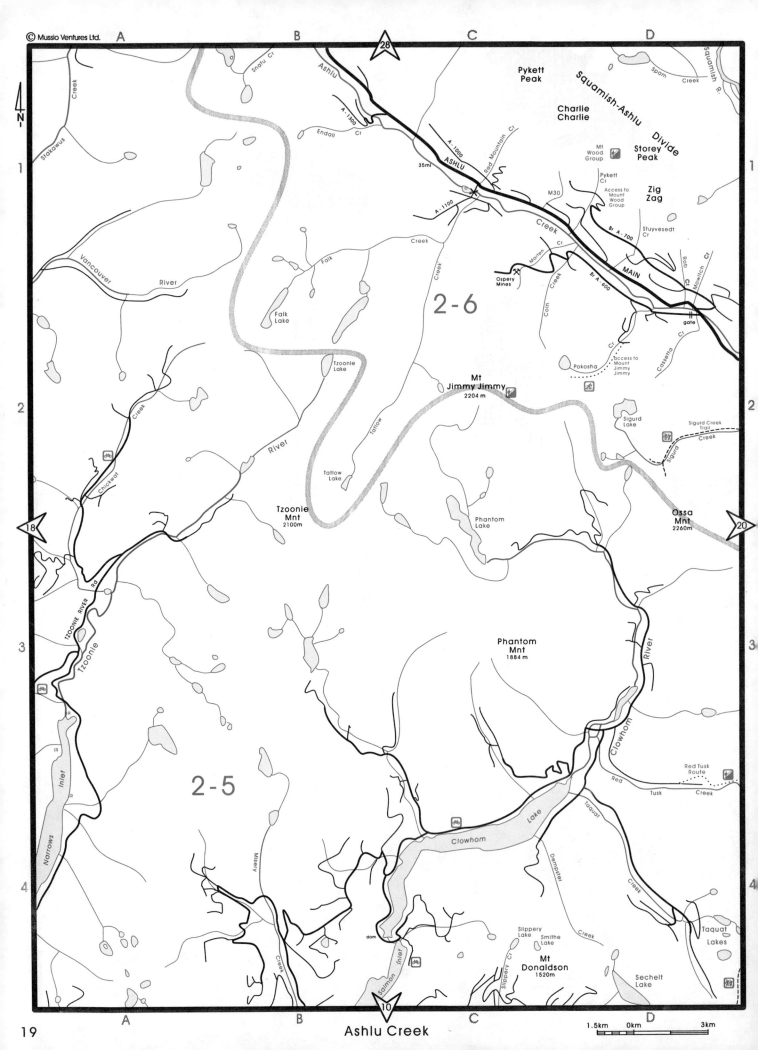

© Mussio Ventures Ltd.

N

A   B   C   D

28

Stakawus Creek
Snafu Cr
Ashlu
Endall Cr
A - 1300
35mi   ASHLU
A - 1000
Red Mountain Cr
A - 1100
Vancouver River
Creek
Falk
Falk Lake
Creek
Creek

Pykett Peak
Squamish-Ashlu
Spam Creek
Squamish R.
Charlie Charlie
Mt Wood Group
Storey Peak
Zig Zag
Pykett Cr
M30
Access to Mount Wood Group
Br A - 700
Stuyvesedt Cr
Rob Cr
Mowitch Cr
Marten Cr
MAIN
Br A - 600
Ospery Mines
Coin Creek
gate

2-6

Cr
Pokosha
Access to Mount Jimmy Jimmy
Cassetta Cr

Tzoonie Lake
Mt Jimmy Jimmy
2204 m

Sigurd Lake
Sigurd Creek Trail
Sigurd Creek

Creek
Chickwat
River
Tatlow

2

Tatlow Lake
Tzoonie Mnt
2100m

Phantom Lake

Ossa Mnt
2260m

8

20

Tzoonie River Rd
Tzoonie
IR
R
IR
R
Narrows Inlet

2-5

Phantom Mnt
1884 m

Clowhom River

3

Red Tusk Route
Red   Tusk   Creek

Misery Creek
Clowhom Lake
Taquat
Dempster Creek

Clowhom

Taquat Lakes

4

dom
Salmon Inlet
Slippery Cr
Slippery Lake
Smithe Lake
Creek
Mt Donaldson
1520m
Sechelt Lake

10

A   B   C   D

19

Ashlu Creek

1.5km   0km   3km

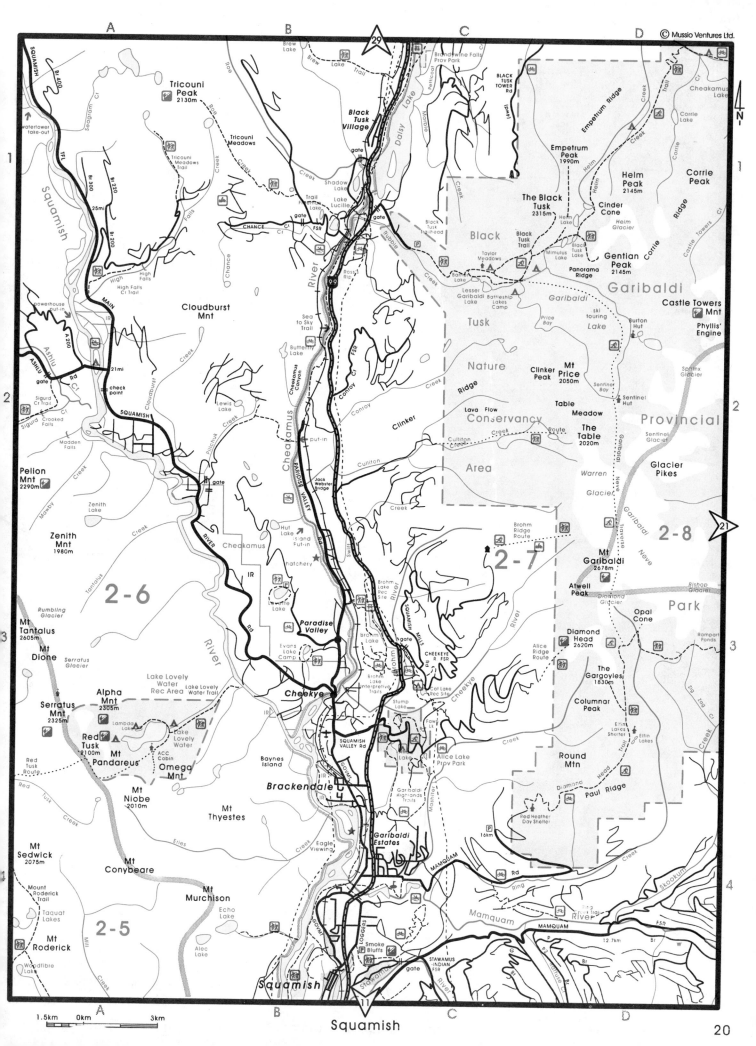

A · B · C · D

SQUAMISH

Br 400

watertower take-out

TFL

Br 300

Br 220

25mi

Tricouni Peak
2130m

Tricouni Meadows Trail

Tricouni Meadows

Brew Lake

Brew Lake Trail

Black Tusk Village

Petticoat Creek

Brandywine Falls Prov Park

BLACK TUSK TOWER Rd (pvt)

Empetrum Ridge

Cheakamus Lake

Corrie Lake

Roe Cr

Seagram Cr

Roe Creek

Shadow Lake

Empetrum Peak
1990m

Helm Peak
2145m

Corrie Peak

Helm

Helm Creek

Corrie Ridge

Castle Towers Cr

High Falls

CHANCE

Chance Cr FSR

Trail Lake

Lake Lucille

gate

gate

Black Tusk Trailhead

The Black Tusk
2315m

Cinder Cone

Black Tusk Lake

Helm Lake

Helm Glacier

Gentian Peak
2145m

Garibaldi

MAIN

IR

High Falls

High Falls Cr Trail

Cheakamus River

99

Rubble Cr

Black Tusk Cr

Taylor Meadows

Black Tusk Lake

Mimulus Lake

Black Tusk Trail

Panorama Ridge

Castle Towers Mnt

powerhouse put-in

Ashlu

A 200

ASHLU Rd

gate

21mi

check point

Sea to Sky Trail

Butterfly Lake

Conroy Cr FSR

P

Barrier Lake

Lesser Garibaldi Lake

Battleship Lakes Camp

Garibaldi Lake

ski touring

Burton Hut

Phyllis' Engine

Sphinx Glacier

Cloudburst Mnt

Cheakamus Canyon

Conroy Creek

Clinker

Black Tusk Nature

Ridge

Price Bay

Clinker Peak

Mt Price
2050m

Sentinel Bay

Sentinel Hut

Provincial

Sigurd Cr Trail

Sigurd Cr

Crooked Falls

Madden Falls

SQUAMISH

Lewis Lake

Pillchuck Creek

put-in

Culliton Creek

Culliton

Lava Flow Creek

Conservancy

Area

Route

Table Meadow

The Table
2020m

Warren Glacier

Glacier Pikes

Sentinel Glacier

Pelion Mnt
2290m

Zenith Lake

PARADISE VALLEY Rd

Jack Webster Bridge

Cheakamus River

2-8

21

Mawby Creek

Zenith Mnt
1980m

Cheakamus

IR

Hut

Island Put-in

hatchery

Swift Cr

Brohm Ridge Route

P

2-7

Mt Garibaldi
2678m

Atwell Peak

Garibaldi Neve

Traverse

Mt Tantalus
2605m

Rumbling Glacier

Tantalus

2-6

RIVER

Rd

Lucille Lake

P

Paradise Valley

Brohm Lake Rec Site

Brohm Creek

Brohm Lake

SQUAMISH MILLS Rd

gate

Diamond Glacier

Bishop Glacier

Park

Rampart Ponds

Mt Dione

Serratus Glacier

River

Evans Lake Camp

CHEEKEYE R FSR

Opal Cone

Diamond Head
2620m

Zag Cr

Serratus Mnt
2325m

Alpha Mnt
2305m

Lake Lovely Water Rec Area

Lake Lovely Water Trail

Cheekye

Brohm Lake Interpretive Trails

Rat Lake Rec Site

Cheekye Creek

Alice Ridge Route

The Gargoyles
1830m

Red Tusk
2100m

Lambda Lake

Mt Pandareus

ACC Cabin

Lake Lovely Water

Stump Lake

Fawn Cr

Columnar Peak

Elfin Lakes Shelter

Elfin Lakes

Red Tusk Route

Omega Mnt

Baynes Island

IR

GOVM

Brackendale

SQUAMISH VALLEY Rd

Alice Lake

Alice Lake Prov Park

Creek

Round Mtn

Diamond Head Trail

Paul Ridge

Mt Niobe
2010m

Mt Thyestes

Garibaldi Highlands Trails

Mashiter Cr

Red Heather Day Shelter

Red Tusk Creek

Eries Creek

Eagle Viewing

Garibaldi Estates

P

16km

Mt Sedwick
2075m

Mt Conybeare

Echo Lake

MAMQUAM

Ring Rd

P

Skookum Cr

Mount Roderick Trail

Taquat Lakes

Mt Murchison

Alec Lake

GOVM

LOGGERS

Mamquam Rd

Ring

Mamquam River

12.7km

FSR

2-5

Mill Creek

Woodfibre Lake

Mt Roderick

Smoke Bluffs

STAWAMUS INDIAN FSR

gate

Stawamus River

MAMQUAM

Squamish

11

1.5km 0km   3km

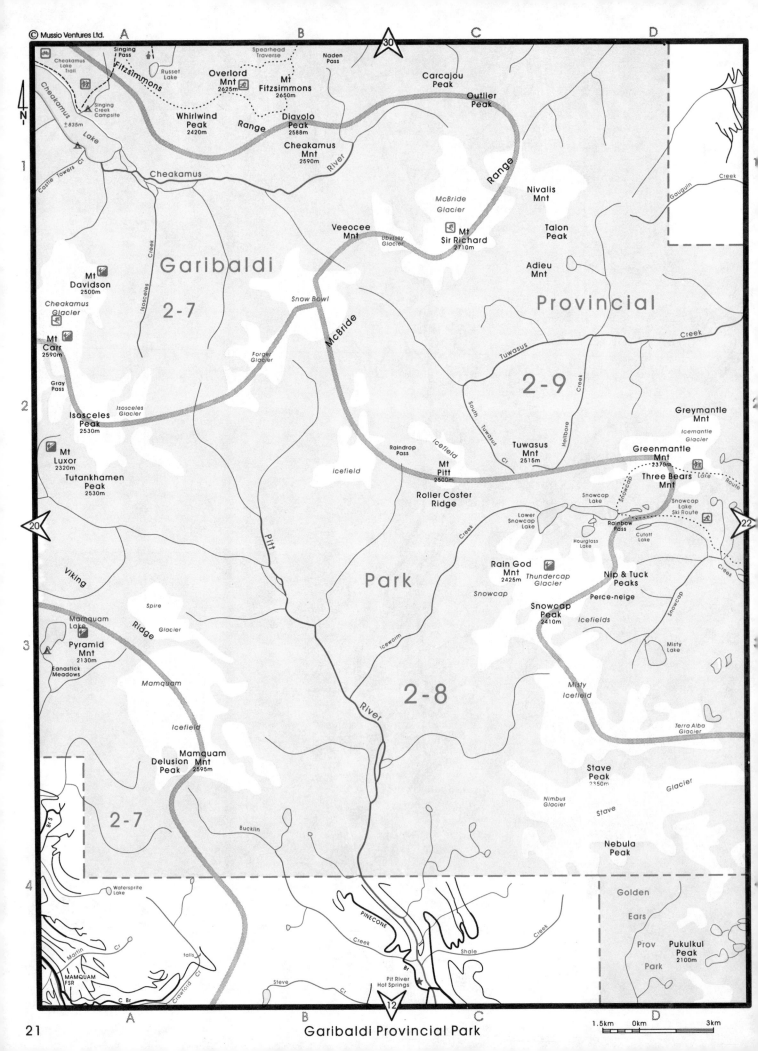

A B C D

Singing Pass
Cheakamus Lake Trail
Spearhead Traverse
Naden Pass
Carcajou Peak
Fitzsimmons
Russet Lake
Overlord Mnt 2625m
Mt Fitzsimmons 2650m
Outlier Peak
Singing Creek Campsite
±835m
Whirlwind Peak 2420m
Range
Diavolo Peak 2588m
Cheakamus Mnt 2590m
River
Range
Nivalis Mnt
Cheakamus Lake
Cheakamus
McBride Glacier
Talon Peak
Castle Towers Cr

Mt Davidson 2500m
Garibaldi
Veeocee Mnt
Ubistey Glacier
Mt Sir Richard 2710m
Adieu Mnt
Provincial

Cheakamus Glacier
2-7
Snow Bowl
Isosceles Creek
McBride
Creek
Tuwasus

Mt Carr 2590m
Forger Glacier
2-9
Greymantle Mnt

Gray Pass
Icefield
South Tuwasus Cr
Hellbore Creek
Icemantle Glacier

Isosceles Peak 2530m
Isosceles Glacier
Raindrop Pass
Icefield
Tuwasus Mnt 2515m
Greenmantle Mnt 2370m

Mt Luxor 2320m
Icefield
Mt Pitt 2500m
Icefield
Snowcap
Three Bears Mnt
Lake
Route

Tutankhamen Peak 2530m
Roller Coster Ridge
Snowcap Lake
Snowcap
Snowcap Lake Ski Route

20
Lower Snowcap Lake
Rainbow Pass
Cutoff Lake
22

Viking
Pitt
Creek
Hourglass Lake
Rain God Mnt 2425m
Thundercap Glacier
Nip & Tuck Peaks

Mamquam Lake
Spire
Glacier
Park
Snowcap
Perce-neige
Misty Lake

Pyramid Mnt 2130m
Ridge
Snowcap Peak 2410m
Icefields

Eanastick Meadows
Mamquam
Iceworm
Misty Icefield
Terra Alba Glacier

3
Icefield
2-8
River

Mamquam Delusion Mnt 2595m
Stave Peak 2350m
Glacier

2-7
Nimbus Glacier
Stave

Br FS
Bucklin
Nebula Peak

4
Watersprite Lake
Golden

Martin Cr
PINECONE
Creek
Ears

falls
Creek
Shale
Prov
Pukulkul Peak 2100m

Crawford Cr
C Br
Steve
Br
Park

MAMQUAM FSR
Pit River Hot Springs

12

A B C D

Garibaldi Provincial Park

1.5km 0km 3km

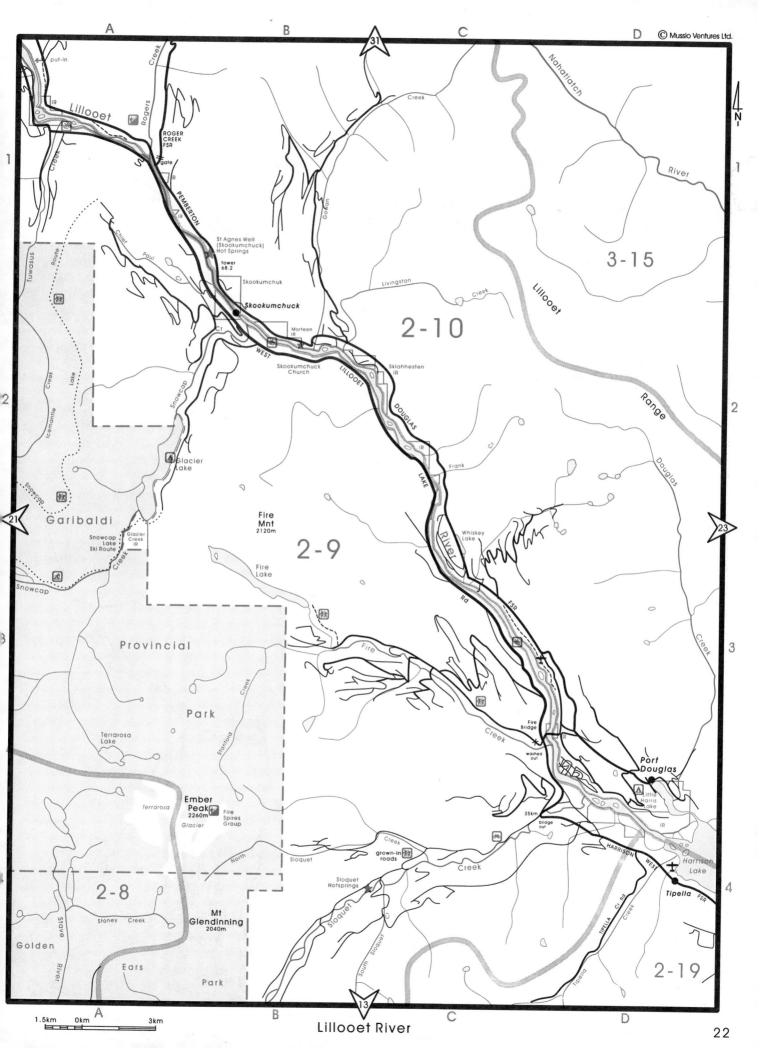

put-in
Lillooet
Creek
Rogers
IR
ROGER CREEK FSR
gate
PEMBERTON
IR
Chief Paul Cr
Snowcap
St Agnes Well (Skookumchuck) Hot Springs
tower 68.2
Skookumchuk
Skookumchuck
Cr
Morteen IR
WEST
LILLOOET
Skookumchuck Church
Sklahhesten IR
DOUGLAS
IR
Frank Cr
LAKE
River
Whiskey Lake

Creek
Nahatlatch
River

3-15
Golan
Livingstan Creek
Lillooet
Range

2-10

Tuwasus Route
Icemantle Creek
Lake
Snowcap

Garibaldi
Glacier Lake
Snowcap Lake Ski Route
Glazier Creek IR
Snowcap Creek

Fire Mnt 2120m
Fire Lake

2-9

Rd
FSR

Provincial

Park

Terrarosa Lake
Stanford Creek

Creek
Fire
Fire Creek
Fire Bridge
washed out
R
Port Douglas
Little Harris Lake
IR

Ember Peak 2260m
Fire Spires Group
Glacier
Terrarosa
North
Creek
Sloquet Creek
grown-in roads
Sloquet
35km
bridge out
HARRISON
Tipella Cr Rd
WEST
Harrison Lake

2-8
Golden
Stave River
Stoney Creek
Ears
Mt Glendinning 2040m
Park
Sloquet Hotsprings
South Sloquet Cr
Sloquet
Creek
HARRISON
Tipella Creek
Tipella FSR
TIPELLA

2-19

1.5km 0km 3km

Lillooet River

22

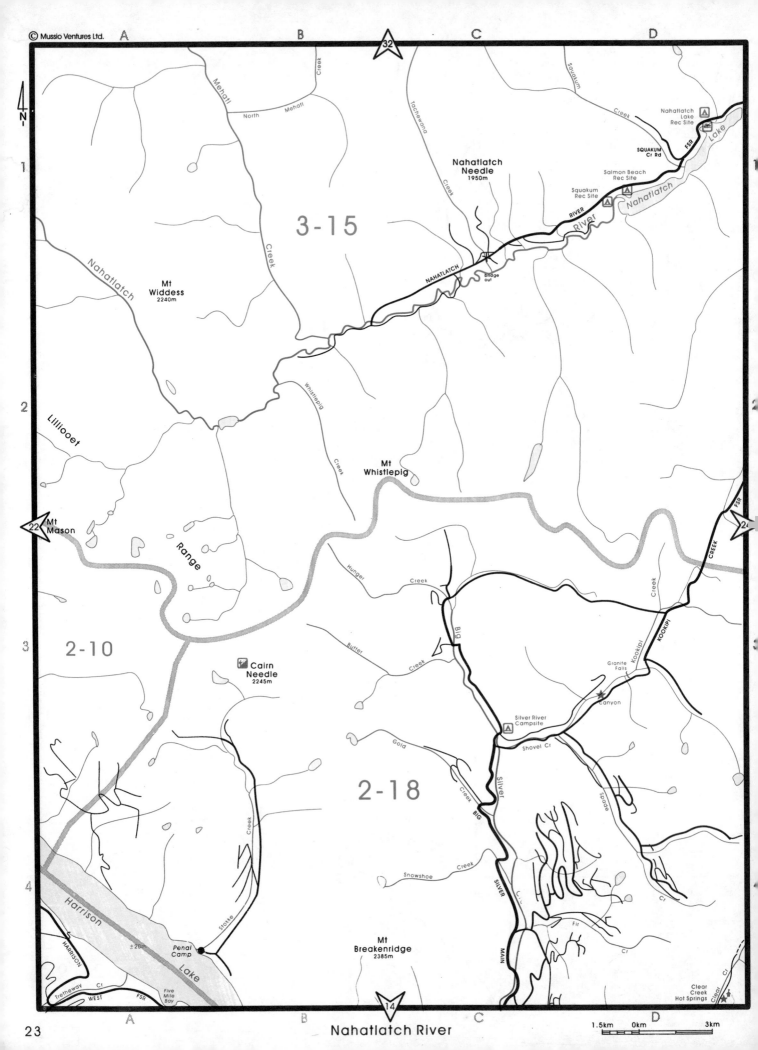

© Mussio Ventures Ltd.

A   B   32   C   D

N

1

Mehalt Creek
North Mehatl
Tachewana Creek

Squakum Creek

Nahatlatch Lake Rec Site

SQUAKUM Cr Rd

Nahatlatch Needle
1950m

Salmon Beach Rec Site

Squakum Rec Site

Nahatlatch Lake

3-15

Nahatlatch

Mt Widdess
2240m

Creek

RIVER River

NAHATLATCH

Bridge out

2

Whistlepig

Lillooet

Creek

Mt Whistlepig

Mt Mason

22

FSR

CREEK

Range

Hunger Creek

Creek

KOOKIPI CREEK

3

2-10

Cairn Needle
2245m

Butter Creek

Big

Kookipi Creek

Granite Falls

Canyon

Silver River Campsite

Shovel Cr

Gold Creek

BIG

Silver

2-18

Spade

Stokke Creek

Snowshoe Creek

SILVER

Cr

Fir

4

Harrison

±2m

Penal Camp

HARRISON

Tretheway Cr WEST FSR

Five Mile Bay

Lake

Mt Breakenridge
2385m

MAIN

Cr

Clear Creek Hot Springs

Clear Cr

14

A   B   C   D

Nahatlatch River

1.5km 0km 3km

23

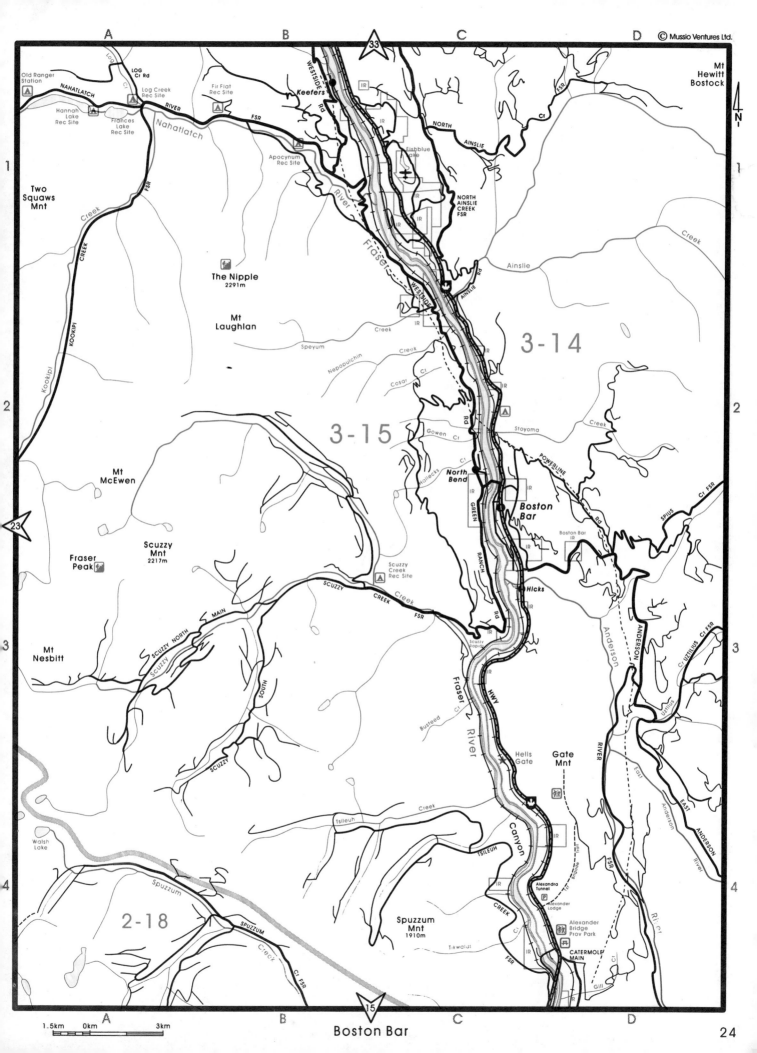

A   B   C   D

Mt Hewitt Bostock

N

Old Ranger Station
NAHATLATCH
LOG Cr Rd
Log Creek Rec Site
Fir Flat Rec Site

Keefers

Hannah Lake Rec Site
Frances Lake Rec Site
Nahatlatch
RIVER
FSR

WESTSIDE Rd

NORTH
AINSLIE

IR

Apocynum Rec Site

Fishblue Lake

NORTH AINSLIE CREEK FSR

Two Squaws Mnt

KOOKIPI CREEK

Fraser River

WESTSIDE Rd

Ainslie
Rd

1

The Nipple
2291m

Mt Laughlan

Speyum Creek

3-14

Nepopulchin Creek

Cosar Ct

Stoyoma Creek

2

KOOKIPI

Mt McEwen

3-15

Gowen Ct

Ct

POWERLINE

Rd

Spius Ct FSR

23

Fraser Peak

Scuzzy Mnt
2217m

Scuzzy Creek Rec Site

Hallecks

North Bend

IR

Boston Bar

GREEN Rd

Boston Bar IR

SPIUS

3

Mt Nesbitt

SCUZZY MAIN

SCUZZY NORTH

SCUZZY SOUTH

SCUZZY CREEK
Creek
FSR

RANCH Rd

Hicks

Scuzzy Rapids

Anderson

ANDERSON

UZILUS Ct FSR

Ct

Uzilus

EAST ANDERSON RIVER

3

Busteed Ct

Fraser River

HWY

Hells Gate

Gate Mnt

RIVER

Walsh Lake

Tsileuh Creek

TSILEUH

Canyon

Spuzzum Mnt
1910m

Brigade Trail

Alexandra Tunnel

Alexander Lodge

East Anderson

FSR

4

2-18

SPUZZUM

Spuzzum Creek

Ct FSR

CREEK

Tikwalus

IR

Alexander Bridge Prov Park

CATERMOLE MAIN

Gill Ct

FSR

A   B   C   D

1.5km 0km   3km

Boston Bar

24

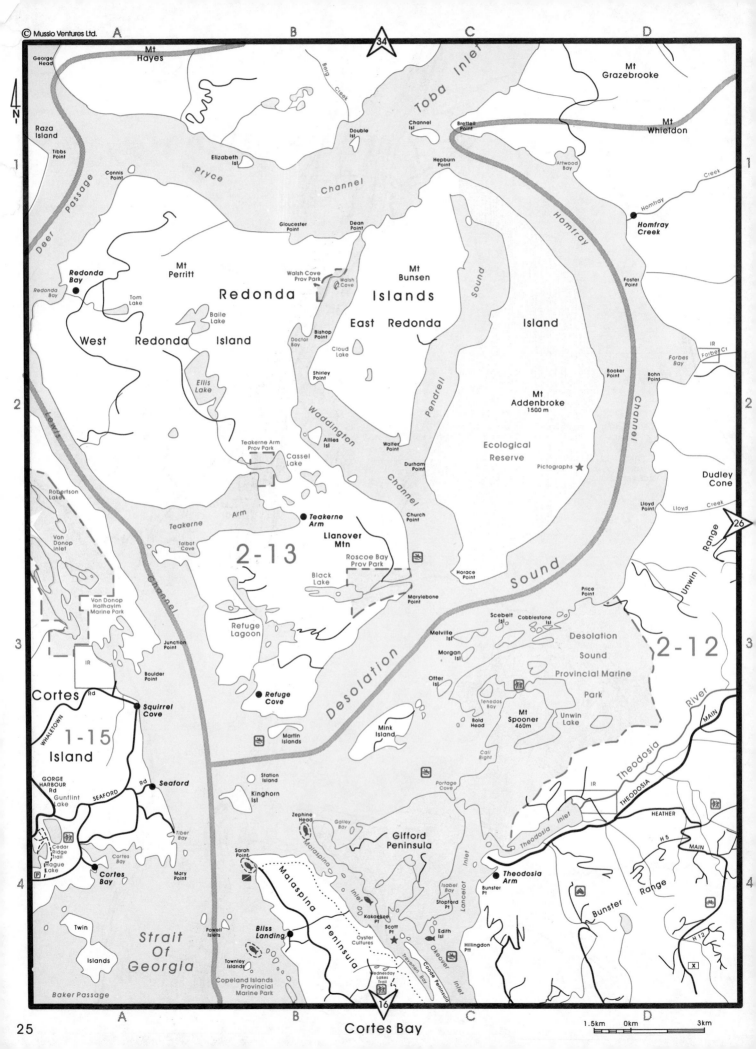

A B C D

George Head

Mt Hayes

Raza Island

Tibbs Point

Connis Point

Elizabeth Isl

Double Isl

Channel Isl

Brettell Point

Toba Inlet

Mt Grazebrooke

Mt Whieldon

Pryce

Channel

Gloucester Point

Dean Point

Hepburn Point

Attwood Bay

Creek

Homfray

Homfray Creek

Deer Passage

Redonda Bay

Redonda Bay

Mt Perritt

Tom Lake

Baile Lake

Redonda Islands

Walsh Cove Prov Park

Walsh Cove

Mt Bunsen

Homfray Sound

Foster Point

Lewis

West Redonda Island

Doctor Bay

Bishop Point

East Redonda

Island

IR Forbes Ct

Ellis Lake

Cloud Lake

Shirley Point

Booker Point

Bohn Point

Forbes Bay

Waddington

Allies Isl

Mt Addenbroke 1500 m

Channel

2

Teakerne Arm Prov Park

Cassel Lake

Walter Point

Durham Point

Ecological Reserve

Pictographs ★

Dudley Cone

Lloyd Point

Lloyd Creek

Range

26

Teakerne Arm

Teakerne Arm

Llanover Mtn

Church Point

Unwin

Arm

Talbot Cove

2-13

Roscoe Bay Prov Park

Horace Point

Sound

Price Point

Pendrell Channel

3

Von Donop Inlet

Robertson Lake

Junction Point

Black Lake

Marylebone Point

Desolation

Scebelt Isl

Melville Isl

Cobblestone Isl

Desolation Sound

Provincial Marine Park

2-12

River

Channel

Boulder Point

Refuge Lagoon

Morgan Isl

Otter Isl

Unwin Lake

MAIN

Von Donop Hathayim Marine Park

IR

Refuge Cove

Bold Head

Mt Spooner 460m

Tenedos Bay

IR

THEODOSIA

Cortes

Rd

Squirrel Cove

1-15 Island

Martin Islands

Mink Island

Cali Bight

Theodosia Inlet

HEATHER

Theodosia Range

GORGE HARBOUR Rd

Gunflint Lake

SEAFORD

Rd

Seaford

Station Island

Kinghorn Isl

Portage Cove

Theodosia Inlet

H 5

MAIN

WHALETOWN

Cedar Ridge Trail

Hague Lake

P

Cortes Bay

Tiber Bay

Mary Point

Zephine Head

Galley Bay

Gifford Peninsula

Isabel Bay

Lancelot Inlet

Theodosia Arm

Bunster Pt

Bunster Range

H 12

Cortes Bay

Sarah Point

Malaspina Inlet

Kakaekae Pt

Stopford Pt

Edith Isl

Hillingdon Ptt

Twin Islands

Powell Islets

Bliss Landing

Malaspina Peninsula

Oyster Cultures

Scott Pt

Okeover Inlet

Coode Peninsula

Strait Of Georgia

Townley Islands

Copeland Islands Provincial Marine Park

Wednesday Lakes Trail

Trevenen Bay

X

Baker Passage

16

A B C D

Cortes Bay

1.5km 0km 3km

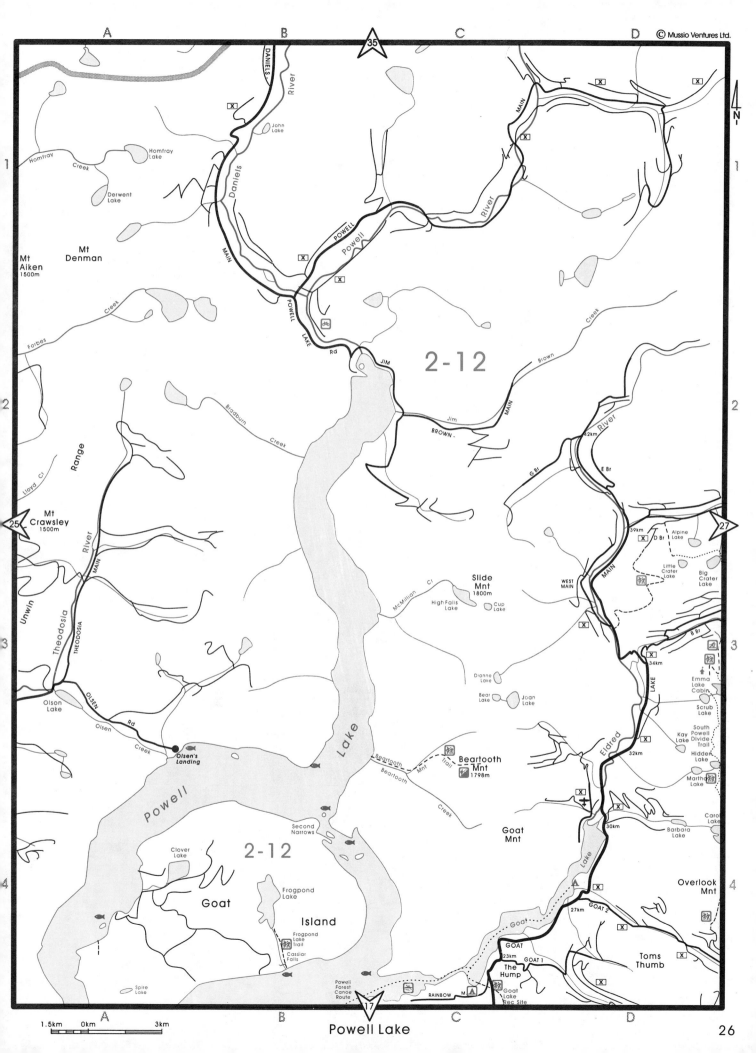

2-12

2-12

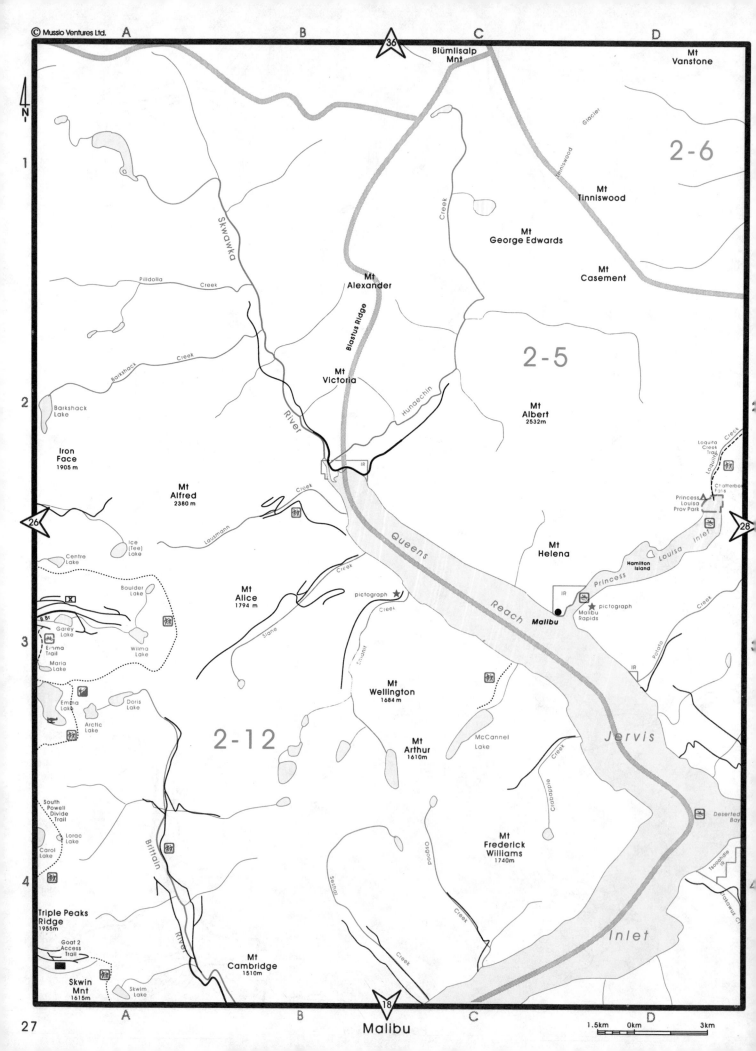

© Mussio Ventures Ltd.

A   B   C   D

36

Blümlisalp Mnt

Mt Vanstone

2-6

Glacier

Mt Tinniswood

Tinniswood

Creek

Mt George Edwards

Mt Casement

Skwawka

Mt Alexander

Blastus Ridge

2-5

Pilldolla Creek

Mt Victoria

Hunaechin

Barkshack Creek

Barkshack Lake

Mt Albert
2532m

Iron Face
1905 m

River

Mt Alfred
2380 m

Lausmann Creek

Creek

IR

Loquita Creek Trail

Loquita Creek

Chatterbox Falls

Princess Louisa Prov Park

26

Centre Lake

Ice (Tee) Lake

Mt Alice
1794 m

Slane Creek

pictograph ★

Queens

Mt Helena

IR

Princess Louisa Inlet

Hamilton Island

pictograph ★

Malibu Rapids

28

Boulder Lake

Garey Lake

Emma Trail

Wilma Lake

Creek

Smanit Creek

Reach

● Malibu

Maria Lake

Emma Lake

Doris Lake

Mt Wellington
1684 m

McCannel Lake

Arctic Lake

2-12

Mt Arthur
1610m

Jervis

Creek

South Powell Divide Trail

Lorac Lake

Brittain

Osgood

Crabapple Creek

Mt Frederick Williams
1740m

Deserted Bay

Carol Lake

Sechal Creek

Tsoohale Cr

Triple Peaks Ridge
1955m

Goat 2 Access Trail

River

Creek

Inlet

Skwin Mnt
1615m

Skwim Lake

Mt Cambridge
1510m

A   B   C   D

18

Malibu

1.5km   0km   3km

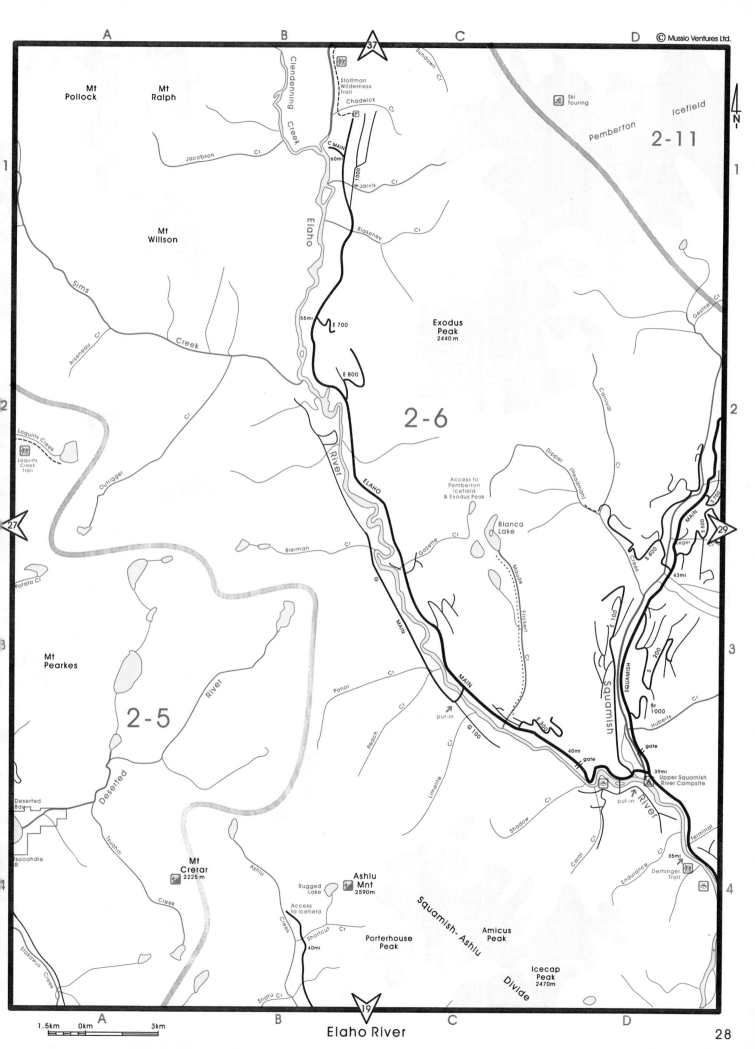

2-11

A   B   C   D

Mt
Pollock

Mt
Ralph

Clendenning Creek

37

Stoltman Wilderness Trail

Chadwick

Sundown Cr

Ski Touring

Pemberton Icefield

Jacobson Cr

C MAIN
60mi

E 1000

E Jarvis

Cr

Mt
Willson

Elaho

Blakeney

Cr

Sims

Creek

Arseneau Cr

55mi   E 700

E 800

Exodus
Peak
2440 m

2-6

Carnival

Cr

27

Loquilts Creek

Loquilts Creek Trail

Outrigger

River

ELAHO

Access to
Pemberton
Icefield
& Exodus Peak

Blanca
Lake

Dipper (Headman)

Cr

S 1000

MAIN

S 500

29

Potato Cr

Cr

Bierman

Cr

Gazette

Cr

Maude

Fickert

Cr

S 400

Jeger

43mi

S 300

Mt
Pearkes

River

G

MAIN

Ponor

Cr

Cr

Peach   Cr

Limelite   Cr

MAIN

put-in

G 100

E 300

Squamish

E 100

S 200

S

Br
1000

Huberts

Cr

2-5

40mi   gate

gate

39mi
Upper Squamish
River Campsite

Deserted Bay

Deserted

Isuahal

Creek

Tsooahdie R

Mt
Crerar
2225 m

Rugged
Lake

Ashlu

Access
to Icefield

Shortcut   Cr

40mi

Ashlu
Mnt
2590m

Porterhouse
Peak

Shadow   Cr

Carol   Cr

Endurance   Cr

put-in

River

Terminal

35mi
Deminger Trail

Squamish-Ashlu

Amicus
Peak

Icecap
Peak
2470m

Divide

Snafu Cr

19

Statawus Creek

1.5km   0km   3km

A   B   C   D

Elaho River

28

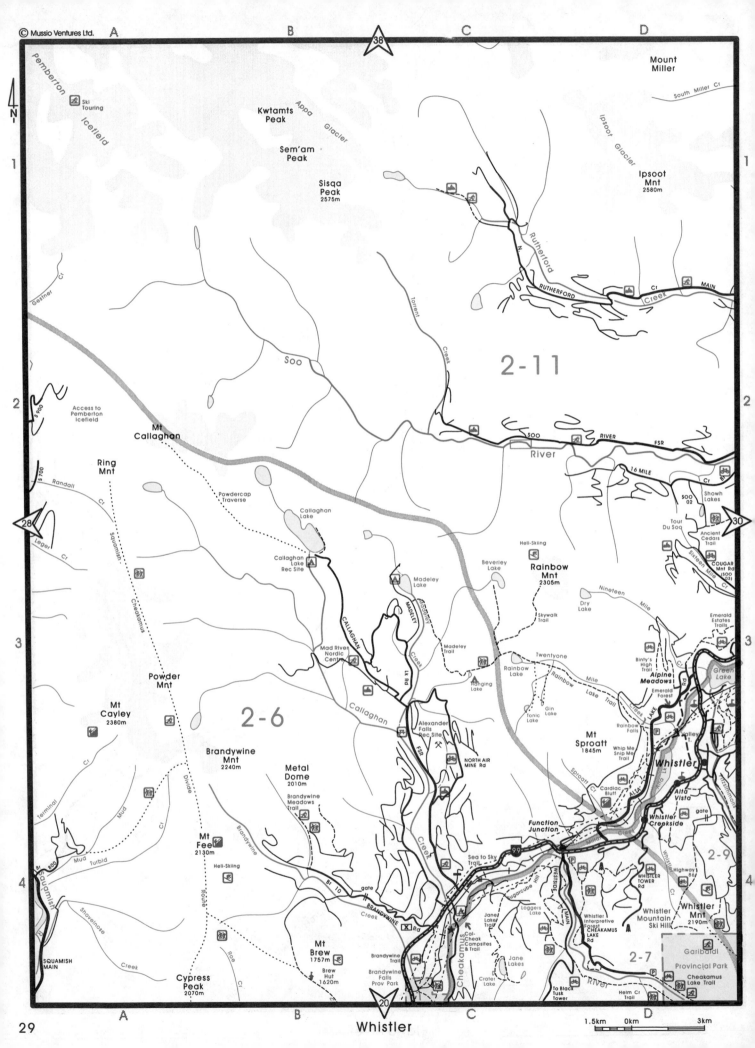

© Mussio Ventures Ltd.

A B 38 C D

N

Pemberton
Icefield

Ski Touring

Kwtamts
Peak

Appa Glacier

Sem'am
Peak

Sisqa
Peak
2575m

Rutherford

Mount
Miller

South Miller Cr

Ipsoot Glacier

Ipsoot
Mnt
2580m

1

Gestner Cr

Soo

RUTHERFORD Creek MAIN

2-11

Torrent Creek

2

Access to
Pemberton
Icefield

Mt
Callaghan

S 700

Randall Cr

Ring
Mnt

Squamish

Cheakamus

SOO RIVER FSR

River

16 MILE

SOO 02 Cr

Showh
Lakes

Tour
Du Soo

Ancient
Cedars
Trail

COUGAR
Mnt Rd
(SOO 03)

Powdercap
Traverse

Callaghan
Lake

Callaghan
Lake Rec Site

Madeley
Lake

Beverley
Lake

Heli-Skiing

Rainbow
Mnt
2305m

Dry
Lake

Nineteen Mile

Binty's
High
Trail

Emerald
Estates
Trails

30

Green
Lake

28

Leger Cr

Powder
Mnt

CALLAGHAN

MADELEY

Madeley Creek

Mad River
Nordic Centre

Lt Rd

Skywalk
Trail

Madeley
Trail

Twentyone

Rainbow
Lake

Rainbow Mile Lake Trail

Alpine
Meadows

Emerald
Forest

LAKE

3

Mt
Cayley
2380m

2-6

Callaghan

Hanging
Lake

Tonic
Lake

Gin
Lake

Rainbow
Falls

Mt
Sproatt
1845m

Whip Me
Snip Me
Trail

Cardiac
Bluff

Valley
T.

Whistler

Alta
Vista

gate

Brandywine
Mnt
2240m

Metal
Dome
2010m

FSR

Alexander
Falls
Rec Site

NORTH AIR
MINE Rd

Function
Junction

Sproatt Cr

ALTA

Whistler
Creekside

2-9

4

Br 800

Mud Turbid

Divide

Brandywine

Mt Fee
2130m

Heli-Skiing

Brandywine
Meadows
Trail

Br 10

gate

BRANDYWINE

Creek

Rd

Sea to Sky
Trail

Cheakamus Creek

99

WESTSIDE MAIN

Sugarcube Hill

Loggers
Lake

Janet Lake
Trail

Jane
Lake

Whistler
Interpretive
Forest
CHEAKAMUS
LAKE Rd

Highway
86

WHISTLER
TOWER
Rd

Whistler
Mountain
Ski Hill

Highway 99

Whistler
Mnt
2190m

Terminal Cr

Shovelnose

Squamish

Mt
Brew
1757m

Brew Hut
1620m

Brandywine
Trail

Brandywine
Falls
Prov Park

Cal-Cheak
Campsites
& Trail

Crater
Lake

Jane
Lakes

RIVER

To Black
Tusk
Tower

Helm Cr
Trail

2-7

Garibaldi
Provincial
Park

Cheakamus
Lake Trail

SQUAMISH
MAIN

Cypress
Peak
2070m

Roe Cr

Cheakamus

20

Whistler

1.5km 0km 3km

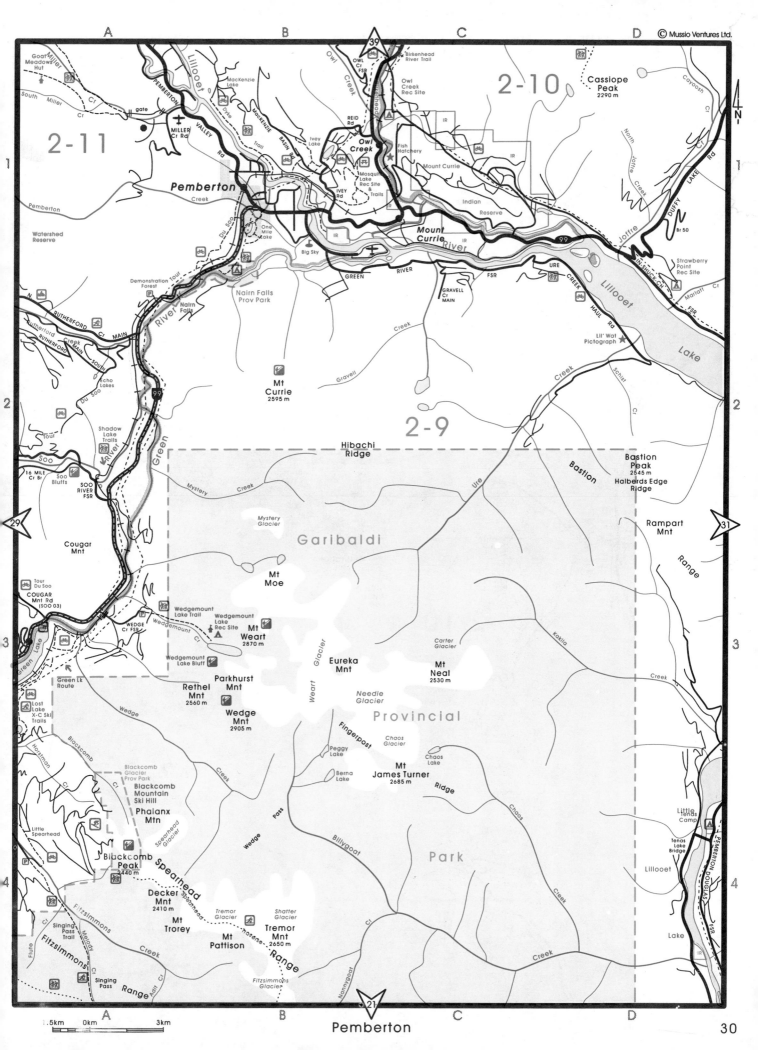

2-10

Cassiope
Peak
2290 m

2-11

Goat Miller
Meadow Hut

South
Miller
Cr

Miller
Cr Rd

gate

Pemberton

MacKenzie
Lake

Owl
Cr
FSR

39

Birkenhead
River Trail

Owl Creek
Rec Site

REID
Rd

Owl Creek

Fish Hatchery

Mount Currie

North
Joffre
Creek

DUFFY
LAKE
Rd

Br 50

N

Pemberton

Watershed
Reserve

Pemberton

Creek

One Mile
Lake

IVEY
Rd

Ivey
Lake

Mosquito
Lake Rec Site
& Trails

Indian
Reserve

Mount
Currie

IR

Strawberry
Point
Rec Site

Marilat
Cr

RUTHERFORD

Rutherford
Creek MAIN

RUTHERFORD
Creek
MAIN
south

Big Sky

Demonstration tour
Forest

Nairn Falls
Prov Park

Nairn Falls

GREEN

RIVER

River

Mount Currie
River

99

GRAVELL
Cr
MAIN

FSR

GRAVELL
Cr
MAIN

URE

CREEK

HAUL
Rd

Lil' Wat
Pictograph

Lillooet

Lake

Echo
Lakes

Du Soo

99

Tour
Du Soo

Soo

Shadow
Lake
Trails

River

16 MILE
Cr Br

Soo
Bluffs

SOO
RIVER
FSR

Green

Creek

Gravell

Creek

2-9

Hibachi
Ridge

Mystery   Creek

Ure

Bastion

Bastion
Peak
2545 m
Halberds Edge
Ridge

Mt
Currie
2595 m

29

Cougar
Mnt

Mystery
Glacier

Garibaldi

Mystery
Glacier

Mt Moe

Rampart
Mnt

Range

31

COUGAR
Mnt Rd
(SOO 03)

Green

Lake

Wedgemount
Lake Trail

Wedgemount
Lake Rec Site

Wedgemount Cr

WEDGE
Cr FSR

Wedgemount Ct

Mt
Weart
2870 m

Wedgemount
Lake Bluff

Weart
Glacier

Eureka
Mnt

Carter
Glacier

Mt
Neal
2530 m

Kakila

Creek

3

Green Lk
Route

Lost
Lake
X-C Ski
Trails

Rethel
Mnt
2560 m

Parkhurst
Mnt

Wedge

Wedge
Mnt
2905 m

Needle
Glacier

Fingerpost

Peggy
Lake

Provincial

Chaos
Glacier

Chaos
Lake

Little Tenas
Camp

Horstman

Blackcomb

Creek

Blackcomb
Glacier Prov Park

Blackcomb
Mountain
Ski Hill

Phalanx
Mtn

Spearhead
Glacier

Berna
Lake

Mt
James Turner
2685 m

Ridge

Chaos

Park

Tenas
Lake
Bridge

PEMBERTON DOUGLAS

Little
Spearhead

Blackcomb
Peak
2440 m

Spearhead

Spearhead

Decker
Mnt
2410 m

Fitzsimmons

Melody

Tremor
Glacier

Shatter
Glacier

Wedge

Pass

Billygoat

Ct

Creek

Lillooet

4

P

Singing
Pass Trail

Mt
Trorey

Mt
Pattison

Tremor
Mnt
2650 m

Napena

Range

Nampoot

Lake

FSR

Flute

Fitzsimmons

Adit Cr

Singing
Pass

Creek

Range

Fitzsimmons
Glacier

21

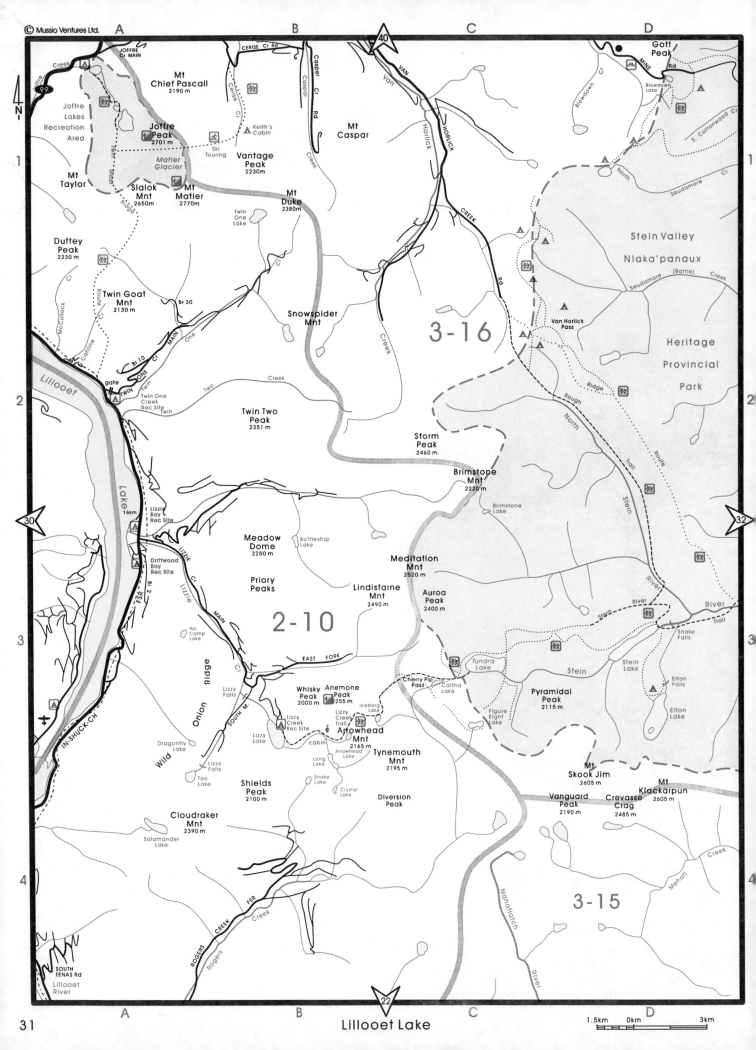

© Mussio Ventures Ltd.

A B C D

N

99

JOFFRE Cr MAIN

Joffre Creek

Mt Chief Pascall
2190 m

CERISE Cr Rd

Casper Creek

40

VAN

Van Creek

MINE Rd

Gott Peak

Blowdown Lake

Joffre Lakes Recreation Area

Joffre Peak
2701 m

Keith's Cabin

Cerise Cr

Casper Cr

Mt Caspar

HORLICK CREEK

Horlick

Blowdown Ct

S. Cottonwood Ct

North

Seudamore Ct

1

Ski Touring

Matier Glacier

Vantage Peak
2230 m

Mt Taylor

Slalok Mnt
2650 m

Mt Matier
2770 m

Mt Duke
2380 m

Twin One Lake

Stein Valley
Nlaka'panaux

Seudamore (Battle) Creek

Duffey Peak
2230 m

Twin Goat Mnt
2130 m

Br 30

Snowspider Mnt

Twin One Ct

MAIN Ct

ONE Ct

Van Horlick Pass

Ridge

Rough

Heritage Provincial Park

2

McCullock Cr

Catline Cr

Route

Br 10

gate

TWIN

Twin One Creek Rec Site

Twin Two Creek

Twin Two Peak
2351 m

Storm Peak
2460 m

Brimstone Mnt
2220 m

North

Stein

Trail

Route

30

Lillooet Lake

16km

Lizzie Bay Rec Site

Meadow Dome
2250 m

Battleship Lake

Brimstone Lake

Rd

River

32

Driftwood Bay Rec Site

LIZZIE Ct

Priory Peaks

Meditation Mnt
2520 m

Stein

3

Br 2

FSR

No Camp Lake

LIZZIE MAIN Ct

Lindisfarne Mnt
2490 m

Auroa Peak
2400 m

Tundra Lake

Stein River

Stein Lake

Elton Falls

IN-SHUCK-CH

EAST FORK

Cherry Pip Pass

Caltha Lake

Pyramidal Peak
2115 m

Elton Lake

Onion Ridge

SOUTH M.

Lizzy Falls

Whisky Peak
2000 m

Anemone Peak
2255 m

Lizzy Creek Rec Site

Iceberg Lake

Lizzy Creek Trail

Figure Eight Lake

Wild

Dragonfly Lake

Lizzy Lake

cabin

Arrowhead Mnt
2165 m

Arrowhead Lake

Tynemouth Mnt
2195 m

Mt Skook Jim
2605 m

Mt Klackarpun
2605 m

Tao Lake

Lizzy Falls

Shields Peak
2100 m

Long Lake

Snake Lake

Crystal Lake

Diversion Peak

Vanguard Peak
2190 m

Crevasse Crag
2485 m

Cloudraker Mnt
2390 m

Salamander Lake

Nahatlatch River

Mehatl Creek

4

ROGERS CREEK

Rogers Creek

FSR

SOUTH TENAS Rd

Lillooet River

22

A B C D

2-10

3-16

3-15

31

Lillooet Lake

1.5km 0km 3km

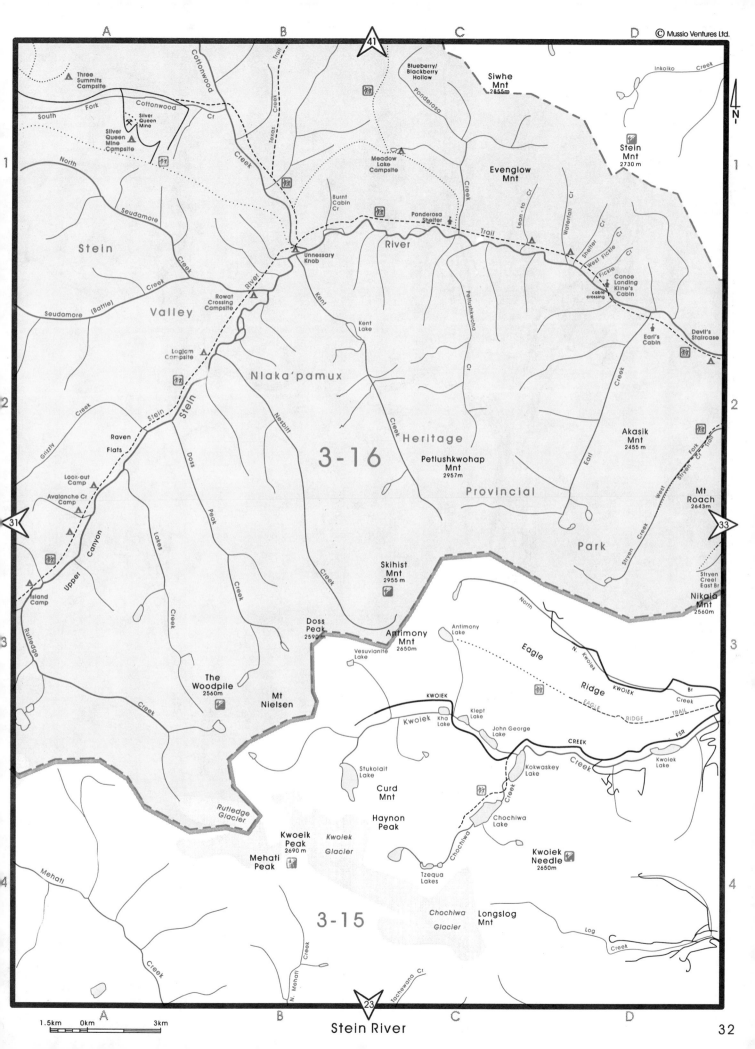

A B C D

N

41

23

31

33

Inkoiko Creek

Stein
Mnt
2730 m

Siwhe Mnt
2855 m

Blueberry/
Blackberry
Hollow

Three Summits
Campsite

Cottonwood Cr

Cottonwood Creek

South Fork

Silver Queen
Mine

Silver Queen
Mine Campsite

North

Seudamore Creek

Stein

Seudamore (Battle)

Creek

Valley

Rowat
Crossing
Campsite

Logiam Campsite

Stein River

Texas Creek

Trail

Meadow Lake
Campsite

Burnt Cabin
Cr

Unnessary Knob

River

Ponderosa

Ponderosa
Shelter

Evenglow
Mnt

Lean-to Cr

Waterfall Cr

Shelter Cr

West Fickle
Cr

Fickle

cable
crossing

Canoe
Landing

Kline's
Cabin

Earl's
Cabin

Devil's
Staircase

Akasik
Mnt
2455 m

Stryen Cr Trail

West Fork

Mt
Roach
2643m

Kent

Kent
Lake

Nlaka'pamux

3-16

Nesbitt

Petlushkwoha
Cr

Heritage

Petlushkwohap
Mnt
2957m

Provincial

Earl Creek

Stryen Creek

Park

Stryen Creel
East Br

Nikaia
Mnt
2560m

Grizzly Creek

Raven
Flats

Stein

Look-out
Camp

Avalanche Cr
Camp

Island
Camp

Rutledge

Upper Canyon

Doss Peak

Lakes Creek

Creek

Creek

Skihist
Mnt
2955 m

The
Woodpile
2560m

Doss
Peak
2590m

Mt
Nielsen

Antimony
Mnt
2650m

Antimony
Lake

Vesuvianite
Lake

North

Eagle

Ridge

N. Kwoiek
Br Creek

KWOIEK

EAGLE RIDGE TRAIL

Rutledge
Glacier

Kwoiek
Peak
2690 m

Mehati
Peak

Kwoiek
Glacier

Stukolait
Lake

Curd
Mnt

Haynon
Peak

KWOIEK

Kwoiek

Kha
Lake

Klept
Lake

John George
Lake

Kokwaskey
Lake

CREEK

Creek

F5R

Kwoiek
Lake

Chochiwa
Lake

Chochiwa Creek

Kwoiek
Needle
2650m

Mehati

3-15

Tzequa
Lakes

Chochiwa
Glacier

Longslog
Mnt

Log Creek

N. Mehati Creek

Creek

Tachewana Cr

1.5km   0km   3km

Stein River

32

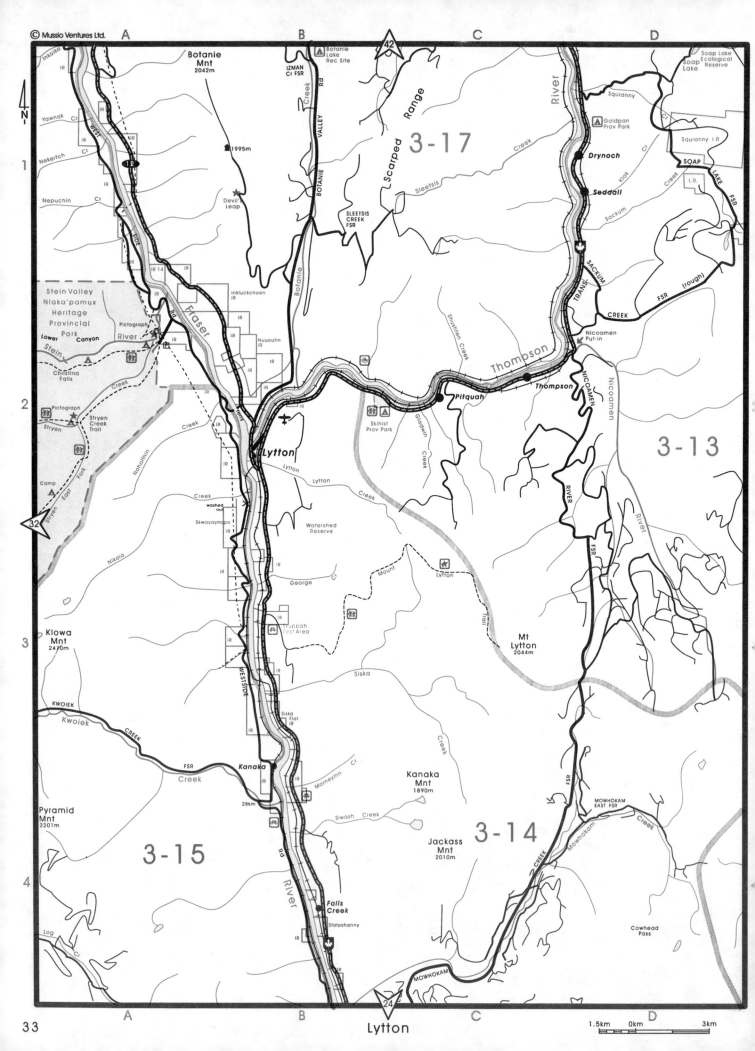

© Mussio Ventures Ltd.

A   B   C   D

42

Botanie
Mnt
2042m

Botanie
Lake
Rec Site

IZMAN
Cr FSR

Soap Lake
Ecological
Reserve

Soap
Lake

Inkolko

Yawnak Cr

Nekertch Cr

Nepuchin Cr

WEST SIDE IR

12

1995m

Devil's
Leap

BOTANIE VALLEY Rd

BOTANIE Creek

Scarped Range

Sleetsis

3-17

SLEETSIS
CREEK
FSR

River

Squianny

Goldpan
Prov Park

Drynoch

Seddall

Squianny I.R.

SOAP

I.R.

SOAP LAKE FSR

Klak Cr

Squianny

Creek

Stein Valley
Nlaka'pamux
Heritage
Provincial
Park

Lower
Stein
Canyon

Fraser
River

Christina
Falls

Pictograph

Inkluckcheen
IR

IR 14

Nuuoutin
IR

Shuhien Creek

TRANS- SACKUM FSR (rough)

CREEK

Nicoamen
Put-in

Sackum

Pictograph

Stryen
Creek
Trail

Stryen East Fork

Nohoithin Creek

Nikola Creek

IR

IR

IR

IR

IR

IR

IR

Skihist
Prov Park

Thompson

Pitquah

Thompson

Gladwin Creek

NICOAMEN RIVER

Nicoamen River

3-13

Camp

32

Klowa
Mnt
2470m

Lytton

washed
out

Skwayaynape

WEST SIDE Rd

Lytton Creek

Lytton Creek

Watershed
Reserve

George Cr

Skuppah
Rest Area

Mount Lytton Trail

Mt
Lytton
2044m

3

KWOIEK

Kwoiek CREEK

FSR

Kanaka

28km

Siska Flat IR

Siska

Morneyinn Cr

Kanaka
Mnt
1890m

Creek

FSR

Pyramid
Mnt
2201m

Log

3-15

Fraser River

Siwash Creek

Jackass
Mnt
2010m

3-14

MOWHOKAM
EAST FSR

CREEK

Mowhokam Creek

Cowhead
Pass

4

Falls
Creek

Stalyahanny

IR

MOWHOKAM

24

Lytton

33

1.5km   0km   3km

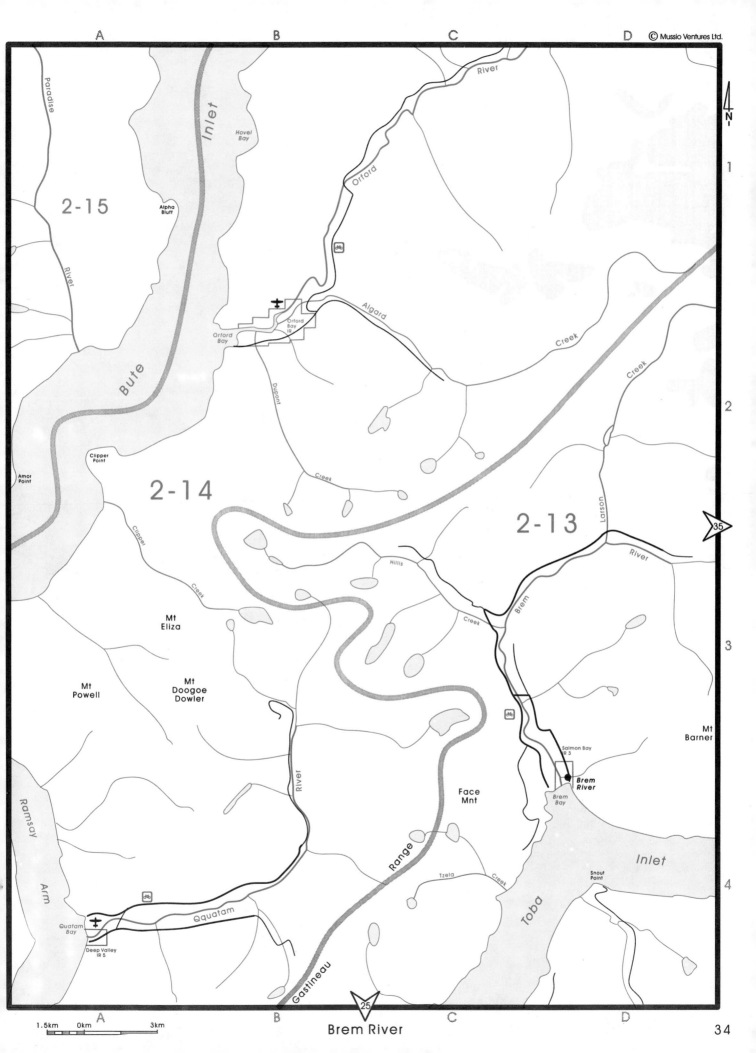

© Mussio Ventures Ltd.

A   B   C   D

N

Paradise

River

2-15

Hovel
Bay

Alpha
Bluff

Orford

River

Inlet

Orford
Bay
IR

Orford
Bay

Algard

Creek

Creek

1

2

Bute

Clipper
Point

Amor
Point

2-14

Dupont

Creek

2-13

Larson

Hillis

River

Creek

Brem

35

Clipper

Creek

Mt
Eliza

Creek

3

Mt
Powell

Mt
Doogoe
Dowler

Salmon Bay
IR 3

Brem
River

Mt
Barner

Ramsay

River

Face
Mnt

Brem
Bay

Inlet

Arm

Qquatam

Range

Tzela

Creek

Toba

Snout
Point

4

Quatam
Bay

Deep Valley
IR 5

Gastineau

25

Brem River

1.5km   0km   A   3km   B   C   D

34

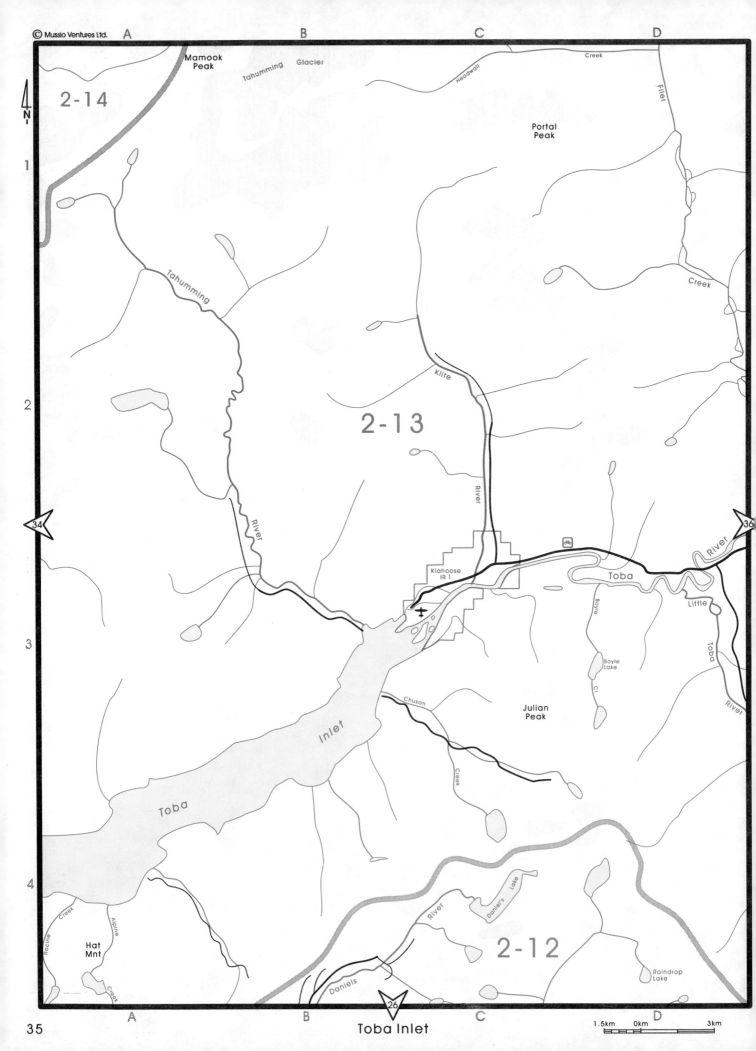

N

2-14

A   B   C   D

1

2

2-13

Tahumming Glacier

Mamook Peak

Portal Peak

Headwall

Creek

Flier

Creek

Tahumming

Klite

River

34

36

Toba

River

Klahoose IR 1

Little

Toba

Boyle

Boyle Lake

River

Cr.

Julian Peak

Chusan

Toba

Inlet

Creek

Daniel's Lake

3

River

2-12

Toba

Racine Creek

Hat Mnt

Alpine Creek

River

Daniels

Raindrop Lake

4

A   B   C   D

26

Toba Inlet

1.5km   0km   3km

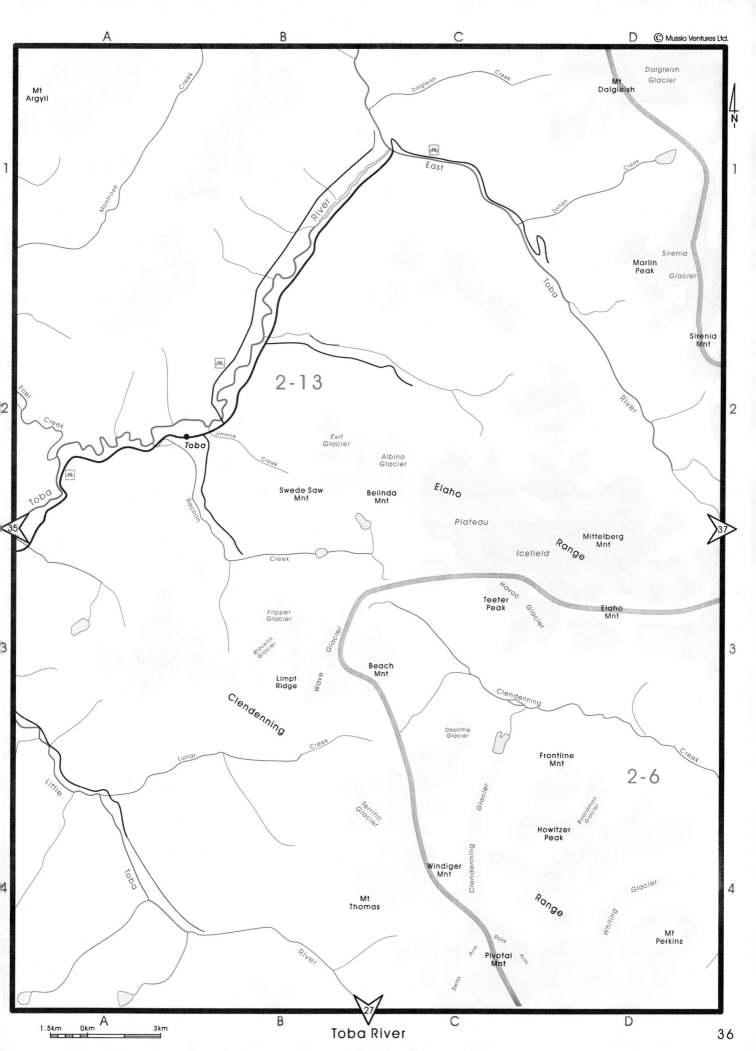

A   B   C   D

N

1

2

35

3

4

Mt
Argyll

Montrose

Creek

Dalgleish

Creek

Mt
Dalgleish

Dalgleish
Glacier

East

River

Toba

Creek

Zoltan

Sirenia

Marlin
Peak

Sirenia
Glacier

Sirenia
Mnt

2-13

Toba

River

37

Filer

Creek

Toba

Toba

Jimmie

Creek

Exit
Glacier

Albino
Glacier

Swede Saw
Mnt

Belinda
Mnt

Elaho

Racoon

Creek

Plateau

Icefield

Range

Mittelberg
Mnt

Havoc
Glacier

Elaho
Mnt

Flipper
Glacier

Teeter
Peak

Blacktin
Glacier

Wave
Glacier

Beach
Mnt

Limpt
Ridge

Clendenning

Clendenning

Doolittle
Glacier

Frontline
Mnt

Creek

2-6

Lunar

Creek

Glacier

Boardman
Glacier

Little

Terrific
Glacier

Howitzer
Peak

Toba

Windiger
Mnt

Clendenning

Glacier

Whiting

Mt
Thomas

Range

Mt
Perkins

River

Ross
Arm

Pivotal
Mnt

Swiss
Arm

27

Toba River

1.5km   0km   3km

A   B   C   D

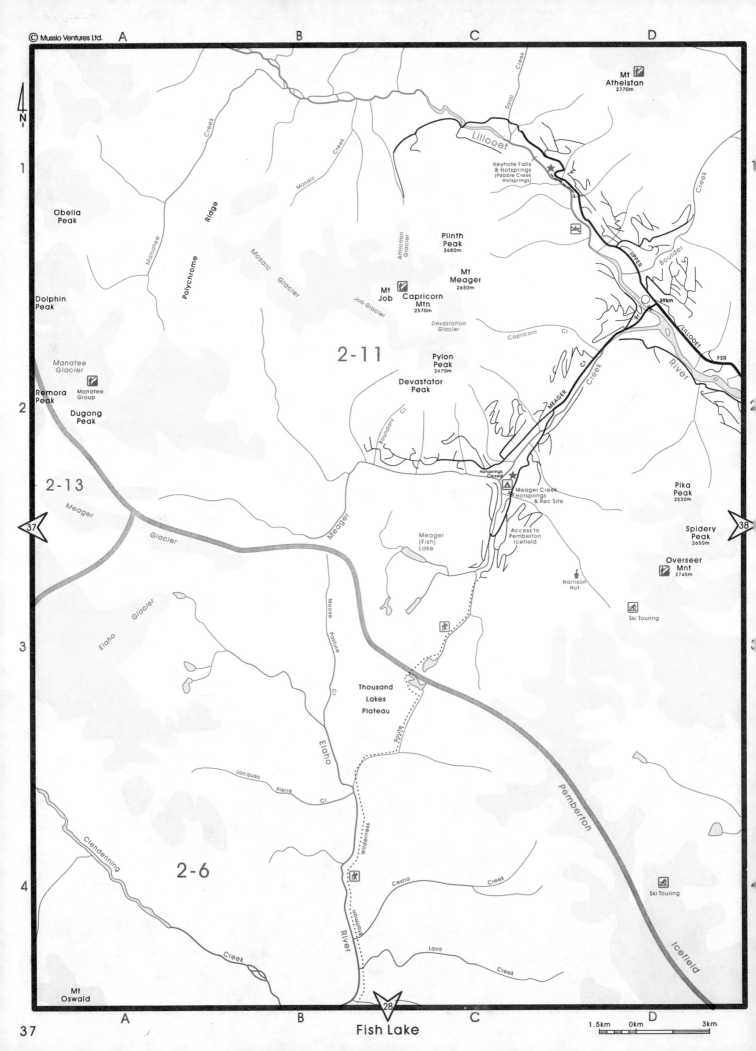

© Mussio Ventures Ltd.

N

A   B   C   D

1

Obelia
Peak

Dolphin
Peak

Manatee Glacier

Manatee
Group

Remora
Peak

Dugong
Peak

2-13

2

37

Meager   Glacier

Elaho   Glacier

Elaho

Jacques   Pierre   Cr

2-6

Clendenning

Mt
Oswald

Creek

Polychrome   Ridge

Mosaic   Glacier

Manatee   Creek

Mosaic   Creek

Affliction Glacier

Job Glacier

Mt
Job

Plinth
Peak
2680m

Mt
Meager
2650m

Capricorn
Mtn
2570m

Devastation Glacier

2-11

Pylon
Peak
2470m

Devastator
Peak

Boundary   Cr

Meager

Moose   Posture   Cr

Thousand
Lakes
Plateau

Poyte

Wilderness

Squamish   River

Lillooet

Keyhole Falls
& Hotsprings
(Pebble Creek
Hotsprings)

Capricorn   Cr

MEAGER   Creek

Cr

Hotsprings
Closed

Meager Creek
Hotsprings
& Rec Site

Meager
(Fish)
Lake

Access to
Pemberton
Icefield

Harrison
Hut

Cesna   Creek

Lava   Creek

Mt
Athelstan
2770m

Salal   Creek

Boulder   Creek

UPPER

39km

LILLOOET

River

FSR

Pika
Peak
2530m

Spidery
Peak
2650m

Overseer
Mnt
2745m

Ski Touring

Pemberton

Ski Touring

Icefield

38

1.5km   0km   3km

A   B   C   D

28

Fish Lake

37

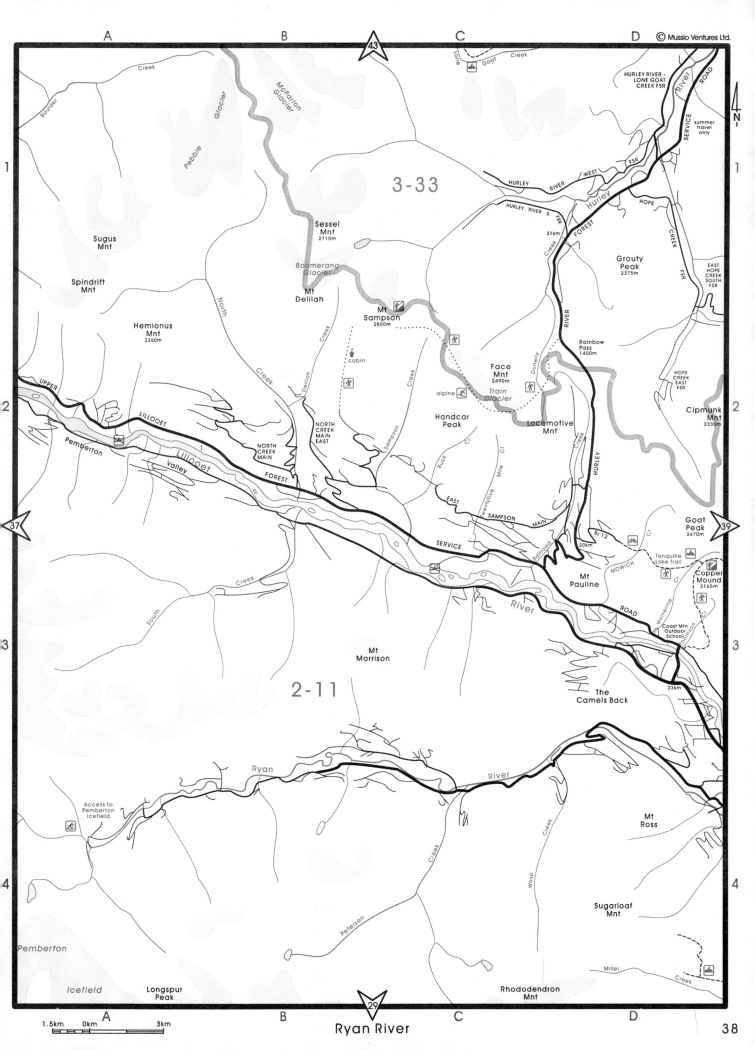

A   B   C   D

43

N

Boulder   Creek

McParlon Glacier

Pebble Glacier

3-33

1

HURLEY RIVER - LONE GOAT CREEK FSR

Lone   Goat   Creek

River

SERVICE   ROAD

summer travel only

Sugus Mnt

Sessel Mnt 2710m

HURLEY   RIVER   WEST   FSR

Hurley

HURLEY RIVER S. FSR

31km

FOREST

Hurley

HOPE   CREEK

EAST HOPE CREEK SOUTH FSR

Spindrift Mnt

Boomerang Glacier

Mt Delilah

Grouty Peak 2375m

Creek

1

Hemionus Mnt 2260m

North

Mt Sampson 2800m

cabin

Delilah   Creek

Creek

RIVER

Rainbow Pass 1400m

Donelly

HOPE CREEK EAST FSR

Cipmunk Mnt 2330m

2

37

UPPER

LILLOOET

Pemberton

Lillooet   Valley

NORTH CREEK MAIN

FOREST

NORTH CREEK MAIN EAST

alpine

Face Mnt 2490m

Train Glacier

Handcar Peak

Sampson   Creek

Buck   Cr

Twentyfive   Mile   Cr

EAST

SAMPSON   MAIN

Locomotive Mnt

Hurley   Creek

20km

Br 12

Goat Peak 2470m

39

Creek

SERVICE

Railroad

Mt Pauline

MOWICH   Cr

Tenquille Lake Trail

Copper Mound 2165m

2

River

Wolverine   Cr

ROAD

Thompson

Coast Mtn Outdoor School

Cr

3

South   Creek

Mt Morrison

2-11

River

The Camels Back

23km

3

Ryan

River

Wasp   Creek

Mt Ross

Access to Pemberton Icefield

Petersen

Sugarloaf Mnt

4

Pemberton

Icefield

Longspur Peak

Rhododendron Mnt

Miller   Creek

4

A   B   C   D

1.5km   0km   3km

29

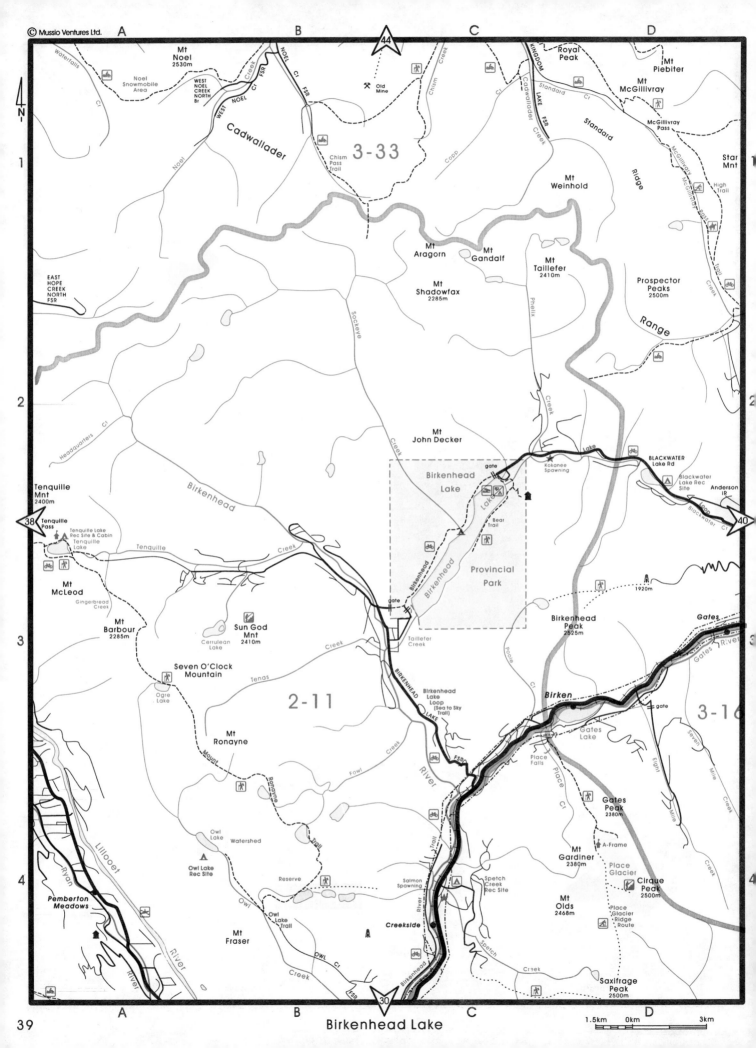

© Mussio Ventures Ltd.

A   B   C   D

N

44

Mt Noel 2530m

Noel Snowmobile Area

WEST NOEL CREEK NORTH Br

Cadwallader

3-33

Chism Pass Trail

Old Mine

Royal Peak

Mt Piebiter

Mt McGillivray

McGillivray Pass

Star Mnt

High Trail

McGillivray Pass

Standard Ridge

Mt Weinhold

EAST HOPE CREEK NORTH FSR

Birkenhead

Mt Aragorn

Mt Gandalf

Mt Shadowfax 2285m

Mt Taillefer 2410m

Prospector Peaks 2500m

Range

Sockeye

Mt John Decker

Birkenhead Lake

gate

Kokanee Spawning

BLACKWATER Lake Rd

Blackwater Lake Rec Site

Anderson IR

40

38

Tenquille Mnt 2400m

Tenquille Pass

Tenquille Lake Rec Site & Cabin

Tenquille Lake

Tenquille Creek

Bear Trail

Blackwater Cr

Mt McLeod

Gingerbread Creek

Birkenhead

Provincial Park

1920m

Mt Barbour 2285m

Cerulean Lake

Sun God Mnt 2410m

gate

Taillefer Creek

Birkenhead Peak 2525m

Gates

3-16

Seven O'Clock Mountain

Ogre Lake

Tenas

2-11

BIRKENHEAD LAKE

Birkenhead Lake Loop (Sea to Sky Trail)

Poole Cr

Birken

Gates Lake

gate

Mt Ronayne

Ronayne Trail

Fowl Creek

River

FSR

Place Falls

Place Cr

Gates River

Eight Mile Creek

Seven Mile Creek

Owl Lake

Watershed

Gates Peak 2380m

Lillooet

Owl Lake Rec Site

Reserve

Salmon Spawning

Spetch Creek Rec Site

A-Frame

Mt Gardiner 2380m

Place Glacier

Cirque Peak 2500m

Ryan River

Pemberton Meadows

Owl Lake Trail

Creekside

Birkenhead

River

Spetch

Mt Olds 2468m

Place Glacier Ridge Route

Mt Fraser

OWL Cr

Birkenhead

FSR

Spetch Creek

Saxifrage Peak 2500m

30

A   B   C   D

39

Birkenhead Lake

1.5km   0km   3km

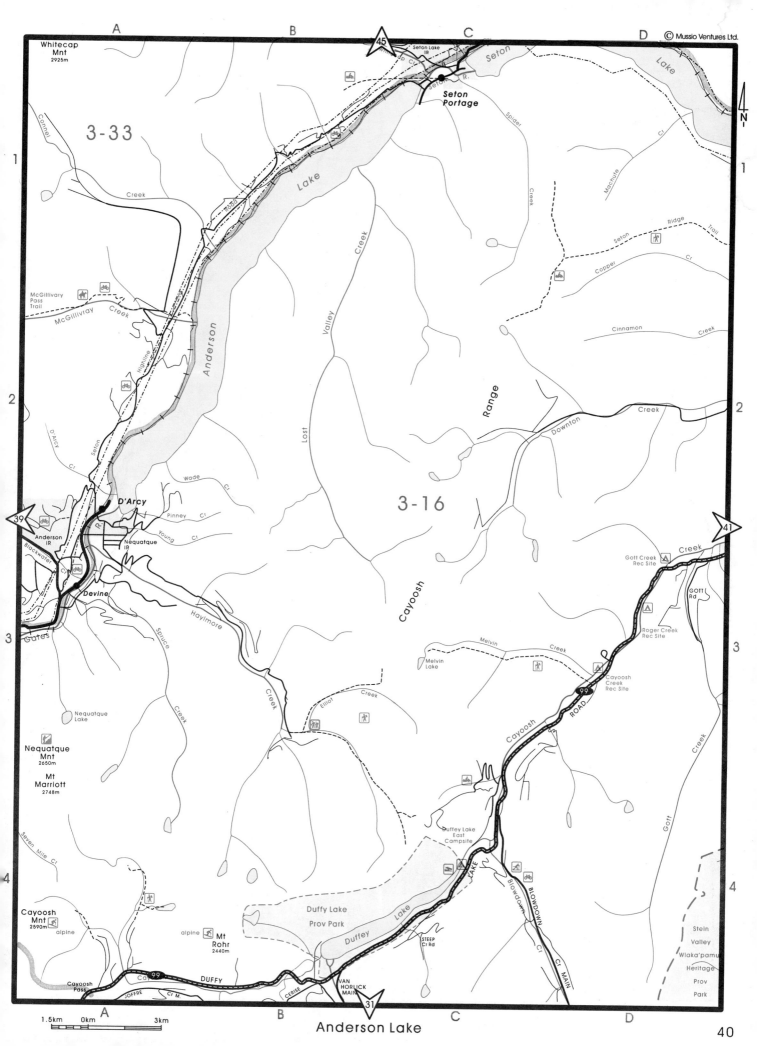

A   B   C   D

Whitecap
Mnt
2925m

3-33

N

Seton Lake
IR

Seton
Portage

Seton
Lake

1

Seton
Creek

Spider
Creek

Machute
Creek

Creek

Anderson
Lake

McGillivray
Pass
Trail

McGillivray Creek

Highline

Seton
Ridge
Trail

Copper
Creek

Cinnamon
Creek

2

Range

Downton
Creek

D'Arcy
Ct

Seton
Rd

D'Arcy

Wade
Ct

Pinney Ct

3-16

Cayoosh

Anderson
IR

Nequatque
IR

young
Ct

39

Blackwater

Cr

Devine

Gates

Haylmore

Spruce
Creek

Creek

Elliot
Creek

Melvin
Lake

Melvin
Creek

Gott Creek
Rec Site

Creek

41

GOTT
Rd

Roger Creek
Rec Site

Cayoosh
Creek
Rec Site

99

Cayoosh

ROAD

Gott
Creek

Nequatque
Lake

Nequatque
Mnt
2650m

Mt
Marriott
2748m

Seven Mile Cr

Duffey Lake
East
Campsite

4

Cayoosh
Mnt
2590m

alpine

alpine

Mt
Rohr
2440m

Duffy Lake
Prov Park

Duffy
Lake

STEEP
Cr Rd

Blowdown
Ct

Blowdown

LAKE

Stein
Valley
Wsáka'pamux
Heritage
Prov
Park

Cayoosh
Pass

99

JOFFRE
Cr M.

Ca

DUFFY

CERISE

VAN
HORLICK
MAIN

Duffy

31

GL MAIN

A   B   C   D

1.5km   0km   3km

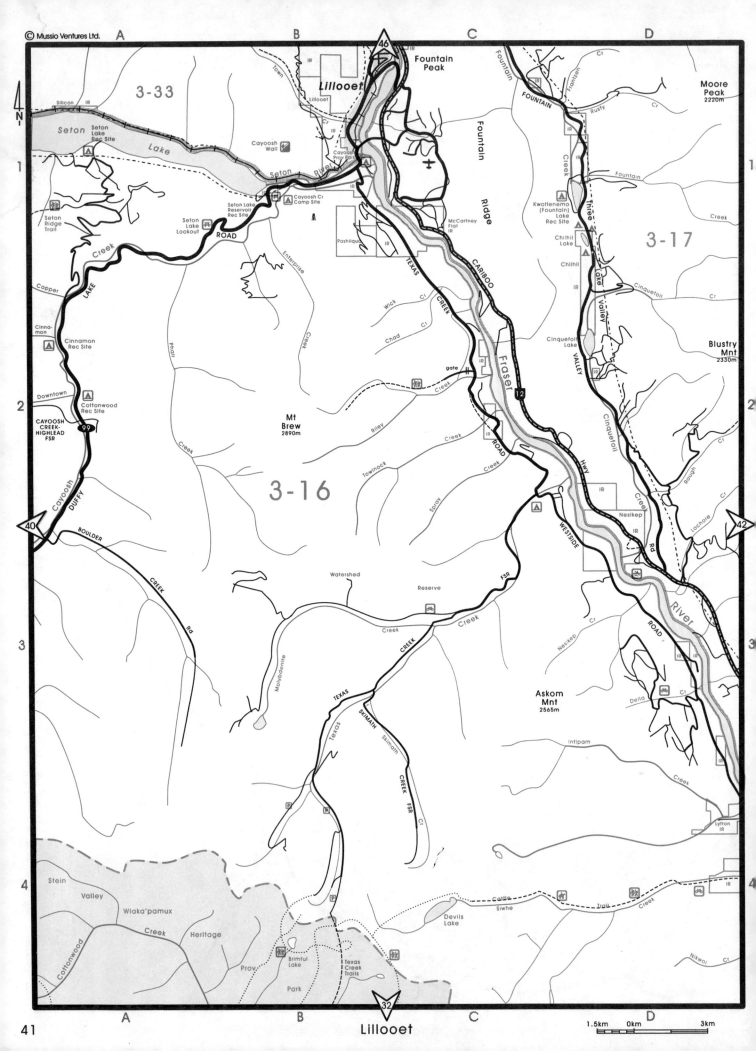

© Mussio Ventures Ltd.

A   B   C   D

N

3-33

Seton Lake

Silicon IR

Seton Lake Rec Site

Seton Ridge Trail

Copper

Cinnamon
Cinnamon Rec Site

Downtown
Cottonwood Rec Site

CAYOOSH CREEK-HIGHLEAD FSR

99

Cayoosh Creek Camp Site

Seton Lake Reservoir Rec Site

Seton Lake Lookout

ROAD

Seton River

Cayoosh Wall

Enterprise

Phair Creek

Creek

Mt Brew
2890m

3-16

Lillooet

46

Fountain Peak

Cayoosh Prov Park

Pashilqua
IR

McCartney Flat IR

Wick Cr

Chad

Riley Creek

Towinock

Spray Creek

Watershed

Reserve

Creek

Creek

TEXAS CREEK

Fountain Creek

Fountain

Moore Peak
2220m

FOUNTAIN

Rusty Cr

Kwotlenemo (Fountain) Lake Rec Site

Chilhil Lake

Three Lake

IR

Chilhil

Cinquefoil Lake

Cinquefoil

3-17

Blustry Mnt
2330m

CARIBOO

TEXAS

CREEK

Fraser

gate

IR

12

ROAD

Hwy

WESTSIDE

FSR

40

DUFFY

BOULDER

Cayoosh

CREEK Rd

42

Nesikep

IR

Cinquefoil Creek

VALLEY

Rough Cr

Lochore

River

ROAD

Nesikep Cr

Askom Mnt
2565m

Intlpam

Della Cr

Creek

Lytton IR

Stein Valley
Nlaka'pamux

Cottonwood Creek

Heritage

Prov. Park

Molybdenite

TEXAS

Texas

SKIMATH

Skimath

CREEK FSR

P

P

Brimtul Lake

Texas Creek Trails

P

32

Lillooet

Cattle Siwhe

Devils Lake

Trail Creek

Nikwoi Cr

41

1.5km   0km   3km

Lillooet

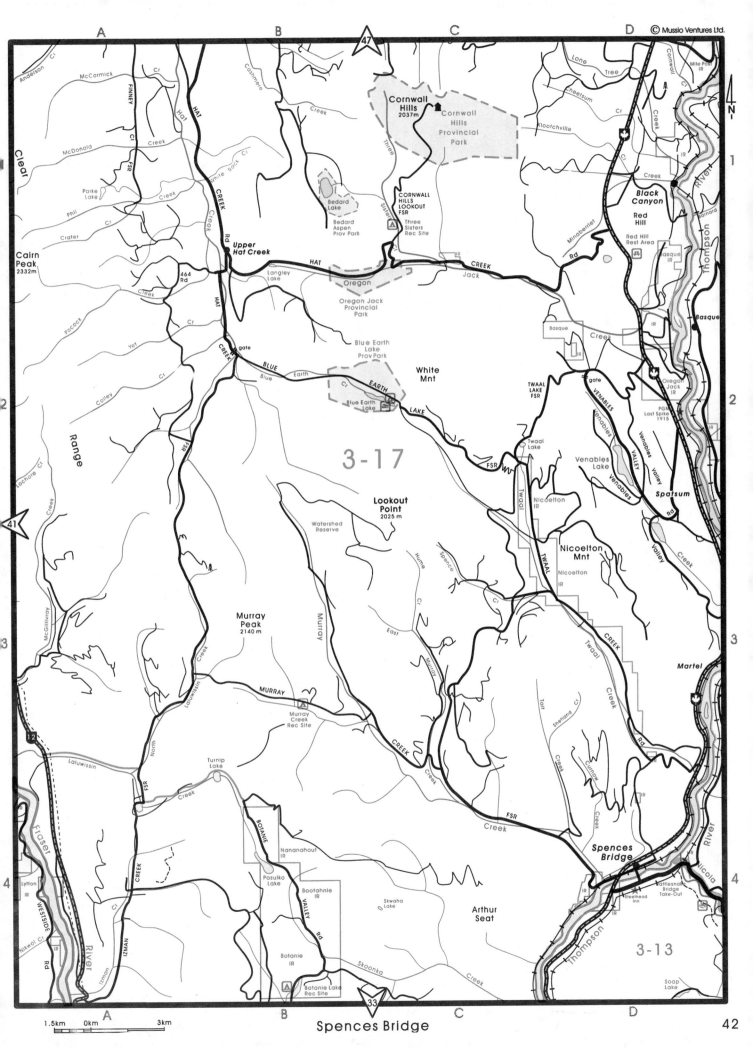

Spences Bridge

3-17

3-13

1.5km 0km 3km

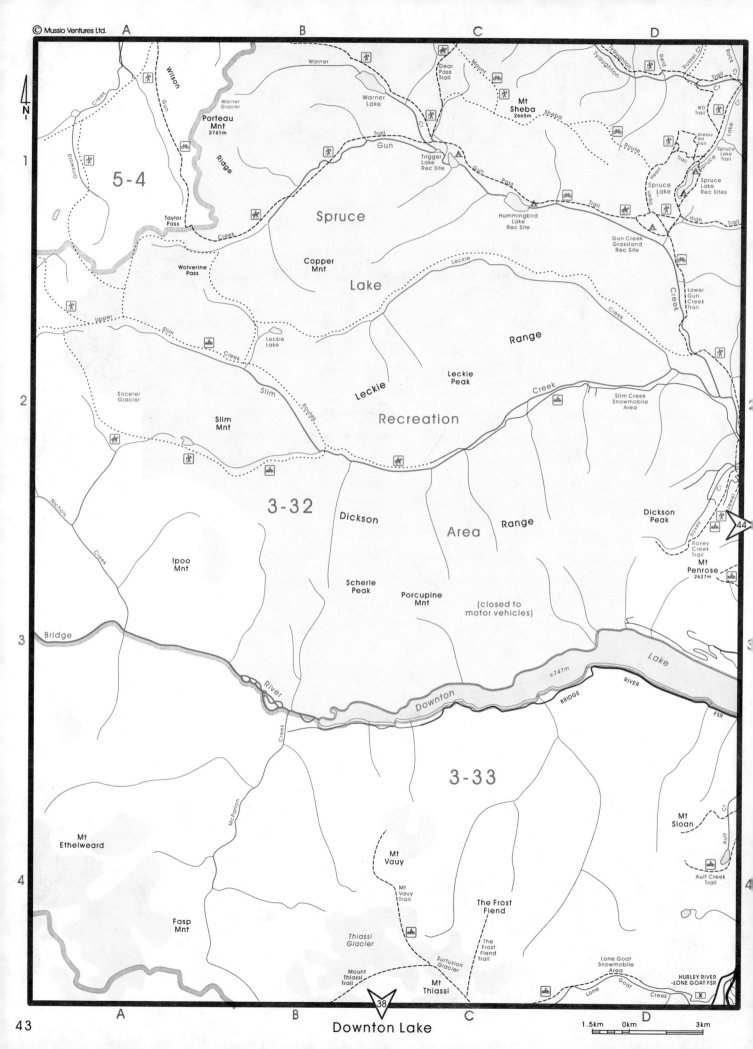

© Mussio Ventures Ltd.

A   B   C   D

N

Wilson

Gun

Griswold

Creek

1

5-4

Warner

Porteau
Mnt
2741m

Warner
Glacier

Warner
Lake

Ridge

Taylor Pass

Creek

Spruce

Gun

Trail

Trail

Gun

Trigger
Lake
Rec Site

Dear
Pass
Trail

Mount

Mt
Sheba
2665m

Sheba

Route

Tyaughton

Reid

Russel Cr

Rock Cr

WD
Trail

Cr

Greasy
Hill
Trail

Spruce
Lake
Trail

Spruce

Lake

Spruce
Lake
Rec Sites

Gun

Pass

Hummingbird
Lake
Rec Site

Gun Creek
Grassland
Rec Site

Lower
Gun
Creek
Trail

Wolverine
Pass

Copper
Mnt

Leckie

Creek

Creek

Upper

Slim

Creek

Slim

Leckie
Lake

Leckie

Leckie

Lake

Range

Leckie
Peak

Creek

Slim Creek
Snowmobile
Area

Socerer
Glacier

Slim

Slim
Mnt

Routes

3-32

Recreation

Dickson

Area

Range

Dickson
Peak

Jewel Cr

Roxey
Creek
Trail

Roxey Cr

Mt
Penrose
2627m

2

44

Nichols

Creek

Ipoo
Mnt

Scherle
Peak

Porcupine
Mnt

(closed to
motor vehicles)

3

Bridge

River

Creek

±747m

Downton

BRIDGE

Lake

RIVER

BRIDGE FSR

Mt
Ethelweard

McParlon

Creek

3-33

Mt
Sloan

Ault Cr

Fasp
Mnt

Mt
Vauy

Mt
Vauy
Trail

The Frost
Fiend

The
Frost
Fiend
Trail

Ault Creek
Trail

4

Thiassi
Glacier

Surfusion
Glacier

Mount
Thiassi
Trail

Mt
Thiassi

Lone Goat
Snowmobile
Area

Lone

Goat

Creek

HURLEY RIVER
-LONE GOAT FSR

A   B   C   D

38

Downton Lake

1.5km   0km   3km

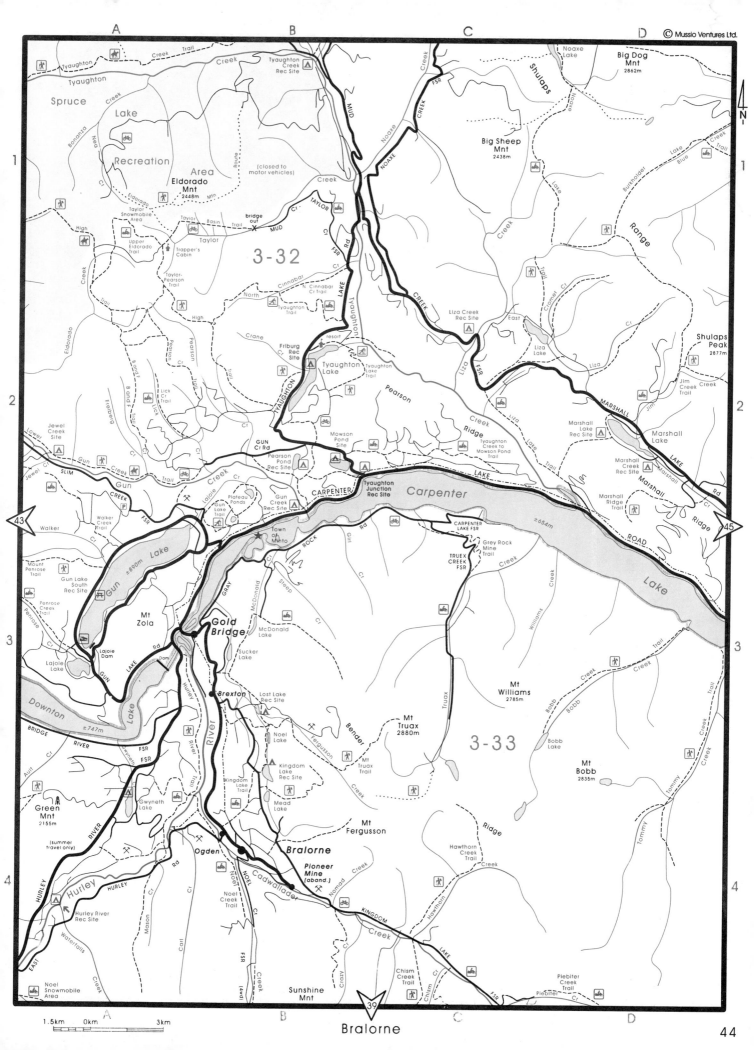

A
B
C
D

N

1

2

43

45

3

4

A
B
C
D

Spruce

Lake

Recreation

Area

Eldorado
Mnt
2448m

Tyaughton

Creek

Tyaughton

Tyaughton Creek
Rec Site

Bonanza

Nea

Cr

Eldorado

Cr

Taylor
Snowmobile
Area

Upper Eldorado
Trail

Trapper's
Cabin

High

Cr

Taylor Basin

Trail

(closed to
motor vehicles)

Route

bridge
out
X

MUD

Taylor

Cr

Cr

Taylor-Pearson
Trail

North

Cinnabar

Cr

N Cinnabar
Cr Trail

Cinnabar Cr Trail

TAYLOR

Cr

LAKE FSR

3-32

MUD

NOAXE

CREEK

Big Sheep
Mnt
2438m

Shulaps

Noaxe

Noaxe
Lake

Big Dog
Mnt
2862m

Creek

Burtholder
Lake

Blue

Lake

Creek

Trail

Range

Crane

Cr

Friburg
Rec Site

resort

Tyaughton
Lake

Tyaughton Lake
Trail

Pearson

Creek

Ridge

Liza Creek
Rec Site

East

Cramer

Cr

Liza

FSR

Liza Lake

Shulaps
Peak
2877m

Jim Creek
Trail

Jim

Cr

High

Cr

Pearson

Cr

Pearson

Trail

B and F

Lick

Cr

Lick Cr
Trail

TYAUGHTON

Jewel Creek
Site

Lower

Gun

Creek

Jewel Cr

SLIM

CREEK

Gun

GUN Cr Rd

Mowson
Pond
Site

Pearson Pond
Rec Site

CARPENTER

Tyaughton
Junction
Rec Site

Tyaughton Creek to
Mowson Pond Trail

Carpenter

LAKE

Liza

Lake

Trail

MARSHALL

Marshall
Lake
Rec Site

Marshall
Lake

Marshall

LAKE

Marshall Creek
Rec Site

Marshall Ridge
Trail

ROAD

2

Walker
Creek Trail

Walker

Cr

FSR

Gun Creek

Trail

Lajoie

Cr

Lajoie Lake
Trail

Plateau
Ponds

Gun Creek
Rec Site

CARPENTER

Rd

ROCK

Cr

Girl

Cr

Lake

±654m

CARPENTER
LAKE FSR

Grey Rock
Mine Trail

TRUEX
CREEK
FSR

Creek

Williams

Creek

Lake

Mount
Penrose
Trail

Gun Lake
South Rec Site

GUN

Gun

Lake

±890m

Mt
Zola

LAKE

Rd

Town
of Minto

GRAY

Cr

McDonald

Gold
Bridge

McDonald
Lake

Steep

Truex

Creek

Mt
Williams
2785m

Bobb

Creek

Bobb

Lake

Bobb

Creek

3

Penrose

Cr

Penrose
Creek Trail

Lajoie
Dam

Lajoie Lake

Dam

Sucker
Lake

Brexton

Lost Lake
Rec Site

Noel Lake

Bender

Fergusson

Cr

Mt
Truax
2880m

Truax

3-33

Mt
Bobb
2835m

Tommy

Creek

Tommy

Creek

Downton

Lake

±747m

BRIDGE

RIVER

Ault

Cr

Gwyneth

Cr

FSR

FSR

Hurley

River

River

Trail

Kingdom Lake
Rec Site

Kingdom Lake
Trail

Mead Lake

Mt
Truax
Trail

Creek

Ridge

Hawthorn Creek
Trail

Creek

Green
Mnt
2155m

RIVER

(summer
travel only)

Gwyneth
Lake

Hurley

Maon

Cr

Noel

Cr

Noel Creek
Trail

Kingdom

Mt
Fergusson

Hawthorn

Creek

4

HURLEY

EAST

Hurley

Waterfalls

Hurley River
Rec Site

Noel
Snowmobile
Area

Cr

Carl

Cr

Rd

Ogden

Noel

FSR

(4wd)

Creek

Cadwallader

Bralorne

Pioneer
Mine
(aband.)

Nomad

Creek

KINGDOM

Creek

LAKE

Crazy

Cr

Chism

Creek

Chism Creek
Trail

Chism

FSR

Cr

Piebiter

Creek Trail

Piebiter

Sunshine
Mnt

39

Bralorne

1.5km   0km   3km
A   B   C   D

44

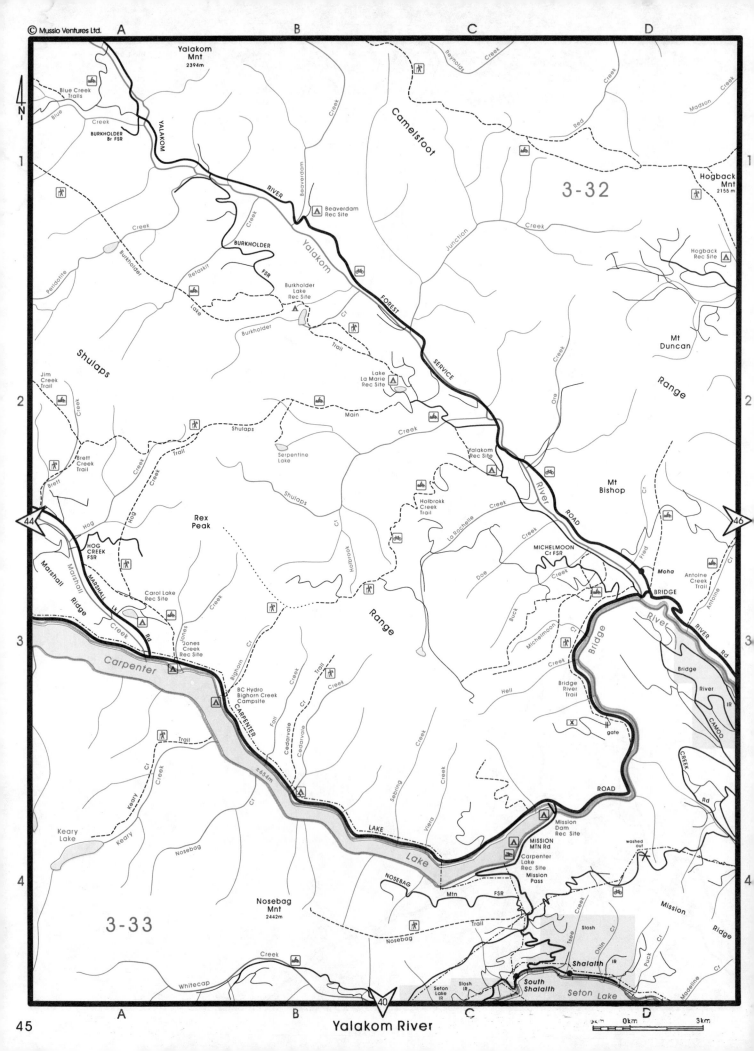

A   B   C   D

N

Yalakom Mnt
2394m

Blue Creek Trails

BURKHOLDER
Br FSR

Blue

Creek

3-32

Camelsfoot

Reynolds Creek

Hogback Mnt
2155 m

1

BURKHOLDER

Creek

Beaverdam Rec Site

Burkholder

Burkholder
Lake
Rec Site

FSR

YALAKOM

RIVER

Yalakom

FOREST

Junction Creek

Red

Madson Creek

Creek

Hogback
Rec Site

Creek

Shulaps

Jim Creek Trail

Creek

Refaskit

Lake

Burkholder

Shulaps

Lake
La Marie
Rec Site

Main

Creek

SERVICE

Ore

Creek

Mt
Duncan

Range

2

Brett Creek Trail

Brett

Shulaps

Trail

Serpentine
Lake

Shulaps

Cr

Holbrokk
Creek
Trail

Yalakom
Rec Site

River

Mt
Bishop

Cr

44

Rex
Peak

Hog

Hog

Holbrook

La Rochelle

Creek

Creek

ROAD

MICHELMOON
Cr FSR

Moha

Antoine Creek Trail

46

Marshall

Marshall Ridge

HOG
CREEK
FSR

Carol Lake
Rec Site

Creek

Jones Lk

Bighorn

Range

Doe

Creek

Buck

Michelmoon

Cr

BRIDGE

Bridge

River

Fred

Cr

Antoine

3

Carpenter

Creek

Jones
Creek Rec Site

BC Hydro
Bighorn Creek
Campsite

Cedarvale

Creek

Cr

Hell

Bridge
River
Trail

gate

Bridge
River
IR

CAMOO

3

Keary

Creek

Trail

Fall

Cedarvale

Sebing

Creek

Viera Creek

ROAD

Rd

CREEK

Keary
Lake

Keary

Cr

Nosebag

LAKE

Lake

Mission Dam
Rec Site

MISSION
MTN Rd

Mission
Pass

washed
out

4

3-33

Nosebag Mnt
2442m

NOSEBAG

Mtn

FSR

Carpenter Lake
Rec Site

Tsee Creek

Slosh

Onin Cr

Mission
Ridge

Puck Cr

Madeline Cr

4

Whitecap Creek

Nosebag

Trail

Shalalth

Seton Lake
IR

Slosh IR

Shalalth

South
Shalalth

Seton Lake

IR

40

45

0km   3km

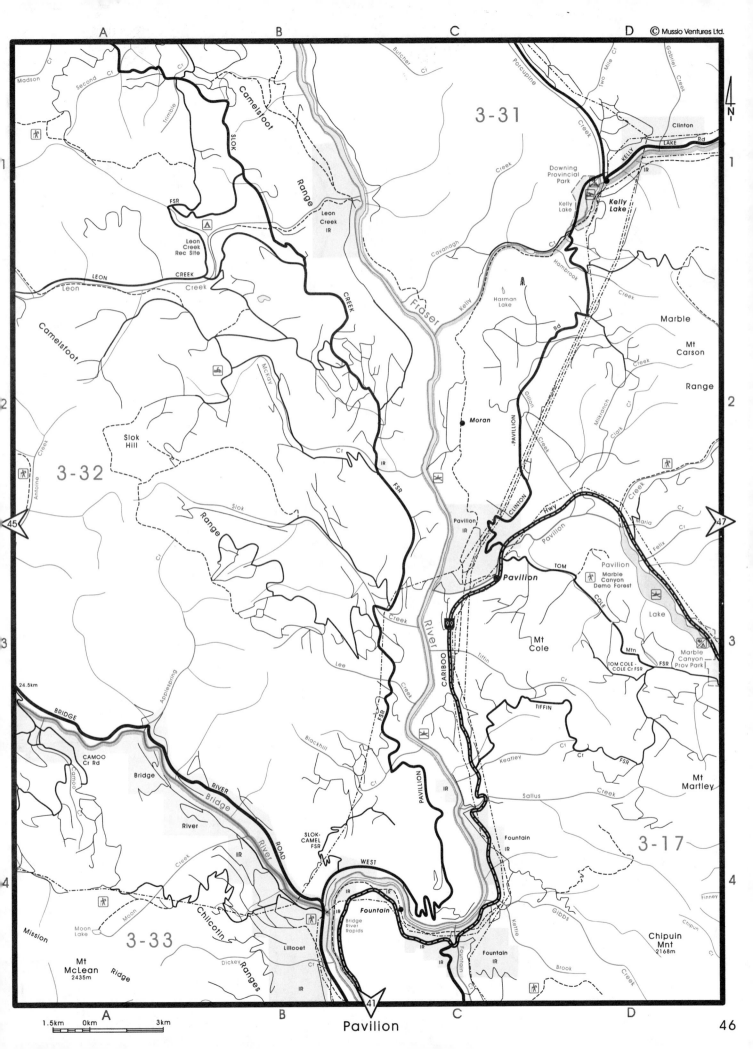

© Mussio Ventures Ltd.

N

3-31

A   B   C   D

1

Madson Cr
Second Cr
Trimble Cr
Butcher Ct
Porcupine
Creek
Two Mile Ct
Gabriel Creek
Clinton
KELLY LAKE Rd
Downing Provincial Park
Kelly Lake
Kelly Lake
IR
Camelsfoot Range
SLOK
FSR
Leon Creek Rec Site
Leon Creek IR
Creek
Cavanagh Creek
Hambrook Creek

2

LEON CREEK
Leon Creek
Camelsfoot
McKay Cr
CREEK
Fraser
Kelly
Harman Lake
Harman Lake
Marble
Mt Carson
Range
Gilon Ct

3-32
Antoine Creek
Slok Hill
Slok Cr
Range
Slok Cr
FSR
Moran
PAVILION
Milkranch Ct
Clark Ct

45
Pavilion IR
CLINTON
Hwy
Pavilion
Maria Ct
Felix Ct
47
TOM
Pavilion
Marble Canyon Demo Forest
Lake

Pavilion
COLE
Marble Canyon Prov Park

3
24.5km
BRIDGE
CAMOO Cr Rd
Bridge
RIVER
Bridge
River
Creek Cr
Lee Creek
Creek
CARIBOO River
99
Tiffin Ct
Mt Cole
TIFFIN
Mtn
TOM COLE - COLE Cr FSR
FSR
3
Mt Martley

Blackhill Cr
FSR
IR
PAVILION
IR
Keatley Ct
Ct
Ct
FSR

3-17

4
Camoo Creek
River ROAD
SLOK-CAMEL FSR
WEST
IR
IR
Fountain IR
Sallus Creek
Fountain
Mission
Moon Lake
Moon Cr
Chilcotin
IR
Fountain
Bridge River Rapids
IR
IR
Kettle Cr
Fountain IR
Gibbs Brook
Chipuin Mnt 2168m
4
Mt McLean 2435m
Ridge
3-33
Dickey Cr
Ranges
Lillooet
IR
Cr
Fountain Cr
Finney Cr

1.5km 0km 3km
A   B
Pavilion
41

C   D

46

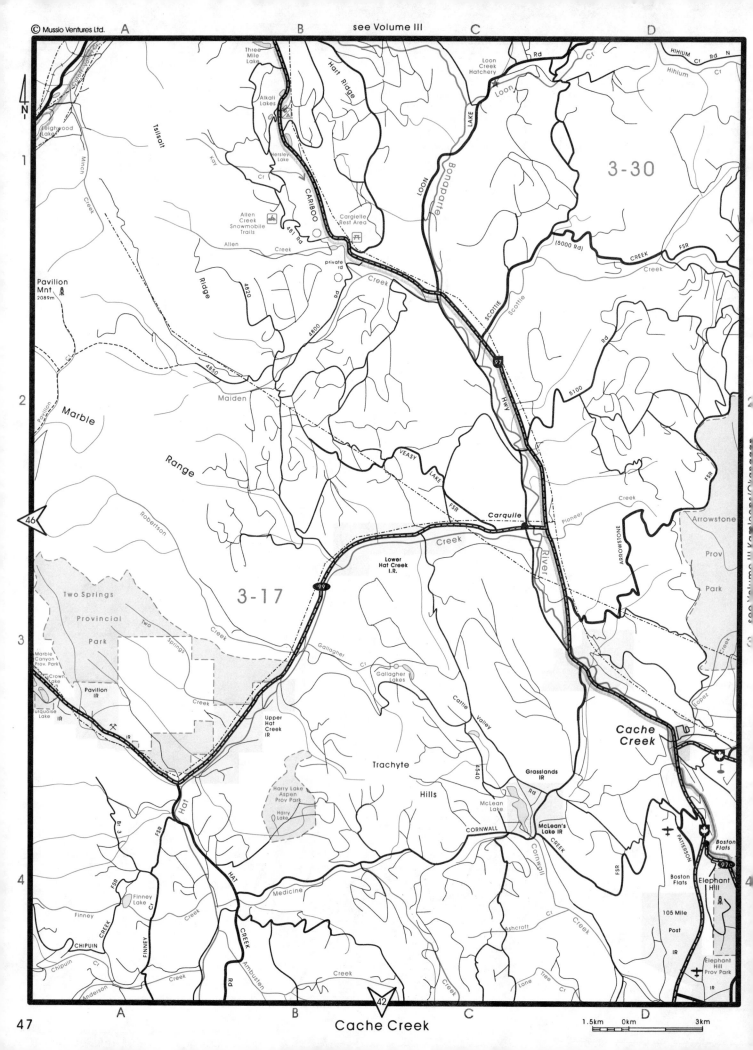

© Mussio Ventures Ltd.

A   B   C   D

N

3-30

Pavilion
Mnt
2089m

1

Marble

Range

46

3-17

Two Springs

Provincial

Park

Marble
Canyon
Prov. Park
Crown
Lake

Pavilion
IR

Turquoise
Lake   IR

3

Lower
Hat Creek
I.R.

Carquile

Arrowstone

Prov

Park

Cache
Creek

Upper Hat
Creek IR

Trachyte

Hills

Harry Lake
Aspen
Prov Park
Harry
Lake

Grasslands
IR

McLean
Lake

McLean's
Lake IR

CORNWALL

Boston
Flats

4

Finney
Lake

CHIPUIN

Elephant
Hill

105 Mile

Post

IR

Elephant Hill
Prov Park

A   B   C   D

Cache Creek

1.5km   0km   3km

Provincial Parks

Between 1993 and 1996, the NDP Government designated several new Provincial Parks during an intense push to preserve 12% of the provincial landbase as parks. Most of the newer parks have little in the way of developed facilities so are really not that attractive for recreation, except for backcountry expeditions. The older, more established parks, however, range from full facility roadside campgrounds to rugged wilderness areas. Regardless of your interests, you are certain to find a park that suites your needs.

Of note, several of the provincial parks in the region provides an opportunity to reserve camping space in advance of attending at the campground. Simply call Discovery Camping at 1-800-689-9025 (689-9025 in Greater Vancouver) and reserve a space so you will not be disappointed when you arrive at the provincial parks and find them to be full during most evenings in the summer. The reservation fee is presently $6/night.

Alexandera Bridge Provincial Park (Map #24/D4)
This small provincial park is a day-use site found in the Fraser Canyon next to Hwy #1. It marks the location of a bridge built in 1926 to replace the old suspension bridge built in 1863 for the Cariboo Wagon Road. The park offers a short trail system for you to explore the area.

Alice Lake Provincial Park (Map #20/C3)
This popular park is located north of Squamish off Hwy #99. Next to Alice Lake, there is a large camping facility (95 units) which is usually full throughout the summer months. There is also a picnic area, boat launch, showers, toilets and a beach at the campsite. Within the park is a total of four fishing lakes that all hold small Rainbow. A large trail network leads through the second growth timber around the lakes.

Apodaca Provincial Park (Map #10/D4)
This is a marine park on the eastern shores of Bowen Island. It has no developed facilities but it is a good place to moor your boat and explore the shoreline.

Arrowstone Provincial Park (Map #47/D3)
This new, 10,503ha park is located in the foothills northeast of Cache Creek. Portions of the provincial park are easily accessed by the Deadman-Cache Creek Road, Hwy #1 or Battle Creek FSR. The park preserves the Arrowstone Creek drainage as well as the Cache Creek Hills. No developed facilities are offered within the park.

Bedard Aspen Provincial Park (Map #42/C1)
This is a new park which contains Bedard Lake. The park has no developed facilities and is found on a 2wd spur road off the Hat Creek Road.

Birkenhead Lake (Map #39/C3)
Birkenhead Lake, which is encompassed by the provincial park, is truly spectacular because it has turquoise coloured water set in a steep valley capped by rugged mountain peaks. There is a campground at the north end of the lake containing over 90 camping site together with a picnic area, wharf, lawn, boat launch and sandy beach. The area receives heavy use throughout the summer months due to its spectacular scenery and well developed trails.

Blue Earth Provincial Park (Map #42/B2)
This new provincial park is easily accessed on the Blue Earth Lake Road and encompasses a track of land set below White Mountain including Blue Earth Lake. The old Blue Lake Rec Site is located at the east end of the lake and offers camping and cartop boat launch facilities.

Brandywine Falls (Map #20/C1, 29/C4)
At the north end of Daisy Lake right on Hwy #99, you will find this small provincial park. There are 15 campsites in the park together with a large pull-out area with picnic tables and toilets. There are several trails through the park, which are accentuated by mature forests. One of the trails leads to the Cal-Cheak Rec Sites and over Callaghan Creek Suspension Bridge (4km one way from the parking lot). Another trail leads to a viewing platform overlooking the 70m high Brandywine Falls.

Bridal Veil Falls Provincial Park (Map #4/D2)
This park is a rest area off Hwy #1. Tourist facilities are nearby (waterslide, children's park, trailer park and gas station). A short hike leads to the falls or for the more adventurous, you can access Cheam Peak along a difficult, steep trail.

Buccaneer Bay Marine Park (Map #9/B3)
This marine park is located at the southern tip of North Thormanby Island and is a great diving area with a broad sandy beach. North Thormanby Island is actually a large sand dune with spectacular sand cliffs. There is limited development at the marine park but large sheltered bay provides safe moorage.

Cayoose Provincial Park (Map #41/B1)
Cayoose Provincial Park is a small park found next to the Fraser River south of Lillooet. It has a campground next to the river as well as a rocky beach. The park is easily accessed by Hwy #99.

Chilliwack Lake Provincial Park (Map #5/C4)
Located at the north end of Chilliwack Lake, this popular park has over 100 camping units together with a boat launch, picnic area and beach. The forested campground is usually full throughout the summer due to its proximity to Greater Vancouver. The lake is easily accessed by the Chilliwack Lake Road. Several popular trails (Post-Greendrop Trail and Radium Lake Trail) lead from the park.

Chilliwack River Park (Map #4/C4)
On the Chilliwack Lake Road (paved), this park is a day-use area complete with picnic tables and a beach. Fishermen, picnickers and kayakers use the park as a stop-over for other destinations within the Chilliwack River Valley.

Copeland Islands Marine Park (Map #16/B1,25/B4)
To the northwest of Lund, this provincial park encompasses scenic Copeland Islands. The area is a sanctuary for birds as well as an excellent area for scuba diving. It is often visited by sea kayakers heading to Desolation Sound. Wilderness camping and protected anchorages are available. There is no developed facilities in the park.

Coquihalla Canyon Rec Area (Map #15/D4)
Formed in 1986, this popular recreation area is found just east of Hope. The main attraction is the spectacular Othello Tunnels, which can be hiked or biked. Forming part of the historic Kittle Valley Railway, the area has also been used in several films including First Blood.

Cornwall Hill Provincial Park (Map #42/C1)
To the west of Ashcroft, the provincial park can be accessed by the Cornwall Lookout Road, which leads to the summit of Cornwall Hill at 2055m. The new park preserves Cornwall Hill together with their surrounding slopes. There are no developed facilities in the new park.

Cultus Lake Provincial Park (Map #4/B4)
Cultus Lake is an extremely popular recreation area complete with private and public campgrounds, water slides, motels, go-charts, mini-golf and restaurants. The park is easily accessed by Vedder Road and Columbia Valley Hwy south of Chilliwack and contains a 300 unit campground. In the park is a large sandy beach, swimming area, boat launch, and picnic area. Water sports are the main attraction to the lake, although hiking and horseback riding trails are found in the hills above the eastern shore of the lake.

Cypress Provincial Park (Map #11/B4)
Cypress Provincial Park is found in the North Shore Mountains. It encompasses Cypress Bowl Ski Area, which is a multi-use area popular with downhill skiers, X-C skiers and snowmobilers in the winter and hikers and mountain bikers in the summer. The park extends northward encompassing the Howe Sound Crest Trail all the way to the Deeks Lake area. The northernmost portion of the park is accessed either by steep trails leading sharply upward from Hwy #99 to Deeks Lake or by hiking the Howe Sound Crest Trail past the Lions. Spectacular scenery and rugged mountain terrain draw hoards of people to this provincial park.

Davis Lake Provincial Park (Map #3/C1)
Davis lake Provincial Park is found on the Lost Creek FSR to the east of Stave Lake. It is a day-use park which is used primarily by fishermen and sunbathers.

Desolation Sound Provincial Marine Park (Map #25/C3)

Encompassing Gifford Peninsula as well as several small islands, this provincial park is one of the premier paddling area on the coast. It receives heavy use during the summer months by ocean kayakers as well as fishermen despite its remote access from Lund or Okeover Inlet. B.C.'s largest marine park is renowned for its warm water and the millions of oysters which multiply on the rocky shoreline of the marine park. There are several designated camping areas for visitors. For more details on the park, consult the fishing and paddling sections of this book.

Downing Provincial Park (Map #46/D1)

This park is accessed off Hwy #12 via Jesmond Road, a good 2wd road. It encompasses Kelly Lake and offers a good alternative to get away from crowded conditions of other provincial parks. A campground and boat launch is situated at the north end of the windy lake, which is located on a broad open pleateau.

Duffey Lake Provincial Park: (Map #40/B4)

This new 2,379ha provincial park surrounds beautiful Duffey Lake. Its facilities include picnic sites and a day use parking. This is a popular spot for fishing, canoeing or kayaking. The existance of a pit toilet is an added bonus.

Elephant Hill Provincial Park (Map #47/D4)

Situated south of Cache Creek, this park was created in 1995. It is easily accessed by Hwy #97 and contains no facilities.

Emory Provincial Park (Map #'15/C2)

Emory Provincial Park is a roadside park next to the Fraser River and Hwy #1. It contains 34 camping units and is used mainly as a stopover for travellers on the TransCanada Highway.

F.H. Barber Provincial Park (Map #5/A1)

The park is a small day-use area on the banks of the Fraser River used by travellers on the TransCanada Highway.

Garden Bay Marine Park (Map #9/B1)

Encompassing an area north of Mt. Daniels, this small marine park has hiking trails as well as a picnic area and tiny dock. It is easily accessed off the Garden Bay Road or by boat into Pender Harbour. Claydon Road leads from the Garden Bay Road to the park entrance. Within the park is a short easy trail that leads to the rocky shoreline. On the rock bluffs next to the ocean is a stand of juniper trees, which is a rare site for the Sunshine Coast.

Garibaldi Provincial Park (Map #20,21,29,30)

Garibaldi Provincial Park is a massive park located east of Hwy#99. It is highlighted by rugged snow-capped peaks, endless alpine and untouched wilderness. Cheakamus Lake, Diamond Head and Black Tusk are the three key access points into the park and give good access to the extensive backcountry trail networks leading into the remote areas of the park. Please refer to the trail and fishing sections of this book for the various recreation options.

Golden Ears Provincial Park (Map #2,3,13)

Golden Ears is a massive park situated between Stave and Pitt Lakes. It is accessed by Fern Crescent from Dewdney Truck Road. The park is noted for its rugged and remote mountain terrain to the north and its multi-use area to the south. Next to Alouette Lake are three different camping areas (Alouette, Gold Creek and North Beach) with a total of 344 camping units. Within the campgrounds are full facilities ranging from boat launches, sani-stations, showers and toilets. There is also a picnic area at the south end of Alouette Lake and a swimming beach at the south end of the day-use area. An extensive multi-use trail network leads through the southern portion of the park.

Goldpan Provincial Park (Map #33/D1)

Located right next to Hwy #1 (and between 2 busy railroads), this 5ha provincial park is best used as a stop over for travellers on Hwy #1. The provincial park is open year round and provides 14 vehicle/tent campsites as well as a day-use area for people who wish to explore the Thompson River for fishing or paddling opportunities. The provincial park is set within the dry pine/sage brush country typical of the Thompson River Valley.

Halkett Bay Provincial Park (Map #10/D3, 11/A3)

This park is reached by boat to Gambier Island. It not only contains over 10 picnic sites but also marks the start of a scenic trail to Mt. Artaban. Mooring buoys, dinghy floats and pit toilets are the other facilities at the park.

Harmony Islands Marine Park (Map #18/B2)

Harmony Islands Marine Park is found in the Hotham Sound. There are no facilities but it is a scenic area to visit given the waterfalls cascading from Freil Lake. The park also marks the location of a fairly good salmon fishing area.

Harry Lake Aspen Provincial Park (Map #47/B4)

This new park is located to the south of Hwy #99 and preserves a small area around Harry Lake. There are no developed facilities in the park.

Indian Arm Provincial Park (Map #2,12)

This newly created 8400ha park encompasses the rugged mountain terrain surrounding the Indian Arm. There is very little access to the park except by boat or by hiking the Dilly Dally Trail. Several diving, fishing and water sport areas are found within the Indian Arm. The Arm is ideal for an afternoon boat trip or a two-three day paddle given the beautiful scenery including some spectacular granite falls.

International Ridge Provincial Park (Map #4/B4)

Located just east of Cultus Lake, the park encompasses the slopes of Mount Amadis. The main attraction to the park is the International Ridge Trail.

Joffre Lakes Rec Area (Map #31/A1)

The rec area is located on the Duffey Lake Road and is marked by a parking lot, which can be used as an overnight pull-out. The popular trail begins at the road and leads past 3 sub-alpine lakes. All 3 lakes provide good fishing for small Rainbow throughout the early summer and fall as well as rustic camping. The last lake, which is set beneath rugged mountain peaks accentuated by glaciers, is truly spectacular.

Kawkawa Provincial Park (Map #15/D4)

This popular provincial park is just east of Hope off the Kawkawa Lake Road. The park has a day-use area complete with a nice beach, warm water and boat launch. The park is busy on sunny summer days.

Kilby Provincial Park (Map #4/B2)

This park is found next to Harrison Bay off Hwy#7. There are a total of 38RV/ tent sites at the park together with a boat launch, picnic area and beach. History buffs and fishermen frequent the area.

Manning Provincial Park (Map #6,7)

Manning Provincial Park is a large high elevation park, which is easily accessed by Hwy #3 east of Hope. Recreationists can enjoy the park year round from any number of different locations. The hub of the park is the Manning Park Lodge and Lightning Lake area. At the lodge you will find full facilities including a hotel, restaurant and stores. Lightning Lake is the main camping area with a total of 143 units crammed into a forested area next to the lake. Ten kilometres further east is the Mule Deer Campground, which has 49 camping units, some of them right next to the Hwyand others along the Similkameen River. Campers can also enjoy the Hampton Campground. All of these campsites fill quickly during the summer months.

Please note that there are no power hook-ups at the campgrounds in the park. For a wilderness camping experience, try Poland Lake. In the winter, there are 73.5km of X-C ski trails available at Cambie Creek and Three Brothers as well as the popular Gibson Pass area which provides groomed X-C trails and a descent downhill area. In the summer, fishing, hiking, horseback riding and mountain biking are all popular activities.

Other attractions include: Cascade Lookout Road, which leads from near the park headquarters to the sub-alpine; Rhododendron Flats and Sumallo Grove both offer wonderful displays of blooming rhododendrons in June. For further information on the extensive trail network in the park, please refer to the trail section of this book.

Marble Canyon Provincial Park (Map #46/D3,47/A3)

This small (335ha) provincial park is situated on Hwy #12 east of Pavilion. It encompasses Turquoise and Crown Lakes, two small scenic lakes set at the base of 1000m high limestone cliffs. There are a total of 34 campsites between the lakes. Picnicking, swimming, fishing and hiking are the primary attractions.

Murrin Provincial Park (Map #11/B1)

Murrin Provincial Park is a roadside park on Hwy #99, which has a large pull-out area as well as a series of picnic tables next to Browning Lake. This small lake provides an opportunity for a family to catch small Rainbow in the 20-25cm range. A rugged trail leads from the parking lot to Petgill Lake to the east.

Mount Seymour Provincial Park (Map #11,12)
The Mount Seymour Parkway winds its way up the mountainside providing spectacular view of Vancouver along the way. At the top, you will enter the 3508ha park, which encompasses Mount Seymour (1453m), Mount Elsay (1418m) and Mount Bishop (1508m). The park is a year round recreation area with downhill skiing and X-C ski trails in the winter and an extensive hiking trail network in the summer (see the trail section of this book for details). Horseback riding and mountain biking are only permitted on the Old Buck Trail. There are four picnic areas within the park but no developed camping. Tenting in the subalpine is permitted north of Brockton Point.

Nairn Falls Provincial Park (Map #30/B2)
Despite its scenic surroundings, the park is not as popular as other parks to the south. There are a total of 88 campsites in the park which are all in close proximity to Green River. A short, easy trail leads to the 60m high Nairn Falls and onto One Mile Lake. The park is easily accessed by Hwy #99 south of Pemberton. Fishing on Green River can produce some Dollies and Rainbows.

Okeover Provincial Park (Map #16/C1)
This small provincial park overlooks Okeover Inlet and a private oyster farm. The park is accessed by the Malaspina Road and a short hike. It has a total of 9 camping spots, which are usually full throughout the summer months, that are very close to one another so there is not much privacy. There is an undeveloped boat launch together with 5 picnic tables, firewood, government wharf and a water pump at the campground. The park is used as a stop-over for paddlers to Desolation Sound.

Oregon Jack Provincial Park (Map #42/C2)
Easily accessed on the Hat Creek Road, this small provincial park preserves a portion of the Oregon Jack Creek drainage. There are no developed facilities in this new park.

Pinecone-Burke Provincial Park (Map #2,12)
This newly created park (1995) encompasses a 36,955ha area to the west of Pitt Lake. The park is considered Vancouver's closest and most rugged protected wilderness with its glacier covered peaks and 500+ year old growth trees. Hiking the Fools Gold Route (see hiking section) is the best way (but not the easiest way) to explore this vast wilderness park. The Burke Mountain Trails also provide access to the southern tip of the park.

Plumper Cove Marine Park (Map #10/C4)
This marine park is located on the northwestern shores of Keats Island. There are 20 rustic tenting pads in the park together with a picnic area, hiking trails and a beach. The park encompasses the highest point on Keats Island and is easily accessed by bike, foot or vehicle from the government wharf which, in turn, is reached by ferry (Dogwood Princess). Alternatively, take your boat to the park and tie up to the wharf or use the mooring buoys.

Porpoise Bay Provincial Park (Map #9/D2)
This small provincial park is located on the shores of Porpoise Bay in Sechelt Inlet. It is easily accessed by the Sechelt Inlet Road and has 84 campsites with full facilities including a sani-dump, 25 picnic tables and showers. Hiking trails and the large sandy beach are the main attractions to the park. The trail network leads to the estuary of Angus Creek for a great view of the Sechelt Inlet as well as a chance to see some waterfowl. Other trails in the park lead through old growth timber. In the fall, spawning salmon can be seen swimming up the creek.

Porteau Cove Provincial Park (Map #11/A2)
This provincial park is located next to Howe Sound right off Hwy #99. It is a popular diving area given the numerous underwater adventures (several sunken ships and a concrete gymnasium). There are 2 concrete boat launches together with a wharf at the park. Slightly to the south of the main parking area is a camping area set in a forest on the shore of the Sound. There are a total of 59 camping spots in the area together with picnic facilities, a sani-station and showers.

Princess Louisiana Provincial Park (Map #27/D2)
This remote provincial park is located at the end of the gorgeous Princess Louisiana Inlet, a fjord-like inlet highlighted by 1500m high sheer granite walls and the spectacular 45m high Chatterbox Falls. Despite its remote access, it is popular with kayakers and boaters. The park provides 5 camping spots together with a trail system leading to the falls and beyond. Its scenic beauty makes this provincial park a must see location if you are interested in a long boat excursion. It takes about 10 hours by powerboat or 5 days by kayak from Saltery Bay or Earls Cove to reach this spectacular inlet.

Roberts Creek Provincial Park (Map #10/A3)
Off Hwy #101 west of Gibsons, this provincial park spans on both sides of the Hwy in a lightly forested area. There are a total of 24 campsites together with sani-facilities, a boat launch, sheltered picnic tables, portable water, washrooms and hiking trails. A nice beach is found next to the ocean.

Rolley Lake Provincial Park (Map #3/B2)
Located to the west of Hayward Lake on Bell Road off the Dewdney Trunk Road, the park has 64 camping units as well full facilities (showers, picnic tables, sani-station, flush toilets and a boat launch). The park receives heavy use throughout the summer with swimming, fishing, paddling and hiking being the main recreation pursuits. A short hike leads around the lake and to Rolley Falls.

Roscoe Bay Provincial Park (Map #25/B3)
Encompassing a small fjord of West Redonda Island, this provincial park has tenting and toilet facilities. Visitors to the park can anchor in the inlet and portage to Black Lake where excellent fishing is offered.

Saltery Bay Provincial Park (Map #17/D3)
This provincial park is found just west of the ferry landing at Saltery Bay. It has 42 campsites at the south end of the park together with two day-use areas, one adjacent to the camping area and one 2km north. The park also has hiking trails, a boat launch and great scuba diving. Of interest is the Emerald Mermaid, Canada's first underwater statue.

Sappers Provincial Park (Map #5/D4)
This tiny park is situated on the southern shores of Chilliwack Lake. There is a small tenting area in the park. Access to the park is via boat or a blocked road past the Depot Creek Rec Site.

Sargeant Bay Provincial Park (Map #9/C3)
This tiny provincial park has a picnic area and beach set in a sheltered, undeveloped bay west of Sechelt. The provincial park is easily accessed on Redroofs Road from Hwy #101. About 15m beyond the parking lot, a trail leads along the waterfront providing a great opportunity to view waterfowl, a small man-

made lake (Colvin Lake) and fishing ladders. In the fall, spawning salmon are the attraction.

Sasquatch Provincial Park (Map #5/A1, 15/A4)
To the east of Harrison Lake, this park is easily accessed by a paved road (Rockwell Drive). There is a picnic ground with a beach, a large parking area, boat launch and tables next to Hicks Lake. The 177 unit campground is located in a forested area next to Deer Lake. The campground, which is almost certainly full during the summer weekends, has full facilities including toilets, sani-station, beach, boat launch, etc. Within the park is a series of descent fishing lakes (Deer Lake, Beaver Pond and Hicks Lake) and a good trail system.

Sechelt Inlet Marine Parks (Map #9/D2)
Along the shores of the Sechelt Inlet, Narrows Inlet and Salmon Inlet are eight small marine parks (Piper Point Marine Park, Tuwanek Point Marine Park, Nine Mile Point Marine Park, Thornhill Marine Park, Tzoonie Narrows Marine Park, Skalakos Point Marine Park, Halfway Inlet Marine Park, Kunechin Point Marine Park). Each of the marine parks have a tenting area for boaters and paddlers exploring the sheltered inlets. The inlets are highlighted by high fjords, steep rock walls and sandy beaches. The parks are also ideal locations for scuba divers. For example, at Kunechin Point, the HMCS Chaudiere, a former warship, was sunk in 1992 providing a great location for diving. Large holes have been cut out of the ship allowing divers to enter the wreck and explore the sea life that has made the wreck its home. Tzoonie Narrows is also an excellent diving site given the currents and the abundance of marine life.

Shannon Falls Provincial Park (Map #11/B1)
This small park is found next to Hwy #99 just south of Squamish. It provides a large parking area used by hikers/mountain climbers accessing the Stawamus Chief or exploring the spectacular waterfall. There are picnic facilities at the popular day-use park.

Silver Lake Provincial Park (Map #5/D1)
Accessed by the Silver-Skagit Road, this small park encompasses Silver Lake. The park has a 50 unit campground complete with a picnic area and boat launch. The park offers fishing, mountain biking and hiking opportunities.

Simson Provincial Marine Park (Map #9/B3)
This marine park covers most of South Thormanby Island and is reached by boat only. There are no docking facilities and so the provincial park is best left for kayakers, small boats or canoes. The closest launch to the provincial park is at Halfmoon Bay. When you reach the park, you can find a trail that traverses the island beginning at Farm Bay on the southeast corner of the island. The trail is 3.6km (1.5hrs) in length.

Skagit Valley Prov Recreation Area (Map #6)
This 27,968ha recreation area is accessed by the Silver-Skagit Road or by trail from the Sumallo Grove Picnic Area on Hwy #3 east of Manning Park. The vast wilderness area is known for its beautiful scenery ranging from old growth stands of timber to rugged mountain peaks. There are two provincial park campgrounds in the area as well as the renowned Centennial and Skagit River Trails. **Ross Lake Campground** is at the north end of Ross Lake and has a 5 unit campground with a picnic area and boat launch. **Silvertip Campground** is found at the junction of Kleslikwa and Skagits River and is shadowed by Silvertip Mountain. It has 4 camping units together with a boat launch. The Skagit River offers excellent fly fishing for Rainbow in July and August.

Skihist Provincial Park (Map #33/B2)
Just to the northeast of Lytton on Hwy #1, this provincial park is mainly used as a stopover for travellers on Hwy #1. It is has 56 vehicle/tent campsites and a day use area with lush green lawns. The provincial park is located on the banks above the Thompson River in a dry ponderosa pine forest. A new trail leads to the bench above the campsite and offers fine views of the Thompson Canyon.

Skookumchuck Narrows Provincial Park (Map #18/C4)
This 123ha provincial park, which is accessed by trail or boat, encompasses the northeast edge of Sechelt Peninsula. The trail leads 4km (1hr) one way from Egmont and is a fairly flat, easy walk. The main attraction to the park is the spectacular rushing water through the narrow, shallow waterway during high water and the tidal pools in low water. There are no camping facilities at the park.

Smuggler's Cove Provincial Marine Park (Map #9/B2)
Smuggler's Cove Provincial Marine Park encompasses the point of land to the north of Halfmoon Bay overlooking the Thormanby Islands. To reach this provincial park requires a 1.3km (one way) hike beginning off Brooks Road and leading through a second growth forest to the ocean. Along the forested shoreline, you will find 5 tenting pads as well as a hiking trail that continues along the

coastline form the campground. The provincial park is also reached by boat from which it is possible to anchor within the cove and explore the shoreline. The cove, during the alcohol prohibition, was used by smugglers bringing rum to the United States.

Stawamus Chief Provincial Park (Map #11/B1)
This 615ha newly created park encompasses the Stawamus Chief, a spectacular sheer granite cliff used extensively by rock climbers. The park is found just south of Squamish and is marked by a of couple parking areas. Hiking trails on the back of the mountain allow visitors to reach the top for a great view of the Squamish Valley.

Stein Valley Niaka'pamux Heritage Provincial Park (Map #31-33, 40, 41)
This vast (65,569ha) park is considered the last remaining untouched watershed in Southwestern B.C. It is accessed by the Stein River Trail from north of Boston Bar or from several locations in the Pemberton area (Blowdown Creek or Lizzie Lake area being the best). The park has no developed facilities and is a great choice for a week long backcountry excursion through an expansive old-growth forest into the subalpine.

Sumas Mountain Provincial Park (Map #3/D3, 4/A3)
This park encompasses the oval shaped mountain seen on the west side of Hwy#1 as you approach Chilliwack from Greater Vancouver. There are no developed camping facilities within the park. The main recreation uses in the park are hiking the Sumas Mountain Trail or fishing Chadsey Lake. The provincial park now forms part of the 1445ha Sumas Mountain Regional Park.

Teakerne Arm Provincial Park (Map #25/B2)
This is a new provincial park within Lewis Channel on West Redonda Island. The main attraction to the park is the 30m high Cassel Falls. There is a dinghy float and pit toilets but no other facilities at the 6,164ha park. Try hiking to Cassel Lake for a beautiful picnic area.

Tetrahedron Provincial Park (Map #10/B2)
This provincial park was established in 1995 to preserve the vast sub-alpine area which is popular with hikers, mountain bikers and backcountry cross country skiers. Within the provincial park is an extensive network of old logging roads and well developed trail systems and several rustic cabins. For details on the trails available in the park, please refer to the trail section of this book.

Two Springs Provincial Park (Map #47/A3)
There are no developed facilities in this new park. The easternmost sections of the park are easily accessed by Hwy #99.

Walsh Cove Provincial Park (Map #25/B2)
This small provincial park encompasses Walsh Cove on West Redonda Island. The park is an undeveloped sheltered anchorage and sees few visitors. Indian pictographs are found on the rock cliffs in the park.

Harrison Lookout Trail

Paddling

River Routes (Whitewater)

We have provided you with information on many different rivers and streams in Southwestern B.C. For each river we have included the put-in and take-out locations. The length of each run, the best season and general comments are also provided. We have used the International River Classification system to grade the rivers:

Grade I: novices in open canoes and kayaks
Grade II: intermediate paddlers (medium rapids)
Grade III: advanced paddlers (scouting required)
Grade IV: expert paddlers; closed canoes & kayaks

Please remember that river conditions are always subject to change and advanced scouting is essential. The information in this book is only intended to give you general information on the particular run you are interested in. You should always obtain more details from your local merchant or expert before heading out on your adventure.

Fraser Valley/ Lower Mainland Whitewater

Alouette River (Map #2/D2)
Put In/Take Out: Neaves Road Bridge
North of Haney, this 15km easy, Grade I, year round paddle extends both north and south of the Neaves Road bridge. The route has the occasional mini-rapids, logs and sweepers to watch out for.

Big Silver Creek (Map #14/C1)
Put In: Clear Creek Branch Road
Take Out: Silver Creek Camp
This is a 7km (2hour) Grade II summer training route for the novice paddler. The creek offers a medium volume of water with continuous flow making the route easy for learning.

Capilano River (Map #1/B1,11/B1)
Put In: end of Capilano Park Road
Take Out: various
This suburban North Shore river offers a 5.5km (2-3hour) Grade III route with a Grade IV drops at high water or a Grade II route with Grade III drops at low water. There is paddling year-round as long as the water flow released from the dam is sufficient for paddling. Along the route, there are up to 20 technical drops as well as a slalom course providing added challenges. The scenic canyon and spawning Coho in the fall add to the experience.

Chehalis River (Map #4/B1)
Put In: trail off Chehalis Road
Take Out: Morris Valley Road bridge
A short trail off the Chehalis Road provides access to the beginning of the route. From there, it is an 8.5km (5hr) Grade IV highly technical kayak route extending to the Harrison River. The river is lined with fishermen in the fall so it is well advised to pick other times of the year to paddle.

Chilliwack River (Map #4,5)
The good fishing, abundant recreation sites, easy access and beautiful scenery makes this an excellent recreational river. The paddler has three routes to choose from.

Put In: Chilliwack Provincial Park
Take Out: Vedder Crossing
This is a 6.5km (2hr) Grade II route for novice kayakers and rafters. The river offers medium flow over gravel bars and past the occasional log jam. Overall, the route is a good training ground anytime between the spring through the fall.

Put In: Slesse Creek bridge
Take Out: Chilliwack River Park
This stretch of the river offers an 18km (3+hr) Grade III (with Grade IV drops) route complete with a slalom course. Be forewarned that there is a 1km portage to avoid Tamihi and Campground rapids unless you are an expert kayaker. The route offers year round paddling but it is best after a good rain.

Put In: Camp Foley
Take Out: West of Slesse Creek
This Grade IV route has a medium volume of water with continuous rapids and drops through a canyon. The route extends 9km (4hr) and requires a portage at the fish hatchery drop.

Cogburn Creek (Map #14/D2)
Put In: Harrison East FSR bridge
Take Out: Bear Creek Logging Camp
Cogburn Creek offers a 3km (0.5hr) Grade IV expert route during spring run-off. It is steep, short and rocky so the route should only be tried by an expert kayaker. Watch for logs and flash floods.

Coquihalla River (Map #15/D4)
Put In: Coquihalla River Park
Take Out: Othello Road
A 13km (5hr) Grade IV route leads through the Coquihalla Canyon just east of Hope. The paddle involves a steady grade with many drops and continuous rapids. There are a number of obstacles to watch out for including logs, sharp rocks and flash flooding. The route is also best taken during spring run-off when the river is at its highest level. Along the way, you can enjoy the spectacular canyon scenery and the Othello Tunnels.

Coquitlam River (Map #2/B1)
Put In: Pipeline Road north of powerline
Take Out: Shaughnessy Street
The Coquitlam River offers an 8km (2hr) Grade III route for intermediate kayakers or experts canoeists in the heart of Coquitlam. The river has a steady grade with plenty of rock gardens making it a real challenge. It is best paddled in the winter after heavy rains.

Fraser River
The mighty Fraser has 1600km of paddling from Yellowhead Pass to Vancouver ranging from narrow gorges to wide flat water. In Southwestern B.C., the Fraser has two extremes. The spectacular canyon from Big Bar to Yale offers Grade IV water for commercial rafters. From Yale to Vancouver, the river provides a swift Grade I paddle through the scenic Fraser Valley.

Kanaka Creek (Map #2/D2,3/A2)
Put In/Take Out: Kanaka Creek Regional Park
This is a 12km (return) Grade I route offering a peaceful and scenic paddle in a rural park setting.

Harrison River (Map #4/C1)
Put-in: Harrison Hot Springs
Take-out: bridge on Hwy #7
This is a popular 15km (4hr+) Grade I easy paddle in a wilderness setting extending from Harrison Lake to Hwy#7. The most notable attraction is the spawning salmon in the fall, which attracts bald eagles and plenty of fishermen.

Nahatlatch River (Map #24/A1)
Nahatlatch River is a small river providing extremely challenging and variable runs set through a series of canyons from Hannah Lake to the Fraser River. Access is provided by the Nahatlatch FSR along the north banks of the river. Several recreation sites provide overnight camping. Although it is not that popular, the river is considered one of the premier whitewater streams in North America. There are three routes to choose from.

Put In: Hannah Lake at the old ranger station
Take Out: west end of Francis Lake
This is a short, 1.5km (1hr) Grade II-III route with steady rapids over a shallow riverbed. It represents a good quick warm-up stretch for longer and more challenging routes downstream. The season runs from April to October.

Put In: east end of Francis Lake
Take Out: Apocynum campground
This is an 8km (3hr) Grade III paddle with Grade IV drops. It is a very demanding stretch of the river with a lot of waves, rapids, holes and rock gardens. The most notable rapids are the Meat Grinder, Rose Garden and Head Wall. Advanced scouting is an absolute must, given the treacherous waters. The season runs from May to October with the best paddling in July.

Put In: Apocynum campground
Take Out: bridge on Nahatlatch Forest Road
This is a 5km (3hr) Grade IV route with close to 20 technical drops (one of which is Grade V and should probably be portaged). This stretch of river is only for the expert and should not be paddled during spring runoff. The best time to paddle the route is May to October.

Seymour River (Map #1/D1,11/D4)
Put In: Riverside Road at Seymour Park
Take Out: ocean
This is a 4km (2hr) Grade II suburban route at low water and Grade III route during high water. It is an excellent training grounds for novice kayakers with several rock gardens to navigate. The route can be paddled year round except in August when the river is at its lowest level. Given that the river is best paddled during higher water, it is well advised to paddle after a good rainfall. Similar to the Upper Seymour Route, a locked gate restricts access to non White-water Kayaking Assoc. of B.C. members from May 15-Sept 30.

Skagit River (Map #6/B3)
Put-in: 26 mile bridge and Ross Lake
Take Out: variable
It is a Grade III-IV route set in a scenic valley with sheer mountain faces and an abundance of wildlife. There are numerous log jams along the route which create a real hazard. The best time to paddle the route is in from July until October (after spring run-off).

Statlu Creek - Chehalis River (Map #4/B1,14/A4)
Put In: trail off Chehalis Road
Take Out: Morris Valley Road bridge
This is a 10km (6hr) Grade III route best paddled during high water. The route offers swift currents over several rock gardens.

Whistler/Pemberton Whitewater

Birkenhead River (Map #30/B1)
Put-in: bridge north of Owl Creek Rec Site on the Pemberton-D'Arcy Road
Take-out: bridge on Pemberton-D'Arcy Road north of Mt. Currie.
The Birkenhead River offers a 5km (2-3hr) Grade IV (Grade III during low water) route for kayakers, rafters or expert canoeists. The route runs along beautiful turquoise water in a spectacular wilderness setting. The river is quite shallow with fast flowing water and continuous rapids. The best time to paddle the river is in June through July or during the fall rains.

Cheakamus River (Map #20,29)
There is easy access to this glacier fed river to the north of Daisy Lake with Hwy#99 following the river all the way to the Whistler Valley. To the south of Daisy Lake, the river enters a scenic canyon, which is good for fishing but not navigable by water. Below the canyon, the river is accessed by the Paradise Valley Road and become navigable again. Overall, there are three routes to choose from:

Put In: Black Tusk Road
Take Out: Hwy #99 bridge
This is a 1.5km (2hr) Grade IV fast and technical route for the expert kayakers only. The best time to paddle the route is in May-October.

Put In: Hwy #99 bridge south of Daisy Lake
Take Out: Hwy #99 salt shed
This is a 4km (2hr) Grade III route (with a Grade IV drop) containing a lot of holes, rock gardens and technical drops. The river flow is dam controlled so the water level is subject to sudden fluctuations. The best time to paddle the river is between May and September.

Put-in: end of Paradise Valley Road
Take Out: Fergie's Lodge
This is a good intermediate Grade II-III paddle that extends 12km (3hrs). The route begins from the end of Paradise Valley Road although it is possible to stop at one of 2 bridges along the road and shorten the paddle. The river is unique because it gives you a feeling that you are in the middle of nowhere because the road is hidden by overhanging trees. Also, the river has a gravel bottom with a good flow ensuring that you do not have to worry about rock gardens. There are 2 short Class III drops, one at Culliton Creek and one at the bridge near Fergie's Lodge. It is best to paddle the route in June through September.

Elaho-Squamish River (Map #28/D4)
Put In: bridge on Elaho Main
Take Out: variable
This is a 12km (2-3hr) Grade III (Grade IV in high water) for expert paddlers and commercial rafting trips. The fast, silty cold water with a few turbulent eddies and big wave rapids are the hallmark of the route. The paddle is very scenic with granite walls and cascading waterfalls. It is best to try the route in June-October or after a heavy rain.

Lillooet River
Lillooet River is a fast flowing glacier fed river that offers year round paddling on four routes. Paddlers can enjoy the mountain scenery, the peaceful valley and the historic gold rush trail along the way. Nearby hot springs are a rewarding destination. Regardless of the time of year, you can expect ice cold murky water.

Above Meager Creek (Map #37/D1)
Put-In: north of Pebble Creek (no trail)
Take-Out: Meager Creek Bridge
Beginning just north of Pebble Creek, the Lillooet River is in a bit of a gorge. As a result, there is a nice 5km (2hr) Grade III and IV route for kayakers, rafters and expert canoeists. The area is noted for its rock gardens and standing waves. It is best paddled in June through October.

Upper Route (Map #37/D1,38/A1)
Put In: Meager Creek bridge
Take-out: bridge on Upper Lillooet River Road
Beginning at the Meager Creek Bridge, this 35km (8hr) Grade II route offers a training ground for novice kayakers as well as a scenic paddle for canoeists. A 200m stretch downstream from the bridge is the swiftest and most treacherous portion of this paddle. After the Lillooet River meets Meager Creek, the river gently flows out into a meandering floodplain. Since the river continuously changes channels, it is best to stay in the deepest water. Also, there are a number of log jams and sweepers to watch out for.

Middle Route (Map #30/A1, 38/D4, 39/A4)
Put-in: first bridge on Upper Lillooet River Road
Take-out: Lillooet River bridge on Hwy#99 east of Pemberton
As the Lillooet River approaches Pemberton, the river widens and increases in velocity. As a result, there is a 23km Grade II paddle which is little more than a float down the river with the current directing your travel. There is no whitewater on the route but the river is still fast flowing and should not be taken lightly. May through July is a better time to paddle if you want a more challenging and faster route because of spring run-off.

Lower Route (Map #30/D4,22/A1)
Put In: Little Lillooet Lake
Take Out: variable
South of Little Lillooet Lake, it is possible to paddle up to 34km (6+hrs) on a Grade II (some Grade III drops) year-round route. Because of the Grade III drops, the route is best left for kayakers, rafters and expert canoeists. The water is cold and murky offering boils but mainly flat slow sections. The main attraction is the old gold rush settlements and hot springs at Skookumchuck.

Mamquam River (Map #20/C4)
Put In: follow signs on Mamquam Forest Service Road
Take Out: variable
This route is a challenging kayak racing area just south of Squamish. It offers a short paddle over Grade III water. The attractions to the route are the proximity to facilities in Squamish and the unforgettable scenery.

River of Golden Dreams (Map #29/D3)
Put In: Wayside Park/ Lakeside Park
Take Out: Green Lake
In the heart of Whistler, the River of Golden Dreams is a good choice for a 9km (2-3hr) slow, easy float. The best place to launch your canoe is on Alta Lake. From there, paddle to the north end of the lake from where the River of Golden Dreams flows northward towards Green Lake. The river winds its way through a marshy area between the two lakes where numerous trees and bush overhang the river. As you float down the river, you will pass under several bridges and you will get glimpses of Whistler and Blackcomb Mountains looming in the background. The route is becoming very popular with inner-tubers.

Squamish River (Map #20/B3)
Put In: powerhouse
Take Out: Brackendale
Beginning at the pumphouse on the Squamish River Road, a 32km (5-6hr) Grade I-II route (with Grade IV rapids) leads to Brackendale along the Squamish River. The river is very swift, cold and murky with log jams and deadheads so it is not an easy paddle. It is well advised to portage around the Grade IV rapids.

Ocean Paddling

An endless coast with numerous sheltered inlets makes ocean paddling one of the most peaceful and scenic ways to explore Southwestern B.C. We have included some of the more popular or scenic routes available.

Before heading out, it is essential to know the marine forecasts, marine charts and tide tables.

Burrard Inlet (Map #1)
Explore Vancouver and the North Shore by water. Lighthouse Park and Jericho Beach are two of the popular destinations. The waters are sheltered from the prevailing winds but boat traffic makes the inlet very choppy.

Desolation Sound Provincial Marine Park (Map #25)
Desolation Sound is B.C.'s largest and most popular destination marine park and is known for its warm, sheltered waters, oysters and spectacular scenery. The area is also rich in native history. The park is best explored in May through October, and can be reached by taking Malaspina Road off Hwy #10 to Okeover Arm. There, one is able to launch a kayak . Please note that Okeover Inlet must be paddled with caution because of tidal currents up to 2 knots.

An alternative to Okeover Inlet is to launch your kayak in Lund and paddle past the Copeland Islands, a 437ha marine park which is home of a diverse range of marine wildlife including harbour seals. Other boat launches are at Squirrel Cove and Cortes Bay on Cortes Island. Overall, you should allow 3-10 days to fully explore the park. Marine campgrounds are scattered on the islands and there are a number of walk-in lakes, which provide excellent fishing. Beach camping is limited due to the rocky shoreline common to the park.

Howe Sound (Map #11)
Spectacular mountain peaks, fishing and island hiking are some of the attractions to the Sound. Popular destinations include Gambier Island, which can be circumnavigated in 2 days, and Anvil Island, a one day trip. Gambier Island also offers good camping and hiking opportunities. The waters are mostly protected except for short crossings between the islands. The best place to launch an ocean kayak or canoe is at Porteau Cove off Hwy #99 or at Port Mellon off of Hwy #101.

Indian Arm (Map #1/D1,2/A1,12/A4)
This newly established marine park offers a beautiful protected inlet that is often overlooked by ocean kayakers. Other than a lot of small boat traffic, it makes an excellent 10 nautical mile (one-way) paddle to the north end of the arm. Along the way, you will pass a marine park at Twin Islands (good camping), Croker Island and the spectacular Granite Falls. The best place to launch a boat is either at Belcarra Bay or Deep Cove. You should allow 2 days to explore the inlet fully.

Jervis Inlet (Map #17/D3,18/A3)
The best place to launch your kayak or canoe is at Saltery Bay on the Powell River side of the inlet or from Earls Cove or Edgmont on the Sunshine Coast. The highlights of the inlet include the popular, breathtaking Princess Louisa Inlet, beautiful Chatterbox Falls and spectacular scenery in a fjord like setting with shear granite walls and Indian pictographs. The winds and tides can cause a problem to paddlers (especially at Malibu Rapids) as can long stretches of rock walls which prevent a shore landing in the event of an emergency. To explore the whole inlet, it is best to allow 6-12 days with the season running from April to October. It is recommended only to paddle on a slack tide.

Northern Gulf Islands (Map #16,25)
Explore Cortes, West and East Redonda Islands and their secluded coves. Warm water, excellent fishing and marine parks make this area of the coast a good paddling destination. Paddlers usually launch from Lund.

Sechelt Inlet (Map #9,18)
Sechelt Inlet is a sheltered inlet, which is very popular with ocean kayakers given its marine parks and scenic surroundings. The best place to start your adventure is to launch at Porpoise Bay. From there, you can either take a day trip or spend a week exploring the waters of Sechelt Inlet, Salmon Inlet and Narrows Inlet. If you are a bird watcher, these inlets are home of a wide variety of birds due to the habitat created by the many bays, creek mouths, rocky crops and estuaries in the inlets. It is also possible to see marine animals such as harbour seals and, if you are lucky, killer whales. The marine parks have tenting sites together with pit toilets and fire rings.

The inlet is generally thought of as a calm body of water since it is protected from the wind and weather systems that make the Strait of Georgia more treacherous to paddle. Therefore, novice ocean kayakers will enjoy paddling the inlet.

Skookumchuck Narrows (Map #18/C4)
Put In: Edgmont boat launch
Passing through the narrows is hard enough with a power boat let alone a kayak or canoe. Therefore, this area is for expert kayakers and canoeists only and should not be tried except during slack tides. In fact, the narrows are rated as Grade IV because the tide can be up to 16 knots and can create waves over 2m high. Phosphorescent plankton and wilderness camping encourage overnight stays.

Ocean/Lake Circuits

Ruby Lk - Sakinaw Lake - Agamemnon Channel Route (Map #9/B1,18/B4)
Put In/Take Out: Earls Cove
Found north of Pender Harbour on the Sunshine Coast, this is a 31km (2-3 day) clockwise route starting at Ruby Lake and ending at Earls Cove. The highlights of the paddle include the coastal scenery & wildlife, Indian Pictographs, wilderness camping and fishing. Be forewarned that there is a 750m portage between Ruby and Sakinaw Lake as well as a 200m portage from Sakinaw Lake to the Channel. Also, winds on Sakinaw Lake and tide action in Channel can make paddling difficult. Further, the Sechelt Indian Band may charge you a fee for using the second portage.

Pender Harbour Route (Map #9/B1)
Put In/ Take Out: Madeira Park boat ramp
Within the popular Pender Harbour Area is a beautiful lake and ocean circuit. This 13km (5hr) clockwise route includes three portages; 200m between the Channel and Sakinaw Lake, 800m between Sakinaw Lake and Mixal Lake and 700m from Garden Bay Lake to the ocean. The highlights of the trip are the coastal scenery together with the Indian Pictographs. Tidal currents, choppy water from power boats and weather can play havoc on the paddler. An alternative route is to portage to Katherine Lake and then camp.

Powell Forest Canoe Route (Map #17,26)
The Powell Forest Canoe Route represents a coastal alternative to the Bowron Lake Canoe Route. It involves a 3-7 day canoe trip passing by 9 lakes and covering 80km of canoeing and 10.7km of portaging. The launch site is located on Lois Lake and is accessed by Branch #41 Road off the Lois FSR. The end point is Inland Lake north of Powell River so two vehicles are a must. The breathtaking scenery and the good Cutthroat fishing are the main attractions to the canoe route.

The main canoe route leads north of Lois Lake to a 1.7km portage along the eastern banks of the Horseshoe River past the Horseshoe Lake Rec Site. An alternative is to paddle to the eastern end of Lois Lake and explore the narrows to Khartoum Lake where another rec site can be found on the northern shores.

Horseshoe Lake is noted for strong winds but there are numerous sheltered bays and coves as well as several islands, which can shelter you from the winds. Once you reach the north end of Horseshoe Lake, the route doglegs to the west into Nanton Lake where you will find a 2.4km portage to Ireland Lake, a cedar wetland full of wildlife.

At the south end of Ireland Lake, which is a small shallow lake, you will find a rec site. Camp here, or paddle to the north end of Ireland Lake and then take the 0.8km portage, which leads uphill to Dodd Lake and the Dodd Lake Rec Site.

Dodd Lake is usually very windy and so it is well advised to remain on the shores and paddle in late afternoon or early morning. At the north end of Dodd Lake, you will find a rec site as well as a 0.7km portage leading to Windsor Lake, the highest lake in the chain at 195m.

Windsor Lake is a very deep and cold lake and so most canoeists do not stopover at the lake. Rather, they travel to the north end of Windsor Lake and take the steep and difficult portage that leads 110m downhill to Goat Lake over a 2.4km trail.

Once at Goat Lake, many canoeists travel northeastward to the estuary of Eldred River. If you wish to stick on the canoe route then travel to the west onto Powell Lake and continue down the southern shoreline. Given that Powell Lake is subject to strong winds, it is well advised to paddle in the early morning or late in the afternoon only. Ultimately, a 0.7km portage leads to Inland Lake and the end point.

Overall, there are twenty rec sites located along the canoe route as well as the adjoining lakes. The area is noted for its diverse ecosystems ranging from cedar or deciduous lowlands to "fjord-like" lakes surrounded by rugged mountain peaks. The canoe route is best travelled in April through November in a counter-clockwise direction so that most of the portages are downhill.

Freshwater Lake Fishing

With the excellent saltwater and river fishing available in southwestern B.C., no wonder lake fishing receives little interest. If you do want to sample some of the local lakes, you should expect fish to be small (less than 30cm). This is because most coastal lakes have acidic, nutrient poor waters resulting in small insect populations and slow growing trout. That is not to discourage you as there are a multitude of options ranging from remote walk-in lakes to some large trolling lakes.

As a general rule of thumb, the lower elevation lakes (lower than 1200m) offer fishing beginning in early April until mid to late June before the waters warm and the fishing tails off into July and August. The fishermen should then focus his/her efforts on higher elevation lakes (greater than 1200m elevation) as the fishing begins in early June and usually does not subside over the summer months. Into the fall, the lower elevation lakes pick up again and by late fall, the higher elevation lakes begin to ice over.

In choosing any lake, a review of the fishing regulations is a must as the coastal lakes are heavily regulated to ensure that the fish stocks are not significantly depleted and remain healthy for years to come.

Harrison Area Lakes

Bear Lake (Map #4/D1)
This tiny (2ha) lake is reached on the Bear Mountain FSR (4wd access) off Rockwell Drive to the east of Harrison Lake. There are good numbers of small Rainbow in the lake. Try a float and bait, small lure or fly for best success any time during the spring or fall.

Campbell Lake (Map #4/D1)
Campbell Lake is 3ha in size and is located at 650m in elevation in the mountains west of Harrison Hot Springs. The lake is accessed by a rough 4wd road then a short hike or a long hike from Harrison Hot Springs. The lake contains good numbers of small Rainbow best caught in the early spring or late fall by spincasting or fly fishing. Since the lake is very shallow, the water warms in the summer making fishing success quite poor. The lake is stocked with Rainbow.

Dickson Lake (Map #4/A1)
This 80ha lake is located on a 4wd road from either the Norrish Creek Road to the south or the Statlu Creek Road to the north. The lake has a fair number of Cutthroat and Dollies to 35cm in size. Trolling a small boat is most effective although fly fishing and spincasting the shallows can be productive. There is a boat launch at the lake which is at 640m in elevation. The lake is best fished in the spring and fall given the elevation.

Elbow / Echo Lake (Map #4/B1)
These two small lakes are found along the Chehalis FSR north of Harrison Mills.

Echo Lake is a small, 5ha lake at 110m in elevation. It has small Cutthroat best caught by spincasting or bait fishing.

Elbow Lake is stocked regularly so it has good numbers of small Rainbow (to 20cm). The 15ha lake is at 170m in elevation.

Fire Lake (Map #22/C3)
Fire Lake is a long narrow lake at 1430m in elevation set below Garibaldi Provincial Park. A newly developed logging road has been cut within a kilometre of the lake making access far easier than the long hike up the overgrown road along Fire Creek. The 155ha lake has many small Rainbow to 30cm (12") which come readily to a fly or lure in the summer through fall. Successful fishing is declining due to the improved access.

Glacier Lake (Map #22/B4)
To the southwest of Skookumchuck is a 4wd road leading to Glacier Lake at 415m in elevation. The 250ha lake, given its difficult access, provides fairly good fishing for Rainbow Trout, Kokanee and Dollies throughout the spring and fall. Trolling is your best bet, although sampling the shoreline with a fly or small lure can be effective.

Harrison Lake (Map #4,14,22,23)
Harrison Lake is a very large (21,780ha) 55km long lake located north of Harrison Hot Springs on Hot Springs Road (Hwy #9). Although two main logging roads run up each side of the lake (the Harrison West FSR and the Harrison East FSR), there are few access points (except at the southern end).

Full facilities can be found at Harrison Hot Springs including hotels, camping, beach and boat launching facilities. There is also a paved boat launch at Green Point. The lake is not well noted for good fishing but you can still produce Cutthroat to 40cm and Rainbow to 1.5kg (3lb) by trolling. The best locations to fish near the south end of the lake are at the mouth of Cascade Bay or along the shores north of the Harrison River outflow. The lake is very deep (up to 200m) and is known for its hostile winds.

Harrison West Lakes (Map #4,14)
Access to this series of lakes west of the Harrison Lake is via the Morris Valley Road and then Harrison West FSR. You will find a total of 4 rec sites in the area and some reasonable fishing for stocked Rainbows. The smaller lakes have an electric motor only restriction on them making a floatation device ideal. The access roads into the lakes off of the mainline are generally steep, making a truck necessary.

Francis Lake has many stocked Rainbow Trout to 30cm in size best caught by fly fishing or spincasting in the spring and fall. The 4ha lake, which has an electric motor only restriction, can be fished from shore. The lake is at 365m in elevation and offers a small rec site.

Grace Lake has many stocked Rainbow in the 30-35cm range. The marshy lake is 6ha in size and is best fished with a float tube since there is no shore fishing possible. There is a rec site at the lake, which is found at 106m in elevation.

Lookout Lake this 10ha lake is located on the west side of Harrison Lake off the Harrison West FSR. The lake is at 650m in elevation and contains a good number of Rainbow to 35cm. A 4wd is recommended to access the lake. Fly fishing and spincasting are your best bets.

Morris Lake is found on a steep road leading just east of the Weaver Creek spawning channel. The 90ha lake has a large channel leading from the outlet to Harrison River which is popular for canoeists. There are a few Cutthroat (to 50cm) which can be caught by spincasting or fly fishing. Try worms, roe or flies.

Sunrise Lake is another small lake found in the hills above Harrison Lake. The 5ha lake is found at 396m and offers excellent shore fishing. The deep lake (up to 14m) also offers good trolling. Access is by a rough 4wd road to the rec site and boat launch on the lake.

Weaver Lake is 81ha in size and has good numbers of Rainbow and Cutthroat that reach 50cm (ave. 30+cm). Weaver Lake receives heavy use during the summer because of its scenic rec site complete with a beach and boat launch. Trolling with a fly or wedding band and worm is popular although the lake, given its numerous bays and undulating shoreline, is well suited to spincasting or fly fishing. Fishing is best on the western side because the water is deeper. For fly fishermen, try a small red Doc Spratley or a half back. The lake is at 260m in elevation and has a trail that circles the lake. Try in May-June or in Sept-October.

Wood Lake is found just off of the Harrison West FSR. Although the road is generally good, the last few kilometres are quite rough, making a 4wd necessary. The lake contains good numbers of stocked Rainbow that are in the 25-40cm range. Fly fishing or spincasting in the spring or fall is quite effective, especially near the deep hole on the north side. The lake is 5ha in size and at 170m in elevation.

Wolf Lake has smaller but more plentiful Rainbow than Weaver Lake. It has a small forest service rec site and is at 105m in elevation. The tiny lake (2ha) is best fished with a float tube due to its marshy shoreline.

Lake Erroch (Map #4/B4)
Lake Erroch is located alongside Hwy #7 and is known more as a recreation lake than a fishing lake. It does have small Cutthroat and Rainbow best caught in the spring or fall. The lake is 30ha in size and at 30m in elevation.

Slollicum Lake (Map #15/4A)
This 25ha lake is reached by a 3km trail off a 4wd road on the east side of Harrison Lake. The lake has numerous small Rainbow (average 15-20cm) which come readily to a fly, bait or lure. Try fishing at the north end of the lake where the fish tend to congregate.

Sasquatch Provincial Park (Map #5/A1,15/A4)
Sasquatch Provincial Park is found on the east side of Harrison Lake and is accessed by Rockwell Drive (good 2wd). The lakes in the park are stocked regularly with Rainbow so they usually offer reasonable good fishing for small Rainbows. Spring is the best time to fish using either a fly, float with a worm or a Flatfish. Camping is offered at Deer Lake and Hicks Lake.

Beaver Pond is a tiny (2ha) pond north of Hicks Lake, which produces surprisingly well for Rainbow and Cutthroat (to 40cm). Since the pond is lined with logs and vegetation, bringing waders or a float tube is a must. Using a float and bait (worm or small eggs) is effective but do not discount fly fishing or spincasting.

Deer Lake has both Rainbow and Cutthroat in the 20-35cm range. The 55ha lake, which is at 265m in elevation, is best fished by boat although shore fishing along the road is possible. Since the fish are plentiful, they are easily caught using a number of methods. Casting from shore using a bobber and bait (worm or salmon flies), trolling a Willow Leaf and worm and casting an attractor type fly (Doc Spratly, Wooly Bugger or Royal Coachman) are all effective.

Hicks Lake is the hub of the provincial park with its camping, beach and warm water. The lake contains fairly good numbers of Rainbow, Kokanee and Cutthroat which are larger than those in the other lakes in the park. The lake is best fished by trolling a fly, small lure or Willow Leaf and worm. Better fishing is found in the spring or fall as the water warms in the summer, especially around the small island or at the mouth of one of the four bays, If you do wish to fish rather than sunbathe on the sandy beach (during the summer), try trolling deep near the centre of the lake. The lake is 150ha in size and at 300m in elevation.

Moss Lake is reached by 4wd access together with a 1.5km hike making the lake a less popular alternative to Hicks Lake. It is definitely worth packing in a float tube in order to enjoy the fast fishing for Cutthroat that average 25-35cm in size. Spincasting and fly fishing both produce good results. The lake is 710m in elevation.

Trout Lake is a small (12ha), shallow lake which has many small Rainbow that take easily to flies. The lake should be fished from an electric motor boat or float tube as shore fishing is limited by the bushy and marshy shoreline. The lake is at 75m in elevation so the water warms during the summer making the spring and fall the best time to fish.

Stacey Lake (Map #4/C1)
This 3ha lake is found on the Mt. Woodside Road (2wd access) and is stocked regularly with Rainbow. The fish are best caught in early spring or late fall by fly fishing or spincasting. The lake is at 890m in elevation.

Statlu Lake (Map #14/A3)
Statlu Lake is located to the north of Chehalis and is reached by a rough 4wd road and then a short hike. The Rainbow tend to be small but plentiful. Fly fishing or spincasting are the preferred methods of fishing at this lake, which is set in a scenic valley below some majestic peaks.

Wilson Lake (Map #14/A3)
On a 2wd forestry road west of Chehalis Lake, Wilson Lake is 50ha in size and contains stocked Rainbow Trout. Trolling is the mainstay of the lake, which is at 815m in elevation.

Lillooet/Goldbridge Area Lakes

Anderson Lake (Map #40/C2)
This large lake is accessed by the road to D'Arcy or by 4wd road from Seton Portage. There are a number of private residents that line the lake. The lake offers good fishing for Rainbow and Dollies mainly by trolling. Try a Wedding Ring with worm, Flatfish, Kitamat or Krocodile.

Burkholder Lake (Map #45/B2)
Located to the west of Yalakom River, this small lake receives light fishing pressure. As a result, it offers some good fishing for small Rainbow. Casting a small spinner or spoon is the preferred method of fishing.

Carpenter/ Gun Lake Area (Map #44,45)
This area is easily accessed by a number of logging roads (Carpenter Lake Road, the Hurley River FSR or the Gun Lake Road). It contains a number of very good fishing lakes that are certainly worth a try.

Carol Lake is easily accessed off the Marshall Creek Road and offers good fishing for small Rainbow. The lake is best trolled slowly with a Wedding Ring and worm. A rec site provides camping and a cartop boat launch.

Carpenter Lake is a long narrow lake which provides reasonably good fishing for Dollies, Rainbow and Kokanee that reach 2kg (4lb) in size. Trolling is the mainstay of the lake although it is possible to spincast or fly fish at the creek mouths. Large spoons such as a Kitimat, Kamlooper or Krocodile are very effective for the Rainbow and Dollies. A gang troll with a Wedding Ring and worm or Flatfish also works for the Rainbow and Dollies as well as for the Kokanee.

Gun Lake is easily accessed on the Gun Lake Road to the west of Goldbridge. The 312ha lake has a resort as well as camping at the rec site on the west side of the lake. The lake has fair fishing for Rainbow to 1kg, small Kokanee and Dollies to 4kg (9lb). Trolling is the mainstay of the lake, which is at 890m in elevation. Try a Willow Leaf and Wedding Ring trolled near the outflow creek.

Gwyneth Lake is found next to the Hurley River FSR. It is a shallow lake that is best fished using a fly (Grizzly King or Royal Coachman) or by spincasting (Flatfish or small spinner with worm).

Kingdom (King) Lake is a small (10ha) lake south of Goldbridge. It provides fishing for many small Rainbow by spincasting or fly fishing throughout the spring and fall. Access is by way of 4wd vehicle or hiking making it less popular than nearby lakes.

Lajoie (Little Gun) Lake is located just south of Gun Lake and provides good fishing for Rainbow Trout and Dollies to 1kg on a fly or with a small lure. The 40ha lake has a cartop boat launch and an electric motor only restriction. It is at 900m in elevation and is best fished in the spring and fall.

Liza Lake is located off the Marshall Creek Road and has a rec site for camping. The lake offers good fishing for small Rainbow best caught by fly fishing. Dry flies such as the Royal Coachman or a stonefly pattern work the best.

Marshall Lake is located north of Carpenter Lake on the Marshall Creek Road. It has good fishing for Rainbow to 1kg primarily by trolling a gang troll with a wedding band and worm. Casting a Krocodile or a Dick Nite also meets with success. Camping is provided at two rec sites on the south end of the lake, which is 65ha in size and at 1150m in elevation.

McDonald Lake is located to the south of Carpenter Lake and offers very good fishing for small Rainbow. The most effective method of fishing is to troll a Wedding Ring with a worm.

Mowson Lake offers Brook Trout best caught in the fall using a small lure (Deadly dick0 and worm. The lake is best fished at the outflow leading to Carpenter Lake. Kokanee to 3kg (6.5lb) and Dollies are also present in the lake.

Pearson Pond is a small (8ha) lake which has Rainbow and Brook Trout to 1.5kg best taken by spincasting or trolling. A cartop boat launch and camping is available at the rec site. The lake, which is found at 825m in elevation, also offers good ice fishing.

Tyaughton Lake has good numbers of Dollies and Rainbow best caught by trolling a Willow Leaf and Wedding Ring. Casting towards shore with a fly or small lure is also effective.

Fountain (Kwotlenemo) Lake (Map #41/D2)

This 40ha lake is located on the Fountain Valley Road. It has a rec site at the lake offering camping as well as a boat launch. The fishing is fairly good for Rainbow to 2kg by trolling slowly with a Flatfish or a wedding band with a worm. The lake is 915m in elevation and has an electric motor only restriction.

Kelley Lake (Map #46/D1)

North of Pavilion, this small, windy lake offers fairly good fishing for Rainbow (to 1kg) on a slow troll using a Flatfish or a Wedding Ring with a worm. The lake is home to Downing Provincial Park, which has camping and day-use facilities.

Mead Lake (Map #44/B4)

Just south of Kingdom Lake, this small lake is accessed by a 4wd vehicle or by a hike. It provides good fishing for small Rainbow by spincasting or fly fishing throughout the spring and fall.

Moon Lake (Map #46/A4)

This tiny lake, which is accessed by trail off a 4wd logging road and is noted for having large Rainbow to 2kg (4.5lb). Spincasting with a small lure or spoon and a worm is the most productive.

Pavilion and Area Lakes (Map #46/D3)

There are three lakes located next to the Cariboo Road (Hwy #99) near Pavilion which provide decent fishing for Rainbow:

Crown Lake is 18ha in size and at 855m in elevation. It has Rainbow to 1kg best caught by fly fishing or casting a small lure throughout the spring or fall. There is a cartop boat launch and camping provided at the Marble Canyon Provincial Park.

Pavilion Lake has fair fishing for Rainbow to 1.5kg primarily caught by trolling a gang troll with a Wedding Ring and worm or a Flatfish. There is also an ice fishing season at the lake. A cartop boat launch is available as is camping and a resort. The lake is 260ha in size and at 825m in elevation.

Turquoise Lake has good fishing for stocked Rainbow growing to 1kg primarily by casting a small lure or by fly fishing. The lake, which is at 855m in elevation and is 10ha in size., offers a cartop boat launch.

Seton Lake (Map #40,41,45/D4)

The short river between Anderson Lake and Seton Lake called the Seton Portage offers Steelhead as well as Rainbow and Dollies (to 2kg). Steelhead fishermen should try near the inflow and outflow using a float and roe. The Rainbow and Dollies are caught at the mouth of Whitecap Creek using bait (roe or worms) or a variety of spoons. Seton Lake hold large Rainbow (to 2kg), Lake Trout (to 5kg) and Dollies to 6kg (13lb). Trolling a large spoon at the drop-off of one of the creek estuaries such as Madelaine, Tsee or Machute Creeks is particularly effective. Casting a large spoon off the Seton Lake Canel Dock just east of Lillooet can also be very effective.

Spruce Lake (Map #43/D1)

This remote back country lake is accessed by hiking into the Spruce Lake Recreation Area. The lake offers excellent fishing for Rainbow that can grow to 1.5kg in size but average 25-30cm. Spincasting and fly fishing from a float tube is your best bet since the lake is quite shallow and shore fishing can be quite difficult. There are private cabins found on the lake.

Lower Fraser Valley/ Fraser Canyon Lakes

Botanie Lake (Map #42/B4)

This lake is accessed by the Botanie Valley Road north of Lytton. It provides decent fishing for Rainbow best caught by trolling or fly fishing.

Chadsey Lake (Map #3/D3)

Chadsey Lake is found within Sumas Mountain Provincial Park at 620m in elevation and is accessed by trail. It is not particularly great for fishing but does hold some small Rainbow (ave. 25cm) which are stocked regularly. Fishing is best in the spring and fall by using a float tube to reach the deeper holes. The lake is 9ha in size and is hard to shore fish. Do not be surprised by the large gold fish which inhabits the lake.

Chilliwack Lake (Map #5/D4)

This 1200ha lake is accessed by the Chilliwack Lake Road (good 2wd access). It is a popular undeveloped, recreation lake with two provincial parks and several rec sites that provide not only camping but beaches and boat launches.

The lake contains Rainbow, Cutthroat, Dollies and Kokanee all growing to 2kg but averaging 30-40cm. The fish are notoriously difficult to catch with trolling being your best bet. Since the lake is glacier fed and at 625m in elevation, the waters remain cold throughout the summer meaning fishing does not decline over the summer months.

Clef Lake (Map #6/A3)

Clef Lake is a small high elevation lake located to the south of the Silver Skagit Road. It is reached by a long trail off the Upper Klesilkwa Creek Road. The 8ha lake has fairly good numbers of small Rainbow easily taken by spincasting or fly fishing in the spring or fall.

Cultus Lake (Map #4/B4)

Cultus Lake is accessed by paved road south of Chilliwack. The 630ha lake is noted more for its water sports than fishing although trolling in the early spring or late fall can produce small Rainbow and the odd larger Cutthroat and dolly. Provincial parks, stores, resorts and water slides are available at this popular summer retreat.

Devil Lake (Map #15/C4)

This lake is near Hope on the west side of the Fraser River. Access to the lake is restricted due to private property. The 4ha lake, which is at 80m in elevation, contains a few small Rainbow and Cutthroat (ave. 25-30cm) best caught in the spring or fall by bait fishing or fly fishing.

Eaton Lake (Map #5/D4)

This 45ha lake is located on a steep trail off the Silver Skagit Road. The lake holds many small Rainbow and Cutthroat (ave. 30-35cm), which come readily to a fly, bait or lure. Since the lake is at 1320m in elevation and is noted for its cold water, fishing holds throughout the summer months. The lake is 45ha in size and is best fished from a float tube as shore fishing is difficult.

Foley Lake (Map #5/B3)

This 11ha lake is accessed by the Chilliwack-Foley FSR at 550m in elevation. The lake offers poor fishing for Rainbow and Dollies to 35cm with the fall being the best time to fish. A rec site provides camping at the west side of the lake. There is lots of debris, but it is possible to shore fish from the south. There is an electric motor restriction on the lake.

Galene Lakes (Map #6/C1)

These high elevation lakes are found at 1873m and are accessed by a day long difficult trail. The lakes offers Rainbow to 35cm.

Garrison Lake (Map #7/C2)

A poorly maintained trail leads off the Sunday Summit FSR leads to two scenic sub-alpine lakes. The lakes total 45ha in size and produce Rainbow Trout to 2kg by fly fishing. The remote access limits fishing pressure. Given the elevation, fishing is best left the early summer through fall.

Hanging Lake (Map #5/C4)

This 25ha lake is located on the border between Canada and the U.S.A. at 1420m in elevation. The lake is reached by a steep trail leading from the south end of Chilliwack Lake. The lake has stocked Rainbow that grow to 45+cm. Fly fishing and spincasting are your best bets.

Kawkawa Lake (Map #15/D4)

This 80ha lake at 45m in elevation, is found just east of Hope and is extremely popular in the summer for water sports. Fishing is best left to the spring for Cutthroat, Dollies and Kokanee (to 40cm). Shore fishing is limited so it is best to bring a boat and try some trolling. Trolling for Kokanee with a Willow Leaf and worm is the most productive. Picnicking facilities, a boat launch and a beach are all available at the provincial park on the lake. The lake is closed to fishing in the winter.

Klahater Lake (Map #15/C3)

This 10ha is located alongside the Trans Canada Hwy north of Hope. The fishing is spotty for small Rainbow and Brook Trout, which are best caught by spincasting or bait fishing. There is a cartop boat launch at the lake.

Lake of the Woods (Schkam Lake) (Map #15/C4)

Off Hwy #1 north of Hope, this 20ha lake is stocked annually with Rainbow which grow to 35cm. Fly fishing, trolling and spincasting can produce good results, particularly in the spring or fall. The lake is at 350m in elevation and has an electric motor only restriction. The Lake of the Woods Resort has a boat launch.

Ling Lake (Map #5/B2)
Ling Lake is accessed by the Chilliwack-Foley FSR to Foley Lake and then a long hike along a washed-out road and then trail to the lake. Once you reach the 14ha lake, you will be rewarded with great fishing for Rainbow (to 1kg). Since the lake is at 1370m in elevation, fishing remains good throughout the summer months and into the fall. The lake is best fished using a float tube and casting a fly or small lure.

Liumchen Lake (Map #4/C4)
You will need a 4wd vehicle to access the trail into this small (2ha) lake. Due to the difficult access and the high elevation (1380m), the fishing is quite good for Trout which average 35 cm.

Manning Park Lakes (Map #6,7)
This extensive Provincial Park has a number of sub-alpine lakes, which provide fast action for small Rainbow (ave. 20-25cm). The success really depends on the access with the more remote lakes providing the better fishing. All the lakes in Manning Park are best fished beginning in the early summer through to the fall, given that the ice is not out until late June.

Flash Lake is southwest of Lightning Lake along the Lightening Lake Chain Trail. It holds Rainbow the largest Rainbow in the park with the average being 30-35cm. The fish come readily to a fly, bait or small lure. The lake is at 1200m in elevation and is 10ha in size.

Lightning Lake is the most popular lake within the Provincial Park. The Gibson Pass Road (paved) provides access to the lake where you will find camping, picnic facilities and a boat launch. The lake contains many small Cutthroat and Rainbow caught by fly fishing or spincasting. For fly fishermen, a caddisfly hatch occurs in early July and a Mayfly hatch occurs in the later part of June. The lake is 50ha in size and at 1245m in elevation.

Nicomen Lake is accessed by the Hope Pass Trail and the Grainger Creek Trail. A small tenting site is located at the 10ha lake. Given the tough access, you can usually expect some great fishing for Rainbow that can grow to 1kg in size. Fly fishing, spincasting or bait fishing all work.

Poland Lake is accessed by the Poland Lake Trail off of the Gibson Loop Road. The lake is at 1740m in elevation and contains many small Rainbow (to 20cm) easily taken by fly fishing or spincasting from the shore or from a float tube. There is a rustic campground next to the lake.

Snowshoe Lake is accessed by the Heather Trail and involves a strenuous 13.5km hike one way. Once you reach the lake, you are certain to find many small Rainbow that take readily to a fly or small lure.

Strike Lake is found along the Lightning Lake Chain Trail. It contains many small Rainbow (to 20cm) best caught by spincasting, bait fishing or fly fishing. The lake is at 1200m in elevation.

Thunder Lake is also at 1200m in elevation and is located on the Lightning Lake Chain Trail north of Lone Mountain. The lake, like its neighbours, contains many small Rainbow (to 20cm) best caught by bait or fly fishing. The lake is 40ha in size.

Twenty Minute Lake is located right along the Gibson Pass Road just east of Lightning Lake. It has the poorest fishing of all the lakes in the park. Rainbow are in the 15-20cm category and are best caught by bait fishing although fly fishing and spincasting can produce. The lake is at 1210m in elevation and is 1ha in size.

Nahatlatch River Area (Map #23,24)
Easily accessed by the Nahatlatch River Road, there are a series of three lakes on the river system (Nahatlatch, Hannah and Frances Lake). None of the lakes are very good for fishing but the area is certainly scenic and well worth the trip. Each of the lakes holds limited numbers of Rainbow, Dollies and Cutthroat with trolling in the spring or fall being your best bet. Several rec sites along the road provide camping for the paddlers and fishermen that frequent the area.

Pierce Lake (Map #5/A4)
This 16ha lake is reached by a steep difficult trail leading from the Chilliwack Lake Road to the lake at 135m in elevation. The hike is certainly worth the effort given the excellent fly fishing and spincasting for large stocked Rainbows that can reach 50cm in size. Dollies can also be found. The lake is quite deep (up to 30m) and allows for shore fishing.

Post-Greendrop Trail (Map #5/C3)
To the mountains north of Chilliwack Lake are 3 hike-in lakes. These lakes are accessed by a series of trails (Post-Greendrop Trail or Flora Lake Trail). Despite their trail access, they are very popular given their good fishing, scenic surroundings and clear waters.

Flora Lake is reached by the most difficult of hikes. You must climb to the summit at 1770m before descending to the lake at 1356m. Given the access, fishing pressure is not heavy. With a float tube, the fishing can be fairly good for Rainbow to 2kg (ave. 25-35cm) primarily by fly fishing. There are camping facilities at the 16ha lake.

Greendrop Lake has fair numbers of Rainbow to 45cm best taken by fly fishing from a float tube. The deep waters (to 40m) ensures that the water temperature remains cold throughout the summer. The lake is 21ha in size and is at 1021m in elevation. It is reached by the same trail as Lindman Lake but is an additional 3km one way to the north of Lindman Lake.

Lindeman Lake, a cold emerald green lake, has good numbers of Rainbow Trout that average 30-50cm in size. Fly fishing is the preferred method although spincasting can be effective. Both methods are possible from shore although a float tube is certainly more effective. The lake is 12ha in size and at 838m in elevation. It is reached by a 3km trail which is acceptable for a family outing.

Ross Lake (Map #6/C1)
On the Silver Skagit Road within the Skagit Valley Recreation Area, Ross Lake sits on the border between Canada and the USA. There is camping, a boat launch and a beach at the Provincial Park. The lake is best trolled for Rainbow and Dollies (average 30-45cm). The lake is at 165m in elevation and is 200ha in size.

Silver Lake (Map #5/D1)
This lake is easily accessed on the Silver Skagit Road (good 2wd access) and is home of a provincial park complete with camping, a boat launch and picnic facilities. The 40ha lake has small Rainbow, Cutthroat and Kokanee as well as a few larger Dollies (to 2kg). Small Steelhead enter the lake in the winter and Coho come through in the fall. For best results, you can cast float with bait from the southern shoreline, fly fish at the creek exit, or troll (but note that the lake is only 12m deep).

Wahleach (Jones) Lake (Map #5/B2)
This man-made lake, at 1655m in elevation, is found south of the Fraser River off the Jones Creek FSR. The road raises sharply from the valley bottom to the lake where you will find fair fishing for small Rainbow and excellent fishing for small Kokanee that can reach 1kg in size. Trolling is the mainstay of the fishery. There is a B.C. Hydro recreation site at the 500ha lake, which provides 30 campsites, a day-use area and a boat launch. There is a B.C. Hydro dam at the north end of the lake.

Wotten Lake (Map #15/B3)
Wotten Lake is a remote lake containing Rainbow which is accessed off the Emory Creek Road to the west of Squeah. The lake receives very little fishing pressure and can offer exceptional fly fishing and spincasting for Rainbow. The fishing is generally best in the spring or fall.

North Shore/ Upper Fraser Valley Lakes

Alouette Lake (Map #13/B4, 3/A1)
Alouette Lake is a large (1650ha) lake located north of Maple Ridge. The lake is more known for its recreation pursuits at Golden Ears Provincial Park than its fishing despite an intensive stocking program. The lake does have some Cutthroat Trout, Rainbow, Kokanee, Dolly Varden and Lake Trout. Some of the Lake Trout can grow to over 10kg and are caught by trolling a plug below the 60ft (18 meter) level. Trolling along the drop-offs at one of the creek estuaries or in one of the many bays is the most effective method of catching all species because the fish are quite scattered throughout the lake. Fly fishermen may have some success at the various tributaries, however. The lake, which is up to 130m deep, but averages close to 60m deep, does not warm significantly in the summer so fishing remains steady throughout the year. The lake is at 125m in elevation and has camping facilities along the western shore as well as at the southwestern end of the lake. The southern portion of the lake is easily accessed by paved road.

Blinch Lake (Map #13/D4)
Blinch Lake is located towards the north end of Stave Lake. The lake is at 765m in elevation and is accessed only by boat and then a lengthy hike/bike along Roaring Creek. Needless to say, the remote and difficult access makes the fishing very good when you arrive. You should expect Rainbow in the 25-35cm class that take readily to a fly or to small lures.

Buntzen Lake (Map #2/A1,12/A4)

Located northwest of Port Moody, Buntzen Lake is immensely popular among sunbathers and fishermen. The lake is easily accessed on the Sunnyside Road and contains Rainbow, Cutthroat, Dollies and Kokanee to 30cm in size. Intensive stocking of Rainbow insures that the fish population is being maintained. Since there is a power boat restriction, it is best to bring a float tube or canoe and try spincasting or fly fishing the edges of the lake. The 180ha lake has steep drop-offs and a trail that circles of the lake (Buntzen Lake Trail), so shore fishing is quite easy. The lake is extremely deep in places (to 200m) and is subject to sudden water level fluctuations because it is a BC Hydro reservoir. The lake, which is at 150m in elevation, has full day-use facilities including a picnic site, a beach and hiking/horse trails.

Cheam Wetlands Ponds (Map #4/D2)

Located within the Fraser-Cheam Regional Park off of the Bridal Veil Falls to Agassiz Hwy, this series of ponds can provide fairly good fishing for small Rainbow in the spring and fall. The cagey fisk make the fishing quite slow. A float-tube is necessary.

Chehalis Lake (Map #14/A4)

North of Harrison Bay on the Chehalis FSR, this large, 629ha lake is 10km long and provides spotty fishing throughout the year for Cutthroat, Rainbow or Dollies (ave. 30-40cm). Trolling is a mainstay of the industry. Since the lake is so deep (up to 150m), the fishing is best around the creek or river mouth, or at the shallower southern end. Three rec sites are scattered along the lake providing camping and boat launch facilities. The lake is at 227m in elevation and can be windy.

Cypress Lake (Map #2/B1)

Cypress Lake is accessed by a trail east of Buntzen Lake. It is 5ha in size and has good numbers of small Rainbow and Cutthroat easily taken on a fly, by bait fishing or by spincasting. The remote access ensures a secluded fishing experience when you arrive.

Davis Lake Area (Map #3/C,13)

To the east of Stave Lakes, Davis Lake is home to a provincial park complete with a campground, beach and boat launch. The 30ha lake provides an opportunity to catch small Cutthroat (to 30cm) primarily in the spring. The lake is at 165m in elevation and is stocked regularly with Cutthroat.

Salsbury Lake is found north of Davis Lake at 425m in elevation. The 80ha lake has small Rainbow and Kokanee (to 30cm) which are stocked regularly. Fly fishing is slow and shore fishing is difficult due to the debris. Trolling produces better, but the lake is shallow. Two rec sites are found at the lake, with the west side offering a gravel boat launch and lakeside camping while the east side only has trail access.

Kenyon Lake is found on a 4wd road leading northward from Salsbury Lake. The 26ha lake is at 700m in elevation and has a rec site near the south end of the lake. Small Rainbow can be caught with reasonable frequency during the spring or fall. The lake is quite deep (up to 40m) and has good fly fishing but trolling and spincasting are your best bets.

Devil's Lake (Map #3/B1)

A short trail leading downhill from 4.9km on the Florence Lake FSR accesses this 46 ha lake. It is a definite advantage to pack in a canoe or float tube as the western shores is very brushy and the deeper, more productive area is off the northeastern shoreline. Spincasting or fly fishing produces the best for the stocked cutthroats that reach 30cm in size. The lake is at 106m in elevation and is best fished in the early spring or fall.

Hayward Lake (Map #3/B2)

Hayward Lake is a 275ha man-made lake easily accessed off Wilson Road to the west of Mission. The lake has been extensively stocked with Steelhead and Rainbow but the fish population has not really grown. The lake is best fished for small Rainbow (to 35cm) towards the south end near the Ruskin Dam where there is a 35m hole reached by boat. The rest of the lake is very shallow and not worth fishing. Shore fishing is possible along the western shores, which are accessed by the Railway Trail or at the north end where the Stave River empties into the lake. There are day-use facilities at the lake together with a concrete boat launch.

Hoover Lake (Map #3/C2)

Found at 440m in elevation, this 4ha lake is accessed by a 3.7km hike from the Dewdney Trunk Road east of Stave Falls Dam. Once you reach the lake, you can expect good fishing for Rainbow and Cutthroat that average 20-30cm in size but can grow to 1.5kg. The lake is best fished in the fall by fly fishing, bait fishing or spincasting from a float tube. Shore fishing, do to the vegetation and floating logs, is very difficult except for a few spots along the east shore.

Isabel Lake (Map #12/D3)

Isabel Lake is worth a try if you want a several day excursion into rarely visited country. The lake is accessed by an unmarked trail from the shores of Pitt Lake which, in turn, is only accessed by boat. Once you reach the 25ha lake, you will be rewarded with very good fishing for Rainbow on a fly or by spincasting. Given the elevation, the fish remain active throughout the summer months.

Mike Lake (Map #2/D1)

This lake is located Golden Ears Park and is accessed by the Mike Lake Road (2wd access) and then a short hike to the lake. The 5ha lake has stocked Rainbow and wild Cutthroat that grow to 30cm in size best caught in the spring given the elevation (235m). Fly fishing, bait fishing or spincasting from a canoe or float tube is your best bet as the shoreline is shallow and marshy making shore fishing very difficult. Casting from the dock may prove fruitful. There is a cartop boat launch at the lake as well as a power boat restriction.

Munro / Dennett Lakes (Map #12/C4)

Follow the Quarry Road to the signed trailhead and hike the steep trail to Munro and Dennett Lakes. Munro Lake has Brook Trout and is 25ha in size. Dennett Lake has small Cutthroat and Brook Trout and is 8ha in size. Both lakes are best left for fishing in the fall when the Brook Trout are about to spawn. This is because the Brook Trout become very aggressive and are easily caught by spincasting (Deadly Dick and worm). Despite the tough access, the lakes still receives a fair bit of fishing pressure.

North Shore Lakes (Map #11)

The extensive hiking trail network that dissects the North Shore Mountains leads past a number of mountain lakes. Most of these lakes do not receive heavy fishing pressure as the hikers seem more interested in enjoying the fantastic scenery than fishing.

Deeks Lake is reached along the Howe Sound Crest Trail from the south or the Deeks Lake Trail from the northwest. Either way, it involves a very strenuous hike to the lake at 1000m in elevation. The 15ha lake has small Cutthroat which are caught by spincasting or fly fishing. Fishing from a float tube is most productive although you can still produce by casting from shore at the inflow and outflow creeks. Given the elevation, fishing begins in late spring and extends into the summer.

Elsay Lake is found towards the north end of Mount Seymour Park. The Elsay Lake Trail, a long challenging trail, passes beneath Mount Seymour and Mount Elsay before reaching the lake. Elsay Lake has good numbers of small Rainbow which take readily to a fly, bait or lure. The lake is 20ha in size and best fished throughout the spring and fall.

Pitt Lake (Map #12/D4)

Rennie Road leads to the south end of Pitt Lake at Grant Narrows Park where you will find a popular boat launch. The lake, which is 5400ha in size, is best fished by spincasting or bait fishing at the creek mouths, deep cliff areas or deeper bays. This is because the waters are often murky especially in the early spring when the salmon fry are returning to the ocean. Try trolling a Bucktail or cast a minnow imitation at that time. The lake contains several salmon species and Steelhead, which migrate through the lake. Resident species are Rainbow, Dollies, sturgeon and Whitefish. Sea-run Cutthroat, in the spring (April-May), migrate to the north end of the lake looking for salmon fry returning to the ocean. Try fly fishing (a silver minnow imitation), bait fishing (small minnow) or casting a small silver lure. When boating, watch for the sandbars, deadheads and winds. No camping is available at the lake.

Rolley Lake (Map #13/B1)

Rolley Lake is home of a popular provincial park complete with camping, a boat launch and a beach. The 23ha lake, which is accessed by Bell Road (paved), has stocked Rainbow (to 30cm) as well as a few larger Dollies and Cutthroat. It is best fished near the north end where there is a deep 30m hole. A float tube or row boat/canoe lets you fish the hole although it is still possible to cast from shore at several places. A 1.5km trail circles the lake providing access to shore fishermen. No powerboats are allowed in the lake which is at 221m in elevation.

Sasamat Lake (Map #2/A1)

Sasamat Lake is located on the Bedwell Bay Road and is found within Belcarra Regional Park at 70m in elevation. The lake is noted more for its great beach and picnic facilities than its fishing. It is still possible in the early spring and late fall to catch wild Cutthroat or stocked Rainbow that can grow to 45cm. Power boats are restricted from the lake from May to September so bring a float tube and spincast or fly fish near the middle of the lake at the 35m 'hole' or along the western shoreline. For shore fishermen, a 200m floating dock at the south end of the 45ha lake or two docks at the outflow are excellent spots. Electric motor boats are allowed in Oct-April and there is a boat launch at the lake.

Silvermere Lake (Map #3/B2)
This is a 110ha man-made lake easily accessed by the Hayward Lake Road and Hwy#7. The lake is very marshy and shallow making it better for catfish and bullheads then Rainbow. The best place to fish for the Rainbow (to 30cm) is near Hwy #7 either from shore or by boat. The east side of the lake is lined by private residents making access difficult. Water skiing is a popular sport on the lake.

Stave Falls Area (Map #3,13)
This area is found between Alouette Lake and Stave Lake and is accessed by the Florence Lake FSR (2wd access). Access to the area may be restricted due to the correction facility and logging activity. Phone the correction facility before heading out.

> **Florence Lake** is heavily regulated lake with fly fishing only, single barbless hooks and catch-n-release restrictions. As a result, the lake has good numbers of Cutthroat, Brook Trout and Rainbow which can grow to 2kg. A float tube or canoe is a must as the western shoreline is overrun with logs and debris making shore fishing near impossible. The lake is 390m in elevation and 32ha in size. No facilities are available at the lake.

> **Morgan Lake** is a catch-n-release & fly fishing only fishery for Brook Trout and Cutthroat (to 2kg). For best results, bring a float tube as shore fishing is very difficult and the lake is quite deep in the middle (45m). The lake, which is reached by bushwacking from about 16.5km on the Florence Lake FSR, is 20ha in size and at 320m in elevation.

> **Sayres Lake** is at 230m in elevation and is accessed by short trail from either 11.3 or 12.7km on the Florence Lake FSR. The 80ha lake has a dock where you can launch a small boat or canoe. There is also a fish hatchery and a correction facility next to the lake but no camping facilities. The lake can be fished from shore but it is better to fish with a float tube or small boat in order to cast/ troll towards the center of the lake where the water depth is 80m. There are rumours of Cutthroat in the 4kg size but the average fish tends to be quite small (30-35cm). There are also some small Dollies, Brook Trout and Rainbow in the lake. There is a bait ban as well as a catch limit and a single barbless hook restriction on the lake.

Stave Lake (Map #14/A3)
Stave Lake is a large (4410ha), 27km long lake that has limited access from either Florence Lake FSR or a forestry road north of Davis Lake. Stave Lake, which is at 82m in elevation, has been damned by B.C. Hydro resulting in fluctuating water levels and very spotty fishing. There are a few Rainbow, Cutthroat, Kokanee, Dollies and Whitefish in the lake, which are best caught by trolling. The Cutthroat can reach 50cm whereas the Dollies can reach 5kg. Several campground including a rec site are located next to the lake. Debris and high winds make boating treacherous at times.

Widgeon Lake (Map #12/C3)
Widgeon Lake, due to its difficult access, provides very good fishing for stocked Rainbow Trout to 2kg best caught by packing a float tube into the lake and spincasting or fly fishing. The lake is very deep (up to 140m) and has a rugged shoreline making shore fishing nearly impossible. The lake is reached by first canoeing across Pitt Lake from Grant Narrows Park and finding the trailhead along the western channel of Widgeon Creek. From there, walk/bike along an old road leading northward and eventually a trail takes off from the road to the lake at 770m in elevation. The lake makes an excellent choice if you want a secluded backcountry fishing adventure.

Whonnock Lake (Map #3/A2)
Whonnock Lake is a 50ha urban lake located north of Whonnock off of 276th Street. It is a marshy lake that is very shallow (up to 10m) and has notably dark but clean water. The lake has Cutthroat, crappies and stocked Rainbow which all grow to 25cm. The marshy shoreline makes shore fishing very difficult so bring a canoe or float tube (no powerboats). Spincasting and bait fishing are the best methods of fishing usually in the early morning or at dusk. There are day-use facilities at the lake making it a popular summer lake.

Powell River/ Texada Island Area Lakes
Freshwater fishing in the Powell River area receives little attention since the focus is on the saltwater fishing. This is despite the fact that the number of freshwater lakes in close proximity to Powell River is truly remarkable.

Cranberry Lake (Map #17/A2)
Cranberry Lake is located just east of Powell River and provides marginal fishing for Cutthroat to 40cm in size throughout the spring and early summer. There is a beach and boat launch at the lake, which is easily accessed by paved road. The lake is at 105m in elevation and is 40ha in size.

Duck Lake (Map #17/B2)
Duck Lake, which is at 155m in elevation, is easily accessed on the Duck Lake FSR. It provides fair fishing for Cutthroat in the 25-30cm range as well as some small Kokanee. Trolling is the preferred method at this 60ha lake.

Freda Lake (Map #17/D1)
Located on the Stillwater Main (good 2wd access), this 50ha lake has a fair number of Cutthroat in the 25-35cm range. The lake provides decent trolling throughout the spring and fall.

Hammil Lake (Map #17/A3)
Hammil Lake is a medium sized (85ha) lake on the Duck Lake FSR. It provides decent fishing for Cutthroat in the spring and fall. A boat launch is at the lake, which is 145m in elevation. A trail circles the lake allowing for shore fishing.

Haslam Lake (Map #17/B2)
This large (1190ha) lake is easily accessed by the Duck Lake FSR. The lake provides fairly good trolling for Cutthroat, Rainbows and Kokanee that average 30cm in size but can grow to 2kg. The lake is at 150m in elevation and has an electric motor only restriction.

Inland (Loon) Lake (Map #17/A1)
This 350ha lake is located on the Inland FSR to the east of Powell Lake. The lake provides good fishing for Cutthroat up to 50cm in size as well as for a few small Kokanee. It is best to troll in the spring or early summer. A well maintained trail circles the lake allowing shore fishing. The lake is at 150m in elevation and has several rustic campsites along its shores.

Powell Forest Lakes (Map #17,26)
A scenic backcountry canoe route links a series of freshwater lakes in the Powell Forest Area. The lakes on the chain provide fairly good fishing for Cutthroat and Rainbow mainly in the spring and fall. The canoe route begins on Lois Lake and is travelled in a counter-clockwise direction. If you do not wish to canoe the route, many of the lakes can be reached via the extensive logging road network in the Powell Forest.

> **Dodd Lake** is accessed by the Weldwood Main. It holds Cutthroat that can reach 3kg although the average size is 25cm. There are also some small Kokanee. Trolling is the preferred method of fishing although casting a fly or a lure in one of the small bays can be productive. The lake is 730ha in size and at 200m in elevation. A rec site provides camping and a boat launch.

> **Goat Lake** has small Kokanee, Cutthroat and Rainbow although some of the cutthroats do grow to 2kg. The 410ha lake offers excellent fly fishing and spincasting for Rainbow when they congregate near the mouth of Eldred River in late April-mid May in preparation for spawning. For the rest of the year, the Rainbow (and Kokanee) are best caught by trolling whereas the Cutthroat are best caught throughout the year by spincasting, bait fishing or fly fishing the shoreline. The lake is at 55m in elevation and has several rustic campspots along the southern shores of the lake.

> **Horseshoe Lake** can be reached by secondary road off the Stillwater Main. The lake has many small Cutthroat, Rainbow and Kokanee that are best caught by fly fishing or trolling. The Cutthroat are known to grow 2kg in size although catching a larger fish is quite rare. It is best to concentrate your fishing efforts in the channel between Horseshoe Lake and Nanton Lake or in one of the many bays or weed beds that line the western shore of the lake. Trolling a Willow Leaf with worm or fly fishing with a leech pattern can be particularly effective. Most attractor type patterns (Wooley Bugger or Doc Spratley) work. Camping is provided at the south end of the 290ha lake.

Ireland Lake is one of the smaller lakes along the canoe route as it is only 25ha in size. The lake can be reached by road (Goat Lake Main) or by paddling. There is a rec site at the south end of the lake providing camping. The lake offers good fishing for small Cutthroat and Kokanee throughout the spring and into the early summer. It is best to fish near the creek inlet leading to Dodd Lake or at the outlet to Nanton Lake.

Khartoum Lake is reached from the east end of Lois Lake and does not actually form part of the canoe route. This lake does not receive heavy fishing pressure and provides good fishing for Cutthroat to 2kg. It is best to concentrate your fishing efforts at the inflow of Lois River or in the channel between Lois and Khartoum Lake. The lake is accessed by the Third Lake Road or by canoe and offers a boat launch as well as camping.

Lois Lake is one of the larger (1415ha) lakes along the canoe route. It is best trolled for the Cutthroat that reach 2kg in size (ave. 30-40cm) or for the small Kokanee. You can also do well spincasting or fly fishing at the inflow and outflow of the lake, around the islands or in one of the sheltered bays.

Nanton Lake is accessed off the Goat Lake Main and is really an extension of Horseshoe Lake. The lake, which is 125ha in size, has camping on the western shores. It has Cutthroat to 30cm in size as well as a few Kokanee. The lake is best trolled in the spring or fall given its elevation (150m). It is renown for holding some pretty large Cutthroat (to 3kg). The lake is best fly fished or trolled near the channel from Horseshoe Lake or at one of the inflow creeks. The May midge hatch is the most productive time for fly fishermen.

Powell Lake is a very large (11,200ha) which is notoriously difficult to fish. The Cutthroat and Rainbow reach 4kg in size and are generally caught by trolling. The lake is at 50m in elevation and has several rustic campsites. It is subject to strong winds making canoeing and boating sometimes difficult.

Windsor Lake can be reached either along the Goat Lake Main Road or by boat from Dodd Lake. The Cutthroat in this lake are very small but the numbers allow fast fishing particularly in the spring. For fly fishermen, the best time to try is in late April-early May during the midge hatch. The lake is at 185m in elevation and is 85ha in size.

Sliammon Lake (Map #16/D2)
Found to the east of Powell River and is accessed by the Wilde Road or by trail. This 180ha lake provides fair fishing for Cutthroat to 2.5kg and for small Kokanee. Trolling is the preferred method although it is possible to catch fish by fly fishing or spincasting in the many bays.

Texada Island (Map #8,16,17)
Texada Island is also more noted for its saltwater fishing than its freshwater lake fishing. However, that is an oversight as the freshwater lakes are very nutrient rich compared to other areas on the coast due to large limestone deposits on the island. The result is, vibrant insect and aquatic vegetation growth means plenty of food for the Cutthroat. Most of the smaller lakes and ponds, due to their lack of fishing pressure, are overpopulated with Cutthroat keeping the fish quite small but certainly plentiful. The three lakes on the island containing the largest fish are listed below.

Emily Lake is located at the north end of Texada Island. The 10ha lake holds a few Cutthroat that grow to 2kg in size. These fish are best caught by fly fishing or spincasting. Access to the lake is by short trail through private property (permission necessary to access the lake).

Paxton Lake is a 10ha lake accessed by a 4wd vehicle off the Iron Mine Road. Cutthroat to 2kg in size are caught in the early summer by spincasting or fly fishing.

Priest Lake is located on the Gillies Bay Road at the north end of Texada Island. The 50ha lake is at 75m in elevation and provides decent fishing for Cutthroat to 2kg. The lake is best trolled.

Unwin Lakes (Map #25/C3)
In Desolation Sound Provincial Marine Park, Unwin Lakes are accessed by boat and then a short 1km portage. The lakes are at 25m in elevation and provide excellent fishing for Cutthroat to 30cm given that they are rarely fished. The lakes total 120ha in size and are best fished with bait, although fly fishing and spincasting certainly work. Early summer is the best time to fish.

Squamish/Whistler Area Lakes

Alice Lake Provincial Park (Map #20/C3)
This provincial park is accessed by a short paved road off of Hwy #99. The park is very popular and receives heavy use throughout the summer months due to its camping facilities and its hiking/biking trails. Stump, Edith and Fawn Lakes all require a short hike from Alice Lake with Stump Lake being the best of the walk-in fishing lakes. Each of those lakes contain stocked Rainbow (to 30cm) and a few wild Cutthroat. Stump Lake was also stocked with splake, a cross between Lake Trout and eastern Brook Trout. The attempt, however, is unsuccessful.

Alice Lake has Dolly Varden as well as Rainbow and Cutthroat. Fishing is best left to the spring with the best time to fly fish being when the black ants hatch in May. That is not to say that other fly patterns do not work throughout the spring and into the fall. The fish in all the lakes tend to be small (to 30cm). All the lakes are between 180 and 300m in elevation and range in size from 1.6ha (Fawn Lake) to 15ha (Stump Lake).

Birkenhead Lake (Map #)
The Blackwater Creek Road provides access to Birkenhead Lake where you will find a provincial park complete with a beach, boat launch and camping facilities. The lake is at 610m in elevation and contains fair numbers of Rainbow, Dollies, Kokanee and white fish. Trolling is the mainstay of the lake with the best time to fish being in the early summer or fall. Try trolling a Flatfish or a gang troll with a Wedding Ring and worm. For the fly fishermen, sampling the inflow or outflow creeks can prove productive. The water is surprisingly clear, making the fly fishing even more exciting when you see a fish rise. Private cabins are found along the northwest shore of the lake, which is 410ha in size.

Blackwater Lake (Map #39/D2)
Blackwater Lake is at 710m in elevation and is next to the Blackwater Creek Road. It is stocked annually with Rainbow and so the fishing remains steady although the fish tend to be small. Your best bet is to fly fish or spincast from a boat or a float tube during the spring or fall. There is a rec site with camping on the northeast end of the 15ha lake. The lake has very dark waters although it is not muddy in nature.

Brandywine Falls Lake (Map #29/B4, 20/C1)
This tiny (1ha) lake is located at the end of a 300m walk from the Brandywine Fall Provincial Park rest area off Hwy #99. The lake, which is actually unnamed, is at 450m in elevation. The lake has a few small Rainbow best taken in the spring or fall.

Brohm Lake (Map #20/C3)
Brohm Lake is located next to Hwy #99 and receives heavy fishing pressure throughout the year given its easy access. The lake still contains good numbers of small Rainbow and a few Cutthroat and Dollies primarily because the Rainbow are stocked annually. You can take advantage of the small cartop boat launch, although it is possible to fish from shore. The lake is at 270m in elevation and is 13ha in size.

Browning Lake (Map #11/B1)
Located in Murrin Provincial Park next to Hwy #99, this small (3ha) lake provides a family recreation opportunity as there is an age restriction to fishing. Even

so, it is not uncommon to see 20-30 fishermen lining the shores to catch the stocked Rainbow in the 20-25cm range. Bait fishing dominates. A day-use area is found next to the lake.

Butterfly & Lewis Lake (Map #17/C1)
An old 4wd road leads along Pillchuck Creek and accesses Lewis and Butterfly Lake. The road is gated so you have to walk or bike all the way from the Squamish River Road. Butterfly Lake is at 420m in elevation and offers very good fly fishing, bait fishing or spincasting for Rainbow that average 25cm in size but can reach 2kg. Lewis Lake also has small Rainbow which are quite numerous and come to a fly or small lure readily. Butterfly Lake is 10ha in size whereas Lewis Lake is 6ha in size.

Cat Lake (Map #20/C3)
On the Cheekeye River FSR, Cat Lake is a scenic little lake (5ha) that provides good fishing for small Rainbow. The lake is at 330m in elevation and has a treed rec site together with a wharf. Fly fishing, bait fishing or spincasting are the preferred methods of fishing the lake.

Callaghan Lake (Map #29/B2)
Accessed by the Callaghan FSR southwest of Whistler, this large (120ha) lake provides decent fishing for Rainbow Trout to 1kg (average 20-30cm). Given the elevation (1200m), the fishing starts in early summer and continues through to the fall. Trolling is the primary method of fishing although spincasting and fly fishing should not be ruled out. There is a rec site with several tenting pads as well as a boat launch at the south end of the lake. The lake is set below some cascading peaks making the setting very attractive.

Daisy Lake (Map #20/C1)
This lake is the uninviting reservoir seen next to Hwy #99 to the north of the village of Garibaldi. The lake is subject to severe drawdown and water fluctuations making fishing less than ideal. The lake does have good numbers of small Rainbow, Kokanee and Dollies (ave. 20-35cm) best caught by trolling. Access is provided at the north end through Brandywine Provincial Park. The area is in the Garibaldi Civil Defence Zone and is a high-risk slide area so fishing is not recommended.

Duffey Lake (Map #40/B4)
This large lake is accessed by Hwy #99 northeast of Pemberton. The lake has Rainbow and Dollies (to 2kg) which are best caught by trolling with a gang troll and a Wedding Ring and worm or a Flatfish. The campsite and a boat launch at the north end of the lake are now part of a new park.

Echo Lake (Map #20/B4)
This tiny (3ha) lake is located on the south Rutherford Main (rough 2wd access). The lake, at 700m in elevation, provides fishing for Rainbow Trout to 30cm throughout the spring and fall. Bait fishing seems to work the best.

Evans Lake Area (Map #20/B3)
Three lakes are located on the road leading past the Evans Lake Camp from the Paradise Valley Road. Up to Evans Lake, the road is very good but as you approach Levette Lake, the road becomes steep with loose gravel making a 4wd vehicle an advantage. After Levette Lake, the road is overgrown and a 4wd vehicle is a must if you want to drive to Hut Lake. It is recommended, however, that you simply walk or bike to Hut Lake.

Evans Lake is 6ha in size and at 115m in elevation. It has stocked Rainbow to 1kg best caught by spincasting, bait fishing or fly fishing in the spring or fall. There are private cabins at the north end of the lake.

Levette Lake is at 425m in elevation and is surrounded by private cabins. The 15ha lake is accessed at the south end where the road leads by the lake and where a steep cartop boat launch is found. The lake contains many small Rainbow that grow to 30cm. Bait fishing from the shore at the south end is possible but you may wish to bring a float tube or small boat in order to spincast or fly fish away from the treed shoreline.

Hut Lake has numerous small (to 30cm) Rainbow Trout, which come readily to a fly, bait or small lure. The lake is 5ha in size and is at 500m in elevation. Spring and fall is the best time to fish.

Garibaldi Provincial Park (Map # 20,21,22,29,30)
This expansive provincial park to the east of Whistler and Squamish is not only home to numerous rugged snow-capped peaks but also several good fishing lakes. The sub-alpine lakes are all accessed by a strenuous hike.

Mamquam Lake is accessed by the Diamond Head Trail and is best left to a multi-day adventure given that you must hike some 22km from the parking lot. The lake is seldom fished so it offers very good fishing for Rainbow

to 50cm (1.5kg). Shore fishing using a small lure, a fly or bait meets with success. The lake is at 1300m in elevation so fishing begins in early summers until October.

Garibaldi Lakes are two spectacular sub-alpine lakes accessed by a steep but well maintained 9km trail (Black Tusk Trail). The lakes provide excellent fishing for small Rainbow beginning in July until October. Shore fishing is possible using bait, flies or spinners. The lake has some Rainbow that can reach the 45-55cm range. It is at 1480m in elevation and is 995ha in size. Lesser Garibaldi Lake holds smaller (ave. 25-30cm) and fewer Rainbow than Garibaldi Lake. It is 10ha in size and at 1390m in elevation.

Cheakamus Lake is at 830m in elevation and is accessed by trail from the end of the Cheakamus Lake Road. The hike is 3km long and involves a gentle climb on a well groomed trail making it possible to pack in a float tube or canoe. The forested shoreline limits fly fishing or spincasting from shore. The 400ha lake offers good numbers of Rainbows in the 20-30cm range as well as a few larger Dollies.

Gates Lake (Map #39/D3)
Gates Lake is located along the road to D'Arcy and is 65ha in size. The lake holds Rainbow and Dollies to 2kg as well as smaller Kokanee and Cutthroat. Given the easy access and the private residents that line the lake, this lake receives heavy fishing pressure and is not particularly great for fishing. Trolling or spincasting using a small lure with a worm is the preferred method of fishing the lake. A resort is located at the lake offering accommodation.

Hixon Creek Lakes (Map #12/A2)
Off the Hixon Creek Road (4wd access), a series of lakes provide fair fishing for Rainbow. The area is reached by travelling southeast from Squamish along the Stawamus- Indian FSR. This road network is not open until late April-early May due to snow accumulation. Given the rough access, bringing a boat into the lakes is a challenge. Better alternatives include spincasting, fly fishing or bait fishing from the shore or from a float tube. All lakes are periodically stocked with Rainbow.

Anne Lake can be reached by trail and is at 900m in elevation. The 25ha lake has a fair number of Rainbow which tend to be quite small.

Belknap Lake is at 710m in elevation and is at 5ha. There are fair numbers of stocked Rainbow in the lake (ave. 25-30cm).

Joseph Lake is 950m in elevation and 10ha in size. It is reached by trail leading past Anne and Little Anne Lakes and has fair numbers of small Rainbow.

Little Anne Lake is located north of Anne Lake and is reached by trail. It has Rainbow that are best caught by fly fishing or spin casting in the spring or fall. It is 10ha in size and is located at 900m in elevation.

Norton Lake is noted for having the largest Rainbow of the series of lakes with reports of fish reahing 2kg but usually averaging 25-35cm. The lake is at 715m in elevation and is 45ha in size. Fishing is best in the spring and fall. It is recommended that you use bait or fly fishing methods.

Young Lake is 5ha in size and at 770m in elevation. It has small Rainbow best caught in the spring and fall.

Jane / Crater Lakes (Map #26/D2)
The old 4wd road to these lakes west of Brandywine Falls Provincial Park is now undrivable because of a new BC Rail fence blocking the road. Therefore, you will have to bike/hike 5km to the lakes at 930m in elevation. The lakes hold Rainbow to 50cm (2kg) which are notoriously difficult to catch. Fly fishing is probably your best option.

Joffre Lakes (Map #31/A1)
Off the Duffey Lake Road near Cayoosh Pass, a trail leads past three sub-alpine lakes. **Upper Joffre Lake** is at 1500m in elevation and has the best fishing for small Rainbow beginning in July and running to October. **Middle and Lower Joffre Lakes** also have small Rainbow but the fish are not as plentiful as Upper Joffre Lake. Rustic camping is available at each lake.

Lillooet Lakes (Map #30/D2, 31/A2)
The Lillooet Lakes are not noted for being great fishing lakes because they are extremely murky due to glacier silt. The best time to fish for the Rainbow, Cutthroat and Dollies is in April in the narrows or at the creek mouths using a fly (an attractor type pattern) or bright lure. After April, the lake becomes extremely murky due to spring run-off and the water does not begin to clear until into late August when fishing picks up again. The Lillooet Lakes are divided into 2 lakes with the small lake called **Tenas Lake**. Good mainhaul logging roads follow both the west and east sides of the lakes. There are several rec sites along the lakes offering boat launches and camping.

Lizzie Lake (Map #31/B3)

The Lizzie Creek Main leads to this scenic sub-alpine lake at 1330m in elevation. This road follows a steep narrow valley to the lake with the last few kilometres requiring a 4wd vehicle. You'll pass by Lizzie Falls along the way which is well worth a look. The area is known more as a staging ground for hikers accessing the Upper Stein Wilderness Area than for fishing. However, the lake does offers very good fishing for small Rainbow best caught by fly fishing or spincasting. A small rec site provides camping.

Lake Lovely Water (Map #20/A3)

To reach this scenic sub-alpine lake, you will require a boat to cross Squamish River and then you will have to endure a steep 5km hike along a poorly maintained and very bushy trail. Once you reach the lake some 5-6hrs later, you can camp on the shoreline and sample some of the great fishing for small Rainbow (to 0.5kg). Shore fishing with bait, a lure or fly is possible.

Loggers Lake (Map #29/C4)

Found on the West Side Main off the Cheakamus Lake Road, Loggers Lake is 2ha in size and at 750m in elevation. Since the access is by a rough 4wd road, the lake receives very little fishing pressure making the fishing reasonably good for Rainbow to 45cm is size. It is best to bait fish or fly fish throughout the spring and fall for the stocked Rainbow.

Lucille / Stanley Lake (Map #20/B1)

Lucille Lake is located west of Hwy #99 across the Cheakamus River Bridge and requires a short hike when you reach the powerline crossing since the road is now blocked by the railway tracks. The 12ha lake produces Rainbow in the 30-40cm range by fly fishing or spincasting with some fish reported to be as large as 2.5kg. There are also a few Brook Trout in the lake, which has an electric motor only restriction and is found at 395m in elevation. Stanley Lake is a tiny lake (1ha) near Lucille Lake, which has Rainbow reaching 40cm. Bait fishing from shore is effective as is spincasting or fly fishing from a float tube.

Madeley Lake (Map #29/B3)

Found to the northwest of Whistler on the Madeley Lake Road (4wd access), this lake produces very well for small Rainbow in the 15-30cm class. There is a small campground at the north end of the lake with a rough cartop boat launch. It is highly recommended that you bring a floattube or a boat you can pack-in as the lake is difficult to shore fish except at the south end. For best results, try bait fishing, fly fishing or spincasting.

Marion / Phylis Lakes (Map #11/B2)

To reach these two mountain lakes, you must walk or bike an old logging road from Hwy #99 just north of Furry Creek. The lakes do not receive heavy fishing pressure and so you can do quite well for small Cutthroat and Dollies particularly in the spring and fall. It is possible to fish from the shore with bait but it is recommended to bring a float tube and spincast or fly fish.

Owl Lake Chain (Map #39/A4)

From the Owl Creek FSR (4wd access), a steep trail leads to the Owl Lake Chain. These lakes have small Rainbow (15-30cm) easily caught by spincasting or trolling. A wedding band with a worm works the best although most small lures are also effective. Casting from shore is possible. Other remote sub-alpine lakes worth a try are Ogre, Fowl and Cerulean Lakes. Each of these lakes can be reached by bushwhacking through rugged terrain. These lakes have Rainbow that are generally small but can reach 50cm in size.

Pemberton Lakes (Map #30/B1)

Around the city of Pemberton are 3 small lakes, which provide some slow fishing for small Rainbows and Cutthroat.

Ivey Lake is a catch and release fishery for large Rainbow to 4kg although the average size is 30-40cm. The fish are very cagey so it may take hours to catch one of these beauties. The lake is 10ha in size and at 410m in elevation. A single barbless hook restriction is in effect.

Mosquito Lake is just east of Ivey Lake and has a rec site with a picnicking area. The lake has stocked Rainbow and Cutthroat to 30cm best caught in the summer and fall. The lake is at 445m in elevation and is 5ha in size.

One Mile Lake is right next to Hwy #99 and has a few Rainbow Trout (to 30cm). The lake is 6ha in size and at 225m in elevation. Fishing is by spincasting or fly fishing from a small boat or float tube throughout the spring and fall. Don't expect great results.

Petgill Lake (Map #11/B1)

This lake is accessed by a steep 2km trail leading from Hwy#99 at Murrin Provncial Park. The lake is 3ha in size and is at 760m in elevation. It contains fair numbers of small Rainbow best caught by spincasting or fly fishing from a float tube. Shore fishing is possible but not as productive as using a float tube. The Rainbow are stocked regularly.

Showh Lake (Map #29/D2)

At 950m in elevation off the Cougar Mountain FSR, this 10ha lake provides a catch and release fishery for Rainbows in the 30-50cm class. The 4wd access limits fishermen so you are likely to be the only one at the lake. The elevation (950m) allows for good summer angling, which lasts until the late fall.

Starvation Lake (Map #20/B2)

Starvation Lake is a small (1.6ha) lake that is reached by an overgrown road leading from the very end of the Paridise Valley Road. The lake produces Rainbow as large as 2kg although the average size is 25-30cm. Spincasting, bait fishing or fly fishing all work. Rustic camping is available at the lake.

Tenquille Lake (Map #39/A3)

This small sub-alpine lake is set beneath Tenquille Mountain. The lake is at 1645m in elevation and is reached by any one of three trails leading from surrounding logging roads. The lake is very popular due to its scenery but the lake still produces well for Rainbow in the 20-30cm range. Fly fishing with a dry fly like the Royal Coachman is your best bet. A rec site provides a lakeshore camping area as well as a cabin.

Whistler Village Lakes (Map #29/D3)

In the heart of the Whistler Valley are 5 lakes, which are not noted for their fishing but rather, their water sports. They do, however, contain some game fish so if you are in the area, you may wish to try fishing one of them. All the lakes are at 620m in elevation and so fishing begins in early May and tails off into the summer (due to warm waters) before picking up into the fall.

Alpha Lake is surrounded by cabins and condominiums but still can produce some good fly fishing in June and early July. Trolling can produce a few small Kokanee and Dolly Vardens. The 15ha lake has an electric motor only restriction.

Alta Lake is a 100ha lake in the heart of Whistler that offers some Rainbow, Kokanee and Dollies that grow to 1kg in size but tend to be quite small. The fishing is very spotty.

Green Lake has Rainbow Trout to 1kg as well as Kokanee and Dolly Varden. The lake is best trolled although, with patience, bait fishing from the shore can produce. The 205ha lake is located next to Hwy #99 north of Whistler.

Lost Lake contains Dolly Varden and Rainbow to 30cm in size. This 20ha lake is best fished in the spring or fall by spincasting or fly fishing. The lake has an electric motor only restriction and since it receives heavy fishing pressure, fishing success tends to be quite spotty.

Nita Lake has small Rainbow and some Kokanee which are best caught by fly fishing or spincasting. The 10ha lake has an electric motor only restriction.

Sunshine Coast Lakes

Black Lake (Map #25/B3)

This 50ha lake is located on West Redonda Island and receives very little fishing pressure due to its difficult access. To reach the lake, you must boat to Roscoe Bay Marine Park and then hike into the lake. Once you reach the lake, try trolling or fly fishing from a float tube or small boat for the Cutthroat that reach 2kg in size. There is a tenting site in the Marine Park.

Carlson / Dragon Lakes (Map #9/C2)

These two lakes are accessed off the Halfmoon FSR (4wd recommended). Both lakes have fair numbers of Cutthroat to 30cm and are at 700m in elevation. They provide good fishing in the early spring by spincasting or bait fishing. Carlson Lake is 20ha in size whereas Dragon Lake is 1ha in size.

Clowhom Lake (Map #19/C4)

This remote 40ha lake is found at the north end of the Salmon Inlet, which is accessed by boat. From there, it is well advised to pack a canoe into the lake and paddle to the north end where the Clowhom River enters the lake. The lake, due to its difficult access, provides very good fishing during the fall (September-early October) for Cutthroat to 2kg in size as well as a few large Dollies. Most fishermen try to fish around the river estuary, using bait, fly fishing or spincasting techniques. It is possible to fish from shore, although using a floatation device is better.

Crowston Lake (Map #9/C2)

A rough logging road leads from Hwy #101 just south of Trout Lake to this 5ha lake. The lake is best fished in the spring and fall as the waters warm significantly in the summer. Fly fishing or spincasting from a small boat or float tube for the stocked Cutthroat (ave. 20-40cm) is your best option since the shore is lined with weeds.

Linfoot Lake (Map #10/D3)

Located on Gambier Island, Linfoot Lake is reached by a rough trail. It provides very good fishing for small Rainbow by spincasting, bait fishing or fly fishing throughout the spring or fall. The lake is 5ha in size and is not often fished.

Lyon Lake (Map #9/C1)

Follow the Halfmoon FSR north from the Sunshine Coast Hwy to this 15ha lake. The road deteriorates significantly as you approach the lake making a 4wd vehicle a must. There are stocked Cutthroat in the 20-40cm range as well as a few larger fish. Fly fishing and spincasting in the spring or fall works. There is a rec site at the south end of the lake providing camping.

Nelson Island Lakes (Map #18/A4)

Nelson Island, to the east of the Sechelt Peninsula, has a number of freshwater lakes. Two lakes worth mentioning are **West Lake** and **Mackechnie Lake**. Mackechnie Lake is 15ha in size and at 25m in elevation. It provides fairly good fishing for Cutthroat to 1kg in the spring and fall by spincasting and fly fishing. The lake is reached by trail from Hidden Basin. West Lake is also reached by trail from Hidden Basin. It is 595ha in size and at 25m in elevation. Although the average size is 30-40cm, the lake has surprisingly large Cutthroat (growing to 3kg). There are also a few Rainbow Trout. The lake is best fished in the spring or early summer using a boat. A resort is at the lake.

Pender Harbour Lakes (Map #9,18)

Most fishermen visiting the area come for the good saltwater fishing. However, that is not to say that trout fishing in the nearby freshwater lakes is not worth trying. In fact, when salmon fishing is slow, many people turn to the lakes. All the lakes are near sea level and the best fishing is in the early spring or late fall.

Garden Bay Lake has stocked Cutthroat to 35cm best caught in the spring (April-May) or the fall. Hotel Lake also has stocked Cutthroat to 35cm best caught in the spring or fall by flyfishing or spincasting. The lake is at 55m in elevation and is 25ha in size. An electric motor only restriction applies.

Katherine Lake Park offers stocked Cutthroat to 35cm in size. The lake is best fished in April-May and again in the fall. Katherine Lake Park has a beach and camping. The lake is 6ha in size and at 25m in elevation.

Klein Lake is accessed off the North Lake Road to the east of Earl's Cove. The 14ha lake has many small Cutthroat easily caught by trolling, fly fishing and spincasting. Its scenic surroundings and good fishing make it a popular destination for locals. A rec site on the north end of the lake provides camping and cartop boat launch facilities.

Kokomo Lake can be reached by portaging a canoe from Sakinaw Lake. Given the difficult access, fishing for small Cutthroat can be quite good. The lake is 10ha in size and has an electric motor only restriction.

Mixal Lake is 45ha in size and offers fishing for small Cutthroat mainly in the spring. It is also possible to catch a Coho in the fall. The lake, which is at

25m in elevation, has full facilities but there is an electric motor only restriction.

North Lake is easily accessed by the paved North Lake Road. The 15ha lake, at 330m in elevation, provides slow fishing for Cutthroat averaging 25-30cm. April-May or October are the best times to fish. The lake has full facilities and has an electric motor only restriction.

Ruby Lake is a popular recreation lake with many summer and permanent residents lining the lake. Despite the heavy fishing pressure, the lake still produces well for Cutthroat in the 25-35cm size and small Kokanee mainly by trolling. In the summer, the waters warm making water sports more enjoyable than fishing. The 470ha lake has resorts, boat launches and camping. It is at 35m in elevation.

Sakinaw Lake is a large (840ha) recreation lake lined with private residents. Fishing is generally slow with the best time to fish being the spring or fall due to the elevation (25m) and warm water in the summer. With patience, it is possible to catch large Cutthroat (to 60cm) and some small Kokanee. Trolling is by far you best choice. Salmon and Sea-run Cutthroat can be caught in the fall near the channel flowing into the ocean at the southwest end of the lake.

Waugh Lake is found on the Egmont Road and is frequently fished for Cutthroat and Rainbow to 40cm. An electric motor only restriction applies at the 55ha lake. The Cutthroat are stocked regularly.

Richardson Lake (Map #9/D2)

This 12ha lake is located on a 4wd road off the Mt. Richardson Road. It involves a steep drive to the lake at 760m in elevation. There is a rec site at the west end of the lake providing camping. The lake is stocked with Cutthroat which grow to 30cm in size. Trolling is the preferred method of fishing, although fly fishing and spincasting both work.

Tannis Lake (Map #10/A2)

Located on the Mt. Richardson Road near the Mt. Steele Backcountry Trail System, this small (10ha) lake is one of a series of small mountain lakes in the area. It provides good fishing for Rainbow (ave. 20-30cm), particularly in the spring or fall by trolling. The lake is at 970m in elevation.

Trout Lake (Map #9/C3)

This small (7ha), productive lake is located next to Hwy #101 just to the east of Honeymoon Bay. Despite its easy access, the lake produces surprisingly well for Cutthroat in the 25-35cm range with some growing as large as 2kg. The lake is at 600m in elevation and is best fished by fly fishing or spincasting towards the weeds on the north end of the lake. An electric motor only restriction is in place.

River/Stream Fishing

In Southwestern B.C., there are numerous rivers and streams which provide good fishing for the various salmon species as well as Sea-run Cutthroat and Steelhead. However, given the proximity to the population belt, most rivers and streams receive heavy fishing pressure especially if they have a decent run. Given that the focus is on migratory game species, most of the fishing occurs in the fall or over the winter. There is also limited opportunity to fish resident Cutthroat, Dolly Varden and Rainbow from the spring through fall.

Please note that the rivers and streams in the region are heavily regulated to preserve depleting stocks. All rivers and streams have a single barbless hook restriction. Further, all wild Cutthroat must be released.

Below we have provided information on some of the better rivers and streams to fish in Southwestern B.C.

Alouette River (Map #13/B4)
This urban river flows from the Alouette Lake into the Pitt River. It have a small run of Steelhead in December through March, Cutthroat in the spring and fall and Coho in late September-October. Given its easy access, the river has been over fished for years which has depleted the fish stocks.

American Creek (Map #15/C3)
American Creek is accessed by Hwy #1 and the American Creek Road. It has small resident Rainbow Trout best caught in July-August after spring run-off. There is a very small number of Salmon that can be caught in early summer (June-early July) near the mouth of the creek.

Anderson River (Map #15/D1)
Anderson River flows into the Fraser River north of Hell's Gate. The river has resident Dollies and Rainbow, which can be caught by bait fishing or spincasting. There is also a small run of Steelhead in the late winter-early summer.

Ashulu River (Map #19/C1, 20/A2, 28/B4)
This creek is easily accessed on the Ashulu Road off the Squamish River Road. Most of its length can be accessed by 2wd vehicle except the upper reaches, which are best left to a 4wd vehicle. Due to the falls, the migratory fish are only found in the lower 3km of the river. In these waters, Steelhead and Dollies can be caught from March through May. There is also Coho in October. Above the falls, resident Rainbow and Dollies can be caught by bait fishing or spincasting.

Big Silver Creek (Map #14,23)
This creek flows into Harrison Lake near the Silver Creek Camp. It is easily accessed by an extensive network of logging roads. The creek is only fishable below the falls 7km upstream where Steelhead can be caught in the winter months and resident Cutthroat throughout the year.

Birkenhead River (Map #39/C3)
The Birkenhead River flows into the northwest end of Lillooet Lake and is accessed by the Pemberton-D'Arcy Road or the Birkenhead Forest Service Road. Sockeye and Chinook Salmon enter the river in good numbers in the fall. There are some resident Dollies and Rainbow as well. Unfortunately, the best fishing is within the indian reserve which does not allow for public access. Also, glacial silt entering the river during spring run-off restricts fishing in May through July. There is a bait restriction so spoons and spinners should be tried. For fly fishermen, use a wet fly such as a Doc Spratley.

Bridge River (Map #43/3B, 36/A4)
This small river flows into the Fraser River to the north of Lillooet. The river has Steelhead, Coho and Chinook in the fall as well as resident Rainbows. Float fishing using roe or crayfish is the most effective although using a large spoon (Deadly Dick, Krocodile or Kitimat) meets with success.

Brittain River (Map #18/B1, 27/A4)
Brittain River is a remote river in Jervis Inlet which is accessed by boat and then by hiking/biking up an old logging road along the river. Due to its limited access, the river is very good for Steelhead from November through March as well as resident Cutthroat in the spring and fall. The farther you walk/bike up the river the better the fishing becomes.

Campbell River (Map #2/C4)
This river flows into Georgia Straight near Mud Bay and, given its urban setting, does not offer great fishing opportunities. There is a very small run of winter Steelhead as well as Coho and Cutthroat entering the river in late fall (October-November). It is possible to catch the Cutthroat until the spring as they often overwinter within the river system to spawn. The Little Campbell River has been extensively rehabilitated by the community hatchery and this has helped somewhat in increasing the salmon, trout and Steelhead returns. Access to the river is where 16th Ave crosses the river near the Peace Portal and Hazelmere Golf Courses.

Chapman Creek (Map #10/3B)
Chapman Creek is located on the Sechelt Peninsula and flows into the ocean at Wilson Creek. The creek is accessed by the West Road along most of its length and provides fishing for Steelhead in February-April, Coho in the fall and resident Cutthroat year round.

Cheakamus River (Map #20/B2)
The upper reaches of the Cheakamus River flow beside Hwy #99 and provide fishing for small resident Rainbow which are best fished using bait. Much of the upper reaches are somewhat impassable due to a canyon. Fishing should be restricted to when the river is not swollen with spring run-off (September-May). The lower Cheakamus River area offers a fairly good spring Steelhead run (April-May).

Coho enter the river in October and can be caught in good numbers throughout the winter. A few Chinook may be caught in the fall (September-November). Resident Dollies and Cutthroat are also present year round. The lower Cheakamus River receives heavy fishing pressure especially near Fergie's Lodge and up the Paradise Valley Road. Roe, lures or flies all work for the salmon and Steelhead.

Chehalis River (Map #4/B1, 14/B4)
This river flows from Chehalis Lake southward into the Harrison River near Harrison Mills and is considered one of the best local Steelhead rivers. The entire length of the river can be accessed by the Chehalis FSR. However, the canyon along most of the river limits fishing. The river provides a good run of winter Steelhead beginning in December until March as well as a few Steelhead in June and July. Both fisheries are enhanced by hatchery stock.

The Steelhead are best caught by a float with roe or by fly fishing using a sinking tip line to ensure that the fly is dragged near the bottom. In addition to Steelhead, there are some summer Chinook running in July through August as well as a very good Coho run (to 7kg) in October through early December so long as there are fall rains. The difficult terrain of the canyon limits fly fishing so spincasting prevails. The lower reaches of the Chehalis near the Harrison River is more open allowing fly fishing as well as spincasting. The lower reaches, given their easy access, receive the heaviest fishing pressure.

Chilliwack (Vedder) River (Map #4/C4)
This river is known as the Chilliwack River above the Vedder bridge and the Vedder River below the bridge. The total fishing length is about 36km all the way to Slesse Creek. The river is easily accessed along the Chilliwack Lake Road and therefore receives heavy fishing pressure making it the most popular river to fish in the Fraser Valley.

The best place to fish the river is above the bridge as there are numerous pools to sample. The river has an excellent Steelhead run from December through March as well as a few Steelhead in the summer months. Chum and Coho fishing can be very good in September to October due to hatchery enhanced Coho stock. Cutthroat fishing can be very good beginning in July until October and Chinook fishing can be decent in July through September. Fishermen use a multitude of different methods but wool, roe, lures and flies seem to work best for the Coho and Steelhead whereas flies and small spinners work best for the Cutthroat. Please make note of the fishing restrictions in place on the river.

Clowham River (Map #19/C4)
Clowham River flows southward into the northeast end of Clowham Lake. It provides Sea-run Cutthroat fishing in the spring and fall as well as Coho fishing in the fall. There are also resident Cutthroat and Dollies available. The river is accessed by the Clowham Lake Road along most of its length.

Cogburn Creek (Map #14/D2)
Cogburn Creek flows into the Harrison River just north of the Bear Creek Camp. It has Steelhead in January-April as well as some resident Cutthroat throughout the year. The fishing is restricted to the first 3km of the creek given some impassable falls.

Coquihalla River (Map #15/D4)
Coquihalla River is accessed by Hwy #5 and provides a fair run of Steelhead in June-September and again in February-March. There are also a few Coho in October and November as well as some resident Rainbow and Dollies. Given the easy access, the river is fished extensively and so you should not expect great fishing.

Coquitlam River (Map #2/B1, 12/B2)
Flowing from Coquitlam Lake into the Pitt River, this shallow, urban river has a small run of Steelhead in December-April, Coho in November-December and Chum in the fall. There are a few small Cutthroat and Dollies that reside in the river year-round.

Deserted River (Map #28/A4)
Deserted River is a remote river flowing into the Jervis Inlet that can only be reached by boat and then bushwhacking up the river. Given its difficult access, there is a good run of Steelhead in the winter as well as Coho in the fall. The farther away from the inlet, you hike the better the fishing becomes.

Elaho River (Map #37,B4)
Elaho River flows into the Squamish River and is easily accessed along most of its length by the Elaho Road (2wd access). A few Steelhead are found in March-May as well as a few Coho in September-October. The river is noted more for its resident Dollies, which can reach 2kg in size, as well as smaller Rainbow.

Emory Creek (Map #15/C3)
Emory Creek flows into the Fraser River north of Squeah. The creek is accessed along most of its length by a good logging road. It has small Rainbow and Dollies best taken after spring run-off. Springs are available at the mouth of the creek between June-July and there is a small run of fall Coho and Steelhead in January-March.

Fraser River (Map # 15/B1, 24/C3, 42/A4, 46/B1)
The Fraser River, between Coquitlam and American Creek, offers excellent fishing for migratory fish and sturgeons. Most of the fishing occurs off one of the many gravel bars that line the river. Access to many of these bars is limited, making the easily accessible area very busy. Spring is really the only time of year when fishing is very poor given the high, murky waters and lack of migratory species in the system.

Sockeye (to 7kg) are now open for fishing and begin entering the river in mid-July. The main runs occur in late August to late September with hundreds of fishermen lining the gravel bars. The sockeye are caught by bouncing a weight and a piece of flourescent green or pink wool off the bottom. Others use small green spin-n-glows or flourescent green or pink flies. Flourescent green outperforms pink in direct contrast to ocean fishing.

Chinooks are caught beginning in June after the spring run-off subsides. Initially, float fishing or spincasting near the creek mouths proves most effective since the water is clearer in the estuaries. Later in the summer, as the spring runoff subsides, the gravel bars begin to appear and the water clears somewhat, fishermen turn to the gravel bars and cast a spin-n-glow or cheater and sinker. As a rule of thumb, use darker coloured spin-n-glows in the early part of the season and a brighter one later in the season as the water clears somewhat. The best of the Chinook fishing ends in July although the fish continue to enter the river until mid-October. Some Chinook can reach 27kg (60lb) but most of them are in the 12-18kg range.

Sea-run Cutthroat (to 50cm) are caught throughout the fall until early spring by fly fishing or drift fishing. Steelhead are available from November-March by float fishing or spincasting. Coho enter the river in late September and provide excellent fishing until December. Bar fishing is the most popular method of catching the Coho. Sturgeon, which can exceed 450kg (1000lbs), are also caught throughout the river system by using a large weight, hook and bait. The fishery is now catch-n-release given the recent decline in the population. Summer and the fall are the best time to fish.

Chum salmon are caught in October and Pink salmon in August and September. Both species are caught in the same manner as the sockeye except Pinks can also be caught by using spoons, spinners or flies. Contrary to popular belief, flies do not have to be hot pink to catch Pinks as flies such as a 52 Buick (a small, green shrimp imitation) work. Fly fishing works best by leaving the fly at a dead drift or by a slow steady retrieve.

Gold Creek (Map #13/A4)
This creek is found in the Golden Ears Provincial Park and flows southward into the Alouette Lake. The creek is accessed by a series of trails and can be fished for small Cutthroat, Rainbows and Dollies which reside in the creek year-round. After spring run-off is the best time to fish using bait.

Gray Creek (Map #9,10)
Gray Creek flows from a series of mountain lakes into the Sechelt Inlet south of Tuwanek. The creek has Cutthroat in the spring and fall and Coho in the fall.

Green River (Map #30/A2)
Green River flows northwest from Green Lake and enters the Lillooet River to the east of Pemberton. Most of the length of the river is easily accessed off Hwy #99. Glacial silt entering the river makes it difficult to fish. It is possible to catch a few larger Dollies (to 1.5kg) and a few small Rainbows.

Harrison River (Map #4/B2)
At the bridge near Harrison Mills, it is not uncommon to see 20-40 fishermen lining the banks in the late summer and into the fall. The reason for the heavy fishing pressure is the excellent fishing. Cutthroat fishing can be particularly effective from March through December, although during spring run-off (May-June) the fishing tails off because the waters are quite murky. The Cutthroat are in the river in the fall to grab salmon eggs and in the spring to feast on the millions of salmon fry making their journey to the ocean. These fish are best caught by casting a fly, bait (worms, roe or eggs) or small lure. For fly fishermen, stick to a flashy type pattern or a small minnow imitation.

The river also offers decent Steelhead fishing in December-January using roe, lures or wool. Coho fishing is active between September-November with the best time being in late October. The Coho take to roe, wool or lures. Pinks can be fished in late August to October. Spoons, spinners or flies all work. Although hot pink flies are the preference of fishermen, do not rule out other patterns such as a 52 Buick (a small, green shrimp imitation). Either try a dead drift or retrieve the fly in a slow, steady manner. The best place to fish for all the species is right near the Hwybridge or near the railway bridge using chest waders and casting from shore. It is possible to launch a boat at Kilby Park off Hwy #7 and troll a fly or lure in Harrison Bay or near the bridges. For best results, simply follow the crowds and you'll get a good idea of where and how to fish.

Hunter Creek (Map #5/D3)
Hunter Creek is a small creek that flows northward into the Fraser River to the west of Hope. Most of the creek is accessed by the Hunter Creek Forest Service Road. Springs are available at the mouth of the creek in June-July whereas Cutthroat and Steelhead frequent the estuary in the winter.

Indian River (Map #11/D2, 12/A3)
Indian River flows into the north end of the Indian Arm and can be accessed either by boat or the Stawamus-Indian FSR. The river offers a small spring Steelhead run as well as fishing for resident Cutthroat and Dolly Varden. The Steelhead enter the river in April when the Stawamus-Indian FSR is inaccessible due to snow accumulation. Therefore, it may be preferable to boat to the Indian Arm and access the river that way. The Cutthroat and Dolly Varden are easiest to catch every second year when the pink salmon fry migrate to the ocean.

Johnson's Slough (Map #5,15)
Approximately 15km east of Aggasiz, this slough is accessed by Hwy #7. It provides decent fishing for Cutthroat in April-June and again in September-October. There are also good numbers of Coho in September-October. Bait fishermen do well with worms and salmon eggs but fly fishing and spincasting should not be ruled out.

www.backroadmapbooks.com

Kanaka Creek (Map #33/B3)
This is a small urban creek, which has a few Steelhead in January-March, Cutthroat in September-April and Coho in the fall. Most of the creek can be easily accessed by paved roads and a good trail system.

Lang Creek (Map #17/B3)
Lang Creek flows from Duck Lake into the ocean just west of Lang Bay. The upper reaches of the creek are accessed off the Duck Lake Forest Service Road whereas the middle reaches must be accessed by trail. There are Steelhead in January-March as well as Cutthroat in the spring and fall in the river. However, the best fishing is now in the shallow estuary for hatchery Springs averaging 20kg. They are fished in mid September to late October by casting a spoon or large fly from the beach. Since the waters are shallow, it is well advised that you use a lure that does not sink too quickly or you will loose a lot of tackle. The occasional Coho and chum is caught in this new fishery.

Lillooet River (Map #22/B2)
The Lillooet River is easily accessed by the Pemberton Valley Road and a number of mainline logging roads. It contains Steelhead (March-May), resident Dollies, Coho (October) and Springs (April-May). However, given the glacial silt that enters the river, fishing is poor during May through October. Therefore, you should restrict your fishing to the early spring or late fall or try one of the many clear water estuaries such as Rogers Creek. Chinook are closed from July 30 to September 30.

Mamquam River (Map #20/C4)
Mamquam River flows westward into the Squamish River just south of Brackendale. The falls at 6km restrict fish migration to the upper reaches of the River. The Mamquam contains fair numbers of Steelhead in March-May with April being the best time to fish. Coho and Dollies are also present in October through early November. The best place to try is at the mouth of the river where it enters the Squamish River or at the estuary of Mashiter Creek.

Maria Slough (Map #4,5/A1)
This water body extends to the west of the Fraser River near Aggasiz. The Seabird Island Road provides access along most of its 10km length. The slough offers some very good fishing for Sea-run Cutthroat in October through March although there are resident Cutthroat throughout the year. Some of the Sea-run Cutthroat reach 2.5kg in size. There is also a good run of Coho beginning in late October until mid-December (check regulations for closures). Resident Dollies are also present. The preferred method of catching the Cutthroat and Dollies is by bait (worms or eggs), lures or flies. Coho prefer lures (Krocodile or Coho lures) or salmon eggs.

Melvin Creek (Map #40/D3, 40/C3)
Melvin Creek is a small creek that flows into Cayoosh Creek. The creek is accessed by trail along its entire length and provides good fishing for small Rainbow on a fly or with a small spoon.

McNab / McNair Creeks (Map #10/A2)
These two small creeks flow into the Thornbrough Canal near Port Melon. McNab Creek, which is accessed by boat, has resident Cutthroat, Coho in October-November and Steelhead in the winter. It is preferable to bring a mountain bike to access the upper reaches of McNab Creek for the best fishing. McNair Creek, which is accessed by Hwy #101, has Cutthroat in the spring and fall, Coho in October-November and Steelhead in the winter.

Miami Creek (Map #4/D1)
This creek runs into Harrison Lake just west of Harrison Hot Springs. The mouth of the creek is the most popular area to fish using bait (salmon roe/eggs and worms) or by casting a small lure. In the summer months, Rainbow can be caught with some fish reaching 0.5kg. In the fall, beginning in late October-November, Cutthroat trout and Coho can be caught. Although the mouth of the creek is the most popular spot, some of the larger pools upstream can be particularly good for Coho and Cutthroat in late November when the waters have risen due to rainfall.

Nahatlach River (Map #31/C4, 22/D1, 24/B1)
Nahatlach River flows into the Fraser River south of Lytton. It provides resident Rainbow and Dollies as well as Steelhead in the winter, Springs in the summer and Coho in the fall.

Nikomekl River (Map #2/B4)
This river flows into Georgia Straight near Mud Bay and, given its urban setting, does not offer great fishing opportunities. There is a very small run of winter Steelhead as well as Coho and Sea-run Cutthroat that enter the river in late fall (October-November). It is possible to catch the Cutthroat until the spring as they often stay within the river system to spawn in the spring.

Norrish Creek (Map #3/D2)
Norrish Creek is easily accessed by the Norrish Creek Road along most of its length. A falls at 7.5km restricts fishing above this mark. There are Steelhead in December-March, Cutthroat in the spring and fall and Coho in October-November. Small resident Rainbow Trout are available year-round.

North Vancouver Rivers (Map #11/C4, 11/D2)
The Capilano River, Seymour River and Lynn Creek offer hatchery produced Steelhead and salmon but they are very heavily fished given their close proximity to the population belt. Each of the water systems have a small run of winter Steelhead beginning in late December and running until early April.

The Seymour and Capilano River also have small summer Steelhead run beginning in June until late July. The Capilano River also has a Coho run which begins in early August. Literally hundreds of fishermen line the shores of the Capilano or fish from boats at the mouth attempting to catch some of these fish.

The Seymour River and Lynn Creek have smaller runs of Coho and some Chinook. Both of these fish must be released if caught. Given the steep terrain, each of the rivers has difficult access. The Seymour River is the easiest to fish as it has a trail (Fishermans Trail) that extends along the river to the Seymour Dam. There are numerous pools to fish with the best fishing being in the upper reaches.

Lynn Creek only has 5km of fishable waters accessed from the park. The Capilano is best fished towards the lower end. Please check the regulation for each of the water bodies as they are heavily regulated.

Pitt River (Map #2/C1, 21/33)
The upper Pitt River provides approximately 24km of good fishing holes, which are seldom visited because of the remote access. The river is reached by boat to the north end of Pitt River and then by biking/walking north along a good logging road. It is preferable to bring a bike as the best fishing holes are well upstream. The river has a good number of resident Dollies, a small run of winter Steelhead (February-March) and a good run of Coho in the Fall (October).

Rainy River (Map #10/C2)
Rainy River is accessed by Hwy #101 to Port Melon and then along a deteriorating logging road (4wd). The river has Steelhead in February-March, Cutthroat year-round and Coho in October-November.

Roberts Creek (Map #10/A4)
Roberts Creek is found on the Sechelt Peninsula and contains Steelhead and Cutthroat. Those fish are best caught near the estuary.

Ruby Creek (Map #15/B4)
Ruby Creek flows southward into the Fraser River. The creek has resident Rainbow and Cutthroat as well as Steelhead in the winter and Coho in the fall. Most of the creek can be accessed by the Ruby Creek Forest Service Road but it is necessary to bring a 4wd vehicle.

Scuzzy Creek (Map #24/A3)
Scuzzy Creek flows eastward into the Fraser River. An extensive logging road network provides access along most of the creek length. There are small resident Cutthroat in the creek that are best caught by bait fishing.

Sechelt Creek (Map #18/C4, 19/D4)
Sechelt Creek is a remote creek located towards the north end of the Salmon Inlet. The creek is accessed by boat and then following a logging road, preferably with a bike. The creek has resident Cutthroat as well as Coho in the fall and Steelhead in the winter.

Serpentine River (Map #2/B3)
This river flows into Georgia Straight near Mud Bay and, given its urban setting, does not offer great fishing opportunities. There is a very small run of winter Steelhead as well as Coho and Sea-run Cutthroat enter the river in late fall (October-November). It is possible to catch the Cutthroat until the spring as they often stay within the river system to spawn in the spring.

Silverhope Creek (Map #15/C4)
This large, fast creek flows into the Fraser River just west of Hope. It has a small Steelhead run in the summer (June-August) and in the winter (January-April). There are also a few salmon that enter the river in the fall and there are some resident Cutthroat and Dollies. For best success, fish at the mouth of the creek or try some of the deep holes along the creek using bait, spinners or flies. Restrictions include barbless hooks and releasing all fish under 20cm in size.

Skagit / Sumallo River (Map #6/C3)
These two rivers are located to the east of Hope and are accessed either by Hwy #3 or the Silver Skagit Road. The rivers offer really the only good Rainbow fishing river in Southwestern B.C. They are similar to some of the rivers and streams found in the interior of B.C.

Sumallo River has small Rainbow which are caught by fly, bait or small spinner. Skagit River is a slow meandering river that is famous for its good fly fishing for Steelhead. Rainbow are also present. Fishermen either walk along the Skagit River Trail from Sumallo Grove or float down the river to sample some of the more remote pools.

Fishing is restricted in both rivers until July with the best fishing being towards August-September, after the river water has subsided. Fly fishermen can do very well using a mayfly imitation (#16 Mayfly), Grizzly King or Royal Coachman later in the summer. The Rainbow in the Skagit River average 20-30cm but can grow as large as 50cm. Dolly Varden enter the river from Ross Lake and can grow as large as 5kg (10lbs). These fish are in the river in the fall but some remain year-round.

Sloquet Creek (Map #13/B1)
Sloquet Creek flows northeast into the Lillooet River. A deteriorating and rough logging road accesses the lower portions of the creek. There are Steelhead in January-April, resident Dollies and Coho in the fall.

Spuzzum Creek (Map #15/C1,24/A4)
Spuzzum Creek flows eastward into the Fraser River south of Spuzzum. The creek has Steelhead in January-April, Springs in June-July and resident Rainbows. Although the creek is accessed by a mainhaul logging road along most of its length, the best place to fish is near the creek mouth.

Squamish River (Map #20,28,29)
This large river flows southward into Howe Sound at Squamish. It has a total of 60km of fishable water. The river, due to glacial silt and spring run-off, is very difficult to fish from early May to the end of July because the water is very murky. Also, the lower reaches of the river below Brackendale are very unproductive. As a result, the best time to fish is in the fall to early spring from below Cheakamus River to the Ashulu Creek estuary. Despite this, the most popular area to fish is from the Cheakamus River estuary to Brackendale.

The river offers Steelhead beginning in January with the best time being in late March. A small run of very large Springs to 25kg (55lbs) enters the river in July through August. Coho are present in October-November and Dollies are available year-round. Most of the river is easily accessed by mainhaul logging roads.

Statlu Creek (Map #14/A4)
Statlu Creek flows eastward into the Chehalis River and is easily accessed by the Statlu Creek Road. The creek provides fishing for Steelhead in the winter as well for Cutthroat year-round.

Stave River (North) (Map #13/B2)
Stave River flows into the north end of Stave Lake and can only be reached by boat and then biking or hiking up the Stave River Forest Service Road. There are resident Cutthroat and Dollies in the river as well as Chinook in the summer, Steelhead in December-March and Coho in the fall. Given the remote access, the river can be very productive for fishing particularly in the late fall.

Stawamus River (Map #11/C1)
Stawamus River is a small stream that flows into Howe Sound at Squamish. It provides slow fishing for Steelhead in April-May and Coho in the fall. There are also resident Cutthroat and Dollies year-round.

Stein River (Map #32/C1, 33/A2)
This river is reached by trail and can provide some very good fishing for Steelhead in the winter, Chinook and Coho in the fall and Cutthroat year-round. The most productive methods of fishing is to cast a large spoon (Kamlooper, Krocodile or Kitimat) or float fish with roe or crayfish.

Sumas River (Map #3/D4, 4/A3)
This river is accessed by Hwy #1 and provides a few Cutthroat in the spring and fall, resident Dollies year-round, Coho in the fall (mid September-December) and Steelhead in the winter. A boat launch is available at the Sumas Pumping Station.

Texas Creek (Map #41/B3)
Texas Creek is found south of Lillooet and flows to the northeast into the Fraser River. Texas Creek Road provides access but if you want to reach the upper portion of the creek you will need a 4wd vehicle. The creek provides excellent fishing for small Rainbow using bait, a fly or small lures.

Theodosia River (Map #25/D3)
This remote river flows into the Thedosia Inlet near Desolation Sound Provincial Marine Park. The river is accessed by boat and then by following the Thedosia Main logging road up the river. Therefore, it is best to bring a bike if you want to try the upper reaches of the river. The river provides Steelhead and Cutthroat in the spring and fall as well as Coho in September-October.

Tingle Creek (Map #13/A3)
This small creek flows into Clearwater Bay and Stave Lake through Mt. Judge Howay Recreation Area. The creek is accessed by boat and then by hiking/biking an old logging road. It provides resident Rainbow, Dollies and Cutthroat fishing in the spring and fall.

Tzoonie River (Map #19/B2)
Tzoonie River is a remote river flowing southward into Narrows Inlet. It is accessed by boat and then by following the Tzoonie River Road preferably by mountain bike. The river provides Steelhead fishing in December-March as well as Coho fishing in the fall. There are resident Dollies and Cutthroat in the river system.

Vancouver River (Map #18/D2)
The Vancouver River is another remote river that flows into Jervis Inlet. A mountain bike can be used to access the length of the river along an old rail line from Vancouver Bay. The river has Steelhead in January-May, Cutthroat in October-November and Coho in the fall. There are also resident Dollies available. Given the remote access, the fishing is usually very good.

Vedder River (4/B4, see Chilliwack River)

Widgeon Creek (12/C3)
This creek drains Widgeon Lake southward into Pitt River. It is accessed by canoe through the Pitt-Addington Marsh. The creek has resident Cutthroat as well as Steelhead in the winter and Coho in the fall.

Yale Creek (Map #15/C2)
This small creek is accessed by Hwy #1 just east of Yale. The creek offers Chinook in June through July at the mouth of the Fraser River.

Saltwater Fishing

Howe Sound/ Vancouver Area

Fishing in the proximity of Vancouver does not measure up to other coastal locations such as the Queen Charlotte Islands or the West Coast of Vancouver Island. But with some patience and some luck, good salmon fishing is possible.

The real advantage of the Howe Sound and Burrard Inlet is the easy access from Vancouver. Boat launches are available near the entrance to False Creek, at Ambleside Beach in West Vancouver, at Horseshoe Bay, at Sewell's Marina, at MacDonald Park in Richmond and several locations along the Fraser River. Most launches charge a hefty fee, around $10.00. It is also possible to access Howe Sound from the Sunshine Coast with boat launches at Langdale and Gibsons being the most convenient.

Over winter Chinook Salmon offer some good fishing in December through April within Howe Sound. A deep troll 25-35m (80-120ft) using a variety of methods (plugs, hoochies, herring or Apex) is the preferred method although mooching and jigging can produce at times. In the spring, you do not generally see the Blueback (Coho) fishing of Vancouver Island especially since the Coho population is severely depleted. Therefore, fishing does not pick up until June when migratory Chinook begin to appear in some areas. Throughout the summer months, there are opportunities to catch Chinook, Coho, Pinks and Sockeye. Chum can be caught in October in some locations.

Please keep in mind that Coho populations are in a decline and so fishing success has suffered over the last four years. The Department of Fisheries, at the time of writing this book, is considering drastic measures such as closing off the entire fishery! Even if they do not, there are still large closures in effect so reviewing the regulations before heading out is a must.

Bowen Island (Map #10/11)
Bowen Island is a 20-30 minute boat ride west of Horeeshoe Bay across Queen Charlotte Channel. The island offers good fishing opportunities throughout the year but in crowded conditions. The better fishing areas are:

Cape Roger Curtis (Map #10/D4)
This area is located at the southwestern end of Bowan Island. Although the area can produce Chinook, it is known more for its Coho fishing. Trolling with a flasher with strip herring near the surface (less than 12m) is best although bucktailing or mooching should not be ruled out. Weather can be a real concern as the point is exposed.

Collingwood Channel (Map #10/D4)
This location often produces very well for winter Chinook in December-April. Trolling all along the west side of Bowen Island can produce at that time. Mooching near the reef off Tunstall Bay is also very effective.

Cowan Point to Cape Roger Curtis (Map #10/D4)
This is a good area for wintering Chinook in December to April. Most fishermen troll deep 25-35m (80-120ft) along the first tide line using hoochies or bait (strip or whole) with a flasher/dodger. If fishing is slow, move further out from the shoreline. Cowan Point also produces well for Chinook in May through July, Coho in late Aug-Oct, Pinks in late August to September (odd years) and Sockeye in September with trolling being your best bet. Mooching live herring or strip casting off Cowan Point also works for Chinook throughout the year. The area is very popular because of its consist fishing success.

Dofman Bay has Chinook and Coho in late July through to early September.

Grafton / Galbrath Bays (Map #10/A4)
Located on the northwest corner of the island and sheltered by Hutt Island, this area holds Chinook most of the year (May-July or Oct-Apr), although it is hit-and-miss. Mooching with live or strip herring in the middle of the channel between Hutt Island and Bowen Island or in the centre of Grafton and Galbrath Bay is most productive. Trollers circle the north end of Hutt Island or troll the two bays. Since the water depth ranges up to 45m (150ft), trollers stick to the 15-25m (60-80ft) level and use plugs or flashers with a hoochie as well as live or cut-plug herring. Coho, in declining numbers, are available off Hutt Island in July or October. Pink, in odd years, can be caught in late August and September.

Seymour Landing, which is on the east side of Bowen Island just north of Cowan Point, has some reasonable fishing for Chinook in May. Troll deep 25-35m (80-120ft) for best success.

Snug Cove is often trolled southward to the Coppermine for Chinook in Dec-March or June-August and for Coho from July to September. Be wary of the ferry traffic.

Tunstall Bay is just north of Cape Roger Curtis and is an area to try in December to April for wintering Chinook. A deep troll using herring (whole or cut) or hoochies is most effective.

Burrard Inlet (Map #1,11)
For fishermen looking for an easily accessed fishing area near Vancouver, there are a number of areas within the Inlet to try:

The Capilano River mouth (Map #1/B1)
is an incredibly popular area to fish. It is not unusual to see 50-100 fishermen casting from the shores of Ambleside Beach together with 20-50 boats all trying to catch the 2-3kg Coho that congregate at the river mouth. If you are fishing from shore for the Coho beginning in June until November, casting any one of a number of lures works (Krocodile, Stingzildas, Buzz-Bombs, No. 4 Colorado or Chrome Flatfish). For boaters, it is best to anchor 20-30m off the lighthouse and mooch with live herring, herring strips or small cut-plug herring on a tide change. A small number of Chinook in the 10-15kg (30-40lb)range also remain in the area in July until mid-September. In December through April, winter Chinooks frequent the mouth and can be caught by mooching 60-80m offshore using a herring strip or small cutplug herring.

Indian Arm (Map #12/A3)
Indian Arm produces an excellent fishery for Pinks in late August- early September primarily in odd years. These fish congregate just south of the Vancouver Yacht Club against the rock cliff. It is best to drift fish while casting a red and white wobbler or similar lure into the school of fish. Where the fish are congregated becomes readily apparent, as you will see the males jumping.

Jericho Beach (Map #1/A1)
This beach is best trolled in December through April for immature Chinook past the drop-off. A dodger with a hoochie, whole herring or Apex is most effective. In July through September, there are occasional Coho that can be caught by trolling.

Point Atkinson (Map #1/A1)
This point is marked by the lighthouse in Lighthouse Park. A rock shelf extends off the point to the 18-25m (60-90ft) level before dropping off to 60m or more. It is at this drop-off that trolling is most effective for Chinook in the winter and July to September as well as for a few Coho and Pinks in August through September. It is best to troll a flasher/ dodger with a hoochie, anchovy or herring in a circular manner around the point and into Caulfield Cove. Casting and mooching can work although both methods are not very popular given the strong currents that pass by the point making anchoring or drift fishing difficult.

Point Grey Bell Buoy (Map #1/A1)

This point use to be a popular area for trolling but is not very productive any more so it receives little interest. The best place to fish is several hundred metres off the Bell Buoy in the deeper waters. Trolling with a flasher and hoochie, herring strip or Apex can produce an immature Chinook in December through May and larger Chinook in September. Bluebacks can be caught in March through April and larger Coho in June through October. The occasional Pink and Sockeye can be taken in September.

The Shipping Lanes and the QB marker (Map #1/B1) are found in the middle of Burrard Inlet and offer some marginal fishing primarily for winter Chinooks between December and April. The area has a sandy bottom and is best to fish 10-15m off the bottom by trolling a flasher/dodger with a hoochie (white preferable), Apex or herring strip.

West Vancouver Waterfront (Map #1/B1)

This region sports an active trolling fishery for Chinook in the winter and early spring and for Coho in August through September. The best place to try is 300m offshore where there is a notable underwater bench where the fish tend to congregate. No one particular area along the West Vancouver waterfront is more productive than another, although fishermen tend to stay in West Bay or off Navy Jack Point.

The typical Coho and Chinook gear (flasher with hoochie or herring strip) seem to produce the best. Some fishermen mooch in the area but it is certainly not as productive as trolling because the fish are not focused in one area and the currents make mooching difficult. The winter Chinook average 4-5kg and are best caught by using a small herring or anchovy in a teaser head. Trolling all the way to the Ambleside boat launch from Navvy Jack Point can prove effective. A deep troll 35-55m (120-180ft) for winter Chinook is preferred. In the summer, Coho have been caught in fair numbers between West Bay and Point Atkinson.

Fraser River Estuary (Map #1)

The Fraser River is the pathway for millions of migrating salmon. It is no wonder the river mouth can provide some of the best fishing anywhere near Vancouver. To fish the Fraser River, you have a number of boat launches to choice from: McDonald Park (on Sea Bird Island), False Creek (behind the Planetarium), and Dyke Road at Gilbert Beach. Each of the launches involves a 20- 30 minute boat ride to the estuary. Once you reach the estuary, simply look for the boats and you will have a good idea where to fish. Between Point Grey Bell Buoy and the QA marker off the North Arm or off the end of the Steveston Jetty in the tide lines are two of the better locations.

By far the best fishery is for Sockeye beginning in mid June and lasting until the end of September depending on the runs. The first run of the year is the Stuart River run which has millions of fish but they all seem to resist taking a lure. After that, there are a number of different runs including the Horsefly River and Adams River runs. To catch Sockeye, troll a small pink hoochie, with only a few strands left, 50-60cm (18-24) inches behind a green or red flasher. Troll very slow in a "S" manner with the tide leaving the flashers 5-15m (20-60ft) down (the deeper the better). If possible, stack the lines so that you have a number of flashers off each downrigger, some of which have no lure so there is plenty of movement to attract the fish. The reason being, the waters of the Fraser are murky making it difficult for the fish to see your lure easily.

Other salmon species do not draw as much attention as the Sockeye. Pinks are in abundance in odd years at the mouth in August. The same set-up for Sockeye catches Pinks. Chinook and Coho can be caught in August to October by trolling a dodger/flasher with a hoochie or bait (herring or anchovy) but watch for the fishing closures that are usually in affect. The best time for the Coho is October when the 6kg (20lb) northerns begin to appear. Believe it or not, sookeye gear does well for Chinook. The occasional fisherman mooches for the Coho and Chinook near the QA Marker or off the Sand Head. Chum, which seem to like a flasher/dodger with a dark hoochie (Army Truck, green, or purple), are present in October to November.

Gambier Island (Map #10/D3)

This island is north of Bowen Island in Howe Sound. Except for the southern end, the waters around Gambier Island, at the time of writing this book, are now closed to fishing between May 31 and Sept 27. The open areas, unfortunately, are usually quite spotty:

Grace (Twin) Islands can be good, on occasion, for immature springs in December to February and for Coho and mature Chinook in July through October. Trolling around the south end of the islands is the best areas. The Coho are fished in 10-20m of water whereas the Chinook tend to be at 15-25m (60-90ft).

Hope Point is the southeasternmost tip of the island. Trolling around the point at 25m (80ft) using a dodger/ flasher and Apex, hoochie or herring (whole or cut), produces Chinook and Coho in July-September. The area is generally hit-and-miss.

Halkett Point is the south eastern most tip of the island. It occasionally produces immature Chinook in November-March, mature Chinook in May-July and some Coho in September-October. Trolling is the best method of fishing as the fish concentration is low and you will have to travel miles to catch one. Mooching off the western tip can produce on occasion.

Howe Sound (Map #1,10,11)

Subject to a change in the regulation, most of Howe Sound is now closed to fishing from March 31 to September 27 from the south end of Gambier Island northward. The Squamish River fishery has been severely affected by years of fishing and by the depletion of the herring population. There is still a spotty winter fishery for Chinook north of the closure and a few descent spots south of the closure that are worth a try throughout the year:

Fishermen's Cove (Map #11/A4) is located several kilometres south of Horseshoe Bay. The area provides a very good fishery for immature Chinook in December through April off the south end of Eagle Island. There are also Chinook and Coho from June to October. The area is somewhat hit-and-miss as it can be excellent for short stretches and then a fish will not be caught for weeks. Since the productive fishing area is quite small and there are shallow reefs towards Eagle Island, it is best to mooch with live or cut herring rather than troll. Some fishermen also try jigging although with less success than mooching.

Grebe Island (Map #1/A1) is also known as Seal Rock and is located south of Fishermen's Cove. It is best trolled on the outside edge as there is an underwater reef leading from Erwin Point to the island making trolling in the inside a very expensive proposition as you are sure to lose your tackle. The area produces some winter Chinook in December through April and some mature Chinook from May to July and Coho from September to October. Pinks are occasionally caught off the island between September and October. A flasher/ dodger with a herring or hoochie works the best for the Coho and Chinook.

Hole in the Wall (Map #11/A4) is a very popular fishing spot just north of Horseshoe Bay. It is marked by a mining test hole on the granite cliff raising above the ocean. The area is notoriously hit-and-miss with some days being absolutely phenomenal whereas on other days, 20 or 30 boats can go without a bite. Mooching with live, whole or strip herring near the bottom is the most productive fishing method for Chinook in November through March and again in July through September. It is best to stay near the cliffs where you will find a 150m ledge. Trollers also work the area in the winter months at 25-35m (80-120ft) using a dodger/ flasher with a hoochie or whole or strip herring. The occasional Coho is caught in the area between July through September. The preferred time to fish the area is in the morning during high water.

Howe Sound (North) (Map #10,11) region is closed to fishing from March 31 to September 27 from the south end of Gambier Island northward. As a result, fishing is restricted to winter springs with the best locations being trolling a few 100ft off the McNab Creek waterfront (Map #10/ D2), the log booms at Port Mellon (Map #10/C2) and the south end of Anvil Island (Map#11/A2). Port Mellon and McNab Creek are usually better in December through February whereas the south end of Anvil Island is better in March through April. Mooching off the Woodfibre Mill (Map #11/A1) is effective in January through March particularly if you

stay close to the pilings off the ferry wharf or nearby to the deep-sea piers. Current is light in the area so a small weight (1-2oz) works. Other options include mooching off Furry Creek (Map #11/B2), mooching herring off the booms in front of Shannon Falls and trolling of Porteau Cove (Map #11/A2). Please note that winter mooching is limited by the lack of available live bait.

Sunset Beach (Map #11/A4) This beach provides the opportunity to troll for immature Chinook in November through March and then for mature Chinook in June. Trolling with a dodger with a hoochie (army truck or white), cutplug herring, anchovy or herring strip all work.

Whytecliff Point (Map #11/A4) Located north of Fishermen's Cove, this spot offers a good place to troll for winter Chinook in March and April. The tides off the point make mooching undesirable.

Keats Island (Map #10/C4)
This small island to the west of Bowen Island is best fished for wintering Chinook in November through April off Cotton Point. Mooching and trolling both work. Trolling around the point at 25-40m (80-140ft) with plugs or whole herring in a teaser head is best. Moochers usually anchor off the point in water up to 180m deep.

Cotton Point can also produce well for Chinook and Coho in June-October. At the south end of Keats Island is Home Island, a small rock outcrop also known as Salmon Rock. This area receives heavy fishing pressure because it is a constant producer for Chinook in March-April and Chinook and Coho in June-September. Mooching with live or strip herring within 15m (50ft) of the southwestern corner of the island is the best spot because the bait accumulates in that area due to tide action. Jigging lures are also effective. Trollers circle around the southern end of the island using flashers or dodgers with a wide variety of lures or bait.

Gibson Gap is a very good producer of Chinook and Coho in June-September. The Gap is a shallow rock shelf (4-15m) that extends from the south end of Keats Island to Cape Byring on the Sunshine Coast. The water on either side of the shelf drops off rapidly to 45m (150ft) and it is at the drop-off where the fish hold. Trolling with herring (cut-plug or whole) with a flasher or mooching with live or strip herring works. The Chinook tend to be in the deeper waters whereas the Coho can be in the deep water or in the shallows. Jigging lures should not be ruled out.

Pasley Island (Map #10/C4)
This island offers very good fishing for immature Chinook in December-April by trolling deep at the south end of the island.

Worlcombe Island (Map #10/C4)
This island is located at the south end of Pasley Island off the southwestern end of Bowen Island. It is a very popular Coho area in July-October with trolling along the southern end being the most productive. A silver bucktail or a dodger with most Coho type lures works as does cut or whole herring. Mooching or strip-casting can also produce if you focus on the outside edge of the island. The occasional Chinook is caught in the summer months or during December to April. Blueblack (Coho) fishing can be good in March.

Tsawwassen (Map #1/C1)
Off the south end of the Coal Port and next to the ferry terminal are two good areas for wintering Chinook as well as mature Chinook and Coho in June through August. There are also a few Pinks and Sockeye in August through September. The area is extremely popular so it is common to see 20-40 boats trolling the terminal when the fishing is decent. The area is not a mooching or jigging spot as the fish are generally dispersed making trolling the best method. A rough boat launch is located next to Hwy #17 along the beach on the jetty leading to the ferry terminal.

Sunshine Coast/Powell River Areas

This area of the coast has much better fishing then around Vancouver. Access to the area is provided by ferry to Langdale and to Saltery Bay. The opportunities range from remote locations up Jervis Inlet to crowded fishing spots off the waterfront of the Sunshine Coast, especially around Pender Harbour.

Like around Vancouver, the Coho population has severely declined in recent years and restrictions on fishing are in the works. Therefore, the focus of the fishery may have to shift to the Chinook.

Bargain Harbour (Map #9/B2)
The mouth of Bargain Harbour is a good place to try in the evening between July-September for Coho. Trolling during March-April for Bluebacks as well as

trolling for wintering Chinook from November to early June can produce. Moochers or strip-casters do very well by anchoring off of Whitestone Islands or by fishing in 15-20m (50-70ft) of water in front of the waterfall. Live herring is by far the most common bait. Trollers stick around Whitestone Islands.

Bjerre Shoals (Map #9/B2)
These series of underwater reefs extends from Harness Island south to McNaughton Point. It is a fairly good Coho area during May-October. Moochers and jiggers anchor off the edge of the reefs. Trollers are restricted to shallow, light tackle or a hook-up is guaranteed. A depth finder is a must.

Camp Byng (Map #10/C4)
Located to the northwest of Gower Point, this area is marked by the Camp Byng sign. It is a popular area given that Coho can be caught in fair numbers from July-September and Chinook can be caught throughout the year from May-September. A large shallow area extends from the beach off Camp Byng some 200m offshore. It is at the drop-off, which goes from 10-65m (30-210ft), where moochers and strip casters focus their efforts. Trolling along the drop-off with a dodger/flasher and a combination of lures including a hoochie or Apex as well or a herring strip seems to work the best. Large swells are common to the area.

Copeland Islands (Map #16/B1, 25/B4)
The Copeland Islands are north of Lund and offer some good fishing for Chinook and Coho. The best location to fish is on the inside passage (Thulin Passage) either by trolling a plug or by drift fishing at 15-25m (60-90ft). The Chinook begin to appear in mid April and can be caught until July. The Coho tend to be near the islands in July and August.

Desolation Sound (Map #25)
Desolation Sound is home of the largest and one of the most popular marine parks in Canada. An early Chinook run begins in April and peaks into May. Mooching at one of the points in the sound (eg. Zephine Head, Price Point, or the tip of Melville Island) or trolling along one of the many islands meets with success.

Earls Cove (Map #18/B4)
This area provides good fishing from May-August for Coho as well as Chinook. It is sheltered from the winds of Jervis Inlet so it makes a good destination for smaller crafts. If you are fishing for Chinook, it is best to try a deep mooch with strip or live herring (20-45m) or try trolling a plug or whole herring in deep water. For Coho, the bluebacks come into the area in May and then you can catch mature Coho until August. These fish take a variety of small Coho lures or bucktails by trolling. Mooching can also produce some Coho.

Egmont Harbour (Map #18/C4)
Egmont Harbour is not a popular fishing location but there is a nice 80ft hole on the west side of the island at the entrance to the harbour. At that location, mooching with live herring and a 1oz weight can produce Chinook if you fish deep or Coho if you fish closer to the surface. Trollers can circle the entrance to the harbour and produce both Coho and Chinook using a flasher and a variety of different lures and baits. There is the occasional winter Chinook although the summer is a better time for the Chinook.

Egmont Point (Map #18/B4)
This point is a spot that fish pass to enter into the Sechelt Inlet so fishing can be quite good throughout the year. Hence, the area is very popular. For Chinook, a deep troll is most effective although mooching with live herring in 15-45m (50-150ft) of water can also produce. Coho tend to take lighter gear and can be caught near the surface trolling a variety of Coho lures, by mooching with live herring or by strip casting. Bluebacks (Coho) are available in March. Moochers tend to stay closer to Earls Cove than the entrance to Sechelt Inlet whereas the trollers tend to troll toward Egmont.

Foley Head (Map #18/B3)
This point provides good fishing for bluebacks beginning in May as well as mature Coho until September. A variety of methods work especially on the Prince of Whales Reach side of the point. Trollers can do well with such things as bucktails or a flasher/dodger with a hoochie or flashtail trolled near the surface with a light weight. Mooching and jigging off the point can also be productive.

Francis Point (Map #9/B2)
On the southern tip of Francis Peninsula, Francis Point marks a good location for trolling for both Chinook and Coho. The Chinook are most prominent in May through June and are best fished deep. The Bluebacks are fairly abundant in May-June and the mature Coho appear in September. The Coho like bucktails or flashtails trolled near the surface.

Gibsons Harbour (Map #10/C4)
There is a popular fishing hole found just east of the piers off at the drop-off. The area is best fished from December-May for wintering Chinook although there are Chinook and Coho in the summer, too. Mooching live herring is the preferred method although it is possible to troll or cast a jigging lure.

Gower Point (Map #10/B4)
Gower Point is the southernmost tip of the Sechelt Peninsula. It is considered one of the premier Coho areas on the Sunshine Coast as the fish must pass by the point on their way to the Fraser River or other rivers of the Burrard Inlet. If you are fishing the area for the first time, trolling with a whole herring or hoochie and a dodger/flasher at 15-25m (60-80ft) is your best bet. Locals fishing the area usually anchor near the drop-off at the south end and try mooching or strip casting. Jigging also works on occasion. Coho are caught from July-September with the evening being the best time of day to try. There are also good numbers of Pinks caught during late July-August in odd years and the occasional Chinook caught in May-September.

Grief Point (Map #17/A3)
Located south of Powell River, this point can be good all year round. The focus, however, is in May to August when the Chinook are found off the point in good numbers. Trolling or mooching are the primary fishing methods.

Halfmoon Bay (Map #9/C3)
This bay is one of the best fishing areas on the Sunshine Coast, as it produces Chinook in Novemeber through March as well as in June-July and again in September. Coho are present in July through September. Both species are best caught by trolling around the points leading into the bay.

Harmony Island / Granville Bay (Map #18/B2)
This area is popular for Chinook fishermen in April through early June as well as Coho fishermen later in the year (July-August). The best place to fish is at the north end of the islands or near the estuary of Freil Lake. Mooching is by far the method of choice using live herring with 1oz of weight. Trollers are best to stay near the drop-off and use a combination of a plug or dodger/flasher with a hoochie or herring (cut or whole). Try fishing for Chinook at first light for best results.

Harwood / Vivian Islands (Map #16/D2)
To the east of Powell River, Harwood Island marks a good area for salmon fishing. The best spots to fish for Coho and Chinook are off the east and southwestern sides of the island using a deep troll. Off the south end of Harwood Island is Vivian Island, which offers Chinook in July and August primarily by trolling. There are also Coho in June through August caught by casting or mooching.

Lasqueti Island (Map #8/C3)
By far the best location to fish around Lasqueti Island is off Young Point, which attracts many moochers. The moochers use live or strip herring and anchor 30-150ft off the point fishing for Coho which are found in 10-15m (30-50ft) of water. Casting lures can also meet with success if the Coho are feeding near the surface. Trollers can circle the point or work their way up to Bull Passage with reasonable success. Coho are the most common fish that are caught with July being the best month. Off the northeastern end of Lasqueti Island from Fegen Islets to False Bay, fishing produces Coho and a few Chinook primarily by a shallow troll. Mooching with live or cut herring or casting jigging lures also produces. At the south end of Jenkins Island is a good spot to troll for Coho in June through October with the northerns coming through in September to October. The occasional Chinook can be caught in July and August.

Lund (Map #16/B1)
Lund is known as a saltwater fishing community and has full facilities to support the fishery. Right off the waterfront, it is possible to catch wintering Chinook in December to April and mature Chinook in May through June. Most fishermen troll along the waterfront all the way to the south end of Copeland Island. Others try off of Hurtado Point just south of Lund. In recent years, the Chinook population has been in a decline so fishermen are turning to Sockeye in July and August.

Merry Island (Map #9/C3)
South of Welcome Beach, this small island offers good trolling for Chinook from May-September, bluebacks in April and Coho from August-September. The best spots to focus your efforts is at the south and north ends of the island in deeper water (over 25m). Mooching with live or strip herring or casting a jigging lure can also produce. Big swells are common to the area.

Myrtle Point / Rocks (Map #17/A3)
Between Powell River and Brew Bay, this area offers good fishing for Chinook from May to July and for Coho in July. Trolling along the shoreline from Myrtle Rock all the way to the point is the principal way of catching the fish.

Mystery Reef / Grant Reefs (Map #16/B2)
Mystery Reef is situated to the northwest of Harwood Island. It is known to produce good numbers of Coho in May through June as well as a few Chinook in July and August. If the bait is near the reefs, anchor off the north or south end of the reef and try some mooching or jigging. Otherwise, try trolling around the reef as the fish are likely scattered. Finding Grant Reefs is half the fun as they are submerged but marked by a series of kelp beds. The best way to locate the reefs is to head east from Mystery Reef and use a depth sounder. The reefs provide good fishing for Coho from May to July by mooching or casting near the kelp beds. Trolling a bucktail or a typical Coho lure off the kelp beds also works. Mature Chinook also hold at the reefs in July and August.

Nelson Island (Map #9/A1, 17/D4)
Nelson Island has a number of good fishing holes off its south end. Ackland Reef, which is several hundred yards off the mouth of Quarry Bay, provides one of the best fisheries for Coho throughout July and August. The area is difficult to find but once you do, it is best to anchor at the edge of the reef in 15-30m (50-100ft) of water and try jigging or mooching. It is also possible to troll the area with lighter gear such as bucktails. Chinook are around in May through August.

Fearney Point (Map #9/A1)
This spot provides a popular fishery for Chinook, Pink and Coho. Most fishermen troll around the point using anything from bucktails for the Coho to a dodger and hoochie for the Chinook. Moochers can use cut or whole live herring by anchoring near the point.

Green Bay (Map #18/A4)
Located in Agamemnon Channel on the southeastern side of the island, this area offers good fishing for Chinook as well as Coho and Bluebacks. Moochers do well by concentrating in the inlet to the bay or on the point to the north of the bay where there is a nice tide rip caused by the point. Live or cut herring work. For trollers, it is best to troll around the point using any one of the typical Coho or Chinook lures or bait.

Quarry Bay (Map #9/A1)
Quarry Bay is a good area to troll a bucktail for Coho in July-August or a hoochie or herring (strip or whole) for Chinook in April-July and November. It also provides good mooching for both Coho and Chinook using live herring. Casting a jigging lure can also produce.

Telescope Pass (Map #17/D4)
Extending between Nelson Island and Hardy Island, Telescope Pass is a seldom fished area but can be very productive for Chinook and Coho. Most fishermen anchor near the entrance to the pass and mooch with live herring at varying depths. Trollers can circle the entrance to the pass if there are not too many boats anchored there.

Pender Harbour (Map #9/A1)
Daniel Point is best trolled or mooched in deep water for Chinook from November to May. The area is hit and miss.

The **"Gap"** leading into Pender Harbour, offers a good place to mooch with live herring for Chinook throughout the year. The occasional Coho will also be caught. It is possible to troll through the area but the confined space and the busy traffic makes trolling difficult. If you want to troll, use a plug.

Hodgson Island provides an area to fish off its east side. The area is best mooched with live or cut herring in deep water fishing near the bottom. The area does not receive the same fishing pressure as other spots near Pender Harbour despite it being a consistent producer of Chinook from November-May. Jigging lures can also be effective in the area. It is best to fish in the outflow tide.

Lee's Bay is located between Daniel Point and Irvines Point. The bay offers one of the most popular mooching areas for Chinook throughout the year. The occasional Coho can also be caught. Fishermen almost exclusively use live herring on a 1oz weight at varying depths depending on the season (deeper for summer and winter and shallower for spring time). The area is also trolled using live herring, plugs or hoochies. The bay is often crowded with 50-75 boats on a summer evening.

Indian Island and the **inside passage** provides two other areas for mooching live herring for wintering Chinook in late November to early June. It is best to anchor near one of the "holes" located off the south end of the island. The area can also be trolled using plugs or whole herring. The best place to fish is off the east end of the island or on the inside passage.

Pirate Rock / Bertha Rock (Map #9/B3)
These small rock outcrops, which may be submerged during high tides, are situated at the south end of South Thormanby Island. Both areas, due to their exposure and distance from Vancouver or the Sunshine Coast, are best left to calm days.

Pirate Rock produces very well for Bluebacks in April and Coho throughout the summer months (late June-September) by trolling around the rock using the typical Coho gear. Stay at least 100ft off shore to avoid hook-ups. Jigging and strip casting is also very effective particularly if anchoring off the southern tip in 50-70ft of water. The odd Chinook is caught in June through September.

Bertha Rock offers one of the best locations for Coho in the strait. Coho are taken from May to October with trolling on the outside of Bertha Rock being the most popular method of fishing. Moochers and jiggers tend to do well in the shallow water extending towards South Thormanby Island.

Porpoise Bay (Map #9/D3)
At the south end of Sechelt Inlet, the bay is mainly fished by locals given its close proximity to Sechelt and difficult access from anywhere else. Mooching off the pier for Chinook starting in March is surprisingly effective although it is best to bring a boat and fish near the drop-off. Moochers tend to use live bait. It is also possible to troll the bay out to Angus Creek. Mooching is the preferred method as there are a few strong currents and it is a sheltered bay. In the late fall (September-October), jigging produces Chum and Coho.

Powell River (Map #17/A2)
The old boat breakwater, known as the Hulks, marks the location of some good Chinook fishing in May through August. Most fishermen begin trolling near the Hulks at dawn and then work their way outward throughout the morning. The opposite is true for the evening fish. Mooching or jigging along the Hulks is also worth a try especially when the Chinook run is at its peak. Another area to try is the Westview waterfront. The occasional wintering Chinook can be caught in December to April on a deep (80-120ft) troll. The better fishing, however, is in May through July for Chinook and Coho.

Roberts Creek (Map #10/A4)
The shoreline extending from Wilson Creek all the way to Gower Point can be a very productive trolling area for Coho from June to October and for Chinook in June and again in September-October. It is also possible to catch wintering Chinook in December to March. Trollers tend to use a dodger/flasher together with a hoochie, Apex or silver coloured lure. Moochers tend to focus their efforts approximately 200m from the wharf at Roberts Creek where there is a noticeable drop-off. Live herring is by far the best producer although herring strips can work as well. The area is subject to large swells.

Saint Vincent Bay (Map #18/A3)
Saint Vincent Bay has a number of fishing holes all the way out to Elephant Point and Culloden Point. Both Culloden and Elephant Point are best for Coho whereas Saint Vincent Bay is best for chinook. The points offer Bluebacks beginning in April until May and then mature Coho throughout the summer. Mooching with live herring at the points or with strip or cut herring works. Trollers tend to circle the points using a variety of gear such as hoochies, live herring, plugs, bucktails or strip herring. Both points are extremely busy during the summer months. In Saint Vincent Bay mooching with live herring can by done throughout the bay as can trolling with a flasher/dodger and bait (herring), hoochie or plug.

Sakinaw Estuary ("A Frame")(Map #9/A1)
The Sakinaw Estuary is also known as the A-Frame. It is either trolled or mooched near the point south of the actual estuary. The best fishing for the Chinook is in December through March although it is possible to catch Chinook year-round. Occasionally, Coho come into the area in the summer (July-August) and can be

caught in good numbers. Trollers use plugs for Chinook whereas bucktails, flashtails and hoochies are used for Coho. Moochers use live herring.

Sangster Island (Map #8/D3)
Sangster Island is located off the southern tip of Lasqueti Island. Due to its exposure, it is best to only fish the area with a larger boat. If you do venture out to the island, it can be extremely productive for Coho throughout the summer months. Fishermen concentrate their efforts off the kelp beds off the southern end of the island. Jigging for both Chinook and Coho as well as trolling anything from a bucktail to a flasher/dodger with a hoochie, plug or bait can be effective. Off the northwestern tip of Sangster Island is another good area, which holds Coho during the summer months. It is best to anchor near the drop-off and mooch or cast lures. Trolling is also possible as long as you stick to the outside.

Sarah Point (Map #25/B4)
Sarah Point marks the northern tip of Malaspina Peninsula. It is a good spot for fishing given that fish entering Desolation Sound must pass by the point. There are some wintering Chinook but the main fishery is from May to June for Chinook and late August-early September for Coho. Trolling around the point seems to work the best although mooching or jigging at the drop-off should not be ruled out.

Sargeant Bay (Map #9/C3)
The bay to the west of Sechelt offers fishing for Chinook and Coho. The Chinook are in the bay in the highest concentration from December to early June whereas the Coho are present in July-September. Trolling along the drop-off of the southwestern side of the bay is the best area to try. Moochers focus on the southwestern point where a series of back eddies and a sharp drop-off exists. Trollers use a variety of lures with a dodger and plugs, hoochies or spoons or bait (strip or whole herring). Moochers mainly use live herring. Jigging can produce at times. Trolling a half kilometre off shore towards Trail Islands is also worth a try. Please keep in mind that the area is subject to strong winds and rough weather conditions.

Savary Island (Map #16/B1)
In July and August, the south side of Savary Island can be trolled using a bucktail/flashtail or a typical Coho lure. The Coho can be found in good numbers all the way along the south side of the island and northward to Hernando Island. Jigging or casting along the kelp beds on the south side of the island can also be effective when the fish are congregating in the area.

Scotch Fir Point (Map #17/C4)
This point marks the beginning of Jervis Inlet and represents the location where migratory salmon must pass. As a result, it offers good fishing throughout the summer months for Coho and in December- March and May for Chinook. Trollers try all the way from Frolander Bay to Thunder Bay but generally focus around the point. Anything from plugs, wobblers, hoochies or bait produce. The moochers, who use live or cut herring, and jiggers focus off the point.

Seal Reef (Map #8/D3)
Fishermen concentrate their efforts on the outside of the reef looking for Coho and the occasional Chinook. Most fishermen mooch with live or cut herring but it is also possible to catch fish by trolling or by casting a lure. Due to the open exposure to winds, the area is best left to larger boats.

Sechelt Inlet (Map #9,18)
This long narrow inlet leads all the way from Egmont south to Sechelt. Within the inlet are a number of good fishing holes which are certainly worth a try.

Silvey's Bay (Map #9/C4)
Located at across from Egmont towards Egmont Point, this area offer very good fishing for both Chinook and Coho near a group of small islands (Sutton Islands). Fishing is good both inside and outside the islands. As a rule of thumb, you should fish closer to the shoreline and move out over the course of the day. The area is best trolled using a downrigger with a flasher/dodger and a variety of bait (whole or strip herring), plugs or hoochies. Moochers, due to the heavy currents of the Skookumchuck Narrows, are best to use at least 4-6oz of weight with live herring. Both Coho and Chinook can be taken throughout the summer months and the occasional Chinook can be taken during the winter.

Sechelt Rapids (Map #9/C4)
These rapids are located at the estuary of Earle Creek. The area is best left to larger boats because the currents can reach up to 15-20knots. Given the strong currents and the difficulty to fish the rapids, the area is also best left to experienced and knowledgeable fishermen. If you do wish to venture out to the rap-

ids, fishing around the islands at the mouth of Earle Creek or on the opposite shoreline during slack tide is your best bet.

Mooching with live bait and 1-2oz of weight or jigging a lure are your best bets. Trolling is not an option. To the south of the Earle Creek Estuary is a bay that forms behind a granite point. In the bay is a strong back eddy which often produces Coho and Chinook by mooching with live herring or using jigging lures. Because of the strong tides, fishing on the slack is highly recommended as is going there with an experienced fishermen who knows the waters. Otherwise, the fishing hole is extremely dangerous.

Skookumchuck Bay (Map #9/C4)
Skookumchuck Bay is situated away from the strong tides of the Sechelt Rapids. For this reason, the area receives heavy fishing pressure and is fished for Chinook early in the morning or in the evening by trolling a plug or dodger with bait (live, strip or cut plug), Hoochie or Apex. Early in the morning, the fish tend to be near the surface whereas over the course of the day, they drop to the 15-35m (50-120ft) level. Coho are also found in the area and are taken near the surface using bucktails or any one of a number or Coho lures. Mooching within the tide flow with live, cut or strip herring often meets with success.

Secret Cove (Map #9/B2)
This area provides some excellent fishing for Chinook when the fish are in the cove. Mooching with live herring near the piers or on the outside is the most popular method of fishing. Trollers are limited to the outside using a Flasher/Dodger with a plug or bait. Chinook season runs from September-June whereas Coho can be caught in October.

Texada Island (Map #8,16,17)
Texada Island offers a number of good saltwater fishing areas:

Anderson Bay (Map #9/A3)is located on the northeast side of the Island, the mouth of the bay offers some good trolling and mooching for Chinook in April to July and Coho beginning in May until August.

Blubber Bay to Davis Bay (Map #16/D3) region marks the eastern most part of the island. The area provides a good trolling area for Coho and Chinook in May through September. The Coho tend to be in the tide lines and can be caught by trolling a bucktail or flashtail. The Chinook congregate in Crescent and Blubber Bay or off Favada Point. Mooching, trolling or jigging all work.

Coho Point (Grilse Point) (Map #16/D3) is found at the northern tip of Texada Island, this point is considered a premier Coho area. The best time to fish is in August by trolling a green and white flashtail with a dodger/flasher. The area is deep with many shoals and so it is easy to troll. The occasional Chinook is caught off the point and towards Cyril Rock.

The Pilings (Map #8/D2) are found on the southeast side of the island just north of Anderson Bay, represent a good mooching area for Chinook throughout the year using live or cut herring. The area is found by locating the pilings from an old logging operation and moving out into the straight some 30-60m (100-200ft). The area is also trolled using live herring, plugs or hoochies. There is Coho that can be caught in May through August.

Mouat Bay (Map #8/B3) is primarily a trolling area for Coho anywhere from Gilles Bay to Mouat Islets. If you wish to mooch, it is best to focus your efforts around Mouat or Dick Islands in the shallows using cut or live herring. The area is quite exposed to winds and should be left to a calm day.

Northeast Point (Map #17/B4) is a good area to fish for Coho in July and August. Trolling in the tide lines using a flasher/dodger with a hoochie, herring or flashtail is fairly good as is bucktailing. Mooching or jigging at the drop-off can also work. Northeast Bay may be worth a try if the point is not producing.

Rebbeca Rock (Map #16/D3) is situated off the north end of Texada Island. Coho and Chinook are present in good numbers from July to September.

Stuart Bay (Map #16/D4) is a holding area for Chinook in the summer months when bait is present in the bay. Given the confined area, mooching and jigging are your better choices. Outside the bay, Coho can be caught from July to September by trolling in the tide lines.

Upwood Point (Map #9/A3) is the southernmost land feature on Texada Island. The Coho season runs from July to October whereas the Chinooks season runs almost year round. The area is best trolled using typical salmon gear such as plugs or flasher/dodger with a hoochie or herring strip. Since it is hard to find concentrations of fish in the area, mooching and jigging are not particularly productive.

Thormanby Islands (Map #9/B3)
Epson Point is the westernmost tip on North Thormanby Island. Like other areas around Thormanby Island, Coho can be taken in good numbers from May - October and Chinook from December-April and again in July to September. The best place to troll is southwest of the point where a prominent drop-off is located. Moochers and strip casters congregate near the drop-off and along the kelp beds. Trollers should try a bucktail, a flashtail, Apex or bait. At the north end of the Thormanby Islands is a bell buoy which marks a good location to catch bluebacks and Coho in May as well as the odd Chinook. Trollers usually circle the fringe to the south of the bell buoy as the buoy marks a sharp drop-off where salmon hold. A shallow troll using weights as opposed to a downrigger together with whole herring or other Coho lures seem to work the best (with or without a flasher/dodger).

Trail Islands (Map #9/D3)
These four islands offer an opportunity to catch Coho and the odd Chinook in the summer months. Trolling at the drop-off on the outside or at the ends of the islands with plugs, hoochies or bucktails is the most efficient way to fish the area. Moochers prefer the inside passage where water depths range from 18-40m (60-140ft) deep using both live and cut herring. The outside fishing grounds are subject to strong winds and adverse weather conditions. The area is not as productive as other fishing holes on the Sunshine Coast.

Vancouver Bay (Map #18/C2)
Located in the Prince of Whales Reach, this small bay is the estuary of Vancouver River. The bay offers a variety of fish including Coho, Cutthroat and Chinook. The Chinook, however, are the main attraction. For best success, troll along the drop-off of the river estuary in 15-45m (50-150ft) of water using whole herring, plugs or hoochies. If you are fishing for the Coho, bucktails can be productive. The Cutthroat are best caught by fly fishing or by trolling a small lure. Mooching, although not a common method of fishing, can produce with live herring at the drop-off.

White Islets (Map #10/A3)
To the south of Wilson Creek, these two small reefs produce Coho during the summer months. The fish are caught off the west and south ends of the islands on a deep troll or by mooching. Since the islets are several kilometres south of the shoreline, the area can be quite exposed so it should be left for larger boats. The area is not noted for being a great producer.

Abbreviations Used Throughout the Book:	**Metric Conversion Table**
2wd: 2 wheel drive	1 kg = 2.205 lbs
4wd: 4 wheel drive	1 cm = 0.3937 in
cm: centimetres	1 km = 0.621 mi
FSR: Forest Service Road	1 m = 3.2808 ft
ft: feet	1 ha = 2.47 acre
ha: hectares	
hr: hours	1 lb = 0.454 kg
Hwy: Highway	
kg: kilograms	1 in = 2.54 cm
Km: kilometres	1 mi = 1.609 km
m: metres	
min: minutes	1 ft = 30.48 cm
Mnt: Mountain	
Mt: Mount	1acre = 0.4047 ha
Prov: Provincial	4047.0 m² = 1 acre
Rd: Road	1 m² = 0.000247 acre
Rec: Recreation	
RV: Recreational Vehicle	
X-C: Cross Country	

INDEX

This comprehensive index is intended to help guide you to the map or reference page you are interested in. If the specific item is not labelled try picking the most prominent land feature in the area. This will guide you to the right map and reference page.

Important Phone Numbers

To Report Forest Fires 1 (800) 663-5555
*5555 (cellular phones)
Tourism BC 1 (800) 663-6000
Travel BC .... www.travel.bc.ca
BC Ferries (Vancouver) .... (604) 277-0277
1 (888) 223-3779

Parks

B.C. Parks .... (250) 387-4550
http://www.env.gov.bc.ca/bcparks
Parks Reservations (Greater Vancouver) .... (604) 689-9025
1 (800) 689-9025
GVRD Parks Department .... (604) 432-6350
FVRD Parks Department .... (604) 702-5000

Road and Trail Conditions

Highway Road Reports 1-800-550-4997
.... www.th.gov.bc.ca/bchighways/jump3.htm
B.C. Off Road .... http://www.bcoffroad.com
Climbers' Media .... http://www.bivouac.com
Mountain Bike Trails ... http://www.orroad.com/bcmtbdir/trails

Chilliwack Forest District

Upper Fraser Valley .... (604) 794-2100
Central Fraser Valley .... (604) 820-2055
Lower Mainland .... (604) 685-5972
Lillooet Forest District .... (250) 256-1200
Squamish Forest District .... (604) 898-2100
Interfor (Squamish Division) .... (604) 892-5244
Sunshine Coast Forest District .... (604) 485-9831

Updates .... www.backroadmapbooks.com

The Authors

Russell Mussio (left) graduated from U.B.C. with a degree in Leisure and Sports Administration. He formed Mussio Ventures Ltd. in 1993 with his brother, Wesley Mussio, in order to publish, distribute and market the Backroad Mapbook Series.

Wesley is a Registered Professional Forester and a Lawyer practicing as a trial lawyer with the law firm of Lindsay Kenney in Vancouver.

Russell and Wesley are avid outdoorsmen. Whenever they are not working on the Backroad Mapbook project, they are enjoying the great outdoors.